SALADIN

AND THE FALL OF JERUSALEM

MINE EYES HAVE SEEN THE DAYS OF HIS MAJESTY,
KING STRONG TO AID; THE SUM OF PIETY,
BANE OF THE CRUCIFIX-IDOLATRY,
BANNERET OF RIGHT AND GENEROSITY
SALAH-ED-DIN,
LORD OF ISLAM AND MUSLIMIN,
SAVING GOD'S HOUSE FROM THE NAZARENE,
SERVING THE HOLY PLACES TWIN,
VICTORIOUS YUSUF, SON OF AYYUB, OF SHADHY'S KIN.
GOD WATER HIS GRAVE WITH SHOWERS OF CLEMENCY,
AND GRANT HIM IN MERCY'S HOME THE MEED OF CONSTANCY.

BAHA-ED-DIN

CRUSADERS PURSUING SELJUKS.

FROM A PAINTED WINDOW AT ST. DENYS, 12TH CENTURY.

SALADIN

AND THE FALL OF JERUSALEM

Stanley Lane-Poole

With a New Introduction by David Nicolle

GREENHILL BOOKS • LONDON
STACKPOLE BOOKS • PENNSYLVANIA

This edition of
Saladin and the Fall of Jerusalem
first published 2002 by Greenhill Books, Lionel Leventhal Limited,
Park House, 1 Russell Gardens, London NW11 9NN
and
Stackpole Books, 5067 Ritter Road, Mechanicsburg,
PA 17055, USA

British Library Cataloguing in Publication Data
Lane-Poole, Stanley
Saladin and the Fall of Jerusalem. – New ed.
1. Saladin, Sultan of Egypt and Syria, 1137–1193   2. Islamic Empire –
History – 750–1258   3. Egypt – Kings and rulers – Biography
4. Syria –Kings and rulers – Biography
I. Title
956′.01′092

ISBN 1-85367-503-2

Library of Congress Cataloging-in-Publication Data available

Publishing History
Saladin and the Fall of Jerusalem was first published in 1898.
It is here republished, complete and unabridged, in a larger format,
with some minor alterations and the addition of new introductory
material by Dr David Nicolle. Dr Nicolle also supplied the images
used in the picture section.

Edited, designed and typeset by Roger Chesneau
Printed and bound in Great Britain by
MPG Books Ltd, Bodmin, Cornwall

CONTENTS

PART V   RICHARD AND SALADIN, 1191–1192

APPENDICES

ILLUSTRATIONS

1. A supposed portrait of Saladin, in Arab costume.
2. The ancient city of Mosul.
3. An Arab-Egyptian army emerges from a fortification.
4. The ruined Roman Temple of Artemis in Jerash.
5. A ceramic statuette representing a Turkish cavalryman.
6. The great brick fortress of Qalaat Jabar, overlooking the Euphrates.
7. A picture from the *Kitab al-Aghani* (*Book of Songs*), showing Badr al-Din Lu'lu.
8. A ruined palace in the city of Raqqa.
9. A picture from the *Maqamat of al-Hariri* showing contemporary costume.
10. The city of Hama, one of the small city-states in Syria.
11. The 'Battle Plate' in Washington, illustrating a battle between rival Islamic armies.
12. The castle and small town of Masyaf.
13. A lustre-ware ceramic plate, perhaps from the time of Saladin.
14. The famous fortified entrance to Aleppo's citadel.
15. A scene from the *Maqamat of al-Hariri*, by as-Wasit.
16. The castle of al-Wu'aira, outside the ancient city of Petra.
17. A detail from the outside of the famous thirteenth-century 'Battle Plate'.
18. Part of the Citadel in Cairo, dating from between 1183 and 1207.
19. A copy of the *Maqamat of al-Hariri* made in Syria in 1222–23.
20. The Citadel of Jerusalem, the strongest part of the city's fortification during the Middle Ages.
21. Inlaid Islamic metalwork, showing cavalrymen.
22. The castle of Marqab, one of the most impressive Crusader fortresses.
23. The Freer Gallery's 'Battle Plate'.
24. Hisn Kayfah, sited on a dramatic cliff overlooking the Tigris.
25. An extract from a copy of the *Kitab al-Baytarah*, a treatise on hippology.
26. The gleaming white Crusader castle of Krak des Chevaliers.

NEW INTRODUCTION

STANLEY LANE-POOLE wrote his biography of Sultan Yusuf Ibn Najni al-Din Ayyub Ibn Shadlhi Abu'l-Muzaffar Salah al-Din al-Malik al-Nasir—better known in Europe and America simply as Saladin—just over a century ago in 1898. Since then it has remained the most readable, generally most sympathetic and often the most accessibe Western biographyof the ruler and military leader, who, by general consent, remains the greatest 'hero' of the Crusades.

Lane-Poole was also the first historian writing in the English language to use all the then available sources, both European and Islamic. These ranged from chronicles and other written texts, through architectural inscriptions, archæological evidence and the numismatic information obtained from coins. The author's enthusiasm for his subject undoubtedly pervades the book. Yet the resulting image has been criticised as being 'untarnished', to use the word of a more recent and less sympathetic biographer, Andrew S. Ehrenkreutz. Some historians have suggested that Stanley Lane-Poole fell under Saladin's 'spell'. Furthermore, his biography of the great Islamic leader has been criticised for perpetuating this 'spell', which supposedly even influenced the thinking of H. A. R. Gibb, a later British scholar and historian of Islamic civilisation.

It seems fair to describe Lane-Poole's biography as the original 'pre-revisionist' account of Saladin's life. The author was himself Professor of Arabic at Trinity College, Dublin, and he wrote in a slightly old-fashioned style which makes his work a delight to read. More importantly, Lane-Poole lived before the rise of anti-Arab prejudice in the twentieth century, and before the increasing tide of Islamophobia which colours so much current writing. On the other hand, his work does reflect a certain Orientalist romanticism and is undoubtedly coloured by those attitudes of cultural superiority which characterise the high imperial period during which he lived. However, as a true scholar who respected as well as loved his subject, Lane-Poole is largely innocent of the implicit racism which can be seen in the writings of so many Western scholars of the late nineteenth and early twentieth centuries.

Indeed, Lane-Poole displays a greater sympathy for the period, cultures and peoples about whom he writes than can be found in the works of many more modern scholars; in fact, he shows genuine respect for his subject—a feeling which seems sadly lacking amongst too many of his successors. I believe that it is this combination of affection and respect that, when combined with the author's profound knowledge of Islamic civilisation, enabled Stanley Lane-Poole to get inside the minds of his medieval Muslim subjects, including Saladin. Furthermore, Lane-Poole was more than merely a fine scholar and an excellent linguist: he knew the Middle East well, especially Egypt, and his other books include *The Story of Cairo* (published in 1902) and *Egypt in the Middle Ages* (published in 1925). These show his depth of understanding for medieval Middle Eastern civilisation, whereas some of his other works on Islamic North Africa (*The Barbary Corsairs*) and the Islamic Iberian peninsula (*The Moors in Spain*) are less satisfactory. Meanwhile, Stanley Lane-Poole's *Mohammedan Dynasties* (published in 1893) remained the standard work of dynastic reference in the English language until superseded by C. E. Bosworth's *The Islamic Dynasties* (1967) and *The New Islamic Dynasties* (1996).

Despite claims to the contrary, I do not believe that Lane-Poole's respect for Saladin, as seen in *Saladin and the Fall of the Kingdom of Jerusalem*, spilled over into idealisation or hero-worship. As a biographer he acknowledged that the Sultan was not a saint, though he clearly did regard Saladin as a very good as well as a very great man. Lane-Poole presents the Islamic ruler as a skilled, occasionally ruthless politician who used what he had at hand, politically, diplomatically and militarily, to achieve ends which he believed to be morally justified. Though patently not a fanatic, Saladm is presented as a man driven by high ideals and genuine religious conviction rather than by the political ambition which most more recent biographers have sought to see in him. Lane-Poole's Saladin was installed with a genuine Islamic desire to 'play by the rules' and to obey the laws of God and man in his dealings with rivals and enemies, both Muslim and Christian.

He is portrayed as highly educated, perhaps more so than his immediate predecessor Nur al-Din and certainly more than Zangi, the founding father of the Islamic fight-back against the invading Crusaders. While it is fair to criticise Lane-Poole's biography as exaggerating the 'simplicity' of Saladin's family background and of his naivety as a youth, history shows that the Sultan did indeed earn the respect of friend and foe alike, Muslim and Christian.

While adopting a generally positive attitude towards the Muslims—Arabs, Kurds, Turks and others—Lane-Poole does not fall into the trap of romanticising the Crusaders, nor of overemphasising their physical heroism Equally, he does not condemn them merely as rude invaders. As such, Lane-Poole's account of the relationship between Muslims and Crusaders, militarily, politically, diplomatically and culturally, similarly avoids the current and perhaps excessive tendency to condemn these European incomers as fanatical and bloodthirsty barbarians. One weakness in Lane-Poole's account is, however, his failure to make sufficient distinction between different groups of Crusaders, from the sometimes undoubtedly brutish northern Europeans to the Italians and some other Mediterranean Crusaders who were, by the twelfth century, on much the same cultural level as the Muslim Kurds and Turks, if not yet the Arabs.

Lane-Poole's descriptions of battles and military operations are vivid and gripping. Yet he is better at analysing and describing broad strategy, both military and political, than he is when coming to grips with tactics and modes of combat In addition to being a very readable and accurate biography of Saladin, this work is also a diplomatic and stategic history rather than a specifically military one. Paradoxically, however, Stanley Lane-Poole proves himself a better historian of the military aspects of the Crusades than most supposedly specialist military historians of his day, including Sir Charles Oman. Clearly, this is because Lane-Poole, while not claiming to be a 'military historian', understood the peoples, cultures, motivation, geography and climate of the Middle East better than most of those military specialists who own experience was rooted in nineteenth-century European and colonial warfare.

Of course, a biography written in 1898 must now be seen to contain some weaknesses, even if only as a result of changing attitudes towards its subject. Many later historians of the Crusades, and of twelfth-century Islamic civilisation in Egypt and the Fertile Crescent, have been very critical of *Saladin and the Fall of the Kingdom of Jerusalem*. Some have taken their criticism to extreme lengths and have consequently undermined their own arguments. Indeed, criticism of Lane-Poole's account started as early as 1930, when Charles J. Rosehault wrote his *Saladin, Prince of Chivalry*. More recent historians have pointed out that, not surprisingly, Lane-Poole had to rely on fewer sources than are available today. On the other hand, newly unearthed or translated material has not fundamentally changed the balance of evidence: generally speaking, such information has merely added details to certain often highly specific aspects of the subject.

Nevertheless, most criticism of Lane-Poole's biography focused on what the criticis have regarded as Lane-Poole's idealisation of Saladin. Certainly, the weakest part of Lane-Poole's account is that dealing with Saladin's early life, childhood background and education within the court circles of Syria, Iraq and south-eastern Turkey. It is also true that the biography exaggerates the young Saladin's simplicity and his inexperience in matters political and military before being sent to Egypt in 1164. Lane-Poole, like so many other historians, similarly over-emphasises Saladin's Kurdish origins. In reality, the young Saladin was brought up and educated in an Arabised Islamic court which was dominated by a Turkish military élite. The Ayyubid family's Kurdish roots were largely irrelevant, except as a source of political and military support once Saladin had become a major player in the power politics of his day. Even then, the Kurdish connection has probably been unduly stressed by some historians who seem bent on denying the Arabs of the Fertile Crescent a significant role in their own twelfth-century history.

Other criticisms of Stanley Lane-Poole's *Saladin and the Fall of the Kingdom of Jerusalem* are more specific, more technical and perhaps less important. For example, the author, though one of the leading Arabists and scholars of his day, occasionally lacks a detailed understanding of military terminology. Sometimes he fails fully to understand the significance of admittedly minor military command or tactical decisions, or of the systems of training which lay behind the actions of Saladin's troops on the battlefield, during sieges or on the march. In these respects Lane-Poole is, in fact, merely old-fashioned and tends to accept too uncritically outdated, romantic and 'orientalist' interpretations of medieval Islamic warfare. His understanding of the naval aspects of the struggle against the Crusaders in the Mediterranean and Red Seas is similarly flawed. Here, however, it should be pointed out that when Lane-Poole was writing, the subject of medieval Mediterranean warfare was still in its infancy.

In conclusion, Stanley Lane-Poole's biography of Saladin has been regarded as the bench-mark against which most other biographies of the Sultan—and indeed many accounts of the Crusades—have measured themselves or been measured by others. If for no other reason, this alone would justify the re-publication of *Saladin and the Fall of the Kingdom of Jerusalem*. Yet there are other reasons why this book, though over a century old, should reappear in a modern, well-illustrated and well-indexed edition. Above all, its reappearance may go some way towards countering the currently fashionable but often excessive citicism of Saladin as a leader, commander and man of genuinely noble stature.

David Nicolle
Woodhouse Eaves
2002

PREFACE TO THE NEW EDITION

SALAH AL-DIN Yusuf Ibn Ayyub—or Saladin, as he is better known in Europe—was born at Tikrit in Iraq in AD 1137 or 1138. By the time he died in 1193 he had become the most famous Muslim military leader against the Crusader invaders of Palestine and Syria—a reputation he retains to this day despite the appearance of several biographies which are far more critical than that written by Stanley Lane-Poole.

Saladin's family or clan, known as the Ayyubids, was of Kurdish origin and originated in the Dwin area of what is now Armenia. They then rose to prominence in Iraq, south-eastern Turkey and Syria. In 1138 Saladin's father Ayyub and his uncle Shirkmli, who controlled the Iraqi castle of Tikjit, entered the service of Zangi, a Turkish ruler of northern Iraq and parts of Syria. After Zangi died, Ayyub entered the service of Damascus while Shirkuh remained with Zangi's son and successor, Nur al-Din. Together these brothers arranged the surrender of Damascus to Nur al-Din, thereby making him the most powerful Muslim ruler on the region. Naturally, their prestige in Nur al-Din's court also helped the career of the young Saladin.

Saladin was not, in fact, a military innocent thrust into warfare against his will. Educated and given considerable military training in the cultivated surroundings of a Turkish court in Arab Syria, the young man had already been allocated an *iqta*, or military fief, of his own. He must soon have done well, because in 1156 he was placed in command of the Damascus garrison. Later Saladin returned to Aleppo as Nur al-Din's senior aide-de-camp, remaining by his ruler's side both in court and on the march.

Saladin's own bid for power resulted from his role during Nur al-Din's take-over of Egypt, though the expeditions which resulted in this take-over had been led by Saladin's uncle, Shirkuk. During the first unsuccessful expedition of 1164 Saladin's own talents proved to be organisational rather than on the battlefield, but in a second and again unsuccessful expedition of 1167 he distinguished himself at the Battle of al-Babayn. He also commanded the defence of Alexan-

dria. On the successful third expedition Saladin played an even more prominent
military role, and when Shirkuh suddenly died in 1169 he was proclaimed leader
by Nur al-Din's senior officers in Egypt. Saladin's appointment as *vizier*, or Chief
Minister, to the shadow Fatimid Caliphate of Egypt was then a mere formality.
In 1171 the last Fatimid, Shi'a Mustini, Caliph of Egypt, died, whereupon Saladin
abolished the Fatimid Caliphate, restored Egypt's allegiance to the Abbasid Sunni
Muslim Caliph in Baghdad and himself became ruler of Egypt under the overall
suzerainty of Nur al-Din.

Saladin's administrative, fiscal, political and military talents now had a chance
to show themselves. He strengthened 'Syrian' control over Egypt, quelled re-
volts, fought off Crusader attacks and revived Egyptian military strength. But in
1172 Saladin stopped declaring that all his actions were carried out in the name
of Nur al-Din. This inevitably led to tension with his nominal overlord, and would
probably have resulted in military action had Nur al-Din not died two years
later. Saladin now declared himself the true successor to the great and highly
respected Nur al-Din. For the next decade Saladin, operating from Egypt and
using its wealth as his power base, extended his authority over Syria and eventually also over northern Iraq. Not surprisingly, this led to several minor wars
with Nur al-Din's descendants, who regarded themselves as his rightful heirs.
In fact, like Nur al-Din himself, Saladin spent most of the first part of his reign
struggling against fellow Muslim rulers. First he took control of Damascus, then
in 1183 Aleppo and then in 1186 Mosul. Meanwhile Saladin generally observed
a truce with the Crusader States, and only occasionally did his army clash with
the Christian occupiers of Palestine.

By 1183 Saladin had created sufficient of a united Islamic front in Syria and
Egypt to turn against the Crusader States. Nevertheless, his first attacks on the
great castle of Karak in southern Jordan both failed. Saladin then fell seriously
ill and spent much of 1185–86 recuperating. This brush with death may have
focused his attention upon religious duties regarding the Crusader-occupied
city of Jerusalem, which became the target of the *jihad* that Saladin now launched,
first summoning his allies and in 1187 undertaking a major offensive. However,
this campaign excluded the Principality of Antioch because Saladin had a truce
with its ruler.

The 1187 offensive culminated in the Muslims' great victory at the Battle of
Hattin on 4 July. In the victory communiqué that Saladin sent to the Caliph in
Baghdad, he wrote; 'The King was captured, and this was a hard day for the
unbelievers. The prince [the notorious Reynald of Châtillon], may God curse
him, was taken and the servant [Saladin himself] harvested his seed, killing him

with his own hand and so fulfilling his vow.' By the time of Hattin, the Crusader Military Orders were also more dangerous than they had been in earlier years, and those captured by Saladin were executed. Furthermore, Saladin had a victory monument erected on the southern Horn of Hattin, though, sadly, all that remains is the foundation of a rectangular structure on the highest point of the hill which may have served as cisterns for a Dome of Victory above.

Five days after the Battle of Hattin, Acre surrendered, and by early September the entire coast of Palestine and southern Syria from Gaza to Jubayl was in Saladin's hands, except for Tyre. Three hundred and fifty miles of the northern Syrian coast also remained in Crusader hands. Now Saladin turned inland and demanded the surrender of Jerusalem, which capitulated on 2 October 1187. It was a strategic watershed and a psychological triumph for Islam. Nevertheless, Saladin had no interest in making Jerusalem his capital, since, despite its religious significance, the city was not a suitable administrative or military centre. Instead, Saladin ruled from Damascus and Cairo when not on campaign.

In 1188 Saladin took several key castles in northern Syria, but not the strategic port of Tyre. He was then faced by a full-scale Third Crusade in response to the fall of Jerusalem. Led by no fewer than three European kings, this massive expedition broke the siege of Tyre, retook Acre after a long siege and regained the Palestinian coast. Nevertheless, it won back virtually nothing inland and did not retake Jerusalem. During his correspondence with Richard the Lionheart, King of England, Saladin replied thus to Richard's insistence that he give up Jerusalem: 'Jerusalem is to us as it is to you. Do not imagine, therefore, that we can waver in this regard.'

In September 1192 Saladin and the Crusaders agreed a truce. Saladin's army was now weary, its munitions almost exhausted, and the Sultan may himself already have been ill. He died on 3 March 1193 and was buried in Damascus. The Muslims by now had the upper hand in relation to the Crusader States. Nevertheless, Saladin's successors, the Ayyubid dynasty, did not press their advantages; instead, they made political alliances with the Crusader States and developed their commercial relations. What Saladin left was a system of collective family rule in which authority was delegated to his relatives and descendants in the major cities of six large but disparate states. These formed a confederacy, with the ruler of Cairo normally at its head, which proved to be a remarkably successful system that broke down only when faced with the Mongol invasions of the mid-thirteenth century.

Saladin's own character, ambitions and appearance remain something of a mystery, despite the huge amount of contemporary information about him. He is, for example, shown as a stylised Islamic ruler on various small coins minted in the south-eastern Anatolian parts of his realm. These follow the numismatic traditions of the area, and on one Saladin appears wearing a Byzantine-Armenian style crown, on another wearing the fur-lined cap of the Turkish military élite. A better known but very simple Fatimid Egyptian-style drawing of him portrays an archetypal Islamic ruler, this time in Arab costume, turban and full beard.

For most of his life Saladin operated within the traditional Middle Eastern Islamic framework of shifting alliances, truces and small-scale warfare, just like other rulers of his day. This entailed almost constant travelling, if not actual campaigning. Saladin was also fully aware of the economic importance of European merchant communities within Islamic cities, and in a letter written to the Caliph of Baghdad he expressed concern about the danger of Muslim merchant caravans being intercepted by Crusader raiders.

As a ruler, Saladin listened to the advice of others, particularly on political matters, and made use of both traditional and new military structures or equipment, while his role as an effective and inspiring leader is clear in several chronicles. Nor was Saladin a bloodthirsty ruler. According to Beha al-Din, when Saladin's children asked if they could execute a prisoner he pointed out, 'I do not want them to get used to shedding blood so young. At their age they do not know what it means to be a Muslim or an infidel, and they will grow accustomed to trifling with the lives of others.' On the other hand, after attempts on his life by Ismaili assassins, Saladin became very concerned for his own physical safety.

Clearly, Saladin was a charismatic leader and his popularity was genuine. According to another contemporary, Abd al-Latif, when Saladin died 'Men grieved for him as they grieve for prophets. I have seen no other ruler for whose death the people mourned, for he was loved by good and bad, Muslims and unbelievers alike.'

As a commander, Saladin was willing to take considerable risks and he had a clear understanding of broad strategy, while he and his immediate Ayyubid successors were responsible for a number of important military reforms. Most were rooted in existing traditions from the Abbasid and Fatimid Caliphates, or the Turco-Iranian Seljuq realm. As part of such reforms, Saladin ordered the writing of three different manuals on warfare and military statecraft. _The Proper Course for the Policy of Kings_, by Abd al-Rahman al-Shayzari, is in the traditional style and contains broad military theory. The better known _Explanation of the Masters of the Quintessence_ [of military knowledge], by Murda Ibn Ali Ibn Murda al-Tarsusi, focuses on the technology and use of weapons themselves, including siege machinery. A third book, *Discussion of the Stratagens of War*, by Abu al-Hasan Ah Ibn Abi Bakr al-Harawi, concentrates on strategies and ruses.

These books reflected Saladin's military career and also the reality of twelfth-entury warfare in the Islamic Middle East. For example, his generosity to the people of Jerusalem and other reconquered cities was fully within traditional Islamic military theory, being used as a sign of power and wealth while undermining the will of other cities to resist. Even Saladin's supposed strategic error in allowing Crusader resistance to crystallise at Tyre after his overwhehning victory at Hattin finds parallels in these military manuals. For example, al-Harawi urged a commander not to become bogged down besieging a strong location and thus jeopardise the momentum of his campaign unless he was absolutely sure of success. Instead, he should attack weaker places first, mopping up resistance and undermining morale in the main centre. This strategy worked at Jerusalem and Acre, while even Tyre had accepted Saladin's terms before the unexpected arrival of Conrad of Montferrat encouraged the beleaguered Crusader garrison to change its mind.

By adhering to such traditional and cautious military principles, Saladin subsequently ground down the Third Crusade. He refused to risk the destruction of his main army in a major battle, and as a result lost only five towns to Crusader reconquest—places which Saladin himself had previously taken in less than a month. Nor is there any doubt that, by the end of the Third Crusade, Saladin had won the moral and psychological struggle. As a result, he became a hero in both Islamic and Christian writing.

Between them Nur al-Din and Saladin re-established a considerable degree of unity in Syria and neighbouring Islamic lands, a cohesion which had been missing for many generations. They also provided continuity of leadership in the struggle against the Crusaders. Comparisons with Nur al-Din were, in fact being drawn in Saladin's own lifetime. Some writers, like Imad al-Din, considered Saladin superior because he modelled himself upon Nur al-Din and then surpassed his model. Others thought Nur al-Din a better man and regarded Saladin as a usurper. Nevertheless, almost all agreed that Saladin was more successful in the struggle against the Crusaders. In reality, both rulers were military commanders who seized power without much legitimate right Both needed legitimacy from the Caliph, and both used their actions in the *jihad* as a means of earning such legitimacy. Several contemporary Muslim biographers already tended to idealise Saladin's character, emphasising his humanity, forgiving nature, piety, love of justice, generosity and courage. These claims may have been exaggerated, but there is no doubt that Saladin made a profound impact upon those around him, and even his Christian foes trusted Saladin's word of honour.

Such Middle Eastern and Western sources together formed the foundation for the legends which grew up about Saladin. Indeed, he became the noble and tragic, though non-Christian, hero of various European tales. Saladin's greatness was such that the European Christians seemed unable to accept that he was a 'mere Saracen'; instead, legends grew up claiming that Saladin was actually the grandson of a beautiful French princess, forced to marry a valiant Turk named Malakia. Traditionally, Saladin has been seen in Europe as a paragon of virtue and as a military hero. Recently, however, more critical interpretations have portrayed him an an ambitious, ruthless and devious politician, and less brilliant as a commander than once thought. In reality, this revisionist view has probably gone too far. Saladin's prudent and half-hearted actions against the Crusaders during the first part of his career may simply have been carried out to avoid provoking a major Crusade—at least, until Saladin felt strong enough to face the Crusaders. Similarly, his unwillingness to continue the struggle in the final years of his life must have reflected the impact of the Third Crusade, which, though it had been contained, had demonstrated just how strong a European invading army could be. Again, Saladin's use of religious law and the rhetoric of *jihad* to enhance his own political position was fully within established Islamic political traditions. He was, in fact, little different from those who came before or after. As so often in history, the truth about the man probably lies between the two extreme views, though all agree that he was the greatest figure in the story of the twelfth-century Crusades.

BIOGRAPHIES AND OTHER WORKS CONCERNING SALADIN

Ahl, Abd al-Aziz Sayyid al-, *Ayyam Salah al-Din* (Beirut, 1961).

Asthor-Strauss, E., 'Saladin and the Jews', *The Hebrew Union College Annual Journal*, XXV (Cincinnati, 1956), pp. 305–26.

Brand, C. M., 'The Byzantines and Saladin, 1185–1192. Opponents of the Third Crusade', *Speculum*, XXXVII (1962), pp. 167–181.

Champdor, A., *Saladin: Leplus pur héros d'Islam* (Paris, 1956).

Ebrenkreuz, A. S., *Nur al Din: un Grand Prince Musulman de Syrie au Temps des Croisades* (Damascus, 1967).

———, *Saladin* (Albany, 1972).

———, 'Saladin's coup d'état in Egypt', in Hanna, S. M. (ed.), *Medieval and Middle Eastern Studies in Honor of Aziz Suryal Atiya* (Leiden, 1972).

———, 'The Place of Saladin in the Naval History of the Mediterranean Sea in the Middle Ages', *Journal of the American Oriental Society*, LXXV (1955), pp. 100–16.

Gabrieli, F., *Il Saladino* (Florence, 1948).

Gibb, H. A. R., 'The Achievement of Saladin', in Gibb, H. A. R. (ed.), *Studies on the Civilization of Islam*, (Boston, 1962), pp. 91–107.

———, *The Achievements of Saladin* (London, 1952).

———, 'The Arabic Sources for the Life of Saladin', *Speculum*, XXV (1950), pp. 58–72.

———, 'The Armies of Saladin', *Cahiers d'histoire Egyptienne*, III (1951), pp. 304–20.

———, *The Life of Saladin: From the Works of Imad ad Din and Baha ad Din* (Oxford, 1973).

———, 'The Rise of Saladin, 1169–1189', in Baldwin, M. W. (ed.), *A History of the Crusades*, Vol. 1 (Philadelphia, 1958), pp. 563–89.

Hamblin, W. J., 'Saladin and Muslim Military Theory', in Kedar, B. Z. (ed.), *The Horns of Hattin* (Jerusalem, 1992), pp. 228–38.

Hamza, A., *Salah al-Din, batal Hattin* (Cairo 1958).

Hillenbrand, C., *The Crusades: Islamic Perspectives* (Edinburgh, 1999).

Hindley, G., *Saladin* (London 1976).

Holt, P. M., 'Saladin and his Admirers: A Biographical Reassessment', *Bulletin of the School of Occidental and African Studies*, XLVI (1983), pp. 235–9.

Jamati, H., *Al-Nasir Salah al-Din* (Cairo, 1962).

Kahle, P., 'Eine wichtige Quelle zur Geschichte des Sultans Saladin', *Die Welt des Orients*, I (1947–52), pp. 299-301.

Khulusi, S. A., 'Saladin—the Man of Destiny', *Islamic Review* (July 1950), pp. 19–25.

Lev, Y., *Saladin in Egypt* (Leiden, 1999).

Lewis, B., 'Maimonides, Lionheart and Saladin', *Eretz-Israel*, VII (1963), pp. 70–5.

———, 'Saladin and the Assassins', *Bulletin of the School of Oriental and African Studies*, XV (1953), pp. 239–45.

Lyons, M. C., and Jackson, D. E. P., *Saladin: The Politics of the Holy War* (Cambridge, 1982).

Minorsky, V., 'Prehistory of Saladin', in Minorsky, V., *Studies in Caucasian History* (London, 1953.), pp. 107–57.

Möhring, H., 'Saladins Politik des Heiligen Krieges', *Der Islam*, LXI (1984), pp. 322–6.

——, *Saladin und der dritte Kreuzzug* (Wiesbaden, 1980).

Nicolle, D., *Hattin, 1187*, Osprey Campaign Series, 1 (London, 1993).

——, *Saladin and the Saracens*, Osprey Men-at-Arms Series, 171 (London, 1986).

Paris, G., 'La Légende de Saladin', *Journal des Savants* (1893).

Qal'aji, Q., *Salah al-Din al-Ayyubi* (Beirut, 1966).

Regan, G., *Saladin and the Fall of Jerusalem* (London, 1987).

Runciman, S., 'Saladin: A Great Leader of Islam', *The Listener* (15 April 1954), pp. 648–9.

Slaughter, G.. *Saladin* (New York, 1955).

Tu'ma, S. J. al-, *Salah al-Din fi'l-shi'r al-'arabi* (Riyadh, 1979).

David Nicolle

EDITOR'S NOTE

Saladin and the Fall of the Kingdom of Jerusalem was first published in 1898 as part of the 'Heroes of the Nations' series, which included amongst its subjects such illustrious and diverse names as Pericles, Mohammed, William the Conqueror, Louis XIV, Nelson, Abraham Lincoln and Bismarck. This reprint is published unabridged, its delightful Victorian prose unaltered except for the correction of a few very minor blemishes. The reader will therefore note a number of stylistic conventions and renderings which are unfamiliar today, for example, the use of parenthetical em rules in conjunction with commas; the use of ligatures ('Cæsarea', etc); the use of the diaeresis mark ('coöperation'); and the presence of what would nowadays be considered archaic forms of spelling ('shew', etc.). A number of obvious typographical errors have been corrected, although other inconsistencies found in the original book have been left untouched (for example, the style in which dates are presented). The original Index contained a number of errors, and these have also been corrected. The folded charts which were to be found in a pocket inside the back cover of the earlier edition have been included in the present work as Appendices, although the size and complexity of the original charts have demanded recourse to a very small (though nonetheless legible) type size. Finally, the line drawings which graced the original publication have also been reproduced here, as space has permitted.

R.D.C

PREFACE

SALADIN IS ONE of the few Oriental Personages who need no introduction to English readers. Sir Walter Scott has performed that friendly office with the warmth and insight of appreciative genius. It was Saladin's good fortune to attract the notice not only of the great romancer, but also of King Richard, and to this accident he partly owes the result that, instead of remaining a dry historical expression, under the Arabic style of "*el-Melik en-Nasir Salah-ed-din Yusuf ibn Ayyub*," he has become, by the abbreviated name of "Saladin," that familiar and amiable companion which is called a household word. The idea, it is true, is vague and romantic. The *Talisman* has given us a noble portrait of the Sultan whose chivalry and generosity excited the admiration of the Crusaders, but the reader is left in uncertainty as to the history and achievements of the hero, and what he is told in those fascinating pages is not always strictly authentic. On the historical relation of the novel to which Saladin owes so much of his fame something is said at the end of this book. The present biography, the first that has been written in English, aspires to fill in, from contemporary sources, the details of the picture.

It is singular that, so far as English literature is concerned, the character and history of Saladin should have been suffered to remain where Scott left them seventy years ago, and that no complete Life of the celebrated adversary of Richard Cœur de Lion should have been written in our language. The materials are abundant, even exhaustive, so far as eastern scholars understood biography. We must not expect the personal details which delight the student of "interviews" : there were no illustrated papers in Saladin's time. But for the essential facts of his life and the qualities of his nature we have the best possible evidence, rich in extent and faithful in detail. The writers of the two chief Arabic records had excellent opportunities of ascertaining the truth, and both were men of learning and high character. Baha-ed-din, who was only seven years younger than Saladin, though he survived him by forty, was an Arab of the celebrated tribe of Asad, born at Mosil on the Tigris in 1145. He went through

21

the arduous course of study by which Moslems in those days qualified themselves for the judicial office of Kady. In the famous Nizamiya college at Baghdad,
founded by the great Vezir Nizam-el-mulk, the friend and schoolfellow of the
astronomer-poet Omar Khayyam, Baha-ed-din attended the lectures of the most
distinguished professors of the day, men who had wandered, like our own medieval scholars, from university to university, from Spanish Cordova to Tatar
Samarkand, teaching and learning as they went. He became a professor himself
at his native city of Mosil, and his wisdom and judgment so commended him to
the Atabeg or ruler of Mesopotamia that he chose him repeatedly to be his ambassador in grave political emergencies.

Baha-ed-din was at Mosil when Saladin twice laid siege to it in 1182 and
1185; he went on an embassy to Damascus in 1184, when Saladin was so much
impressed by his ability that he offered him a judgeship, which was loyally declined by the envoy; but they met again at Harran in the spring of 1186, when
Baha-ed-din assisted in drawing up a treaty of peace between his sovereign and
Saladin. After making the pilgrimage to Mekka, and to Jerusalem, then newly
recovered from the Christians, he visited the Sultan once more, and from that
time forth he seldom left his side. Entering his service on 28th June, 1188, he
was present throughout his subsequent campaigns, witnessed the siege of Acre
from the beginning to the end, accompanied him as he harassed Richard's march
down the coast, took a prominent part in the engagements at Jaffa in 1192, and
was at Saladin's bedside during his fatal illness. After the Sultan's death, he
accepted the high dignity of judge of Aleppo, and there he devoted his zeal and
his savings to founding colleges and training doctors to be learned in the law.
One of his pupils has left a touching description of the venerable Kady, as he
knew him, when a heated alcove and heavy furs could not warm the chilled
blood of 85; but the old scholar still loved to teach the students who came to him
after Friday prayers, when he could no longer go to the mosque, and when even
in his private devotions he could scarcely keep his feet. "He drooped like an
unfledged bird for weakness," says his biographer, and in 1234 he died, twoscore
years after the events he related in his Life of his master.

For the last five years of Saladin's career, Baha-ed-din is an incomparable
authority, an eye-witness of what passed, and an intimate friend and counsellor
of the Sultan. For the earlier periods he is less accurate and much less detailed;
but even here he is able to record several important transactions at first hand,
and his familiar intercourse with Saladin and his officers and kinsmen must
have supplied him with much of his information. He writes, it is true, as an
avowed panegyrist, but though in his eyes the King can do no wrong, he is so

frank and guileless in his narrative, and so obviously writes exactly what he saw and thought, that the biography has not suffered by the writer's hero-worship. It bears the unmistakable stamp of truth, and its personal bias and oriental hyperbolism are easily discounted. As our sole first-hand witness to the negotiations between Richard I. and Saladin, Baha-ed-din's simple veracity is especially a quality of importance.

If Baha-ed-din is an avowed hero-worshipper, in the other prime authority we find a useful corrective to undue admiration. Ibn-el-Athir had every political reason to decry the supplanter of his local lords, and his annals contain criticism of Saladin's generalship and one or two graver accusations. Ibn-el-Athir, who was also an Arab, of the tribe of Sheyban, was fifteen years younger than Baha-ed-din, and was born in 1160 at Jezirat-ibn-Omar on the Tigris, over which city his father was Waly or prefect. The historian spent most of his life in laborious study at Mosil, where his brother was a distinguished councillor of the Atabeg who ruled Mesopotamia. Another brother held a post in Saladin's chancery. Ibn-el-Athir, like Baha-ed-din, was present when Saladin besieged Mosil in 1185, and he accompanied the contingent which the Mesopotamian princes afterwards sent to join the Sultan's army in his north Syrian campaign of 1188; he was also a traveller, and in his journeys to Damascus, Jerusalem, and Aleppo, he had means of verifying his information. His *History of the Atabegs of Hosil*, completed in 1211, is as much a panegyric as Baha-ed-din's biography of Saladin, but it is a panegyric of Saladin's enemies; its author can never forgive him for supplanting the dynasty of the Atabegs in Syria, and making even the great lord of Mosil his vassal. Thus, if anything can be urged in disparagement of Saladin, we may be sure that Ibn-el-Athir will not pass it over. Yet, with this natural bias in favour of his family's old masters and benefactors, he is not usually unfair. He recognises Saladin's great services to Islam, and in his later work, the *Kamil*, or *Perfection of History*, which is brought up to within three years of his death in 1233, he shows a more impartial spirit than in his special eulogy of the Atabegs of Mosil.

These two historians must be the prime authorities for a Life of Saladin; but there are others of great value for particular portions or aspects of his career. Of these Imad-ed-din of Ispahan, generally known as el-Katib, "the Scribe," Saladin's chief secretary or chancellor for the Syrian provinces, is of the first importance; but unfortunately only a small part of his work has been printed. He was with his master at the siege of Acre, and his writings, despite their intolerable rhetoric, have the merit of first-hand documents. The *Autobiography* of Osama, an Arab prince and poet, of the castle of Sheyzar on the Orontes, who witnessed the

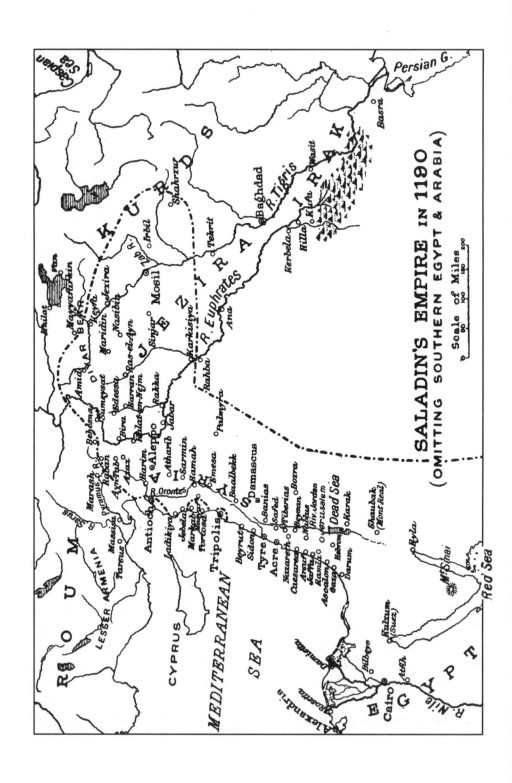

SALADIN'S EMPIRE IN 1190
(OMITTING SOUTHERN EGYPT & ARABIA)

Scale of Miles
0   50   100   150   200

greater part of the Crusading period from his birth in 1095 to his death in 1188, presents a vivid picture of the times; but although in his old age he lived for some years at Damascus in frequent intercourse with Saladin, his reminiscences in this regard are disappointing: the old Arab was too full of himself to give much space to the sayings and doings of others. Ibn-Khallikan, the assiduous biographer of eminent men, and Abu-Shama, the author of *The Two Gardens*, were neither of them contemporaries; but both knew people who knew Saladin, and their writings sometimes supply what was missing, or amplify what was meagre, in the contemporary records.

Among the Christian chroniclers we are fortunate in the presence in Palestine of the incomparable Archbishop William of Tyre, whose *Historia*, far transcending in vividness, grasp and learning all Latin or Arabic annals of the time, deals with the events in the East from 1144 to 1183 from personal knowledge. The Archbishop left no successor of his own calibre, and that he should not have lived to carry his history ten years further, to the end of the Third Crusade, is a loss which every student of the period, and not least the biographer of Saladin, must lament. The various continuators of his work cannot lay claim to his great qualities as an historian, but their merits are not to be undervalued, and the Chronicle of Ernoul in particular supplies valuable contemporary evidence. Ernoul was squire to Balian of Ibelin, who played a prominent part in the Holy War and was frequently in personal relations with Saladin; and the squire doubtless attended his master to the memorable field of Hittin and afterwards in the defence of Jerusalem. Ernoul's narrative, which is full of vivid personal touches, is thus extremely valuable as representing the Christian side of events which the Arabic writers describe from a Mohammedan point of view. It is also useful, in a less degree, in checking the exuberant Ricardolatry of the *Itinerarium Regis Ricardi*, which forms our fullest authority for the Third Crusade, and, despite its exaggerations and party spirit, is a marvellously graphic recital of the achievements of the English hero.

These then are the chief sources from which the present Life of Saladin is drawn. They are nearly all contemporary, and a large part of the story is told by actual eye-witnesses, whilst in no instance has an authority been relied upon who was more than one generation removed from the events he relates. References to these sources are given when a statement seemed to require authentication, and in the later chapters, when it is important to distinguish the testimony of Christian from that of Moslem witnesses, such footnotes are frequent; but in the earlier part, where nearly everything rests upon the authority of Ibn-el-Athir and Baha-ed-din, references are given only when there is a serious discrepancy between the two. In an historical study founded upon original research such verification is, of course, essential; but where none is given, some confidence, it is hoped, will be placed in the biographer. There is not a line in this volume that cannot be substantiated by practically contemporary evidence.

It has been remarked as strange that such abundant materials should not long ago have been utilised in an exhaustive Life of Saladin, but it would not be fair to ignore the admirable labours of M. Marin, "un écrivain aussi connu par la douceur de ses moeurs que par l'étendue de ses lumières et l'élègance de sa plume." M. Louis-François-Claude Marin was born in Provence, where he eventually held the posts of Censeur Royal et de la police, and Sécretaire général de la Librairie et des Académies de Marseille et Nancy. In 1758 he published in two charmingly printed duodecimo volumes an *Histoire de Saladin, Sulthan d'Egypte et de Syrie* (Paris, chez Tilliard, Libraire, Quai des Augustins, à l'Image Saint Benôit). The book appears to be almost unknown, or it would surely have found a translator. At once scholarly, philosophic, and written with that light touch by which the French, preëminently, are able to carry off the ponderous effect of real learning, M. Marin's biography has only to be read to be admired. He made a full use of the Crusading chronicles, and of Schultens' edition of Baha-ed-din, and he consulted Ibn-el-Athir's *Atabegs* in an Arabic manuscript at Paris. So far as his contemporary materials go, he is excellent; but he relied overmuch on later writers, and on unequal though learned compilations such as Herbelot's *Bibliothèque Orientale*; and of course a great deal has been discovered and published since his time. Still, considering his necessary limitations, he achieved a remarkable success, and the only serious fault to be found with his manner of dealing with such authorities as he was able to use is a tendency to read more "between the lines" than the text really justifies. M. Marin employed what is called "the historical imagination" over freely, and despite his frequent references to original sources one can detect a personal equation which has to be eliminated. It is much more interesting to give oneself a free hand in writing history, but the temptation must be subdued and the letter of the text must be respected.

Some authors, in treating of the history of Mesopotamia, have thought it necessary to prepare their readers by beginning at the Flood. M. Marin considered that his Life of Saladin demanded an introduction which went back to Mohammed and the first preaching of Islam. I have not tried the patience of the reader quite so severely, but without some account of the course of history in western Asia during the eleventh and twelfth centuries, the political situation in which Saladin began his career would be unintelligible. Especially important is the position achieved by his great forerunner, Zengy, the conqueror of Edessa, whose unfulfilled ambitions prepared the way for the imperial realisations of Saladin. The introductory chapters, however, have been reduced to as small a compass as possible.

Oriental names are naturally a stumbling-block to western readers, and the use of accents, long marks, dots, and the like, does not seem to be of much assistance to the unlearned. In the present work, therefore, the names are written as simply as possible, and the reader is only asked to pronounce the vowels after the Italian manner. Those who are curious as to the more precise transliteration will consult the index, where every name is furnished with the proper accents and distinguishing marks, and can be at once converted by the scholar into the Arabic character. In the text, the article *el* is generally omitted before the well-known names of towns, such as el-Mosil, el-Ramla, and western names are given when familiar, as in the case of Edessa (for er-Ruha), Aleppo (for Halab), and Cairo (for el-Kahira). When a town has two names, one used by the Arabs, the other by the "Franks" or Crusaders, both are given on its first occurrence, and Crusading names are retained so long as the place remained in the hands of the Crusaders.

Tables of contemporary sovereigns and princes in western Asia, of Saladin's family, and of the chief Crusading houses, will help the reader to understand the political situation. The maps are based upon the "Survey of Western Palestine," Thuillier and Rey's "North Syria," and the Arab geographers. Much assistance has been derived from Mr. Guy Le Strange's valuable work on *Palestine under the Moslems*; the notes contributed by Gen. Sir Charles Wilson and Lieut.-Col. Conder, R.E., to the Palestine Pilgrims' Text Society's translation of Baha-ed-din have been consulted; but the text of that work, not being directly translated from the Arabic, has not been cited. The author is specially indebted to Mr. T. A. Archer, not only for ready help in any difficulty that arose in connexion with the Crusading chronicles, but also for permission to quote his translation of parts of the *Itinerary of King Richard*, originally published in his fascinating little book, *The Crusade of Richard I.*, in the series of "English History from Contemporary Writers," edited by Professor York Powell. His thanks are also due to Mr. E. B. Knobel, late President of the Royal Astronomical Society, for kindly investigating the chronology of the eclipses recorded in the course of Saladin's campaigns, and to the editor of the *Quarterly Review* for permission to reprint part of an article on "The Age of Saladin."

M. Paul Casanova has kindly permitted the reproduction of three of the photographs which illustrate his valuable *Histoire et description de la Citadelle du Caire*; to Dr. F. J. Mackinnon is due the illustration of the tomb of Saladin at Damascus, as restored in Ottoman times. The author is also obliged to the Council of the Royal Institute of British Architects for the use of two views of the Omayyad Mosque of Damascus, before the fire, from sketches by Mr. R. Phenè Spiers, F.S.A.

PRINCIPAL AUTHORITIES

Ibn-el-Athir (1160–1233), *el-Bahir:* History of the Atabegs of el-Mosil, written in 1211 (*Recueil des historiens des Croisades: historiens orientaux*, tome ii., 2, Paris, 1876)

Ibn-el-Athir (1160–1233), *el-Kamil fi-t-tarikh:* General History, written up to 1231 (ed. Tornberg, 14 vols., Leyden, 1866–76; *Recueil*, tome i., 1872; tome ii., 1887).

Baha-ed-din, Ibn-Sheddad (1145–1234), *en-Nawadir es-Sultaniya wa-l-Mahasin el-Yusufiya:* Life of Saladin (ed. Schultens, Leyden, 1732; *Recueil*, tome iii., 1884; and Palestine Pilgrims' Text Society, ed. Sir C. W. Wilson, K.C.B., R.E., 1897).

Ibn-Khallikan (1211–1282), *We-fayat el-A'yan:* Biographical Dictionary (trans. de Slane, 4 vols., Paris, 1834–71).

Osama ibn Munkidh (1095–1188), *Kitab el-I'tibar:* Autobiography (ed. and trans. H. Derenbourg, 2 vols., Paris, 1886–93).

'Imad-ed-din el-Katib (1125–1201), *el-Feth el-Kussy* (ed. Landberg, vol. i., Leyden, 1888).

Abu-Shama (ob. 1267), *Kitab er-Rodateyn:* History of Nur-ed-din and Saladin (2 vols., Cairo, 1870–71).

William of Tyre (*c.* 1137–1185), *Historia rerum in partibus transmarinis gestarum* (*Recueil: historiens occidentaux*, tome i., Paris, 1844).

Ernoul (fl. 1187), *Chronique* (ed. Mas Latrie, Paris, 1871).

Itinerarium Peregrinorum et Gesta Regis Ricardi (1190–92) (ed. Stubbs, Rolls Series, vol. xxxviii. a, London, 1864).

Archer, T. A., *The Crusade of Richard I.* (London, 1888)

Le Strange, Guy, *Palestine under the Moslems* (Palestine Exploration Fund, 1890).

Rey, E., *Les colonies franques de Syrie* (Paris, 1883).

Other works are also referred to in the footnotes.

PART I

THE LIFE OF SALADIN

CHAPTER I

SALADIN'S WORLD

I N THE YEAR 1132 a broken army, flying before its pursuers, reached the left
bank of the Tigris. On the other side, upon a steep cliff, stood the impregnable Fortress of Tekrit, defended landwards by a deep moat and accessible
only by secret steps cut in the rock and leading from the heart of the citadel to
the water's edge. The one hope of the fugitives was to attain the refuge of the
castle, and their fate turned upon the disposition of its warden. Happily he
chose the friendly part, and provided a ferry by which they crossed to safety.
The ferry boats of the Tigris made the fortunes of the house of Saladin. The
flying leader who owed his life to their timely succour was Zengy, the powerful
lord of Mosil; and in later days, when triumph returned to his standards, he did
not forget the debt he owed Tekrit, but, ever mindful of past services, carried its
warden onward and upward on the wave of his progress. This warden was
Saladin's father.

Ayyub (in English plain Job), surnamed after the fashion of the Saracens
Nejm-ed-din, or "Star of the Faith," the fortunate commandant at this critical
moment, although an oriental and a Mohammedan, belonged to the same great
Aryan stock as ourselves, being neither Arab nor Turk, but a Kurd of the Rawadiya
clan, born at their village of Ajdanakan near Dawin in Armenia. From time immemorial the Kurds have led the same wild pastoral life in the mountain tracts
between Persia and Asia Minor. In their clannishness, their love of thieving,
their fine chivalrous sense of honour and hospitality, and their unquestioned
courage, they resembled the Arabs of the "Days of Ignorance" before Islam, or
the Highland Scots before the reforms of Marshal Wade. They have ever been a
gallant and warlike people, impervious as a rule to civilisation and difficult for
strangers to manage, but possessed of many rude virtues. At least, they gave
birth to Saladin. Of his more distant forefathers nothing is known. His family is
becomingly described by his biographers as "one of the most eminent and re-
spectable in Dawin," but even if true this is at most a provincial and limited
distinction. Dawin, formerly called Dabil, was the capital of Inner or Northern

31

Armenia in the tenth century, long before Tiflis attained to its greater importance. It was a large walled city, the residence of the governor of the province,
and its inhabitants were chiefly Christians, who carried on a rich trade in the
goats' hair clothes and rugs which they wove and dyed with the brilliant crimson
of the kirmiz worm. Jews, Magians, and Christians dwelt there in peace under
their Mohammedan conquerors, and the Armenian Church stood beside the
Mosque where Moslems prayed.

But Dawin was already in its decline when Saladin's grandfather, Shadhy,
son of Marwan, inherited the family position of "eminence and respectability" ;
and having a large number of sons he resolved to seek careers for them in the
more stirring life of Baghdad, where the courts of the Caliph and the Sultan
offered prizes to the ambitious. Shadhy is but a name; nothing is known of his
character or history, except that he had a close friend in the Greek Bihruz, who
rose from slavery at Dawin to high office at the Persian court, became the tutor
of Seljuk princes, and was rewarded with the important government of the city
of Baghdad. To this old friend Shadhy resorted, and Bihruz out of his large
patronage presented his comrade's son Ayyub to the post of commandant of the
castle of Tekrit. Probably the whole family accompanied the fortunate nominee;
certainly Shadhy and his son Shirkuh joined Ayyub; and if the last justified his
patron's trust by the wisdom and prudence of his rule, Shirkuh, ever hasty and
passionate, wrecked, as it seemed, the good fortune of the family by an act of
chivalrous homicide: he killed a scoundrel to avenge a woman's wrong. Bihruz
was already annoyed at the escape of Zengy, whom he did not love; and he was
not inclined to overlook the violence of Shirkuh. The brothers were commanded
to seek employment elsewhere. They departed from Tekrit, oppressed with a
sense of misfortune, and drew a sinister omen from the fact that on the very
night of their flitting a son had been born to Ayyub. Never, surely, was augury
worse interpreted; for the infant whose first cries disturbed the preparations of
the journey that night in the castle of Tekrit in the year of Grace 1138, was
Yusuf, afterwards renowned in East and West under his surname of "Honour of
the Faith," *Salah-ed-din,* or, as we write it, SALADIN.*

Before attempting to relate whither Ayyub carried the baby Saladin, or what
befell them, we must glance briefly at the political conditions in which the future
leader of the Saracens would have to shape his career. The eastern world of that
day was widely different from the old empire of the Caliphate; it had vitally

* The Mohammedan year 532, in which Saladin was born, corresponds to the interval between 19
Sept. 1137 and 8 Sept. 1138. The month of Saladin's birth is not recorded, and he may of course
have been born in 1137.

changed even in the lifetime of Saladin's father. The flaming zeal which had at first carried the armies of Islam, like a rushing prairie fire, from their ancient Arabian musterground to the desert of Sind in the east and the surge of the Atlantic on the west, had not availed to keep together, in a well-knit organisation, the vast empire so suddenly, so amazingly, acquired. The Caliphate lasted indeed for over six hundred years, but it retained its imperial sway for scarcely a third of that time. In the seventh century, the soldiers of the Arabian Prophet had rapidly subdued Egypt, Syria, Persia, and even the country beyond the Oxus, and early in the eighth they rounded off their conquest of the Barbary coast by the annexation of Spain. Such an empire, composed of contentious and rival races, and extending over remotely distant provinces, could not long be held in strict subjection to a central government issuing its patents of command from Damascus or Baghdad. The provincial proconsul of the Mohammedan system was even more apt to acquire virtual independence than his Roman prototype. The very idea of the Caliphate, which was as much an ecclesiastical as an administrative authority, encouraged the local governors to assume powers which were not irreconcilable with the homage due to a spiritual chief; and the religious schisms of Islam, especially the strange and fanatical devotion inspired by the persecuted lineage of Aly, led by a different road to the dismemberment of the state.

Already in the ninth century the extremities of the Mohammedan empire were in the hands of rulers who either repudiated the authority of the Abbasid Caliph of Baghdad, or at least tendered him, as Commander of the Faithful, a purely conventional homage. The Caliph's writ—or its Arabic equivalent—even in the days of "the good Harun er-Rashid," did not run in Spain or Morocco, and met but a qualified respect in Tunis. Egypt on the one hand, and north-east Persia on the other, soon followed the lead of the extreme west, and by the middle of the tenth century the temporal power of the Caliph hardly extended beyond the walls of his own palace, within which his authority was grievously shackled by the guard of mercenaries whom he had imprudently imported in self-defence. This state of papal impotence continued with little change until the extinction of the Baghdad Caliphate by the Mongols in 1258. Now and again, by the weakness of their neighbours or the personal ascendency of an individual Caliph, the Abbasids temporarily recovered a part of their territorial power in the valley of the Tigris and Euphrates; yet even then, although the Caliph had a larger army and possessed a wider dominion than his predecessor had enjoyed, his authority was restricted to a narrow territory in Mesopotamia, and his influence, save as pontiff of Islam, was almost a negligible quantity in Saladin's political world.

This political world was practically bounded by the Tigris on the east and the Libyan desert on the west. For a century and a half before Saladin began to mix in affairs of state, Egypt had been ruled by the Fatimid Caliphs, a schismatic dynasty claiming spiritual supremacy by right of descent from Aly the son-in-law of the Prophet Mohammed, and repudiating all recognition of the Abbasid Caliphate of Baghdad. Still more nearly affecting the politics of the Crusades was the situation in Syria and Mesopotamia. The whole of these districts, from the mountains of Kurdistan to the Lebanon, are in race and politics allied with Arabia. Large tribes of Arabs were settled from early times in the fertile valleys of Mesopotamia, where their names are still preserved in the geographical divisions. Bedawy tribes wandered annually from Arabia to the pasture lands of the Euphrates, as they wander to this day: and many clans were and are still permanently settled in all parts of Syria. The decay of the Caliphate naturally encouraged the foundation of Arab kingdoms in the regions dominated by Arab tribes, and in the tenth and eleventh centuries the greater part of Syria and Mesopotamia owned their supremacy; but by the twelfth these had all passed away. The Arabs remained in their wonted seats, and camped over all the country to the upper valleys of Diyar-Bekr as they do now; but they no longer ruled the lands where they pastured their flocks. The supremacy of the Arab in those regions was over for ever, and the rule of the Turk had begun.

The Turks who swept over Persia, Mesopotamia, and Syria in the course of the eleventh century were led by the descendants of Seljuk, a Turkman chieftain from the steppes beyond the Oxus. In a rapid series of campaigns they first overran the greater part of Persia; other Turkish tribes then came to swell their armies; and the whole of western Asia, from the borders of Afghanistan to the frontier of the Greek empire and the confines of Egypt, was gradually united under Seljuk rule. Persians, Arabs and Kurds alike bowed before the overwhelming wave of conquest. But wide as was their dominion, the significance of the Seljuk invasion lies deeper than mere territorial expansion. Their advent formed an epoch in Mohammedan history by creating a revival of the Moslem faith.

"At the time of their appearance the Empire of the Caliphate had vanished. What had once been a realm united under a sole Mohammedan ruler was now a collection of scattered dynasties, not one of which, save perhaps the Fatimids of Egypt (and they were schismatics), was capable of imperial sway. The prevalence of schism increased the disunion of the various provinces of the vanished empire. A drastic remedy was needed, and it was found in the invasion of the Turks. These rude nomads, unspoilt by town life and civilised indifference to religion, embraced Islam with all the fervour of their uncouth souls. They came to the rescue of a dying State and revived it. They swarmed over Persia, Mesopotamia, Syria, and Asia Minor, devastating the country, and exterminating every dynasty that existed there; and, as the result, they once more reunited Mohammedan Asia, from the western frontier of Afghanistan to the Mediterranean, under one sovereign; they put a new life into the expiring zeal of the Moslems, drove back the re-encroaching Byzantines, and bred up a generation of fanatical Mohammedan warriors to whom, more than to anything else, the Crusaders owed their repeated failure."8

Melik Shah, the noblest of the Seljuk emperors, was one of those rulers who possess the power of imposing their minds upon their age. To belong to his household, to hold his commands, was not merely an honour and a privilege; it was also an apprenticeship in principles. In serving the Sultan, one grew like him; and a standard of conduct was thus set up, modelled upon the life of the royal master, the pattern and exemplar of the age. It is recorded by an Arab historian that a chief or governor was esteemed by public opinion in accordance with the degree in which he conformed to the Sultan's example; and the standard thus adopted formed no ignoble ideal of a prince's duties. Justice was the first aim of Melik Shah; his chief effort was to promote his people's prosperity. Bridges, canals, and caravanserais bore witness to his encouragement of commerce and inter-communication throughout his dominions. The roads were safe, and it is stated that a pair of travellers could journey without an escort from Merv to Damascus. Generous and brave, just and conscientious, he fulfilled the ideal of a Moslem Prince, and his example impressed itself far and wide upon the minds of his followers.

Great as he was in character and statesmanship, Melik Shah owed much of his principles and his successful organisation to the still wiser man who filled the highest office in the realm. Nizam-el-mulk stands among the great statesmen of history. His Mohammedan eulogists dwell fondly upon his spiritual virtues, and recount with unction how he could repeat the entire Koran by heart at the age of twelve; but the supreme testimony to his ability is seen in the prosperity and progress of the great empire for nearly a third of a century committed to his charge. His capacity for affairs was joined to a profound knowledge of jurisprudence and an enlightened support of learning and science. He it was who encouraged Omar Khayyam in his astronomical researches,—less famous to-day but certainly not less important than his well-known *Quatrains,*—and founded the famous Nizamiya college at Baghdad. And it was he who in his *Treatise on the Principles of Government,*† drawn up at the bidding of Melik Shah and adopted by the Sultan as his code, set forth an ideal conception of kingship that embod-

---

* S. Lane-Poole, *The Mohammedan Dynasties*, 149, 150.
† Published by M. Schefer with the title of *Siasset Naheh*, Paris, 1893.

ies an uncompromising doctrine of Divine Right. The sovereign, he holds, is without doubt God's anointed; but the doctrine is tempered with a stern insistence upon the king's responsibility to God for every detail of his conduct towards the subjects entrusted to his protection. Παστι δε ω εδοθη πολυ, πολυ ζητηθησεται παρ αυτου, "For unto whomsoever much is given, of him shall be much required," is the Vezir's principle, as it was of a greater Teacher before him, and his ideal of a true monarch savours of a counsel of perfection. He defines the character of a king by a quotation from an old Persian anecdote:

> "He must subdue hatred, envy, pride, anger, lust, greed, false hopes, disputatiousness, lying, avarice, malice, violence, selfishness, impulsiveness, ingratitude, and frivolity; he must possess the qualities of modesty, equability of temper, gentleness, clemency, humility, generosity, staunchness, patience, gratitude, pity, love of knowledge, and justice."

One weighty judgment, it is alleged, is of more service to a king than a mighty army. He is cautioned to avoid favouritism and disproportionate rewards, to eschew excess in wine and unkingly levity, and recommended to be strict in fasting, prayer, almsgiving, and all religious exercises. In every circumstance he is to "observe the mean" ; for the Prophet of Islam said, unconsciously quoting Aristotle, that in all things "the mean" is to be followed.

The most striking feature in the system of government outlined by Nizam-el-mulk is his constant insistence on the duties of the sovereign towards his subjects, and the elaborate checks suggested for the detection and punishment of official corruption and oppression. Twice a week the Sultan was obliged to hold public audience, when anybody, however humble and unknown, might come to present his grievances and demand justice. The Sultan must hear these petitions himself, without any go-between, listen patiently, and decide each case in accordance with equity. Various precautions are recommended to ensure the free access of the subject to the king. The example is cited of a Persian sovereign who held audience on horseback in the middle of a plain, so that all might see and approach him, when the obstacles of "gates, barriers, vestibules, passages, curtains, and jealous chamberlains" were thus removed. Another king made all petitioners wear red dresses, so that he might distinguish and take them aside for private audience; and the example is approved of a Samanid prince who sat alone and unattended all night during heavy snow, in the middle of the great square of Bokhara, on the chance that some oppressed subject, who might have been turned away by his chamberlains, should see him and come for redress.

Extraordinary pains were to be taken lest the maladministration of local governors should escape detection:

"When an officer is appointed to a post, let him be benevolent to God's creatures. One must not exact from them more than is right, and one should demand it with gentleness and consideration. Taxes should never be claimed before the fixed legal day, else the people, under pressure of need, will sell their goods at half-price, and become ruined and dispersed."

Constant inspection of the tax-gatherers and other officials is recommended, and severe punishment is to be meted out to the unjust. "Spies," he says, "must perpetually traverse the roads of the various provinces, disguised as merchants, dervishes, etc., and send in reports of what they hear, so that nothing that passes shall remain unknown." Another precaution was to change all tax-gatherers and agents every two or three years, so that they should not become rooted and overbearing in their posts. Further, inspectors of high character, above suspicion, paid by the treasury and not by local taxation, were appointed to watch the whole empire; "the advantages which their uprightness brings will repay an hundredfold their salaries." A prompt and regular system of post-messengers maintained rapid communications between the inspectors and the central government. Finally, the good behaviour of vassal chiefs was ensured by their sending hostages, relieved every year, to the imperial court, where no fewer than five hundred were constantly detained.

These provisions for just administration and frequent inspection were all the more necessary in an empire which was founded upon a military organisation, wherein the government was vested in the hands of foreigners. The Seljuk power rested on an army composed, to a great extent, of hired or purchased soldiers, and officered by slaves of the royal household. Freemen were not to be trusted with high commands, at least in distant provinces; native Persians and Arabs could not, as a rule, be expected to work loyally for their Turkish conquerors; and it was safer to rely on the fidelity of slaves brought up at the court, in close relations of personal devotion to the Seljuk princes. These white slaves or *mamluks*, natives for the most part of Kipchak and Tartary, formed the body-guard of the Sultan, filled the chief offices of the court and camp, and rising step by step, according to their personal merits and graces, eventually won freedom and power. They were rewarded by grants of castles, cities, and even provinces, which they held of their master the Sultan on condition of military service. The whole empire was organised on this feudal basis, which seems to have been usual among the Turks, and which was inherited from the Seljuks and carried into Egypt by Saladin, where it was for centuries maintained by the Mamluk Sultans. The greater part of Persia, Mesopotamia, and Syria was parcelled out in military fiefs, and governed by Seljuk captains—quondam slaves in the mamluk bodyguard—who held them in fee simple by letters patent, revocable at the Sultan's will, and who levied and lived on the land tax, on the sole condition of furnishing troops at the Sultan's call.

The greater feudatories in turn let out portions of their fiefs to sub-vassals, who were bound to furnish troops to their overlord, just as he was required to bring his retainers to the support of his sovereign. We read of a primitive method of summoning the military contingents, by sending an arrow round from camp to camp, or village to village, as a signal for assembly. After a campaign the feudal troops were dismissed to their homes, whither they always retired during the winter, under an engagement to join the colours in the spring. In the interval a general was obliged to be content with his own immediate followers, his bodyguard, and any mercenaries who could be induced to remain in the field. Saladin, as will be seen, invariably observed this custom. When living on their lands, the vassals were only allowed to collect the legal tax, amounting apparently to about one-tenth of the produce, and were straitly enjoined not to oppress the people or seize their goods. "The land and its inhabitants are the Sultan's," wrote the great Vezir, "and the feudal lords and governors are but as a guard set for their protection." No doubt, so long as the Seljuk empire held together, the omnipresent spy kept license and corruption at bay; but when there was no supreme government, during the troublous times that preceded the establishment of Nur-ed-din's and Saladin's organised rule, much misery, instead of "protection," must have come in the train of feudalism. We read constantly of the barons or emirs setting forth on the war path, followed by their retainers, and such a party was as likely as not to meet a rival troop somewhere along the rugged tracks of Mesopotamia, with the usual result of a skirmish, perhaps a victory, and then slaughter and pillage. The life of the shepherd, the husbandman, and the trader, must have been sufficiently exciting, and not a little precarious, in the midst of the valorous activity of neighbouring chiefs; and the equitable precepts of Melik Shah and his wise Vezir must often have been forgotten in the flush of victory.

The Arab chronicler, however, prone as he is to dwell upon feats of arms, never quite overlooks the condition of the peaceful population; and it is worth noticing that in signalising the virtues of a great lord he puts prominently forward the justice and mildness he displayed towards his subjects. The "Gyrfalcon" (Ak-Sunkur) of Mosil is held up to admiration as a wise ruler and protector of his people.* Perfect justice reigned throughout his dominions; the markets

---

* Ibn-el-Athir, *Atabegs*, 29, 30.

were cheap; the roads absolutely safe; and order prevailed in all parts. His policy was to make the district pay for its own misdeeds, so that if a caravan were plundered, the nearest villages had to make good the loss, and the whole population thus became a universal police for the traveller's protection. It is recorded of this good governor that he never broke his word, and the same might be said of more Moslem than Christian leaders of the Crusading epoch. The example of a just and virtuous chief naturally inspires emulation among his retainers, and it is not difficult, in many instances, to trace the effects of such influences. The constant endeavour of a great baron was to surround himself with a loyal body of retainers and minor feudatories, who could be trusted to support his arms, extend his dominions, and carry out his policy in the management of their domains. Upon their loyalty depended the succession of his family. When a baron died, his vassals and mamluks would rally round his heir, obtain for him the succession in the fief, and uphold him on the throne. No feeble ruler, however, had a chance in that strenuous age; he must be strong in war and firm in peace. It sometimes happened that an emir failed to satisfy the demands or retain the loyalty of his followers, who would then transfer their services to a more popular master.

In spite of its military character and the truculence of many of its leaders, nothing is more remarkable in Seljuk civilisation than the high importance attached to education and learning. Although colleges existed before in Mohammedan countries, we must ascribe to Seljuk patronage, above all to the influence of Nizam-el-mulk, the great improvements in educational provision in the East during the eleventh and twelfth centuries. The celebrated Nizamiya *medresa* or university at Baghdad, founded by the Vezir himself, was the focus from which radiated an enthusiasm for learning all over Persia, Syria, and Egypt, where it met a kindred stream of erudition issuing from the Azhar university of Cairo. To found a college was as much a pious act among Seljuk princes, as to build a mosque or conquer a city from the "infidels." The same spirit led the great vassals and the numerous dynasties that sprang up on the decay of the Seljuk power, to devote particular attention to questions of education, and by Saladin's time Damascus, Aleppo, Baalbekk, Emesa, Mosil, Baghdad, Cairo, and other cities, had become so many foci of learned energy. Professors travelled from college to college, just as our own medieval scholars wandered from university to university. Many of these learned men and ministers of state (the two were frequently united) were descendants or household officers of Seljuk Sultans. The Atabeg Zengy of Mosil, with all his vast energy and military talent, could scarcely have held the reins of his wide empire without the aid of his Vezir

and right-hand-man Jemal-ed-din, surnamed el-Jawad, "the Bountiful," whose
grandfather had been keeper of the coursing leopards in Sultan Melik Shah's
hunting stables. So ably did he administer the several governments successively
committed to his charge, and so charming were his manners and conversation,
that Zengy received him into the intimacy of his friendship and advanced him to
the post of Inspector-General of his principality and President of the Divan or
Council of State. His salary was a tenth of the produce of the soil and he spent
his wealth in boundless charity; ministered lavishly to the necessities of the
pilgrims at Mekka and Medina; built aqueducts and restored mosques; and kept
a gigantic roll of pensioners. When he died, "the air resounded with the lamentations" of widows and orphans and of the countless poor who had hailed him
benefactor.*

The ranks of the wise and learned were recruited from all parts of the Moslem world. Professors from Nishapur delighted audiences at Damascus. Persian
mystics like es-Suhrawardy met traditioners like Ibn-Asakir, whose funeral
Saladin himself attended in 1176. In the same year there arrived at Cairo a
stranger from Xativa in distant Andalusia, drawn eastward by the fame of the
revival of learning; it was Ibn-Firro, who had composed a massy poem of 1173
verses upon the *variæ lectiones* in the Koran, simply "for the greater glory of
God." This marvel of erudition modestly confessed that his memory was burdened with enough sciences to break down a camel. Nevertheless, when it came
to lecturing to his crowded audiences, he never uttered a superfluous word. It
was no wonder that the Kady el-Fadil, chief judge and governor of Egypt under
Saladin, lodged him in his own house and buried him in his private mausoleum.
The presence of such philosophers tempered with cool wisdom the impetuous
fire of the predatory chiefs. Many of the great soldiers of that age delighted in the
society of men of culture; and though the victorious Atabeg might exclaim that
to him "the clash of arms was dearer far than the music of sweet singers, and to
try conclusions with a worthy foe a greater delight than to toy with a mistress,"
yet he loved the company of his wise counsellor el-Jawad. His successor Nur-ed-
din was devoted to the society of the learned, and poets and men of letters
gathered round his Court; whilst Saladin took a peculiar pleasure in the conversation of grave theologians and solemn jurists. The most bloodthirsty baron of
them all could not do without his poet and historian. It was the same in later
centuries with the Mamluk Sultans of Egypt. Barbarous and savage as they
seemed, prone to deeds of blood and treachery, they loved the arts, encouraged

---

* Ibn-Khallikan, iii. 295–9.

belles-lettres, and made Cairo beautiful with their exquisite architecture. It would seem that in the East, at all events, violence may go hand in hand with taste and culture, and it was not Saul alone whose moody fits were relieved by the music of sweet singers.

The effects of the Seljuk domination reached far and wide; but the dynasty itself was shortlived. Less than half a century after they had entered Persia as conquerors, the vast fabric they had audaciously planned and splendidly maintained split up into fragments. Three Seljuk emperors in succession held their immense dominions under their personal rule without fear of rivalry or revolt; but when Melik Shah died in 1092, civil war broke out between his sons, and the empire was divided. Seljuks continued to rule at Nishapur, Ispahan, and Kirman; Seljuks at Damascus and Aleppo; Seljuks in Anatolia: but they were divided planks of the mighty bole, unable long to resist the forces which pressed upon them from within and without. Their overthrow was the inevitable consequence of their feudal organisation; they were hoist with their own petard. The slaves whom they imported for their defence became their destroyers, and the great fiefs that they had constructed for the protection of the empire proved to be its chief danger. The prime defect of European feudalism was equally conspicuous in the Seljuk system. The slave owed his master service, the vassal was bound to his overlord, but the service and loyalty did not extend beyond the immediate superior. If a chief vassal found himself strong enough to rebel against his overlord, his retainers, sub-vassals, and slaves followed him; they owed no service to the overlord. Nor was there any equivalent to a direct oath of allegiance to the sovereign, though one sometimes finds the sentiment of loyalty that induced sub-vassals to leave a rebellious overlord and go over to the side of the Crown. As the sovereign power grew weaker, this sentiment ceased to operate, and the great feudatories were able to found independent kingdoms of their own with the full concurrence of their vassals. When the empire became divided against itself, the captains who had fought its battles and reaped its rewards became independent princes; the mamluks who had won victories for their emperors became regents or governors (Atabegs) of their emperors' heirs; and the delegated function was presently exchanged for the full rights of sovereignty and the transmission of hereditary kingship.

The twelfth century saw the greater part of the Seljuk empire in the hands of petty sovereigns who had risen from the ranks of the mamluks and converted their fiefs into independent states. In Persia, and beyond the Oxus, a cupbearer and a *major domo* had founded powerful dynasties; and the slaves of these slaves, a generation of "gentlemen's gentlemen," had established minor principalities on the skirts of their masters' dominions. In this way a slave became regent over his master's heir and on his death assumed regal powers at Damascus; thus Zengy, founder of the long line of Atabegs of Mosil, was the son of one of Melik Shah's slaves; and the Ortukids and other local dynasts of Mesopotamia traced their fortunes to a similar source. However servile in origin, the pedigree carried with it no sense of ignominy. In the East a slave is often held to be better than a son, and to have been the slave of Melik Shah constituted a special title to respect. The great slave vassals of the Seljuks were as proud and honourable as any Bastard of medieval aristocracy; and when they in turn assumed kingly powers, they inherited and transmitted to their lineage the high traditions of their former lords. The Atabegs of Syria and Mesopotamia carried on the civilising work begun by the wise Vezir of Melik Shah. The work was interrupted, indeed, by internal feuds, but its chief hindrance during the twelfth century came from the Crusades.

STORMING OF ANTIOCH, 1098.
FROM A PAINTED WINDOW AT ST. DENYS, 12TH CENTURY.

CHAPTER II

THE FIRST CRUSADE
1098

MELIK SHAH, the great Seljuk Sultan, died in 1092, and civil war immediately broke out between his sons. Four years later, the First Crusade
began its eastward march; in 1098 the great cities of Edessa and Antioch
and many fortresses were taken; in 1099 the Christians regained possession of
Jerusalem itself. In the next few years the greater part of Palestine and the coast
of Syria, Tortosa, Acre, Tripolis, and Sidon (1110) fell into the hands of the
Crusaders, and the conquest of Tyre in 1124 marked the apogee of their power.
This rapid triumph was due partly to the physical superiority and personal courage
of the men of the North, but even more to the lack of any organised resistance.
Nizam-el-mulk had died before his master, and there was no statesman competent to arrange the differences between the emperor's heirs. Whilst the Seljuk
princes were casting away their crown in fratricidal strife, the great vassals,
though on the road to independence, had not yet learned their power: all were
struggling for pieces of the broken diadem, each was jealous of his neighbour,
but none was yet bold enough to lead. The founders of dynasties were in the
field, but the dynasties were not yet founded. The Seljuk authority was still
nominally supreme in Mesopotamia and northern Syria, and the numerous governors of cities and wardens of forts were only beginning to find out that the
Seljuk authority was but the echo of a sonorous name, and that dominion was
within the reach of the strongest.

It was a time of uncertainty and hesitation—of amazed attendance upon the
dying struggles of a mighty empire; an interregnum of chaos until the new forces
should have gathered their strength; in short, it was the precise moment when
a successful invasion from Europe was possible. A generation earlier, the Seljuk
power was inexpugnable. A generation later, a Zengy or a Nur-ed-din, firmly
established in the Syrian seats of the Seljuks, would probably have driven the
invaders into the sea. A lucky star led the preachers of the First Crusade to seize
an opportunity of which they hardly realised the significance. Peter the Hermit
and Urban II. chose the auspicious moment with a sagacity as unerring as if

43

they had made a profound study of Asiatic politics. The Crusades penetrated like a wedge between the old wood and the new, and for a while seemed to cleave the trunk of Mohammedan empire into splinters.

Seven years before the birth of Saladin, when Fulk of Anjou ascended the throne of Jerusalem in 1131, the Latin Kingdom was still in its zenith. Syria and Upper Mesopotamia lay at the feet of the Crusaders, whose almost daily raids reached from Maridin and Amid in Diyar-Bekr to el-Arish and "the brook of Egypt." Yet the country was not really subdued. The Crusaders contented themselves with a partial occupation, and whilst they held the coast lands and many fortresses in the interior, as far as the Jordan and Lebanon, they did not seriously set about a thorough conquest. The great cities, Aleppo, Damascus, Hamah, Emesa, were still in Moslem hands, and were never taken by the Christians, though their reduction must certainly have been possible at more than one crisis. The only great city which the Crusaders held in the interior, besides Jerusalem, was Edessa, and this they were soon to lose. The Latin Kingdom, with its subordinate principalities, counties, baronies, and fiefs, was more an armed occupation than a systematic conquest; yet even as an occupation it was inefficient. At the time of its greatest extent, the "Frank" dominion extended along a zone over five hundred miles long from north to south, but rarely more, and often less, than fifty miles broad. In the north the County of Edessa (er-Ruha, Orfa) stretched from (and often over) the borders of Diyar-Bekr to a point not far north of Aleppo, and included such important fiefs as Saruj, Tell-Bashir (Turbessel), Samosata, and Ayn Tab (Hatap). West and south of the County of Edessa lay the Principality of Antioch, which at one time included Tarsus and Adana in Cilicia, but usually extended from the Pyramus along the sea-coast to a little north of Margat, and inland to near the Mohammedan cities, Aleppo and Hamah; among its chief fiefs were Atharib (Cerep), Maarra, Apamea, with the port of Ladikiya (Laodicea). South again of Antioch was the County of Tripolis, a narrow strip between the Lebanon and the Mediterranean, including Margat (Markab), Tortosa, Crac des Chevaliers, Tripolis, and Jubeyl. Over all these states, as overlord, stood the King of Jerusalem, whose own dominions stretched from Beyrut past Sidon, Tyre, Acre, Cæsarea, Arsuf, Jaffa, to the Egyptian frontier fortress Ascalon, and were bounded generally on the east by the valley of the Jordan and the Dead Sea. The chief subdivisions were the County of Jaffa and Ascalon (including also the fortresses of Ibelin, Blanche Garde, and Mirabel, and the towns of Gaza, Lydda, and Ramla); the Lordship of Karak (Crac) and Shaubak (Mont Real), two outlying fortresses beyond the Dead Sea, cutting the caravan route from Damascus to Egypt; the Principality of Galilee, including

Tiberias, Safed, Kaukab (Belvoir), and other strongholds; the Lordship of Sidon; and the minor fiefs of Toron, Beysan (Bethshan), Nablus, etc.*

A glance at the map will show that a large proportion of these Christian possessions were within a day's, or at most two days', march of a Mohammedan city or a garrisoned fort, from which frequent raids were to be expected in retaliation for the incursions of the Franks. The autobiography of one of Saladin's elder contemporaries, the Arab Osama, reveals a perpetual state of guerilla encounters, alternating with periods of comparative friendliness and tranquillity. The general tendency of the original settlers of the First Crusade was undoubtedly towards amicable relations with their Moslem neighbours. The great majority of the cultivators of the soil in the Christian territories were of course Mohammedans, and constant intercourse with them, and social and domestic relations of the most intimate nature, tended to diminish points of difference and emphasise common interests and common virtues. In the present day a European family can rarely live to the third generation in the East without becoming more or less orientalised. The early Crusaders, after thirty years' residence in Syria, had become very much assimilated in character and habits to the people whom they had partly conquered, among whom they lived, and whose daughters they did not disdain to marry; they were growing into Levantines; they were known as *Pullani* or creoles. The Mohammedans, on their side, were scarcely less tolerant; they could hardly approve of marriage with the "polytheists," as they called the Trinitarians; but they were quite ready to work for them and take their pay, and many a Moslem ruler found it convenient to form alliances with the Franks even against his Mohammedan neighbours.

We find this interesting approximation between the rival races clearly appreciated in the fascinating memoirs of the nonagenarian Osama, the Arab prince of Sheyzar. As an historical witness, Osama was fortunate in his epoch. He was born in 1095, three years before the capture of Antioch gave the Franks their *point d'appui* whence they advanced to the conquest of Jerusalem; and he died in 1188, when the Holy City had just been retaken by Saladin. He witnessed nearly the complete tide, the flow and ebb, of Crusading effort. His long life of ninety-three years embraced the whole period of the Latin rule at Jerusalem, and only just missed the Crusade of Richard Cœur de Lion. His family, the Beny Munkidh, were the hereditary lords of the rocky fortress of Sheyzar, the ruins of which still overhang the Orontes. Strong as the castle was, shielded by a bold bluff of the Ansariya mountains, approachable only by a horsepath, which crossed

---

* Archer and Kingsford, *Crusades*, ch. vii.

the river, then tunnelled through the rock, and was again protected by a deep dyke crossed by a plank bridge, its situation in the immediate neighbourhood of Christian garrisons, half-way between the Crusading centres of Antioch and Tripoli, brought it into perilous contact with the forays that passed perpetually beneath its battlements.

Sheyzar was one of those little border states, between the Moslem and the Christian, which found their safest policy in tempering orthodoxy with diplomacy. No better post of speculation could have been chosen from which to observe the struggle that went on unceasingly throughout the twelfth century; no witness more competent or more opportune could be found than the Arab chief who surveyed the contest from his conning-tower of Sheyzar. He knew all the great leaders in the war, and often took part in the fray. His first battle was fought under that truculent Turkman, Il-Ghazy, the man who did more than anyone, before the coming of Zengy, to spread dismay through the Christian ranks. Osama served under Zengy himself, and was actually present in the famous flight over the Tigris into Tekrit when the timely succour of Ayyub made the fortunes of the house of Saladin. He had seen Tancred more than once, when the prince led an assault against Sheyzar; and he remembered the beautiful horse which the Crusader received as a present from its castellan. King Baldwin du Bourg was a prisoner in the fortress for some months in 1124, and rewarded his host's kindness, *more Francorum*, by breaking all his engagements the moment he was released. Joscelin of Courtenay was another well-known figure in the armed expeditions which passed in perpetual procession over the Orontes; the autobiographer even saw the Emperor John Comnenus lay siege to his own eyry on the "Cock's Comb." Later on he visited King Fulk at Acre and explained to him through an interpreter, for Osama knew no *lingua Franca*, that he too, Arab though he was, might call himself "knight, after the fashion of my race and family; for what we admire in a knight is that he be lean and long." Nor was Osama's acquaintance limited to such high personages as he chanced to meet at Sheyzar or visited during brief excursions into Frank territory. He lived for long years at Damascus, at the court of Nur-ed-din, for whom he conducted a diplomatic correspondence with Egypt; he became for a time the guest of the Fatimid Caliph at Cairo, and farmed a fief near by at Kom Ashfin, where he kept two hundred head of cattle, a thousand sheep, and reaped rich harvests of grain and fruit; and in his latter days he was intimate with Saladin, who delighted in his poetry and impromptu recitations.

Osama draws a firm line of distinction between the settled Franks, the families of the first Crusaders, who had grown accustomed to oriental life and become friendly with their Moslem neighbours, and the new arrivals, a set of big-oted pilgrims and needy adventurers, whose indiscreet zeal and lust of plunder embroiled the good understanding which had been established between the two creeds in Palestine. "Those Franks," he says, "who have come and settled amongst us and cultivated the society of Moslems are much superior to the others who have lately joined them. . . . The new-comers are invariably more inhuman than the older settlers, who have become familiar with the Mohammedans." Personal friendships were frequent between the settled Crusaders and the neighbouring Moslems, and it was not unusual for a Mohammedan to enjoy the hospitality of a Christian knight. Osama himself had acquaintances among the Templars, whom he called his "friends," and whom he preferred above all other Franks. When he visited Jerusalem, they gave him one of their oratories, close to the christianised mosque el-Aksa, wherein to say his Moslem prayers; he walked with them in the Sanctuary, and was taken to the Dome of the Rock and House of the Chain. Of the hospitality of the knights of St. John, too, he does not stint his praise. He was a witness of an ordeal by battle and ordeals by water, which did not increase his respect for Christian jurisprudence, and he cannot conceal his indignation at the frequent breaches of sworn faith by the Crusaders, who seldom kept pact with the "infidel." Whilst generously admiring their valour, he lays special stress upon their defensive tactics, their cautious, orderly move-ments, their precautions against ambushes and surprises, and their self-con-trol after victory in denying themselves the delights of a headlong pursuit. Like a grave oriental, however, he cannot approve the idle merriment, jovial roars of laughter, and mad pursuit of pleasure, which he noticed among Franks of all degrees. An eastern gentleman can never understand childish buffoonery or broad grins among men of sense and position. Still less can he tolerate the slightest public display of that gentle passion which, like a true Moslem, he conceals behind the curtains of his harim. He has no patience with the amazing liberty allowed by Crusading husbands to their wives.

> "They know not what honour means," he writes, "nor jealousy neither. If they walk abroad with their wives and meet another man, they let him hold the wife's hand and take her aside to talk, whilst the husband stands aloof till the conver-sation be done! If the lady prolongs it overmuch, her spouse walks off and leaves her alone with her friend!"

So peaceful a scene of mutual toleration and goodwill between Christian and Moslem was not likely to last long. The first breath of fanaticism would of course blow all this fine cobweb to pieces. It came from both sides. In proportion as the first Crusaders became more tolerant and easy-going—not to say careless and licentious—the later visitors found more reason for a display of zeal. To a political adventure, and a military annexation, succeeded an age of pious pilgrimage, attended by thinly veiled freebooting. As soon as the early Crusaders had made Palestine a safe field for devout tourists, the shrines were besieged by pilgrims whose narrower experience could not stomach the worldly toleration assumed by the earlier Christian settlers. Added to the fanaticism of honest bigots came the lawlessness of palmer-adventurers, freelances who disguised the lust of plunder under a pious cockle-shell. Both classes exasperated the Moslem population and incited the Crusading leaders to unprovoked forays. Describing the situation at the end of the first quarter of the twelfth century, a Mohammedan historian says:

> "The Franks raided the country day by day; they worked unspeakable harm to the Moslems and brought ruin and desolation upon them. . . . Their forays pressed on into Diyar-Bekr, as far as Amid; they spared neither orthodox nor heretics; in Mesopotamia they despoiled the people of all the silver and valuables they possessed. As for Harran and Rakka, they oppressed them with contumely and shame, and gave them daily to drink of the cup of death. . . . All the roads to Damascus were cut, save that which passes Rahba and the desert, and merchants and travellers were forced to suffer the dangers and fatigues of a long journey across the wastes, in peril of life and property from the wandering Bedawis. The Franks even exacted black-mail from all the towns in their neighbourhood, and went so far as to send agents to Damascus to liberate Christian slaves. At Aleppo they forced the inhabitants to pay tribute up to the half of their revenue—even to the proceeds of the mill at the Garden Gate."*

On the other side, the Saracens, at least the Turkish Moslems, though for the moment divided and unable to offer any resolute opposition to the enemy, were by nature and training soldiers, and by race and teaching fanatics. The military system of the Seljuks bred up a nation of fighters; and their recent conversion to Islam, their ignorance and consequent subjection to the influence of fanatical *mullas*, imbued them with the convert's proverbial zeal. Every little court that assumed regal attributes on the decline of the central power became a nursery of warriors, each one of whom was a strenuous upholder of Islam. As with their Christian opponents, booty and Paradise no doubt combined to stimulate their enthusiasm for a religious war; but, whichever motive was uppermost, it was certain that only combination and a leader were needed to convert these straggling forces into a formidable army ready to die for the Faith. It was but

---

* Ibn-el-Athir, *Atabegs*, 59ff. We may make some allowance for oriental prejudice and exaggeration, bit it must not be forgotten that the writer of the foregoing indictment lived soon after the events he describes, and that his father was an eye-witness of many of these scenes.

necessary to preach the *Jihad*—the Holy War—and to show them a commander whose courage and military genius all must respect, and the Turkman chiefs and vassals would at once become a Church Militant with whom the Crusaders would have very seriously to reckon. The leader was found in Imad-ed-din Zengy.

ROBERT OF NORMANDY UNHORSES A SARACEN.
FROM A PAINTED WINDOW AT ST. DENYS, 12TH CENTURY.

CHAPTER III

THE HARBINGER
1127

A MONG THE NUMEROUS Seljuk officers, once slaves of Melik Shah, who were rewarded for their services with valuable appointments, Ak-Sunkur held a high place. As court chamberlain he was wholly in the confidence of his royal master, and enjoyed the special privilege of standing at his right hand at all public levees and councils of state. Later, as governor of the province of Aleppo, his rule was clement and enlightened*; his name became a proverb for loyalty and uprightness; and he died for his faithfulness to his old master's son (1094). He left a boy of ten, Zengy, surnamed Imad-ed-din or "Pillar of the Faith," round whom the retainers rallied. The greatest man then ruling in Mesopotamia was Kurbugha, lord of Mosil and many other cities, a vassal-in-chief of Melik Shah's son and successor. Kurbugha had not forgotten his old friend the "Gyrfalcon," and he summoned Zengy and his mamluks to his court. "Bring the lad," he wrote, "for he is the son of my comrade in arms, and it behooves me to see to his nurture." So they went to Mosil, were assigned becoming fiefs, and followed their new lord on his campaigns. Once near Amid, when the issue of a battle trembled in the balance, Kurbugha embraced Zengy before the army, and then consigned him to his own mamluks, saying, "Behold the son of your old master; fight for *him*!" They closed round the boy and set-to with such fury that the day was won. This was Zengy's first battle-field, and he was then about fifteen.

Henceforward for many years he lived the life of a privileged favourite at the court of Mosil under successive leaders—a notable squire of the fighting lords who held the borderland between the Crescent and the Cross. He had grown tall and distinguished-looking, of swarthy complexion and piercing eyes, and his character was as upright as his carriage. Up to his thirty-eighth year he continued to play a secondary part in the wars and politics of Mesopotamia. Five great barons, one after the other, held the government of Mosil with the defence of the

---

* See above, pp. 38–9.

marches, and each of them treated him like a son, endowed him with rich fiefs, and gave him high command in their constant expeditions against the Franks. On one of these occasions, at the siege of Tiberias, Zengy distinguished himself by a conspicuous deed of valour. At the head of his men he had repulsed a sortie of the garrison, and pursued them to the gate of the city, which he dinted with his lance. Then facing about, he found he was alone; his troop had halted after the engagement, and left him to follow the enemy singlehanded. For some time he maintained his hazardous position, and kept the Franks busy, in the hope that his men would come up and join in an assault; but when none appeared, he reluctantly beat a retreat, and slowly returned to the lines unhurt. The fame of his exploit was noised abroad and he was known thereafter by the name of esh-Shamy, "the Syrian."*

In 1122 "the Syrian" was rewarded by the Seljuk Sultan for his military services by the gift of his first direct government, the fief of Wasit, then a large and important city, together with the post of warden of Basra.† He quickly justified the Sultan's choice. The Arabs of "the Swamps" in Lower Mesopotamia, into which the Euphrates and Tigris in those days poured their waters, were eager to recover their lost supremacy in the fertile fields watered by the Great River; but so long as Zengy commanded the frontier, they were held in check. The Arab historian gives a graphic picture of the critical battle fought on March 1st, 1123, between the Arabs and the Turks. The former were led by the famous Emir of the Asad tribe, Dubeys, son of Sadaka, who had settled at Hilla, attacked Madain (Ctesiphon), and even marched upon the "City of Peace," Baghdad itself, the seat of the Abbasid Caliphate. The Caliph el-Mustarshid was no laggard; he put himself at the head of his Turkish guard, marshalled his troops, and clad in his black robe and turban, with the cloak of the Prophet on his shoulders and the sacred staff in his hand, he embarked in his galley. On landing on the other side he was received by his great vassal, el-Bursuky, the lord of Mosil, Zengy of Basra, the chief Kady, the head of the noble Seyyids, the chief of the Ulema, and other noted warriors and dignitaries, who, as soon as they saw the well-known baldachin surmounting the Caliph's horse, fell on their knees and kissed the ground before him. El-Mustarshid received them in his tent, and one after the other the barons took the oath of faithfulness. Then they marched upon Hilla, the enemy's stronghold. Dubeys met them by the canal

---

* Ibn-el-Athir, *Atabegs*, 34, 35.

† It was a settled principle of the Seljuk administration that no one was eligible for a governorship until he was thirty-six; Zengy was now thirty-seven, and had therefore gained his promotion almost at the earliest possible date.

called "Nile," which connected the Euphrates and Tigris, and both sides prepared for battle.

The Arabs numbered ten thousand horse and twelve thousand foot; the Caliph and his lords mustered but eight thousand horse, and their infantry did not exceed five thousand. The Commander of the Faithful stationed himself with his staff behind the line of battle but in full view of the combatants. In front of him stood his chaplains, each with an open Koran before him; all Baghdad was on its knees that day, reciting the Holy Word and seeking the protection of God; and if it was read once, the Book was read right through a thousand times in that hour of stress. The right wing of the Caliph's army was under the command of Zengy and another emir, and received the brunt of the enemy's attack.

Antar led his Bedawy horsemen in two brilliant charges, and had almost put the Caliph's troops to flight, when Zengy, Imad-ed-din, Atabeg of Mosil, by an adroit movement, took the Arabs in flank, and, aided by el-Bursuky, drove the enemy into the canal. The rout was complete, the prisoners were slaughtered without mercy, their leader fled, and his women fell into the hands of the conquerors.

After the victory Zengy resolved to try his luck at court. He was tired of standing at the beck and call of temporary superiors. He called his henchmen and comrades together and addressed them: "Our position," he said, "is become unbearable. New governors are continually appointed, and we are to obey their whim and pleasure! They send us now to Irak, now to Mosil, to-day to Mesopotamia, tomorrow to Syria. What do ye advise me to do?" Then Zeyn-ed-din Aly, the friend whom Zengy trusted most of all, spoke up: "My lord, the Turkmans have a saying, 'If so be a man must needs set a stone on his head, let it be quarried withal out of a high mountain.' In like manner, if it be necessary that we serve somebody, let it be the Sultan himself." Zengy took this advice and went to Hamadhan, to the court of the Seljuk Mahmud. Here he remained in waiting, without gaining any reward beyond his father's privilege of standing in the post of honour next to the throne. This honour he enjoyed until his pockets were empty. "O Aly, my friend," he said to Zeyn-ed-din, "we have indeed put the stone on our heads, as you proposed, and, faith, it is heavy enough!"

At length one day the Sultan rode forth to play polo, attended by his court. When it came to choosing partners, he singled out Zengy and handed him the *chogan* mall, saying "Come and play." After the match he turned to the other courtiers and upbraided them for their boorish jealousy.

"Are ye not ashamed?" he asked. "Here is a well-known man, whose father held an exalted place in the state, and not one of you has so much as offered him a gift, or bidden him to his table! By Allah, if I have left him so long without providing for his charges or allotting him a fief, it was only that I might see what ye would do." Then to Zengy: "I give you to wife Kundughly's widow, and my people shall supply you with gold for the wedding."

Kundughly had been the richest noble of the court, and his widow was endowed like a king's daughter. The day after his marriage the fortunate Emir rode forth in great pomp, surrounded by his own and his wife's retainers.

Zengy's visit to court had succeeded, and he returned in 1124 to the double fief of Basra and Wasit, which he ruled with a firm yet generous hand. When the Sultan and his spiritual suzerain came to blows, Zengy defended Wasit against the Caliph's army, and then, seizing every boat he could lay hands on, embarked his troops and brought a timely reinforcement to the Sultan, who was then outside Baghdad, and was equally amazed and relieved when he suddenly saw the device of his trusty baron displayed on the approaching flotilla. In the result the Caliph was forced to make peace; the Seljuk graciously consented to take up his undesired abode in the City of Peace; and Zengy received the long coveted post of warden of Baghdad, with the control and patronage of the whole of Irak (Chaldæa). In the autumn of 1127 he was appointed to the government of Mosil and Jezira (the "Island," Mesopotamia). Nor was he merely a great feudatory and ruler of broad lands; he was also given the important charge of bringing up two of the Sultan's sons, and by virtue of this office he attained the dignity of an *Atabeg* or Governor of Princes. The new position placed him in the forefront of the struggle with the Latin power. Henceforward we shall see him as the champion of the Faith against the Franks—the Cid Campeador of the East. His encomiast recites his achievements in rhyming prose:

> "He ravaged the Franks in the midst of their domain; and wreaked revenge for the true believers' pain; till the crescents of Islam waxed full, after their wane; and the suns of faith, of late extinct, flashed forth again; and the Moslems trod proudly, arrayed in victory's dress; and drank of the ever-flowing wells of success; deprived the Trinitarians of keep and fortress; and dealt back their lies and wickedness; so the worship of the One was restored in the 'Island' and Syrian regions; and there flocked to the cause of Islam defenders in legions."

Before he could measure swords with the Crusaders, however, he had to make good his position in his new and important government. Hitherto he had been but one of many peers—a great captain but no king. But at Mosil, two hundred miles away up the Tigris, he was practically independent, and permitted no interference in his government. His system was that which had received the sanction of the ideal emperor, Melik Shah, and which formed the model for the administration of all the states that sprang up from the ruins of the Seljuk empire. It depended upon direct personal rule, carried out by an elaborate network of inspectors, whose reports were checked by an army of spies. Zengy had agents at the capitals of all the neighbouring princes and even at the imperial court, and he knew exactly what the Sultan was doing from morning to night. Each day brought couriers from various parts with despatches, and he was always the first to hear of any news. The widest hospitality was extended to visitors, but it was combined with strict surveillance. No envoys passed through his territory without due notice and permission, and when they came they were furnished with a trusty escort to check inconvenient questioning of the people and spying out of the land. His subjects were not permitted to leave his dominions, lest they should betray the weak points in his defences; if any escaped, he compelled their surrender. When a company of peasants migrated from Mosil to Maridin, he called upon the Ortukid Prince of that city to send them back. Timurtash objected: "We treat our *fellahin* well," he wrote, "and take but a tithe of their produce; had you done the like, these peasants would not have quitted you."

> "Say to your master," replied Zengy to the messenger, "if thou didst take but one-hundredth of the produce it would be too much, seeing that thou livest in luxury and sloth on thy crag of Maridin; whereas if I taxed my people up to two-thirds, it would be nothing for my services. For I have not only mine own enemies to fight but must wage the Holy War withal, and but for me thou couldst not drink even a cup of water in security at thy Maridin, for the Franks would have gotten, possession of it. Wherefore, unless those peasants are sent back, verily I will bring out every clodhopper from Maridin and dump him down at Mosil."

The emigrants were hastily sent back. Another time Zengy made the Sultan deliver up a fugitive noble; the unhappy man was cast into prison and heard of no more.

Evidently this was no lenient governor. The story is told how Zengy once surprised a boatman asleep at his post, when he ought to have been alert and awaiting him; on being roused the man was so terrified to see his dreaded master standing before him that he dropped dead on the spot. His slaves complained, with too much reason, of his cruelty, and his servants went in such fear that they dared not ask him to repeat an order which they had not understood. It is told how he gave one of his waiting-men a rusk to hold, and the man did not dare to let it go. Nearly a year had passed when Zengy suddenly called for it; the man instantly produced it, carefully wrapped in a napkin. His obedience was rewarded by a rich appointment.

Zengy was a shrewd judge of men, and whenever he found a capable servant or officer, that man was sure of steadfast trust and support. Moreover, severe as he was himself, he allowed no one else to tyrannise over his subjects; "there can be only one tyrant at a time in the land," he said. Once, on a campaign, when he discovered that one of his favourite captains had turned a Jewish family out into the winter's cold, to make his quarters in their house, Zengy faced round on the man and gave him a single look,—and that emir went humbly forth from the city and pitched his tent in the mud and rain. Oppression and licence were never permitted among his officers, and no one in that age more rigorously punished assaults upon women. The wives of his soldiers, he held, were under his special protection, and no man insulted them with impunity during their husbands' absence at the war. He discouraged his followers from acquiring property. "So long as we hold the country," he said, "what boots your estate, when your military fief serves as well? If the country be lost to us, your estates go too. When a Sultan's followers own lands, they oppress and harass and despoil the folk." He never allowed his armies to trample on the people's crops,—they marched, says the chronicler, "as it were, between two ropes," —and no soldier was permitted to take even a truss of straw from a peasant without paying for it. Acts of violence were rigorously punished by crucifixion. He was lenient in his taxation towards the poor, but rich cities like Aleppo were heavily mulcted for the cost of his campaigns.

After all he gave them a good return for their money. The effects of his severe and resolute rule were seen in the security and prosperity of his dominions, and especially in the revival of his capital. The father of the historian Ibn-el-Athir relates:

> "I saw what Mosil, the Mother of the 'Island,' was when our martyred* lord first came. The greater part of the city was in ruins, and waste land stretched from the Quarter of the Drummers as far as the Citadel and Palace. . . . The old mosque was deserted, and all the houses near the ramparts were abandoned to the distance of a stone's throw. . . . But as the Martyr's reign went on, the country enjoyed protection, the designs of the wicked were frustrated, and the powerful were restrained from tyranny. The tidings of improvement spread abroad, and the folk flocked into his territory and settled there. Verily 'Generosity breeds attachment.' Buildings multiplied at Mosil and the other towns, insomuch that the very cemeteries vanished under new suburbs."

Zengy built the great Government House opposite the Almeida,† doubled the height of the ramparts, deepened the fosse, and erected the gate called after him

---

* Zengy did not die in battle for the Faith, which is the highest title to the name of *Shehid* or "Martyr" : but the term is also applied to those Moslems who fall, as he did, by assassination, and other causes.

† Almeida, Arabic *Meydan*, is a large square or open space used for horse-racing, polo matches, and other sports.

el-Bab el-Imady. Before his time Mosil was so poor in fruits that when a merchant sold grapes he cut off little bunches with scissors to make the weight exact; but when Zengy restored its prosperity, fertile gardens grew up around it, pomegranates and pears, apples and grapes abounded, insomuch that last year's gathering was hardly exhausted before the new crop was ready to be plucked.*

* Ibn-el-Athir, *Atabegs,* 137–142.

A PARTY OF CRUSADERS RETURNING FROM A FORAGING EXPEDITION.
FROM A 13TH-CENTURY MS. OF WILLIAM OF TYRE.

CHAPTER IV

THE FALL OF EDESSA
1127–1144

ZENGY'S HISTORICAL IMPORTANCE rests not upon his benefactions to Mosil and its dependencies, but upon his championship of Islam against the Crusaders, at a time when the Mohammedan cause seemed desperate. The Turkman chiefs of Mesopotamia were disunited and as prone to fight each other as to "go on the Path of God," and they were in nowise disposed to follow the leadership of the new governor of Mosil. The whole country was parcelled out in military fiefs, corresponding to Zengy's own tenure, each with a number of vassals, and among the great feudatories were some of old standing and renown. The Ortukid princes had been settled at the castles of Keyfa and Maridin since the beginning of the century. The two sons of Ortuk, Sukman and Il-Ghazy, had been famous in their raids upon the Franks; and the latter had held the high office of warden of Baghdad. No leader so far had inspired half the terror in the Christian ranks that this truculent Turkman had aroused. From his mountain fastness he had raided northern Syria; and when Aleppo put itself under his protection, he marched to the relief of the city at the head of three thousand horse and nine thousand foot, and storming the hill of Ifrin, where the Franks were strongly posted, he won a signal victory, in which Roger of Antioch was slain. Il-Ghazy died in 1122,—the very year of Zengy's first appointment,— but his son Timurtash succeeded to his eyry at Maridin and afterwards to Aleppo; and though he was an easy-going prince, who preferred a quiet life, he was not likely to forget what was due to his father's son—at least, until he had received a lesson in deportment.

A more powerful and energetic leader of the Ortukids was his cousin David, who had succeeded to the castle of Keyfa in 1108 and became the most renowned chief in all Diyar-Bekr. When he sent one of his arrows round among the Turkmans, everybody girded his loins in delighted anticipation of the fray, and soon twenty thousand men mustered under his banners. Such a prince was not disposed to resign the first place to a new-comer, and Zengy soon found that he had to reckon with David before he could venture into wider fields. Diyar-

Bekr must be subdued or disarmed, or he could never safely advance into Syria without fear of a flank attack. His first move was against the town of Jeziret-ibn-Omar, which had recently shaken off the yoke of Mosil; he took his army across the Tigris, some swimming, some in boats, and, aided by treacherous inhabitants, entered the town just in time; for the next day there was a spate to the height of a man, and the river became impassable. From Jezira he marched against Nisibin, once a famous capital, from whose conquest Trajan derived his title of Parthicus. It was now one of the Ortukid cities, and Zengy won it by an unworthy artifice; he caught one of the enemy's carrier-pigeons, which commonly served as messengers in Mesopotamia and Syria, and substituted a false message, which procured the immediate surrender of Nisibin, quickly imitated by Sinjar.

Here a fresh danger awaited him. The cities commanding the upper course of the Euphrates, Edessa, Saruj, Bira, etc., formed outposts of the Christians, and, in the hands of Joscelin de Courtenay, their garrisons were a *corps d'élite*. They could not be left safely in the rear without precautions. Zengy met the difficulty by arranging an armistice with Joscelin, who was probably glad enough to postpone a struggle with so formidable an adversary; and the Atabeg was left free to advance into Syria. He was engaged in establishing order in his new territories when he received an appeal from Aleppo for deliverance from the exactions of the Franks. It was the very opportunity he was seeking. He straightway crossed the Euphrates (1128), passed through Manbij, and was welcomed with thanksgivings at Aleppo. The only Syrian lord who had been able to make any head against the Crusaders was Tughtigin, the Atabeg of Damascus; and he was just dead. In the very nick of time, Zengy, now "the Syrian" *par excellence*, came to take his place and to champion the despairing Moslems against the infidels.*

Master of Aleppo, Zengy stayed more than a year in northern Syria, doing as much mischief as possible to the Christians. Armed with the Sultan's letters-patent as Governor of all the Western Provinces, he laid siege to the strong castle of Atharib (the "Cerep" of the Franks), a day's journey from Aleppo, to which it had long been a standing menace. Its garrison was full of picked warriors, and from its position and the mettle of its defenders it was one of the most formidable of the Latin strongholds. For a long time Zengy's furious assaults were steadily repulsed, but he drew his lines closer and never lost heart. The

---

* A melancholy incident marred his arrival. Turning over the treasury and wardrobe of the governors of Aleppo he chanced to light upon a bloody tunic. It was the very coat in which his father had been executed; and the wife who stood by his side was a grand-daughter of the Seljuk Tutush who had ordered the deed. In uncontrollable aversion Zengy put ther aside, and in spite of her entreaties and the remonstrances of the judge she was sternly divorced.

besieged were in sore straits, and King Baldwin at Jerusalem held a council of war, whether or not he should advance to their relief. Some thought it a trifling matter and made sure that the Saracens would beat a retreat, as they had been used to do of late; but one of the council, "a devil to know," says the chronicler, saw something more serious in Zengy's movements: "A blaze will follow these sparks," said he, "and there is flame under this smoke. Is not this the young lion who left his spoor at Tiberias?"

Baldwin finally resolved to relieve the beleaguered city, and marched "with his horsemen and foot, his banners and crosses, his princes, knights, and counts," to meet the lion of Tiberias. Zengy's counsellors advised a retreat to Aleppo, but he would none of their counsel: "Let us put our trust in God, and meet them, tide well or ill." Instead of waiting for the relieving army, he went forth to the encounter, and a furious battle ensued. Zengy at the head of his men charged the enemy again and again, shouting the words of the Prophet, "Take a taste of Hell!" The Crusaders were utterly routed: "the swords of God were sheathed in the necks of his foes," and few indeed escaped to tell of the field of shambles. They turned to fly, but what could avail when "the bottle was hung on the peg, and the locust had ended its song" ? No quarter was given; the "Martyr" plunged through a sea of blood, cleaving heads and laying bones bare, till the field was covered with mangled corpses and severed limbs. Only those escaped who hid under the heaps of slain, or "mounted the camel of night."

Deprived of its last hope, Atharib was taken by assault, its fortifications razed, and its garrison enslaved or put to the sword,—the piles of their bones could be seen for years. Thus was the terror of Cerep abated. The loss was not all on one side, however, and Zengy was anxious to get his wounded home and give his men rest. After making terms with the neighbouring fortress of Harim (Harenc), he returned to Mosil in 1130, the most famous leader in Islam. His deeds were bruited over the land, and his name became a proverb for valour and ferocity. *Sanguineus* the Christians wrote his name, and he had signed it in blood on the field of Atharib.

Four years Zengy rested from the Holy War. He had much to occupy him at Mosil, in maintaining his supremacy over the neighbouring chiefs; and the death of his sovereign the Sultan in 1131 brought about another war for the Seljuk succession, in which Zengy took his share. It was in this campaign that he encountered the defeat from Karaja the Cupbearer which sent him and his army flying pell-mell to the Tigris, where the ferry-boats of the governor of Tekrit saved them from destruction. The Caliph sought to profit by this reverse and to pay off old scores against the Atabeg; but his siege of Mosil in 1133 was literally circumvented by Zengy, who completely surrounded the besiegers, and after three months of futile attack his Holiness retired. The eastern horizon being once more serene, the Atabeg turned his eyes again to Syria. To wage the *Jihad* with success, it was essential to have possession of Damascus, the heart of Syria, yet now little better than an outpost of the Franks. Damascus must be his,—and then, massing the armies of Syria and the "Island," he would drive the "dogs of Christians" into the sea.

It was a dream destined never to be realised by the dreamer, though it came to pass after his death. His first attempt in 1135 was successfully repulsed. Then the able statesman who governed Damascus in the name of a series of nominal lords, Muin-ed-din Anar (the Ainardus of the Latin chroniclers), took the only possible measure to defeat Zengy's design: he made common cause with the Franks. The Crusaders themselves stood in no little dread of the furious champion of Islam, and were glad to aid Damascus in checking his advance. When Zengy again arrived in Syria in the summer of 1137 he found the Franks on the side of Anar, and his first act was to drive them, along with the King of Jerusalem, into the castle of Barin (Mont Ferrand). The Arab historians describe the fortress as "high as the crest of Orion, loftier than the mountain-peaks," the giddy summit of which was unattainable by the weary-winged birds; and the Franks held it impregnable. Nevertheless, after Zengy's mangonels* had played upon its walls, Mont Ferrand was forced to lower its flag. The Atabeg presented King Fulk—"*ab hoste satis humane tractatus*," as William of Tyre admits—with a robe of ceremony, and the exhausted and dispirited garrison was suffered to march out with the honours of war.

This unwonted clemency was the result of common prudence. Zengy had learned that strong reinforcements from Europe were landing in Syria, and hastily patching up a truce with Damascus he retreated to Mosil. In fact a formidable combination was gathering for his discomfiture. The Emperor John Comnenus brought an army into Syria, and was joined not only by the Crusading states, but by the Moslem lord of Damascus and its dependencies. John began by exchanging friendly embassies with Zengy, and we read of gifts of falcons and hunting-leopards, and a treaty that guaranteed the immunities of Aleppo. But such facts were not worth their parchment in days when Christian ecclesiastics laid down the rule that an oath to an infidel was null and void. The Emperor next took Bizaa and Kafar Tab, and then laid siege to Sheyzar, Osama's family

---

* A mangonel or stone-sling was a machine for throwing stones worked by means of twisted ropes. The other chief siege-engine of the day, the catapult (ballista) resembled a huge arbalest or crossbow.

fortress on the Orontes, in April, 1138. Zengy was summoned to the rescue, and pressed on with forced marches. Though not strong enough to drive the enemy from their position on the heights, his harassing skirmishes, the rumoured advance of David of Keyfa, together with some skilful diplomacy and the passing of hard cash, changed the imperial mind, already disgusted at the indifference and frivolity of the Latin princes; for on the twenty-fourth day of the siege "the Dog of the Romans" departed, abandoning his siege-train, including eighteen huge mangonels, which Zengy instantly appropriated. "It was thus," quoth Ibn-el-Athir, that "*God sufficed the faithful in the fight.*"*

The Emperor's interposition had proved futile; but the understanding between Damascus and Jerusalem held good. In vain Zengy tried to conciliate the rulers of the Syrian capital by marrying the Lady Emerald (Zumurrud Khatun), the widowed mother of the reigning lord, and giving his own daughter to the emir himself. The young man was murdered soon after, and everything had to be begun over again. Nothing could tempt or intimidate Anar, the real ruler of the city, not even the savage execution of the garrison of Baalbekk—his personal fief—after it had surrendered in October, 1139, to Zengy's solemn pledge of safe-conduct on the Koran and the Triple Divorce. This treacherous butchery only strengthened the alliance with the Christians, which was now cemented by a formal treaty, whereby Anar agreed to pay the King of Jerusalem a monthly subsidy of 20,000 gold pieces and to give him Banias, if he would aid in taking it from Zengy and driving him out of the land. The town was duly taken by the strange allies, but Zengy saved them from the trouble of carrying out the last part of the agreement by himself withdrawing his army from Syria. Leaving Saladin's father as warden of Baalbekk in reward for long and tried services, he once more left Damascus unsubdued, and returned to Mosil.

The resistance of Damascus defeated Zengy's plans in Syria. He now developed an attack upon the Crusaders from a different quarter. Repulsed in the south, he would swoop upon them from the mountains of the north. His preparations were deliberate. He protected his rear and flank by overawing the Kurds, seizing Shahrzur and Ashib (which he rebuilt and named after himself el-Imadiya, Amadia, as it is called to this day), and allying himself by marriage with the Shah of Armenia. Then he gradually advanced towards the enemy. One after the other, the towns of Diyar-Bekr fell into his hands, until his army lay before the strong walls of Amid, to which he began to lay siege for no juster cause than the Arab adage, "The sword is a better title-deed than parchments." But Amid was

---

* *Koran*, xxxiii., 25.

not his objective; his eyes were elsewhere; and as the Eastern chronicler says, he "but coquetted with Amid to conceal his desire for Edessa."

So long as his old antagonist, Joscelin de Courtenay, had held the famous episcopal city, Callirrhoe of the sweet waters, Zengy had not dared to approach it. The restless Count had been a terror throughout Diyar-Bekr and Syria: a very "devil amongst unbelievers," the Mohammedan annalist called him; and Edessa had been the strongest outpost of the Christian state. But Joscelin was dead, and a second and very different Joscelin sat in his seat. Valiant like his father, but only by fitful impulses, ordinarily sluggish and pleasure-seeking, Joscelin II. preferred the comfortable ease of his fief at Tell Bashir (Turbessel) to the rigours of the hill-country, and Zengy's ruse of a siege of Amid was quite enough to determine the Count to go away to his pleasant Syrian estate. His Latin followers were nothing loth to follow his example, and Edessa was left to the care of Chaldee and Armenian merchants, *imbelles viri*, unskilled in arms, who relied upon the protection of mercenaries whose pay was often a year or more in arrears. With such defenders the strongest walls were little worth.

Zengy's opportunity had come, and when the city lay deserted by its lord and the picked Crusading chivalry, he suddenly raised the siege of Amid and advanced upon Edessa with a vast array. He first summoned the garrison to surrender, being loth to injure so queenly a city:but when they refused—mindful, no doubt, of the fate of Baalbekk—he took counsel with the Koran, and obtaining a favourable augury, gave the order for the siege. He had brought mangonels and skilled sappers, and covered the approaches of the engineers with a devastating bombardment and incessant assaults, till the besieged realised the words of the Koran, "*The earth, all spacious as it is, became too strait for them.*"8 An Arab poet sang of him:

> He rides in a billow of horsemen,
> > they roll o'er the earth like a flood;
> His spears flash speech to the foeman-
> > incarnadined tongues of blood.
> Dark as the night is his beauty,
> > but his brow has a morning light;
> Mercy he uses at pleasure,
> > but not in the stress of the fight
> Heart to the Heart of his host,
> > and wings to its Wings, is his might.*

---

* *Koran*, ix., 119.
* Ibn-el-Athir, *Atabegs*, 121.

After repeated storming parties had been sent in vain, the engineers at last brought their mines, stuffed with burning faggots, up to the walls. Zengy himself inspected the trenches, and then said, "Let no man sup with me to-night unless he will ride with the into Edessa in the morning." After a month's siege, a breach of over one hundred ells was made and the Turkman troops poured into the devoted city (23 December, 1144). They were mad with the intoxication of victory, and burning to avenge the thousand insults which the lords of Edessa had forced down Moslem throats; now was the time to blot out in blood the raids and massacres, the sacking and burning, which had made the knights of Baldwin and Joscelin a terror throughout the country side. In their first fury they spared nothing: "they murder the widow and the strangers and put the fatherless to death" ; crosses were overturned, monks and priests cut down, everything destroyed and trampled under foot, save only the girls like gazelles, the youths fit for slaves, and the treasures of the merchants. It was ruthless but did not the Koran picture righteous punishments such as this? "*Even such was the heavy hand of thy Lord God, which He laid on the cities that had wrought wickedness: of a surety His grip is deadly, fearsome!*"8

Then Zengy himself entered the city, and was amazed at its beauty and stateliness, and grieved that it should suffer at his hands. He stopped the soldiery in their destructive rage, and made them give up their prisoners, the youths and girls like gazelles, and the treasure and goods they had taken. He restored the inhabitants—all that was left of them—to their homes, that the city might recover its prosperity, and he spared no pains to undo the mischief he had begun.

Edessa, in the words of the Arabic historian, was "the conquest of conquests" ; the stoutest prop of the Latin Kingdom was uprooted; Saruj and the other satellites of the great city immediately surrendered; and the valley of the Euphrates was finally freed from the oppression of the infidel. *Truth is come and Falsehood vanished away*† was proclaimed through the length and breadth of the land; for Islam had triumphed. The victory was the common talk of the civilised world, and people delighted to relate strange portents of the wonderful event. Far away, a holy man, who afflicted his body with abstinence and rigour, came forth one day from his cell with a face transfigured with joy, and said to the people, "One of the brethren has told me that Zengy has taken Edessa this day." After a time, some of the men who had fought in the siege chanced to come to his retreat: "O master," said they, "we knew that we should triumph, from the

---

* *Koran*, xi., 104.
† *Koran*, xvii., 83.

moment that we saw thee standing on the ramparts and shouting the battle-cry, 'Allahu Akbar.' " The saint denied that he had been at Edessa, but they all swore with great earnestness that they had recognised him on the wall. Still more strange were the words of the pious Moslem sage at Palermo, over whom King Roger of Sicily was exulting in respect of some recent successes of his troops over the Saracens: "Where was your Prophet," he asked, "that he came not to the aid of his Faithful?" The sage made answer, "He was helping in the conquest of Edessa!" The courtiers burst into laughter, but the king sternly checked them: the words impressed him strangely. Soon afterwards they were only too clearly explained.*

The great Atabeg did not long survive his crowning triumph. The next two years were spent, no doubt, in organising his new dominions, for he never returned to Mosil. In furtherance of his schemes of Syrian empire, he was actively besieging Castle Jaabar, hard by the Euphrates, in 1146, when one night as he was sleeping, being heavy with wine, some of his slaves stole into his tent and began drinking what was left. The noise roused Zengy, who roundly abused the fellows, and then fell asleep again. It seems that the men dreaded the punishment that was certain to follow in the morning; but the Atabeg was often so cruel a master that little was needed to drive them to desperation, even if the governor of the besieged fortress had not offered them blood-money. They plucked up heart and stabbed him as he lay. The eunuch Yaruktash gave the fatal blow, and then all three turned and fled into the castle. When the alarm was raised, the great Emir was in the very article of death. One who was present told how he had found his master still breathing;

> "On seeing me he thought I had come to give him the final stroke, and he raised a piteous finger, as though praying for mercy. I stopped short, crying out, ' O my master, who hath done this?' But he had no strength to answer, and that instant he breathed his last." (14 September, 1146.)

So died Imad-ed-din Zengy, "King of Emirs," "Pillar of the Faith," at the age of sixty-two, by the sword which he had used without mercy—his great ambition unsatisfied, his goal unattained. As he lay there stark, treacherously slain by men who had eaten at his table, none regarded him; his sons and henchmen were all eager to claim their inheritance, or secure the favour of his successor; the army, paralysed by the crime and the loss, disbanded in dismay; and the man who had led them and fed them, and conquered a kingdom with them, was left alone in his cold tent. It was reserved for strangers from Rakka to compose

---

* Ibn-el-Athir, *Atabegs*, 132.

his limbs and bury him hard by on the field of Siffin, where so many of the Faithful had fallen five hundred years before. In calmer times, his sons built a dome over the grave, and admiring chroniclers called him hero and "Martyr." It even fell to a saint of those days to see him in a vision, his face all glorified with peace, and to ask him concerning his state: "How hath God treated thee?" — "With forgiveness." —"For what cause ?" —"Because of Edessa."

Meantime the Crusaders punned on the tragic end of "Sanguin" in their doggerel Latin:

> *"Quam bonus eventus! fit sanguine sanguinolentus*
> *Vir homicida reus nomine Sanguineus."*

But they rejoiced too soon. Zengy indeed was dead, but he had done a work that all the princes in Christendom could not undo, and he left in his son Nur-ed-din, and his follower Saladin, leaders who knew how to crown the task he had begun. Forty years after the great Atabeg's death, the Holy Land belonged to Saladin, and Jerusalem had fallen again into the keeping of the Moslems, who have held it to this day.

BATTLE BETWEEN CRUSADERS AND KURBUGHA.
FROM A PAINTED WINDOW AT ST. DENYS, 12TH CENTURY.

PART II

EGYPT
1138–1174

CHAPTER V

SALADIN'S YOUTH
1138–1164

W E LEFT AYYUB in 1138 sadly departing from the castle of Tekrit, with his brother, on the very night of Saladin's birth. They betook themselves to Zengy at Mosil, and were not disappointed of their welcome. The great Atabeg had not forgotten the ferry on the Tigris, and was never the man to turn away a good sword. The two brothers served in his armies in many wars, and when Baalbekk fell, in October, 1139, Ayyub became the governor of the conquered city. Baalbekk, or Heliopolis, the old "city of the Sun," was celebrated not only for its antiquity and its temples, but for its lofty situation. It stood between Lebanon and Antilibanus, overhanging the valley of the Litany, at a height of four thousand feet above the sea, and was said to be the coldest town in Syria. A legend tells how men asked the Cold, "Where shall we find thee?" and it answered, "My home is Baalbekk." Though far from being the magnificent city that it was in the days when Antoninus Pius built the great temple of which a part still stands, Baalbekk in the time of Ayyub was yet an important town, surrounded by fertile fields, orchards, and gardens, and defended by a strong wall, with a citadel, or acropolis, on the west. It had not yet suffered the vandal touch of the Mongols, or the final upheaval of earthquake, which reduced it to its present ruined state. Its "presses overflowed with grapes," sweet water ran through the town, and mills and water-wheels all around bore witness to fertility.* To be placed in command of so great and prosperous a city was a convincing proof of Zengy's confidence, especially when it happened to be the southernmost outpost over against the hostile city of Damascus, distant only thirty-five miles.

Here the governor's son Saladin spent some years of his childhood; and, according to the saying, they ought to have been happy years, because they have no history. We know absolutely nothing of the family of Ayyub between 1139 and 1146, the period of their residence at Baalbekk. No doubt Saladin

---

* El-Idrisy, writing in 1154.

received the usual education of a Moslem boy; probably as the son of the commandant he had the best teaching within reach. Ayyub was particularly devout,
and even founded a convent for Sufy recluses at Baalbekk. His son was doubtless drilled for years in the Koran, in Arabic grammar, and the elements of
rhetoric, poetry, and theology; for, whatever the race of the Saracen rulers of
those days, their educational standard was Arabian; and to instil the Koran and
traditions, to teach a pure Arabic style and the niceties of Arabic syntax, formed
the chief aim of the learned but limited men who were entrusted with the training of distinguished youth.

Whatever schooling Saladin had at Baalbekk must have been meagre compared with his later opportunities. He was not yet nine years old when his father's
patron was murdered, and the death of the great Atabeg was of course the signal
for the recovery of Baalbekk by its old Damascus owner. Ayyub made no effort to
defend the town. He was ever a diplomatic, prudent sort of man, keenly alive to
his own interests. He saw that the two sons of Zengy, who shared their father's
dominions, were occupied in watching each other, and had no time to look after
Baalbekk. Mosil was distant, and Aleppo timid. On the other hand, Damascus
was near, and was resolved to get back her own. When her troops entered
Baalbekk, Ayyub made terms from the citadel, and before he surrendered he
had arranged to receive a handsome fief, including ten villages near Damascus,
a good sum down, and a house in the capital. Here his statecraft and sagacity
soon procured him a high position at the court of Abak, the grandson of Tughtigin, and in a few years he rose to be commander-in-chief of the Damascus
army.

Ayyub held this exalted post when Zengy's son, the King of Aleppo, Nur-ed-
din Mahmud, marched against Damascus in April, 1154. The name of Nur-ed-
din (Noradin) is second only to Saladin among the great defenders of Islam. After
the catastrophe at Jaabar, the Atabeg's kingdom had fallen into two parts: his
eldest son, Seyf-ed-din Ghazy, succeeded him at Mosil, whilst a younger, Nur-
ed-din, ruled the Syrian province. Hardly had he established himself upon the
throne of Aleppo, when he was called upon to defend Edessa. Immediately after
the death of Zengy, the Armenian inhabitants invited their former Count, Joscelin
de Courtenay, to retake the city, and in November, 1146, he surprised the
Turkman guard in their sleep, and the town was his. The citadel, however, held
out till Nur-ed-din's arrival, when Joscelin and his troops prudently retired,
whilst the Armenians who sought to flee under his protection were caught between the garrison and the relieving army and cut to pieces. *Foris gladius et
intus pavor.*

"It was pitiful to see, and lamentable to tell,—the helpless crowd, the peaceful populace, old men and sick, matrons and tender maids, ancient grandams, and little children even at the breast, in the jaws of the gate, some trodden down by horsemen, some smothered in the press, some slain by the merciless swords of the enemy."

Very few escaped with the outgoing army, which Nur-ed-din pursued and harassed as far as the Euphrates.

Joscelin himself was captured later on, blinded, and cast into prison at Aleppo, where he died after nine years' misery. His failure was followed by the complete extinction of the Frankish power throughout the County of Edessa and along the northern frontier. The disastrous Second Crusade, led by the Emperor Conrad and Louis VII., still further depressed the courage of the Christians. They came at the preaching of St. Bernard to wipe out the disgrace of Edessa; but they only disgraced themselves before Damascus, in 1148, where the vigilant Anar, no longer afraid of Zengy, and aided no doubt by Ayyub, held them at arm's length and eventually saw their forces evaporate.

"From the place of muster at Tiberias, the host, with the Holy Cross at its head, marched across Jordan; first went the barons of the land under King Baldwin, next the French, and last the Germans. The mud wall that surrounded the famous gardens of Damascus offered no bar to the advance of such an army. But the thick orchards with their narrow foot-paths and their growth of fruit and herbage formed a far better protection to the city. Everywhere throughout the length and breadth of this vast stretch of green and trees the ambushed Saracens opposed the invaders' progress; or, penned up in lofty buildings, which here and there rose up like stone islands out of a sea of green, shot down their arrows from above. At last, after long fighting, the woods were cleared, and the Christians, wearied out with heat and thirst, made for the river, only to find a fresh army drawn up against them. 'Why do we not advance?' cried Conrad from the rear, and, learning the cause, burst through the French battalions to the van. There, in true Teutonic fashion, he and his knights leaped off their war-horses, and, closing up behind their shield-wall, soon swept back the enemy within the city.

" ' The siege now began in earnest, and would have been brought to a successful issue,' says William of Tyre, 'had it not been for the greed of the great princes, who commenced negotiations with the citizens.' At the advice of traitors, the camp was shifted to the south-west, where, so ran the rumour, the wall was too weak to withstand the feeblest onslaught. But here the Crusaders found a more deadly enemy than strong fortifications; for in their new position they were cut off from the river and deprived of the orchard fruits; and through lack of food and leadership despair fell upon the host, until men began to talk of retreat. There was jealousy, likewise, between the Syrian Franks and their Western allies, and out of this too fertile source of evil, Anar, the Vezir of Damascus, was not slow to reap profit for himself. He pointed out to the former the folly of helping their brethren to seize Damascus, the capture of which would be but the prelude to the seizing of Jerusalem also. His arguments, supported as they doubtless were by bribes, brought about the abandonment of the siege."*

By Easter, 1149, this valiant Crusade was on its way home.

In such a crisis no man who could bear a sword could have been idle in Damascus. Ayyub, though he probably did not attain the rank of commander-in-chief until after Anar's death in the August following the siege, must have played a prominent part in the defence. Saladin was of course too young to be more than an absorbed spectator. It is true that Western legend tells how Eleanor of France carried on her amours with the future "Soldan"; but as he was then but eleven years old, King Louis's jealousy found a more probable accomplice for the divorce, which afterwards took place, than a good little boy at school.

Five years later, Ayyub was the chief agent in changing the dynasty and admitting the son of his old patron to the capital of Syria. It happened that whilst the elder brother had made terms with Damascus and had there risen to high power, the younger, Asad-ed-din Shirkuh, the "Mountain-Lion," had taken service with Nur-ed-din, and such was the valour he showed in every engagement, that his master not only gave him valuable cities in fief—such as Emesa and Rahba,—but placed him in command of the army which was destined for the conquest of Damascus.

The great opportunity seemed at last to have come. The Franks were discredited and dismayed after the miserable collapse of the Second Crusade; Mesopotamia was quiet under the magnanimous rule of Zengy's eldest son; the indomitable Anar, who had repeatedly withstood the great Atabeg himself, was dead, and in his stead had risen Ayyub, whose brother was Nur-ed-din's trusted marshal; and already the Prince of Damascus had humbly paid homage to the King of Aleppo. If ever the hour had struck for the realising of Zengy's dream of a Syrian empire, centred at Damascus, it was now.

In April, 1154, Nur-ed-din's army appeared on some pretext before the unconquered city. Shirkuh opened negotiations with his politic brother within the walls. In six days all was arranged; Ayyub did justice to his old devotion to the house of Zengy,—and espoused the side of the strongest battalions. *Il devint traitre pour n'etre point ingrat.* The people of Damascus, like sheep astray, now that Anar was dead, abandoned their hereditary lord, and following Ayyub's advice opened their gates to the powerfulest sovereign of the age. Nur-ed-din

* Archer and Kingsford, *Crusades*, 217–219.

entered Damascus without a blow, and the brothers were duly rewarded. Ayyub alone of all the court* was granted the right to be seated in the presence of the king, and was made governor of Damascus; Shirkuh was established at Emesa, with the viceroyalty over the whole Damascene province. The ferry on the Tigris had proved a sovereign talisman; but if they owed their first advance to a stroke of fortune, both brothers evidently possessed the talent and courage to use their opportunities.

From 1154 to 1164, Saladin lived at Damascus, at the Court of Nur-ed-din, with the consideration that belonged to the son of the commandant. As to what he did, what he studied, how he passed his time, and with whom, the Arab chroniclers maintain an exasperating silence. We are informed that he showed himself a youth of "excellent qualities," that he learned from Nur-ed-din how "to walk in the path of righteousness, to act virtuously, and to be zealous in fighting the infidels." As the favoured governor's son, he naturally enjoyed a privileged position, but, far from exhibiting any symptoms of future greatness, he was evidently a shining example of that tranquil virtue which shuns "the last infirmity of noble minds." This is all we are told of Saladin up to the age of twenty-five. The Syrian nobles—and Saladin's rank was now high—spent their youth in study, and their manhood in war and hunting and the cultivation of letters. Stalking the lion was the king of sports, but coursing and hawking were practised with unflagging energy. We read of setters and falcons imported regularly from Constantinople, where they were bred with great care and science. But we are not told a word to favour the supposition that Saladin as a youth was a mighty hunter; all we know tends to the belief that he preferred a quiet seclusion, and like his sagacious father, rather than his impetuous uncle, governed his life on principles of prudence and placidity. When it came to a choice of ways, the one arduous but leading to honour and renown, the other to peaceful insignificance, Saladin, as we shall see, endeavoured to choose the latter; nor was it a case of a formal *nolo episcopari*, but rather the protest of a retired nature against the rush and press of an ambitious career. He was one of those who have greatness thrust upon them; and though, when once fairly launched, he missed no opportunity of extending his power, it may well be doubted whether he would ever have started at all but for the urgency of his friends. An uneventful youth might have gently passed into a tranquil old age, and Saladin might have remained plain Salah-ed-din of Damascus with a name too obscure to be Europeanised.

---

* Ibn-el-Athir, *Atabegs*, 314.

Nor is it likely that he would have distinguished himself as a scholar or poet. To judge by later years, his literary tastes tended to the theological; he loved poetry indeed, but less than keen dialectic; and to hear holy traditions traced and verified, canon law formulated, passages in the Koran explained, and sound orthodoxy vindicated, inspired him with a strange delight. Like his father Ayyub, he was above all things a devout Moslem; and at Damascus he had ample opportunities for cultivating divinity. Learning in those days meant theological armory more than anything else, and wise men came in throngs from the East and from the West, from Samarkand and from Cordova, to teach and be taught in the mosques and *medresas* of Damascus. They must have brought with them the knowledge of other lands and other customs and arts. Perhaps Saladin sat and listened in the west corner of the Great Omayyad Mosque, when Ibn-Aby-Usrun was holding his lectures there. He could have no better master than one who was styled a "leader of his age in talents and legal learning," and whom Nur-ed-din not only brought with him to Damascus, but even built colleges in most of the great cities of Syria for him to lecture in, that his wonderful gifts might be known of all. He became a judge in Mesopotamia, and it speaks well for Saladin's faithfulness to early ties that, when the old man lost his sight, the Damascus youth who had become the greatest of Sultans refused to let him be deprived of his honourable office.

A negative proof of the retired life led by Saladin in youth and early manhood is found in the fact that Osama, who spent nearly the whole of the ten years, 1154-1164, at Damascus in intimate relations with the court (when it happened to be there), does not once mention him, and when at last he met him in 1174 it seems that a formal introduction had to be made.* Had Saladin been constantly at court, Osama must have known him. At the same time it must be remembered that the Arab chief was between sixty and seventy at the period of his earlier Damascus residence, and would hardly have paid much attention to a mere youngster; and further, that the old poet's impulsive Bohemian nature could have had little in common with the staid young man who preferred the society of divines. Saladin possibly thought Osama a sad warning, and the wild old Arab perhaps retorted with the opinion that the governor's discreet son was no better than a prig.

The fact that Saladin, who was afterwards the most renowned leader of his time, was apparently a completely obscure individual up to the age of twenty-five, is the more curious when it is remembered that his uncle Shirkuh, who

---

* Derenbourg, *Ousama*, 368.

afterwards brought him into public life, was Nur-ed-din's right-hand man, a conspicuously able and ambitious general, and was even spoken of as almost his colleague in sovereignty.* When in 1159 Nur-ed-din was apparently dying of a malady which kept him stretched for months on a bed of sickness at Aleppo, Shirkuh, then unquestionably the premier noble of Syria, was on the point of seizing the crown itself, and was only deterred by the ever-prudent counsels of Ayyub, who suggested that it might be wise to wait and see whether their master was really going to die or not.

In 1160 Shirkuh acted as leader of the Damascus caravan of pilgrims to Mekka, and displayed extraordinary pomp on the occasion; yet we do not hear of Saladin among his brilliant staff, nor did the latter, despite his religious instinct, ever perform that journey which to Moslems is the crowning act of grace. Shirkuh of course took a prominent part in the wars of Nur-ed-din, in the conquest of Harim (Harenc) from the Franks in 1164, and, the ensuing capture of fifty Syrian fortresses, whereby the kingdom of Zengy's cautious son was extended to Marash on the border of the Seljuk Sultanate of Rum on the north, and southward to Banias at the foot of Mount Hermon, and to Bozra in the Hauran.

In all this Saladin had no share: if he had taken the smallest part in any warlike operation we may be sure his admiring biographers would have recorded it. It was not until Shirkuh made his memorable expeditions to Egypt that the future "Sultan of the Moslems" emerged from his voluntary retirement and stepped boldly into his uncle's place as the true successor of Zengy in the role of Champion of Islam.

---

* Ibn-el-Athir, *Atabegs*, 305.

CHAPTER VI

THE CONQUEST OF EGYPT
1164–1169

OR TWO CENTURIES Egypt had suffered the rule of a dynasty of heretical Caliphs who boasted a descent from Fatima, the daughter of the Prophet Mohammed, and were hence known as the Fatimids. They professed the peculiar mystical philosophy of the Shiïtes, maintained the incarnation of the Divine Reason in the Imams sprung from Aly and Fatima, and believed in the coming of the Mahdy, the last inspired leader of the same elect descent. Notwithstanding the rigid orthodoxy of the vast majority of the Egyptians, who followed the teaching of the great Sunnite Imam esh-Shafiy,—whose tomb in the desert, outside the southern wall of Cairo, is still an object of profound reverence,—the Fatimid Caliphs imposed their authority with little difficulty upon a people accustomed to submission and pliable in matters of faith; and for several generations wielded a power which stood unrivalled among Mohammedan states. Their navies disputed the command of the Mediterranean with those of the Caliphs of Cordova; they successfully occupied Sicily, and raided Sardinia and Corsica; their ships frequented the Red Sea and the Indian Ocean, and even coasted West Africa through the Straits of Gibraltar; their caravans traded with Asia and Europe, and penetrated the heart of Africa even to Lake Chad; their armies held Syria and Arabia as well as Egypt, and excited perpetual alarm in their decayed rivals, the orthodox Abbasid Caliphs of Baghdad. Their wealth, the fruit of the great Indian trade, which passed through their customs-houses to the merchants of Venice and Pisa, was fabulous, if we may credit the amazing inventory of jewels and treasure recited by the Arab historians; the luxury and prodigality of their court were the wonder of foreign envoys; the walls and gates and mosques of Cairo bear witness to their splendid conception of what was due to the royal city, yet what remains of their architecture is but a vestige of the noble works upon which they are known to have lavished all the resources of decorative art.

Egypt has proved herself the Capua of more than one conquering race. The Fatimid Caliphs, abandoning the simplicity of their early days, when they ruled as missionaries among the simple hardy Berbers of Kayrawan, revelled in the wealth and luxury of their beautiful palaces at Cairo, and were content after a while to devote themselves to the unique pursuit of pleasure, and to leave the obnoxious labour of government to their servants. Their vezirs gradually usurped all sovereign powers, and even assumed the title of King, whilst the Fatimid pontiff, buried in the cushions of his harim, retained only the mysterious spiritual authority with which the "true Imam" was invested in the eyes of all devout followers of the sect of Aly. The Caliph of Cairo, on his jewelled throne, became as much a puppet as his rival of Baghdad. Cabals and factions were the natural consequences of bureaucratic rule, and the Fatimid kingdom, divided against itself, with a population imperfectly reconciled to the Shiïte sect, might easily have fallen a prey to any determined invader. The long immunity of Egypt was due chiefly to the weakness of her neighbours. The Seljuks had indeed deprived her of Syria, but the Seljuk empire had split into fragments before an invasion of Egypt had been attempted. The only power that menaced the Fatimid government in the first half of the twelfth century was the Kingdom of Jerusalem. The Franks were not only in possession of the Syrian coast and many inland fortresses, but were ambitious fighting men, bent upon plunder. Fortunately for Egypt, the Crusades fought at least as much for gold as for glory, and there is no doubt that the later Fatimids procured their indulgence by a prudent application of subsidies, if not a settled annual tribute.*

The arrival of Nur-ed-din upon the scene of Syrian politics, especially after his conquest of Damascus, introduced a highly disturbing influence. The King of Syria and the King of Jerusalem were now rival powers: neither could allow the other to increase his strength by the annexation of Egypt, and thus to acquire a vantage-ground from the south. Each coveted the delta of the Nile, and each watched his rival with jealous vigilance. The Egyptian vezirs, the real governors of the country, fully alive to the possibilities of the situation, set themselves to coquet with both parties, and to play off one against the other. In the end they carried the game too far, and gave Saladin an opportunity which he did not neglect.

The cause of Nur-ed-din's first interference in arms in the affairs of Egypt was an appeal from a deposed vezir. In a time of frequent assassinations and changes of ministers, Shawar, the Arab governor of Upper Egypt, made his way to the vezirate in January, 1163, only to be deposed in seven months' time and driven out of the country by Dirgham, the Warden of the Gate and commander

---

* *Annuam tributi pensionem*, William of Tyre calls it (xix., 5).

of the Barkiya battalion. Shawar fled to Nur-ed-din at Damascus and implored succour. It was not the first time that an Egyptian vezir had proposed terms of alliance to the Syrian King, but Shawar's proposals were the prodigal pledges of desperation. He offered to pay the whole cost of an invasion, and afterwards to give Nur-ed-din a third of the Egyptian revenue in annual tribute. The King of Syria was not indifferent to the importance of obtaining a hold upon Egypt: he knew that it was the master-key of the political situation, and would form a prolific source of revenue. Yet he hesitated to accept Shawar's overtures. Distrust of the man himself, and apprehension of the risks to which an expedition would be exposed when marching through the desert on the Crusaders' flank, made him pause.

Events, however, moved too fast for his prudence. Dirgham quarrelled with Amalric over the yearly subsidy, and the new King of Jerusalem with prompt decision invaded Egypt in September, 1163, to exact the usual tribute. Dirgham, after a severe defeat near Bilbeys, ingeniously avoided total discomfiture by breaking down the dams and causeways and flooding the country with the imprisoned waters of the Nile, then at its height. Amalric had already retired to Palestine, but half satisfied with some sort of composition, when Dirgham, hearing of Shawar's negotiations at Damascus, perceived his error in not conciliating the Latin King, and hastened to proffer an eternal alliance, to be cemented by increased tribute. This step must have been known to Nur-ed-din: fortified by an auspicious consultation of the Koran, he immediately cast his former scruples to the winds; and before Amalric could intervene, Shawar was on the march to Egypt (April, 1164), supported by a strong force of Turkmans from Damascus, led by Asad-ed-din Shirkuh, with Saladin on his staff. The Egyptians were defeated at Bilbeys, but rallied again under the walls of Cairo.

For several days indecisive conflicts took place, Shawar holding Fustat, and the other the castle of Cairo. Then, to raise funds, Dirgham possessed himself of the *wakf*, the "money of the orphans," and at once the people began to fall away from him. Worse still, he was deserted by the Caliph and the army. Driven to bay, for the last time he sounded the "assembly." In vain "the drums beat and the trumpets blared, *ma-sha-llah!* on the battlements": no man answered. In vain the desperate Emir, surrounded by his bodyguard of five hundred horse, all that remained to him of a powerful army, stood suppliant before the Caliph's palace for a whole day, even until the evening call to prayer, and implored him by the memory of his forefathers to stand forth at the window and bless his cause. No answer came; "the guard itself gradually dispersed, till only thirty troopers were left. Suddenly a warning cry reached him: 'Look to thyself and save thy life!'—and lo! Shawar's trumpets and drums were heard, entering from the Gate of the Bridge."

Then at last the deserted leader rode through the Zuweyla gate out into the streets beyond, calling on the people, who had once adored him and battened on his favour, to rise and do battle in his cause; they only hooted and cursed, as is the manner of the multitude towards fallen favourites. Still he rode on, till his horse, maddened by the tumult, threw its rider, beside the sacred chapel of "our Lady Nefisa." Instantly the fickle folk hacked off his head, and bore it in triumph through the streets; his body they left to be worried by the curs. Such was the tragic end of a brave and gallant gentleman, poet, and paladin; courteous and comely in face and bearing, cultivated in mind and accomplished in every manly sport; "one who could write like Ibn-Mukla, and composed poems with double rhymes"; "the best horseman of his age," and as stout an archer as ever drew bow in Egypt.

Shawar, restored to power, in May, 1164,* was eager to see the backs of the allies who had effected his reinstatement. He cautiously excluded Shirkuh from the fortified city of Cairo, and kept him in the suburbs. Then safe, as he thought, within his own strong walls, he defied his ally, broke all his promises, and re-fused to pay the indemnity. Shirkuh was not the man to forego his rights or condone broken faith; he sent Saladin to occupy Bilbeys and the eastern prov-ince. This hostile movement compelled Shawar in turn to appeal to Amalric. Now the King of Jerusalem plainly foresaw the ruin of the Christian cause in Palestine, penned in "between the devil and the deep sea," if Nur-ed-din should once gain a firm footing in Egypt, and he willingly sent the same army with which he had intended to support Dirgham against the very man whom he was now to protect. The tables were thus turned: the Franks were now the allies of their former enemy, and the saviour of the Egyptian vezir had become his foe.

On the arrival of the Crusaders the Syrian army entrenched itself at Bilbeys, where it resisted all the assaults of Amalric for three months. A fortunate diver-sion at last came to its relief. Nur-ed-din was waging a successful campaign in Palestine. After a reverse at the hands of Gilbert de Lacy and Robert Mansel, he had taken Harim (Harenc) and was laying siege to Banias (Cæsarea Philippi) then commanded by Walter Chesney; and Amalric was sorely wanted at home to protect his own kingdom, always dangerously exposed upon its eastern marches. Nor was Shirkuh less anxious to extricate himself from a situation where, at-tacked all day and every day, penned in behind weak earthworks, and running

---

* In his chronology of the first expedition to Egypt, Baha-ed-din is a year too early (1163). I follow Ibn-el-Athir in his *Kamil.*

short of food, his position was neither safe nor agreeable. An armistice was accordingly arranged, and the two parties came to terms. On the 27th of October, the Syrians marched out of their camp and filed off between the lines of the allied Crusaders and Egyptians, Shirkuh himself, battle-axe in hand, bringing up the rear. A Frankish officer, surprised at this warlike attitude, asked the truculent old warrior whether he was afraid that the Christians would attack him in spite of their pledge. "Let them try!" said Shirkuh, and passed on. In accordance with the agreement, the army returned to Damascus, where they found that Nur-ed-din's victories had been crowned by the surrender of Banias in mid October, and the capture of Bohemond Prince of Antioch, Raymond Count of Tripolis, with Hugh of Lusignan, and other noted knights, who were led in chains to Aleppo.*

The expedition to Egypt had ended without glory, but it had accomplished its object; it had spied out the land, and Shirkuh was able to report favourably on the possibility and advantages of annexation. Egypt was a country, he said, "without *men*, and with a precarious and contemptible government." Its wealth and defencelessness invited aggression. The ambitious general was devoured by desire for a viceregal throne at Cairo, and from this time forth he persistently urged Nur-ed-din to authorise the conquest of Egypt. The bolder spirits at court supported his importunity, and the Caliph of Baghdad accorded his blessing and encouragement to a project which involved the deposition of his heretical rival. Nur-ed-din, ever cautious, resisted these influences for a while, but at last gave way,—possibly because rumours had reached him of a closer union between Shawar and the Franks, which soon proved to be well founded.

It was, in fact, a race for the Nile. Shirkuh started first, at the beginning of 1167, with two thousand picked horsemen, and, taking the desert route by Gazelle Valley (Wady-el-Ghizlan) to avoid a collision with the Franks, but encountering on the way a violent and disastrous sandstorm, reached the Nile at Atfih, some forty miles south of Cairo, where he might cross to the west bank without fear of molestation. He had hardly carried his army over, however, when Amalric appeared on the east side, having hurried from Palestine as soon as he heard of the enemy's movements. The two armies followed the opposite banks down to Cairo, where Amalric pitched his camp close to Fustat, whilst Shirkuh took up a position exactly facing him at Giza. There each waited for the other to begin operations. Meanwhile Shawar had recovered from his surprise at the sudden irruption of the Franks whom at first he had not recognised with cer-

---

* William of Tyre, xix., 9.

tainty as foes or friends, and began to testify his gratitude for their protection in a substantial form. Amalric took the opportunity of the vezir's amicable dispositions to place their alliance on a more formal basis. Convinced of the unstable character of the Minister, he resolved to have a treaty ratified by the Caliph in person. The conditions were that Egypt should pay the King two hundred thousand gold pieces* then and there, and a further like sum at a later date, in return for his aid in expelling the enemy. On this agreement Amalric gave his hand to the Caliph's representatives, and claimed a like ratification from the Caliph himself.

The introduction of Christian ambassadors to the sacred presence, where few even of the most exalted Moslems were admitted, was unprecedented; but Amalric was in a position to dictate his own terms. Permission was granted, and Hugh of Cæsarea with Geoffrey Fulcher the Templar were selected for the unique embassy. The vezir himself conducted them with every detail of oriental ceremony and display to the Great Palace of the Fatimids. They were led by mysterious corridors and through guarded doors, where stalwart Sudanis saluted with naked swords. They reached a spacious court, open to the sky, and surrounded by arcades resting on marble pillars; the panelled ceilings were carved and inlaid in gold and colours; the pavement was rich mosaic. The unaccustomed eyes of the rude knights opened wide with wonder at the taste and refinement that met them at every step;—here they saw marble fountains, birds of many notes and wondrous plumage, strangers to the western world; there, in a further hall, more exquisite even than the first, "a variety of animals such as the ingenious hand of the painter might depict, or the license of the poet invent, or the mind of the sleeper conjure up in the visions of the night,—such, indeed, as the regions of the East and the South bring forth, but the West sees never, and scarcely hears of." At last, after many turns and windings, they reached the throne room, where the multitude of the pages and their sumptuous dress proclaimed the splendour of their lord. Thrice did the vezir, ungirding his sword, prostrate himself to the ground, as though in humble supplication to his god; then, with a sudden rapid sweep, the heavy curtains broidered with gold and pearls were drawn aside, and on a golden throne, robed in more than regal state, the Caliph sat revealed.

The vezir humbly presented the foreign knights, and set forth in lowly words the urgent danger from without and the great friendship of the King of Jerusalem. The Caliph, a swarthy youth emerging from boyhood,—*fuscus, procerus*

---

* In Arabic, *Dinars*. The dinar was a gold coin weighing a few grains more than the present half-sovereign, and containing a larger proportion of gold (.97).

corpore, facie venusta,—replied with suave dignity: He was willing, he said, to confirm in the amplest way the engagements made with his beloved ally. But when asked to give his hand in pledge of faithfulness, he hesitated, and a thrill of indignation at the strangers' presumption ran through the listening court. After a pause, however, the Caliph offered his hand—gloved as it was—to Sir Hugh. The blunt knight spoke him straight: "My lord, troth has no covering: in the good faith of princes, all is naked and open." Then at last, very unwillingly, as though derogating from his dignity, the Caliph, forcing a smile, drew off the glove and put his hand in Hugh's, swearing word by word to keep the covenant truly and in all good faith.*

The treaty thus ratified, Amalric attempted to throw a bridge of boats across the Nile; but the presence of the enemy on the other side defeated the plan, and he resorted to another. Finding the place where the river forked into its two main streams, he conveyed his army over to it by night and thence to the other side, in ships. Shirkuh discovered the movement too late to oppose, and finding the enemy landed he retreated to Upper Egypt. The King pursuing came up with him at "the two Gates" (el-Baban), ten miles south of Minya. Here was a plain, on the border where the cultivated land touched the desert, and numerous sandy hills gave cover to the combatants. Shirkuh's captains at first advised him not to risk a battle; but one of them stood forth and said stoutly, "Those who fear death or slavery are not fit to serve kings: let them turn ploughmen, or stay at home with their wives." Saladin and others applauded; and Shirkuh, always ready for hard knocks, gladly gave battle (18th April, 1167). He put the baggage in the centre, covered by Saladin's troop, which was to bear the first brunt of the attack. Saladin's orders were to fall back when pressed and draw the enemy in pursuit, and then to press them in turn, as the fight might allow. Shirkuh himself took command of the right wing, composed of a body of picked horsemen, which was to cut up the enemy's rear, consisting of the less warlike Egyptians. It fell out as he expected. The Franks were drawn away by Saladin; the Egyptians were cut up and routed; and when the Crusaders, returning from the pursuit, found their allies fled, they also hastily retreated, abandoning their baggage and leaving Hugh of Cæsarea among the prisoners.† The victors, however, were not strong

---

* William of Tyre, *Historia rerum in partibus transmarinis gestarum*, lib. xix., cap. 19, 20. The embassy is not recorded by the Arabic chroniclers.

† Ibn-el-Athir, *Kamil*, 548: according to his *Atabegs* it was a month earlier. The numbers engaged are variously estimated. The Arab historians give Shirkuh only 2000 horsemen. William of Tyre, on the other hand, puts the Saracen force at 9000 men mailed (*loricis galeisque*), 3000 archers, and at least 10,000 Arabs armed with spears. The Latins, he says, had only 374 knights, an uncertain number of light infantry (Turcopoles), and a body of Egyptians who were more of a burden than a help (xix., 25).

enough to follow up the success, march on to Cairo, and run Shawar and Amalric to earth. Taking the lesser risk, Shirkuh went north by a desert route and entered Alexandria without opposition. Here he installed Saladin as governor, with one half of his army, while with the other he again turned southwards to levy contributions in Upper Egypt.

The joint forces of the Franks and Egyptians now invested Alexandria, whilst the Christian fleet held the coast. The defence of the city was Saladin's first independent command, and he quitted himself well. He had but a thousand followers of his own in the midst of a mongrel and partly foreign populace, who, as malcontents, were not sorry to take part against a feeble government, or to defend their city against the savage and bloodthirsty Franks; yet, as merchants and tradesmen, could not conceal their terror of the siege-machines and infernal engines which the "infidels" brought against their walls. Provisions, moreover, ran short; and short rations make a humble stomach. At last they rose in a tumult and openly talked of surrender: "Why suffer we these things for a stranger and a cause which is not ours?" Saladin meanwhile had sent to his uncle for help, and Shirkuh was hurrying down from Kos laden with treasure The news put fresh heart into the people, already spurred on by Saladin's spirited exhortations and the promise of reinforcement, or frightened into a desperate courage by his tales of the monstrous barbarities inflicted by the Franks upon the vanquished. They held out for seventy-five days, in spite of hunger and incessant assaults, till it became known that Shirkuh was at the Abyssinians' Lake, laying siege to Cairo. On this, Amalric gave up all thoughts of Alexandria, and a peace was arranged (4 August, 1167), by which both parties* agreed to leave Egypt to the Egyptians. Alexandria was surrendered to Shawar; prisoners were exchanged; and Shirkuh led the exhausted remnant of his two thousand troopers back to Damascus. Before leaving, Saladin was honourably entertained in Amalric's camp for several days but rather, one suspects, as a hostage than as a guest. The experience, nevertheless, may have been valuable. He must have seen something of knightly order and discipline, and may here have formed a friendship with Humphrey of Toron, who was on terms of brotherliness (*fraterno fœdere junctus erat*†) with at least one Saracen emir. It is even probable that this was the occasion when Saladin received Christian Knighthood at Humphrey's hands.‡

---

* It is fair to state that the Franks did not fully admit this pledge for their part of the treaty of peace.

† William of Tyre, xvii., c. 17.

‡ *Itinerarium Regis Ricardi*, i., c. 3. See below, Chap. XXIII.

The Christians claimed the campaign as a triumph, and the evacuation of Alexandria as a surrender; but if the Arab chroniclers are right in saying that Amalric paid Shirkuh fifty thousand pieces of gold to go away, the advantage would appear to have been on the side of the Moslems. On the other hand, the Franks, in violation (apparently) of their agreement, not only left a Resident or Prefect at Cairo, but insisted on furnishing the guards of the city gates from their own soldiers; they also increased the annual subsidy to be paid by Shawar to the King of Jerusalem to one hundred thousand gold pieces. The apparent inconsistency of these arrangements at Alexandria and Cairo may be explained by the supposition that the Christians, alarmed by the news of Nur-ed-din's successes in Palestine, were eager to get home at all costs, and therefore abandoned their chances against Shirkuh, however propitious; yet did not leave Egypt without clinching their hold upon the shifty vezir at Cairo.

Not content with this hold, the more impetuous among Amalric's counsellors presently began to urge the complete conquest of Egypt, and their advice was strongly supported by the garrison they had left at Cairo and Fustat, who had naturally the best means of discovering the weakness of the defences. The King of Jerusalem withstood these counsels in vain. He had doubtless discovered by this time that the only safe policy was to conquer Damascus first, and make the Kingdom safe on the east, with the great Syrian desert for its frontier, before attempting to annex Egypt—since invasion meant exposing his rear to the assaults of Nur-ed-din. Moreover, Egypt, he said, was their milch cow; and he pointed out the bad policy of turning a friend into an enemy and throwing Shawar into the arms of Nur-ed-din—with whom he was already supposed to be intriguing,—but he argued to no purpose. His captains were bent upon invasion and confident of success, and at last he allowed himself to be persuaded. In open violation of his word, as understood by the Saracens, and at least without the shadow of an excuse, he once more marched into Egypt; but now he entered as an enemy where before he had been bidden as an ally. Arrived at Bilbeys on the 3d of November, 1168, he added to perfidy the crime of wholesale massacre,—he spared neither age nor sex, says the Latin chronicler, in the devoted town.

This barbarous act at once ranged the Egyptians on the side of Nur-ed-din, and inspired them to heroic exertions. They took advantage of the Christians' foolish loitering, to marshal their forces and strengthen their defences. The old city of Fustat, for three hundred years the metropolis of Egypt, and still a densely populated suburb of Cairo, was by Shawar's orders set on fire, that it might not give shelter to the Franks (12 November, 1168). Twenty thousand naphtha barrels and ten thousand torches were lighted. The fire lasted fifty-four days, and its traces may still be found in the wilderness of sandheaps stretching over miles of buried rubbish on the south side of Cairo. The people fled "as from their very graves," the father abandoned his children, the brother his twin; and all rushed to Cairo for dear life. The hire of a camel for the mile or two of transit cost thirty pieces of gold.* The capital itself was in a tumult of preparation for the attack. Amalric did not keep it long in suspense, but he was forced to abandon the usual camping ground (the Birket-el-Habash) on account of the suffocating smoke from Fustat. The assault, however, was postponed by the negotiations which Shawar adroitly contrived, to buy off his greedy assailants. There was more pretence than honesty in his diplomacy, for he was sending at the same moment couriers to Damascus to implore the aid of Nur-ed-din. The young Caliph of Egypt wrote himself, and even enclosed some of his wives' hair as a supreme act of supplication which no gentleman could resist.†

This time the King of Syria did not hesitate; he was nettled at the poor results of the two previous expeditions, and indignant with the Franks for what he held to be a flagrant breach of faith. He might even have gone in person, but that he was preoccupied with the unsettled state of Mesopotamia. He lost no time, however, in despatching a force of two thousand picked troopers from his own guard, with six thousand paid Turkmans of approved valour, under the command of Shirkuh, supported by a large staff of emulous emirs. The only one to hold back was, strange to say, Saladin himself. He had been his uncle's right hand in the former campaigns, but he still loved his old retirement and the discourse of pious men; and when Shirkuh, in the presence of Nur-ed-din, said "Now, Yusuf, make ready for the march," Saladin answered "By Allah, if the sovereignty of Egypt were offered me, I would not go: what I endured at Alexandria I shall never forget." Then Shirkuh said to Nur-ed-din, "Needs must he come with me," and Nur-ed-din turned to the young man and repeated the words, "*La budd min mesirik maa ammik*," "Needs must that you go with your uncle." In vain Saladin pleaded his aversion to the campaign and his lack of means; Nur-ed-din would not listen, but supplied him with horses and arms and bade him make ready: "So I went," said Saladin, recounting the scene in later years, "I went like one driven to my death." Thus were accomplished the words of the Koran‡: *"Perchance ye hate a thing although it is better for you, and perchance ye love a thing although it is worse for you: but God knoweth and ye*

---

* *Kamil*, 555; el-Makrizy, *Khitat*, i., 286; Wüstenfeld, *Geschichte der Fatimiden Chalifen*, 338–339.
† Ibn-el-Athir, *Kamil*, 556.
‡ *Koran*, ii., 113; *Kamil*, 563.

know not." Nur-ed-din himself superintended the marshalling of the army at the Spring Head, a day's march from Damascus, and gave every man a present of twenty gold pieces, whilst he committed to Shirkuh two hundred thousand dinars for his military chest.

On the 17th of December, 1168, the third expedition began its march to Egypt, once more to rescue Shawar, in name, but in fact with far larger designs. Amalric, always needy and greedy, was still waiting before Cairo for more of the vezir's promised gold, when Shirkuh suddenly effected his junction with the Egyptians (8 January, 1169), evading the Frank army which had gone out to intercept his advance. Deceived by Shawar and outgeneralled by Shirkuh, the discomfited king retired to Palestine, without offering battle, having gained, as the proverb has it, nothing better than the "boots of Honeyn." The Syrians entered Cairo in triumph, and were welcomed as deliverers. The grateful Caliph gave audience to Shirkuh and invested him with a robe of honour, clothed in which he returned to display himself to the army. Shawar, inwardly devoured by jealousy and alarm, rode out daily to the Syrian camp, in great state, with all his banners, drums and trumpets, and overwhelmed the general with protestations of devotion; but meanwhile he took no steps to perform his engagements to Nur-ed-din, but was actually meditating a treacherous arrest of Shirkuh and his officers at a friendly banquet. The Syrian leaders soon determined that he was not to be trusted, and Saladin and Jurdik resolved to get rid of him. As the vezir was riding out to visit the general, who chanced to be paying his respects to the venerated tomb of the Imam esh-Shafiy, Saladin and his men dragged him from his horse and made him prisoner. Whatever doubts Shirkuh may have entertained as to the fate of Shawar were set at rest by a peremptory order from the Caliph himself, who, like a slave emancipated from a rigorous master, demanded the head of the vezir. It was sent, and thus ended the brief and checkered career of a remarkable and politic minister; an Arab chief, moreover, of ancient lineage, with all the Bedawy's daring and the ancestral love of poetry—insomuch that he once filled Omara's mouth with gold in delight at an ode—and, it must be added, with the Arab's full share of falsehood and deceit.

The Caliph el-Adid, who was much impressed by the gallant bearing of his deliverers, immediately appointed Shirkuh to the vacant office, clad him in the robes of vezir, invested him with plenary powers, and gave him the titles of "Victorious King" and "Commander-in-chief" (18th Jan., 1169). The people were as pleased as the pontiff; they had liked the jolly soldier as he rode over the country a year and a half ago, even though he was levying taxes; and the Cairenes appreciated the liberal manner in which he had disbursed from his heavy military chest, and had refreshed them with the looting of Shawar's palace, where they left not so much as a cushion for his lavish successor to sit on! The Arab poet saw more clearly when he remarked that the claws of "the Lion"* were now fastened in his prey. The "Lion of the Faith," however, lived scarcely more than two months to enjoy his quarry, but died suddenly on the 23rd of March, 1169— the result of over-eating; for he was a mighty trencherman and addicted to heavy feeding. In person, Shirkuh was short and stout, choleric of face, and fierce by nature; nor had Allah endowed him with a superfluity of intelligence. Yet he was a bold and capable soldier, emulous of glory, patient under hardships, liberal beyond his means, and beloved of his men; and he had the grace to die at the right moment. The way was now open for Saladin.†

---

* Asad-ed-din, "Lion of the Faith," was the Arabic surname of Shirkuh, which is itself Persian for "Mountain-Lion."

† William of Tyre's portrait of Shirkuh is worth quoting: it was evidently drawn by one who knew him. He describes him as "virum industrium, et in armis strenuum, liberalem supra vires patrimonii sui, gloriæ cupidum, et in re militari admodum exercitatum, militibus carum, efficiente munificentia, et acceptum. . . . Erat autem homo jam senior, pusillus statura, pinguis multum et corpulentior . . . in altero oculorum habens albuginem; laboris patientissimus, sed et sitim et famem æquanimiter tolerans, supra id quod ætas illa soleat sustinere."—*Hist.*, xix., 5.

EAGLE ON THE WALL OF SALADIN'S CITADEL AT CAIRO.

CHAPTER VI

VEZIR OF EGYPT
1169–1171

"I MEANT AMR; but God meant Kharija," is the Arab version of *l'homme pro-pose et Dieu dispose.* Saladin had been dragged to Egypt against his will, foreseeing nothing but misery; and now the very step he had tried to avoid was to lead him to the pinnacle of fame. The Prophet indeed said truly, "*God will make men wonder when they see folk hauled to Paradise in chains.*" In such happy bonds was Saladin led to the throne. The Fatimid Caliph chose him from among all the Syrian captains to be the successor of his uncle, and on the 26th of March, 1169, three days after Shirkuh's death, he was invested* with the mantle of vezir and decorated with the title *el-Melik en-Nasir,* "The King Strong to aid." His comrades in arms, many of whom were older and more experienced than himself, were not easily reconciled to the promotion of the young man of thirty over their heads. They thought him a well-behaved and intelligent sub-altern, too quiet and unambitious for high command;—it was indeed this opinion of Saladin's docility that had procured him an office where a tractable tool was wanted:—but to raise him above the war-worn captains of Nur-ed-din's campaigns was more than they could stomach. It needed all Saladin's tact and diplomacy, supported by the specious arguments of el-Hakkary the lawyer, and a liberal opening of treasury coffers, to induce the jealous warriors to submit; and several of them returned to Syria rather than serve under their junior.

On his side, Saladin began to order his life more rigorously. Devout as he had always shewn himself, he became even more strict and austere. He put aside the thought of pleasure and the love of ease, adopted a Spartan rule, and set it as an example to his troops. He devoted all his energies henceforth to one great object—to found a Moslem empire strong enough to drive the infidels out of the land. "When God gave me the land of Egypt," said he, "I was sure that He meant Palestine for me also." It may well be that natural selfish ambition quick-

---

* The actual diploma of appointment is preserved at Berlin, and runs to ninety-eight folios.

88

ened his zeal; but the result was the same; thenceforward his career was one long championship of Islam. He had vowed himself to the Holy War.

The new vezir's position was curiously anomalous. He was at once the prime-minister of an heretical (Shiite) Caliph, and the lieutenant of an orthodox (Sunnite) King. With admirable inconsistency, the two names were duly prayed for every Friday at the mosque. The anomaly would have to be abolished, but only by degrees: violent changes might be fatal so long as the people of Egypt retained the affection for the (Shiite) doctrines which two centuries of Fatimid rule had instilled, and which was fostered by the very nature of the tenets. Saladin's relations with Nur-ed-din were also delicate. The King of Syria congratulated him, indeed, on his appointment, and confirmed him in his command of the Syrian army in Egypt, but was clearly resolved to keep him in his place. His despatches from Damascus were addressed merely "To the Emir Salah-ed-din, Commander-in-chief, and the other Emirs," to show him that he was but *primus inter pares*, liable to be recalled or degraded at his sovereign's pleasure. To gradually strengthen his own position without awakening the distrust of the people of Egypt or the jealousy of Nur-ed-din, was the prudent policy which Saladin must necessarily pursue.

His first step was to surround himself by his family. Like another Joseph, also vezir of Egypt, but under a Pharaoh instead of a Caliph, he sent for his father and brethren from Syria, and made them share his splendour. He even offered to surrender his high office to his father,* but Ayyub refused the honour. "My son," said he, "God had not chosen thee for this great position hadst thou not been fitted for it; it is not well to play with one's luck." Ayyub, however, took upon himself the duties of treasurer, and his other sons loyally supported their brother in his difficult situation. They had their reward, for Saladin gave them the fiefs of obnoxious Egyptians, whom he banished to places where they could do no hurt. His plan was to weaken the Caliph's party, and he did not care how much he was hated by the Egyptian courtiers and officers, so long as he gained the confidence of the people. This he set himself seriously to win, and his Arab biographer says that the folk came from all parts of Egypt to see him, and seldom went away empty-handed: there was ever a petitioner at his ear, and none appealed to him in vain.

He needed all his popularity among the people; for the palace, with its numerous troops and dependents, was openly hostile. The Caliph had discovered that he was mistaken in Saladin's character,—that he had adopted not a slave

---

* Ayyub arrived in Egypt in the middle of April, 1170, a year later than his sons (Ibn-Khallikan, i., 245).

but a master; and intrigues were soon a-foot to destroy the new vezir. Nejah, the chief black eunuch and major domo, headed a conspiracy among the upholders of the Fatimid dynasty. They planned an understanding with the Franks, who were to invade Egypt and entice Saladin from Cairo, when the conspirators would take him in rear, and thus attacked on both sides he and his Turkmans would perish. An accident revealed the plot to Saladin, and he had the chief eunuch watched, until at length he succeeded in catching him at his country house, outside the protection of the palace, and the unlucky Black was quickly be-headed (July, 1169). This summary execution of their countryman and leader aroused the fury of the Caliph's troops, then (as in modern Egypt) composed largely of Sudanis; and fifty thousand, it is stated, of these Blacks rose up to avenge him. A bloody struggle ensued in the wide quadrangle that divided the palaces (Beyn el-Kasreyn), and many houses and streets were set on fire; but at last the Blacks were overcome, their quarter, el-Mansuriya, was burnt, and they were compelled to beg for mercy. They were sent over the Nile, to Giza, and thence away to Upper Egypt, where rebellion smouldered for several years. In the winter of 1171–2, Saladin's eldest brother, Turan Shah, reduced them to temporary submission, but in the following winter he had to fight them again, and even pursued them into Nubia, where he took the city of Ibrim (Primis), near Korosko, pillaged the church of the monophysite Christians, tortured the bishop, and slew seven hundred of the pigs which were found there in great abundance, to the proper disgust of all pious Moslems. In 1174 there was a formidable rising of the Blacks at Aswan, led by Kenz-ed-daula; and it needed some hard fighting before he was defeated and killed in September by Seyf-ed-din (el-Adil), another of Saladin's brothers. Yet another insurrection, at Koptos, had to be suppressed by the same general in 1176. After this we read no more of risings among the Blacks, but, as the Arab historian piously concludes, "God made an end of their villainy." It is evident that the struggle was obstinate, and that Upper Egypt was for six years in a state of intermittent rebellion; and there can be little doubt that the Blacks who repeatedly revolted were stirred up by the fugitive Sudany slaves and other partisans of the Fatimids.*

Hardly had Saladin expelled the mutinous Blacks from Cairo, when a still more urgent danger arose. The Crusaders were not slow to grasp the signifi-cance of the political change in Egypt. The possession of the Nile by Nur-ed-din's

---

* See the ingenious memoir of M. Paul. Casanova on *Les derniers Fatimides* in the *Mémoires de la mission archéologique française au Caire*, tome vi., fasc. 3; and Ibn-el-Athir, *Kamil*, 566–8; Baha-ed-din, 56; Abu-Salih, *Churches and Monasteries of Egypt*, ed. Evetts, f. 96.; Mrs Butcher, *Church of Egypt*, ii., 104.

general placed the Kingdom of Jerusalem as it were in a cleft stick, squeezed on both sides by armies controlled by the same power. The harbours of Damietta and Alexandria gave the Moslems the command of a fleet, and enabled them to cut off the communications of the Crusaders with Europe, stop the annual pilgrim ships, and seize their supplies. Every effort must be made to break this fatal chain, which threatened the very existence of the Latin power in Palestine. Accordingly the most formidable attack that Saladin ever had to meet in Egypt was organised, probably in connexion with conspirators in Cairo. Amalric joined hands with the Eastern Emperor, and a Greek fleet of 220 sail co-operated with a strong land force of Crusaders in besieging Damietta. Fortunately for the defenders, contrary winds delayed the fleet on its way from the Golden Horn, and Saladin availed himself of this respite to strengthen the garrison and prepare for the attack. At the same time he sent messengers to Nur-ed-din to report the state of affairs, and especially to point out the risk of leaving a hostile faction behind him at Cairo whilst he went himself to the assistance of Damietta. In response, the King of Syria poured troops into Egypt, battalion on battalion, and began to distract the attention of the enemy by a demonstration against Palestine.

The siege of Damietta was begun in November, 1169. Amalric took up a position between the sea and the town, and awaited the arrival of the Greek fleet. In three days it appeared, but an iron chain guarded by an impregnable tower prevented its entering the harbour, and it was unable to render the aid that had been expected. *Nocuit differre paratis:* the chances of success were weakened by delay; and when at last, led in person by their gallant king, the Franks attacked with all their elaborate machinery of mangonels and fighting towers,* the garrison was more than equal to repelling them, and sallying forth burnt their siege engines and even set fire to part of the fleet. Saladin meanwhile had brought up his troops, with ample stores and munitions of war, and a million gold pieces in his chest, and perpetually harassed the besiegers. The garrison was easily kept supplied, since the arm of the Nile was open and protected by the troops from Cairo; but the Franks ran short of bread; a diet of fruit disordered their unaccustomed stomachs, and disease and famine thinned their

---

* "The movable towers [*castra or castrella*] or 'belfreys' [*berefrida*], were brought in pieces, which were framed together. They were then pushed across the ditch of the fortress, which was filled up with hurdles and fascines to facilitate their passage. The towers protected the 'besieging engines' with which the walls were battered, and the mining operations" (Sir C. W. Wilson, R.E., note to Baha-ed-din). They were the *machinæ, par excellence*, of medieval warfare. They ran on wheels, and were often protected from fire by a covering of raw hides. Mr. Archer states (*Crusade Rich. I.*, 88) that Almaric's *machina* at Damietta was seven stories high.

ranks. The Greeks on the ships were starving, and the Latins ashore could spare them nothing.

The very elements seemed to conspire with the improvidence of the commanders to complete their discomfiture. Heavy rains swelled the Nile, flooded the plain, and saturated the camp. The storm upset their tents and siege-scaffolds, and the garrison took advantage of their plight to pelt them with stones slung by powerful catapults. Murmurs arose in the ranks; the wretched soldiers, half starved and half drowned, begged to go home; and after fifty days of fruitless efforts, Amalric was forced to give up the siege. Peace was made, and the generous and businesslike Alexandrians opened their markets to the famished invaders, who, when they had well eaten, set out in great dejection on their return to Palestine (19 December). To crown the disaster, a tempest wrecked nearly the whole fleet, and the dead bodies of the Greeks were cast up on the coast which they had come to conquer. As the proverb says, "The ostrich set out to find itself horns, and came back without ears."* Henceforward, instead of going forth to attack, the Latin Kingdom was on its defence.

Encouraged by the failure of the Franks at Damietta, Saladin took the field in the following year—a year memorable for the earthquake which devastated Syria and laid low many of its ancient cities,—and began the series of attacks which continued until his treaty with Richard of England, twenty-two years later. His first raid was against Gaza, the frontier city of the Latin Kingdom. On his way he laid siege to the small castle of Darum, the southern outpost of Christianity, which had been recently fortified by Amalric, and was held by the Knights Templars. Their commander, Ansel de Pass, made a vigorous defence, and gave time for Amalric to come up with 250 knights of both the military orders, and 2000 foot-soldiers, who speedily dislodged the Saracens from their positions. Saladin did not wait for a pitched battle: at dead of night he slipped away, and almost before they were awake the inhabitants of Gaza found their town taken. The citadel, however, a strong fortress built by Baldwin III., held out, and its warden, Milo de Planci, sternly refused to admit the fugitive citizens, who were thus forced to stand outside the gates and fight to the death. Saladin had no mind for a long siege, and after plundering the town left the castle alone, and returned to Egypt with the spoils. On his way he passed close to Amalric, who got his men under arms, but was relieved to see him depart without offering battle. The year's successes ended in December, 1170, with the taking of Eyla at the head of the gulf of Akaba,—the same Elath whence Solomon's fleet sailed to

* *Kamil*, 568–70.

Ophir,—the key of the Red Sea route for pilgrims to Mekka. In order to rescue this important post from the Crusaders, Saladin had ships built in sections at Cairo, carried the parts on camels to the Red Sea, where he put them together, and took the fort after a combined attack by sea and land.

These successes against the "infidels" brought Saladin much renown among the Egyptians, who were ready enough to forget their jealousies and religious differences when a campaign was on foot and booty within sight. As their champion against the common enemy, Sunnites and Shiïtes, Egyptians and Turkmans, eagerly followed the banners of the young leader, against whom they had no less willingly plotted when no Holy War was at stake. Saladin's valour and generalship convinced the army of his right to command, and the mass of the people, so far as they understood at all, recognised in him a powerful protector. His authority was now so firmly established that he could venture upon a momentous step. The anomalous situation of a Sunnite vezir holding office under a Fatimid Caliph was peculiarly distasteful to a man of Saladin's orthodox views. For some time the King of Syria and the Abbasid Caliph of Baghdad had pressed him to do away with this political and theological inconsistency by introducing the name of the true instead of the false Caliph in the public Friday prayer (*khutba*)—the recognised form of allegiance. Hitherto Saladin, despite his religious tenets, had combatted this proposal on the ground that the change might cause a revolution in Egypt. Another reason, which he did not mention, was that his popularity among the heterodox Egyptians might prove a valuable support in the very probable event of a rupture with Nur-ed-din.

In 1171, however, his position had become much stronger, and he could afford to run some risk. The Fatimid Caliph was no longer personally a factor in politics. Since the assassination of his black chamberlain, he and his palace had been placed under the vigilant control of the white eunuch Karakush, Saladin's right-hand man, whose name, curiously enough, instead of being associated with acts of fidelity and severity, has become in the Turkish empire the designation of the ridiculous puppet, Punch. The seclusion and impotence of the Caliph had lowered the influence of Shiïte doctrine in Cairo, and Saladin had provided sound religious instruction according to the Sunnite rules by founding colleges* and establishing approved teachers of orthodoxy in the capital and the chief provincial towns.

The ground was thus prepared, and advantage was taken of the illness of the helpless captive who still called himself Imam, or God-directed leader, to

---

* The Nasiriya or Sherifya and the Kamhiya colleges near the mosque of Amr in Fustat, were founded by Saladin in 1170.

carry out the long-determined change in the Caliphate. On the first Friday in the sacred month Moharram, the first month of the year of the Flight 567 (the 10th of September, 1171), a bold divine from Mosil, anticipating the regular preacher in the chief SS, recited the bidding-prayer for the preservation and prosperity of the orthodox Caliph of Baghdad:

> "O God, assist him and assist his armies; O Thou Lord of the Faith and of the world present and the world to come, O Lord of the beings of the whole world. O God, assist the forces of the Moslems and the armies of the worshippers of Thee Only. O God, frustrate the infidels and polytheists, Thine enemies, enemies of the Faith."

This ecclesiastical revolution took place without a sign of opposition,—"there was not so much as the butting of two goats," says the chronicler; nothing worse than surprise was shown by the crowded congregation. The Caliph at Baghdad was overjoyed, illuminated his capital, and sent Nur-ed-din and Saladin robes of honour and the famous black flags borne by the Abbasid legions. To Nur-ed-din he sent, besides, two swords, one for the dominion of Syria, the other for Egypt, and hailed him Sultan. Meanwhile the person most affected lay dying in his great palace at Cairo. El-Adid, the last of the Fatimid Caliphs, never heard of his supersession in the public prayers; Saladin had forbidden his servants to tell him, saying, "if he recover, he will learn the truth soon enough, but if not, let him die in peace." He died three days later, not quite twenty-one years old. On his deathbed he had asked to see Saladin, but the vezir suspected a plot, and excused himself. Afterwards, when he found the wish was sincere, he repented his neglect, and spoke highly of the young Caliph's many virtues, his gentle character, his good qualities, and friendly advances.

Thus ended in feebleness and neglect the Fatimid dynasty, which had been the greatest Mohammedan power on the shores of the Mediterranean for nearly three centuries. The family indeed survived for two generations, but they could do nothing against the assured authority of Saladin. El-Adid left eleven sons, four sisters, four wives, and other relations, to the number altogether of one hundred and fifty-two; but Karakush, the major domo, shut them up under strict guard, the men in one place, the women in another, according them the luxuries and respect to which they were accustomed. The great palace of the Fatimids owned a new master.

CHAPTER VII

SALADIN AT CAIRO

1171–1173

VISITORS TO MODERN CAIRO see very little of Saladin's capital. Besides the three ancient gates, three ruined mosques, and part of the old walls, nothing remains of the city he traversed when he first rode out from the Fatimid palace at the head of his guard. The most conspicuous feature of the present Cairo, the Citadel, with its slender Turkish minarets and commanding battlements, did not exist: only a rounded spur of Mount Mukattam suggested the place where a fortress should be built. Most of the wide expanse, now covered by the European houses of the Ismaïliya quarter, between the Ezbekiya and the river, was under water; for in Saladin's day the Nile ran much further east and almost washed the city wall at the part where the river-suburb of el-Maks then stood. Bulak and its island were not as yet risen above the surface of the water, and there was no Abbasiya suburb on the north. Houses and streets indeed stretched then, as now, beyond the old Zuweyla Gate, towards the south, as far as the chapel of "our lady Nefisa," and there were many buildings or ruins of former habitations beyond this, where we now see only hill after hill of rubbish-heaps smothered in sand—the melancholy memorials of what was once the stately city, bowered in gardens, of old Fustat, and still older Babylon.

These suburbs and ruins were not then part of Cairo. The real Cairo, the city of the Fatimid Caliphs, was never more than an immense royal castle, called "The Victorious," el-Kahira, the Cahere of William of Tyre, which Italians corrupted into our modern Cairo. It was also known as "the city" el-Medina, and it was founded, in 969, expressly for the residence of the Caliph and his vast harim and slave-household, with quarters round his palace for the separate brigades of his army, the vezir and officers of state, and the departments of government. The spacious enclosure of the castle, guarded by massive walls and imposing Norman-like gates, was forbidden ground to all but high functionaries of state. Even ambassadors of foreign powers were required to dismount outside, and were led to the Caliph's presence by both their hands in the manner of the old Byzantine and the medieval Ottoman courts.

The chief buildings were the "Great East Palace" the Caliph's personal residence, where he kept his women, children, slaves, eunuchs and servants, estimated at from eighteen to thirty thousand in number, and the "Lesser West Palace," or pleasure-house, which opened on the spacious garden of Kafur, where a *meydan* or hippodrome provided exercise for the court. The two were separated by the square called "Betwixt the Palaces "(*Beyn el-Kasreyn*) where as many as ten thousand troops could parade; the name is still preserved in part of the Suk-en-Nahhasin or Coppersmiths' Market. An underground passage connected the two palaces, by which the Caliph could pass without violating that mysterious seclusion which was part of his sacred character. Hard by were the mausoleum where lay the bones of his Fatimid ancestors, brought from far Kayrawan; and the mosque (el-Azhar) where the Caliph was wont to lead the Friday prayers as Prince and Precentor of the Faithful; and near this, the Arab historian remarks, as if it were a common architectural feature, was "the well into which the Caliph used to throw the slain." The people believed that something more valuable than corpses of murdered caliphs, slaves, or disgraced favourites, was hidden in its gloomy depths; but when they searched for gold and precious stones, they were supernaturally repelled; and since no man can safely contend with "the Jinn," the well was filled up, lest worse should happen.

Of the size and splendour of the Great Palace the Arabic historians speak with bated breath. We read of four thousand chambers;—of the Golden Gate which opened to the Golden Hall, a gorgeous pavilion where the Caliph, seated on his golden throne, surrounded by his chamberlains and gentlemen in waiting (generally Greeks or Sudanis), surveyed from behind a screen of golden filigree the festivals of Islam;—of the Emerald Hall with its beautiful pillars of marble;—the Great Divan, where he sat in state on Mondays and Thursdays, at a window beneath a cupola,—the same window, perhaps, under which Dirgham stood suppliant in his downfall;—and the *sakifa* or Porch, where the Caliph listened every evening, while the oppressed and wronged came below and cried aloud the *credo* of the Shiïtes, till he heard their griefs and gave orders for their redress. The historians say little of the splendour within the palace, but some idea may be formed of its treasures by the marvels observed by Hugh of Cæsarea,* and from the statement that among the amazing wealth of jewels and precious stones which Saladin discovered on the death of el-Adid were an emerald four fingers long, and a ruby known as "the Mountain," the weight of which, in our terms, was over 2400 carats ("I have seen and weighed it myself," says Ibn-el-

---

* See above, page 81.

This supposed portrait of Saladin is on a page which must originally have come from a larger manuscript. Here the great Sultan is shown in Arab rather than Turkish costume, and, judging from its style, this simple illustration was probably executed in Egypt or Syria in the late thirteenth or early fourteenth century. (Private collection)

The ancient city of Mosul lies next to the River Tigris in northern Iraq. Before the region was devastated by the Mongols in the mid-thirteenth century, Mosul was a large and thriving commercial centre as well as being the capital of a state or large province. Its freedom depended on how much independence its ruler could wring from neighbouring powers. Despite the ravages of time and war, the medieval centre of Mosul still contains many buildings. including mosques, churches, ruined palaces and the remains of a citadel which existed when Saladin claimed sovereignty over the city.

An Arab-Egyptian army emerges from a fortification in a fragmentary manuscript painting from the ruins of Fustat in southern Cairo. Their enemies include a twelfth-century western European knight who is falling from his horse, so the picture was probably painted around the time that Saladin siezed control of Egypt. Most of the Muslims wear turbans rather than helmets, and three of them are also protected by the same sort of mail hauberks used by the Crusaders, including the man who is falling from his saddle. (Dept. of Oriental Art, British Museum, London)

The ruined Roman Temple of Artemis in Jerash in Jordan was the largest structure amid the rubble of what had been the city of Gerasa. By the twelfth century this site had been largely abandoned, though there was a large Arab village on a neighbouring hill. Not surprisingly, when the Muslims needed to construct a castle quickly in the face of the Crusader threat, they used the remains of the Roman Temple. Walls were erected between the columns of the Temple itself, while an outer defence was made by rolling the drums of fallen columns between the bases of surviving columns.

Islamic art is widely believed to ban three-dimensional representations of living creatures, especially human beings, yet in the medieval period this was clearly not the case. Here a large ceramic statuette represents a Turkish cavalryman, with a sword, circular shield and segmented hat or helmet, fighting a serpent which has curled around his horse. It was found at Raqqa in northern Syria, where it was probably also made. (National Museum, Damascus)

The Crusaders were not the only people to build large and imposing castles in the Middle East: the Byzantines, Armenians and of course the Muslims also did so. The great brick fortress of Qalaat Jabar overlooked the River Euphrates in northern Syria. Most of what still stands dates from the twelfth and early thirteenth centuries. When this photograph was taken, the view from Qalaat Jabar's shattered towers was much as it would have been in Saladin's day. Now, however, the valley had been turned into the man-made Lake Assad, and Qalaat Jabar is surrounded by water.

The *Kitab al-Aghani*, or *Book of Songs*, by Abu'l Faraj al-Isfahani is an anthology of poems. One of the earliest and most magnificent versions was made in northern Iraq in AD 1217–18, probably in Mosul. Each volume has a different frontispiece. This particular picture shows Badr al-Din Lu'lu, the ruler of Mosul, with a Turkish military governor wearing a fur hat, and a Christian bishop wearing a turban. In fact, the Muslim rulers of the Fertile Crescent made great efforts to retain the support of their indigenous Christian populations. (National Library, Ms. Fars, 597/4, Cairo)

Several centuries before the Crusades, the city of Raqqa overlooking the Euphrates in northern Syria was the occasional capital of the Abbasid Caliphs; as such, it was the centre of an empire which stretched from the Atlantic Ocean to the borders of Tibet. Some fragments survive from those glory days, perhaps including part of this ruined palace. It was, however, rebuilt several times, and the remaining stucco decoration is more likely to date from the twelfth century.

One of the most popular non-religious books in the medieval Arab Middle East was the *Maqamat of al-Hariri*. It was a collection of comic tales about a clever rogue who constantly tricked the authorities, both secular and religious. Many copies were made in the thirteenth century. Some were superb works of art while others, like this version from Mosul made in AD 1256, were much simpler, but each contains pictures illustrating contemporary life and costume. (British Library, Ms. Or. 1200, f. 81r, London)

When the Crusaders arrived in the Arab Middle East, Syria was fragmented into numerous small city states. The city of Hama was one of them, and, being so close to the frontiers of two Crusader states (Tripoli and Antioch), it felt very vulnerable. Yet it was Saladin and his precedessors, Zangi and Nur al-Din, who ended the independence of mini-states like Hama, uniting them into a larger realm which was at last strong enough to defeat the invading Crusaders.

The so-called 'Battle Plate' in Washington was made in Iran in the early thirteenth century, and it illustrates a battle between rival Islamic armies rather than a clash between Muslims and Crusaders. In addition to cavalry and foot soldiers, there is a turbanned Arab or Persian engineer operating a siege weapon on top of the tower. Otherwise the men are dressed and armed in the same manner as those Turks and Kurds who faced the Crusaders on the battlefield. (Freer Gallery of Art, inv. 43. 3, Washington)

(Right) This lustre-ware ceramic plate might have been made in late twelfth- or early thirteenth-century Iran, but the warrior's sword and distinctive flat-based infantry shield make it more likely that it comes from Egypt, perhaps from the time of Saladin himself. This shield was called a *januwiya*, and it was normally used during siege warfare. (Keir Collection, London)

(Above) In the foothills of the Syrian coastal mountains stands the castle and small town of Masyaf. In the twelfth and thirteenth centuries it was the capital of a tiny state squeezed between the powerful Islamic cities of the interior and the warlike Crusader states of the coast. Masyaf was, however, ruled by the Isma'ilis, adherents to one of the many sects of Shi'a Islam, and as such it was generally regarded as an enemy by both sides. Its ruler was sometimes called The Old Man of the Mountain, and his followers were called *Hashishin* (Hashish users) by orthodox Muslims—a name which the Crusaders corrupted to 'Assassins'.

At the time of the Crusades, Aleppo was, as it is today, the most important city in northern Syria. Its massive citadel stood on top of an ancient *tel*, the remains of millenia of human habitation, while the city was also surrounded by a sturdy wall. The famous fortified entrance to Aleppo's citadel, seen here, was constructed by al-Malik al Zahir Ghazi, Saladin's son, who governed Aleppo from 1186 to 1216.

The finest of all copies of the *Maqamat of al-Hariri* was made in Baghdad in 1237, and was illustrated by an excellent artist whom we only know as al-Wasiti ('the man from Wasit'). His numerous lively and detailed pictures show aspects of life in Iraq before the catastrophic Mongol invasion. Some illustrate everyday scenes, while others show special events. Here, for example, a caravan of Muslim pilgrims sets out from Iraq for the annual journey, or *Haj*, to the holy cities of Mecca and Medina. (Bibliothèque Nationale, Ms. Arabe 5847, Paris)

The little castle which the Crusaders constructed outside the ancient Arabian city of Petra in southern Jordan is now called al-Wu'aira. Its defences are largely natural, since the site is almost surrounded by cliffs and chasms, but walls and towers were added to the weaker points, plus this remarkable rock-cut gate-house.

The outside of the famous early thirteenth-century 'Battle Plate' in Washington is decorated with scenes of hunting, and princes with their attendants. Here one such leader carries a distinctive animal-headed mace, a weapon which seems to have been reserved for rulers or men of senior rank. (Freer Gallery of Art, inv. 43.3, Washington)

When Saladin took control of Egypt he set about making it an effective military powerbase. As a result, he started the construction of the massive Citadel which now overlooks the Egyptian capital. The extensive walls and towers were not actually completed within Saladin's own lifetime, but those seen here, on the eastern side of the Citadel, date from between 1183 and 1207.

This copy of the *Maqamat of al-Hariri* is slightly older than the more famous version illustrated by al-Wasiti, having been made in Syria in 1222–13. It is interesting to note that the ships shown in al-Wasiti's version, which was made in Iraq, reflect the sewn construction and angled hulls of Indian Ocean craft, whereas those made in Syria like this one reflect the traditional curved hulls of Mediterranean ships. (Bibliothèque Nationale, Ms. Arabe 6094, Paris)

The Citadel of Jerusalem was the strongest part of the city's fortifications during the Middle Ages. After Saladin liberated Jerusalem in 1187, the fortifications were allowed to fall into disrepair and the Citadel was the only part which remained usable. The tower which exists today largely dates from the fourteenth-century Mamluk period.

In addition to manuscripts and ceramics, inlaid Islamic metalwork also provides pictures of Muslim warriors. Some are armoured, usually wearing the sort of lamellar cuirass seen here. One cavalryman has a pointed helmet with a neck protection or *aventail*, while the second horseman on the right clearly wears a helmet of segmented construction. (Staatliche Museen, Berlin)

The Freer Gallery's 'Battle Plate' clearly illustrates a real event, as many of the figures are named, but scholars have not been able to agree what event it was. The commander of the attacking army rides forward, bow in hand, and is followed by both horsemen and infantry. Several of the latter are armed with pairs of javelins. (Freer Gallery of Art, inv. 43. 3, Washington)

The castle of Marqab, overlooking the coast of Syria, is one of the largest and most impressive Crusader fortresses. Unlike the blinding white stonework of the even more famous Crusader castle of Krak des Chevaliers, Marqab is made of sombre black basalt, relieved only by some decorative lines of limestone. Saladin failed to capture Marqab in 1188, but this massive Crusader outpost eventually fell to the Muslims just under a century later.

Hisn Kayfah, or Hasankeyf as it is now called, is sited on a dramatic cliff overlooking the River Tigris in south-eastern Turkey. During the medieval period there was also a magnificent stone bridge spanning the river, though this has now collapsed. Saladin did not annex the little state of which Hisn Kayfah was the capital, but his successors did so: instead, Hisn Kayfah remained a relatively peaceful city—a place of scholars rather than soldiers.

The artists who decorated books of Arabic poetry and of comic stories also illustrated manuals of medicine, veterinary science and horse management in much the same styles. Here, in a copy of the *Kitab al-Baytarah*, a treatise on hippology written by Ahmad Ibn al-Ahnaf, an artist working in Baghdad in 1210, is an accurate picture of the horse harness and riding costume as it appeared at the time. (Topkapi Library, Ms. Ahmet III, no. 2115, Istanbul)

Unlike the dark basalt fortress of Marqab, the gleaming white Crusader castle of Krak des Chevaliers lies some way inland. It guards a strategic gap between the Syrian mountains to the north and the much higher Lebanese mountains to the south. It is also the most famous of all Crusader fortresses, but, whereas Marqab is largely unchanged since Crusader times, much of Krak was rebuilt after it fell to the Mamluks in the thirteenth century.

The fortress of Yilanlikale stands on a rocky hill overlooking the road from the Cilician plain in what is now southern Turkey, across the mountains to Syria. This was one of the most important roads in the medieval Middle East, and so it is not surprising that the Armenian rulers of Cilicia constructed this massive castle, most of which dates from the twelfth and thirteenth centuries. Over its inner gate there is also a carving of an Armenian king, who sits cross-legged in the style of a Muslim Turkish ruler.

(Left) Astrological figures were popular subjects in the medieval art of the Islamic Middle East. They appear in carvings on buildings, in astrological manuscripts, and even as inlaid metalwork. Some figures are armed, and occasionally armoured, as is this warrior in a mail hauberk. He carries a scorpion representing Scorpio, and he is found on an early thirteenth-century inlaid brass writing box probably made in northern Iraq. (Franks Bequest, British Museum, London)

(Right) Another figure painted on the outside of the early thirteenth-century Iranian 'Battle Plate' in Washington shows a heroic warrior slaying a lion. He strikes with an iron-headed mace, and his helmet has a long neckguard. In addition there is a bowcase attached to his belt, though any armour is hidden beneath his highly decorated coat. (Freer Gallery, no. 43. 3, Washington)

Saladin was burried in Damascus following his death in 1193, and three years later a mausoleum was erected over his grave. As the centuries passed, this gradually fell into ruin. Then, in 1898, the German Kaiser, Wilhelm III, paid for its complete renovation as part of his efforts to promote an alliance between Germany and the Ottoman Empire. Twenty years later, on the eve of the fall of Damascus to an Arab army led by Lawrence of Arabia, a new white marble tomb was also provided. The original wooden sarcophagus still stands next to it, bearing the inscription, 'O God, receive this soul and open to him the Gates of Paradise, the last conquest for which he hoped.'

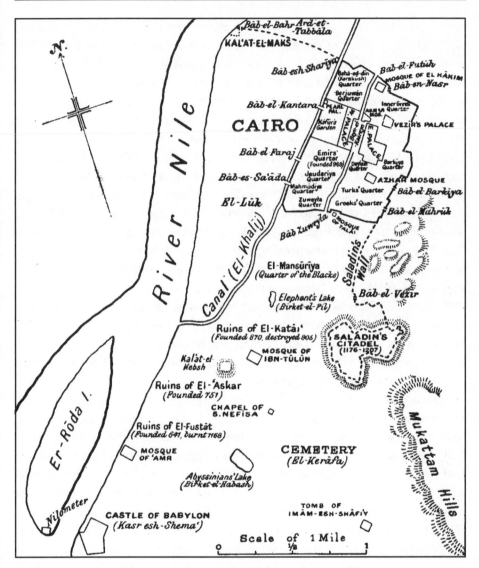

CAIRO IN THE DAYS OF SALADIN – 1170.
Dotted Lines show additions to the Fortifications made by Saladin.

Athir). The wealth of the Fatimids in jewels and works of the goldsmith's art had long been proverbial. In the inventory of the treasures of one of these Caliphs we read of quantities of emeralds and pearls, cut crystal vases, chased and enamelled gold plate; coffers inlaid with designs in gold; furniture and ornaments of sandalwood, ebony, and ivory, adorned with precious stones; cups and pitchers of fine porcelain filled with camphor and musk; metal mirrors framed in silver and gold with borders of emeralds and carnelian; tables of sardonyx; countless vessels of bronze inlaid with silver and gold; tapestry, silk, and brocade, heavy with gold embroidery, and adorned with the portraits of kings.

Of all the treasures that he found, Saladin kept nothing for himself. Some he distributed among his followers, or presented to Nur-ed-din; the glorious library of 120,000* manuscript volumes he gave to his learned chancellor the Kady el-Fadil; the rest of the treasure was sold for the public purse. Nor did it suit his simple and austere mode of life to take up his residence in the stately palace of the late Caliph. Silken divans and "Pavilions of Pearls" were nothing to him. He remained in the "House of the Vezir," and gave up the Great Palace to the captains of his army, allotting the western pleasure-house to his brother el-Adil. No longer a royal residence, the beautiful mansions of the Fatimids gradually fell into decay. "O censurer of my love for the sons of Fatima," cried Omara the poet of the Yemen, "join in my tears over the desolate halls of the twin Palaces!" One of the doorkeepers remarked that he had seen no wood brought in, and no rubbish thrown out, for a long time; and when the woodwork is used for fuel and the refuse is left to accumulate, the end of a building is not far off. So it happens that not a vestige remains of these once splendid palaces, which were the wonder and envy of princes.

Outside the "city" or castle of Cairo there was a large population to the south-west, and when Saladin rode forth to visit the holy tomb of the Imam esh-Shafiy in the desert, he passed by the sites of three earlier capitals. Going out of the Zuweyla gate, he would first traverse the comparatively recent quarters which had sprung up since the building of the royal and official "city" ; he would pass by the ruins of the Mansuriya, out of which he had smoked the rebel Blacks like a nest of hornets. Further on, the "Lake of the Elephant," long since dried up, would be on his right, whilst on the left the craggy spurs of the Mukattam range prompted the building of the citadel which he afterwards began. All the way his road lay through the crowded suburbs of the populace, whose houses covered the site where once had stood the famous city of "the Wards" (el-Katai), where Ibn-Tulun three centuries before had kept his kingly state. El-Katai was, like the "city" of Cairo, essentially an official capital, and was inhabited chiefly by the king and his court, his soldiers, and his purveyors, each class in a separate "ward." It was the third capital built since the Arabs conquered Egypt, and of all its magnificence nothing remains but the ruined mosque of Ibn-Tulun, of which

---

* Some say 2,600,000 volumes, including 1220 copies of one book, the famous history of Tabary. The numbers and statistics of Oriental writers are seldom to be trusted.

the grandeur and admirable designs reveal something of what has been lost. Beyond, still to the south-west, once stood el-Askar, "the Camp," another official centre, where the governors dwelt who were sent from Baghdad to rule Egypt in the days when the Abbasid Caliph held undivided sway from the borders of India to the Atlantic Ocean. Furthest south of all, between the Abyssinians' Lake and the Nile, lay what remained of the oldest capital of Mohammedan Egypt, at once the official centre and the metropolis of commerce, called el-Fustat, "the Tent," in memory of the pavilion of the Arab conqueror. In spite of the devastations of the great fire of 1168, the inhabitants had begun to return to their ruined homes and were trying to re-people the desolate streets. But Fustat never recovered its lost prosperity, when its bazars were renowned for wealth and commerce, and its houses reared their six stories aloft, and gardens of fruit and flowers stretched all around. Now nothing remains but the old Mosque of Amr, so often repaired and altered that its founder would not know it, and the Roman fortress of Babylon, the "Castle of the Beacon" of the Arabs, now a hive of Coptic churches served by Coptic drones, but once the guardian of a busy Christian city, the ancient and populous "Babylon of Egypt." The scanty suburb of "Old Cairo," or Masr* el-Atika, is not a relic of Fustat, for it stands on ground which was covered by the Nile in the days when Fustat was a city.

The history of the capital of Egypt under its Mohammedan rulers had thus been a series of transplantings from the south to the north-east. First *el-Fustat*, "the Tent," was founded by Amr the conqueror in 641; then *el-Askar*, "the Camp," was built, as a government centre, on the site of the camp of the Abbasid general in 750; thirdly, *el-Katai*, "the Wards," was laid out, still further to the north-east, in 869, by Ahmad ibn Tulun, as the capital of his dynasty; and lastly, in 969, Johar, the general of the Fatimid Caliph of Kayrawan, after annexing Egypt, founded *el-Kahira*, "the Victorious," as a fortified residence for his master. Saladin carried on the tradition of building, in which every great eastern ruler took pride; but, instead of pushing the capital still further to the north-east, he sought to unite the sites of all the four capitals, and to build a Citadel—the famous "Castle of the Mountain"—on the westernmost spur of Mount Mukattam, to be the centre of government and to form a military stronghold capable of overawing the whole city and resisting assaults from outside. His plan was to connect this

---

* The capital of Egypt was called by the Arabs by the same name as Egypt itself—*Misr*, and this name was commonly used for Fustat, which remained the commercial metropolis long after the building of Cairo. Misr is now pronounced *Masr*, and it is possible that it was so pronounced as early as the time of Saladin, for we find in William of Tyre, who certainly knew Arabic, the spelling *Macer*.

fortress by a bastioned wall with the old fortifications of the Fatimid "city," and
to extend it so as to enclose the site of Fustat and Katai, and thus to sweep
round to the river; but the plan was not completed, and even the Citadel was not
finished till long after his death. Saladin's enlargement of the area of the city
was accompanied by the demolition of whole suburbs between the old "city" and
the shrine of Nefisa. These were replaced by pleasure gardens, and it is recorded
that the tall Zuweyla gate could be seen from the door of Ibn-Tulun's mosque.
Jehan Thenaud, who accompanied an embassy from Louis XII. to Cairo at a
later period, found these gardens still a striking feature of the city:

> "moult somptueulx et grans jardins plains de tous fruictiers: comme cytrons,
> lymons, citrulles, oranges, aubercotz, cassiers et pommes de musez on d'Adam
> pour ce que l'on dict estre le fruict duquel Adam oul trepassa le commandement
> de Dieu. Lesquelz jardins tous les soirs et matins sont arrousez de l'eau du Nil
> que tirent beufz et chevaulx."*

Traces of some of these pleasure grounds may even now be seen from the battlements of the Citadel.

It has been supposed that Saladin designed the Citadel of Cairo to protect
himself against a possible insurrection of the partisans of the late dynasty. A
sufficient explanation, however, is found in his early associations: every Syrian
city had its citadel or fortress, and experience had shown many a time that the
town might be taken whilst the citadel remained impregnable, a refuge for the
people and a means of recuperation. Therefore Cairo must have a citadel too. It
might soon be needed as a tower of defence against his liege-lord Nur-ed-din
himself. Saladin had propitiated the King of Syria with presents from the treasures of the Fatimid palace; prayers were offered for him as sovereign lord every
Friday in the mosques, above all in the great mosque of el-Hakim, which now
supplanted the Azhar as the chief mosque of the city; and his name appeared on
the coins struck by Saladin at Cairo. But in spite of this nominal subjection and
the absence of all symbols of personal sovereignty, Saladin was virtually his own
master; and supported as he was by a strong army commanded by his brothers
and nephews, he was in fact King of Egypt. Nur-ed-din was well aware of this,
but his difficulties with the Franks, with the Seljuk Sultan of Rum, and with
various contentious rulers in Mesopotamia, left him no leisure to clip the wings
of his vassal in Egypt. He could not even count upon Saladin's coöperation in
the Holy War; for, whether rightly or wrongly it is difficult to decide, Saladin was
convinced that if once his suzerain had the chance of seizing his person, there

---

* *Le voyage et itinaire de oultre mer faict par Frère Jehan Thenaud*, cited in Schefer's *Nassiri Khosrau*,
133.

would be an end of his power; and nothing could induce him to venture within Nur-ed-din's reach. Not only this, but he seems to have carried this dread so far that he preferred to have the Franks on his borders as an obstacle to Nur-ed-din's advance.

An instance occurred immediately after the death of the Egyptian Caliph. Amalric was absent at Constantinople, concerting further measures against the Saracens with his wife's uncle, the Emperor Manuel Comnenus; and Saladin, probably acting on orders from Damascus, seized the opportunity for an attack upon Mont Real (esh-Shaubak), an irritating little fortress built by Baldwin I. in 1115. Its glittering white battlements crowned a hill clothed with olives, and its gardens of apricots below formed a delicious oasis in the desert south of the Dead Sea. But it stood like a sentinel on the frontier between Syria and Egypt, and commanded the caravan road between the two countries to the perpetual annoyance of their commerce. To hold it or destroy it was for many years an object dear to Saladin, but it constantly eluded his grasp. On this first attempt he set out on the 21st of September, 1171, and established his leaguer round the white walls with little opposition. Indeed after a brief defence the garrison asked for an armistice of ten days, to arrange terms of capitulation, or more probably to gain time for rescue. During this interval Nur-ed-din himself left Damascus to join his Egyptian viceroy; whereupon Saladin broke up his camp and retreated to Cairo. Writing to his liege-lord he pleaded a convenient rumour of a conspiracy in favour of the late dynasty as an excuse for his sudden retreat. It was true, but insufficient; his brothers were fully competent to deal with the rising of the Blacks in Upper Egypt. Nur-ed-din was not deceived, and resolved to invade Egypt and make an end of such contumacy.

Rumours of the coming attack soon reached Cairo, and an anxious council was held by the family of Ayyub and the leading captains of the army, to whom Saladin communicated the news. There was a dead silence. Then a fiery young nephew, Takied-din Omar, spoke up: "If Nur-ed-din comes," said he, "we will fight him and drive him out of the land." But Ayyub, prudent and sagacious as ever, sternly rebuked the hot-headed youngster, and turning to Saladin said:

"I am thy father, and here is Shihab-ed-din thy mother's brother: bethink thee, is there one in this assembly who loves thee and desires thy welfare as we do?" "No, by Allah!" exclaimed Saladin. "Know then," said Ayyub, "that if I and thine uncle were to meet Nur-ed-din, nothing could stop our dismounting and kissing the ground at his feet. Even should he bid us cut off thy head with the sword, we should do it. From this, judge what others would do. All whom thou seest here, and all the troops, must needs do homage to Nur-ed-din, should he come. This land is his, and if he would depose thee, we must instantly obey. This therefore is my counsel: write to him, and say: 'News has reached me that you intend to lead an expedition to this country; but what need is there for this? Let my lord but send hither a courier on a dromedary, to lead me to you by a turban about my neck; no one here will offer to resist.' "

Then he dismissed the meeting: "Retire and leave us. We are Nur-ed-din's mamluks and slaves, and he may do with us as he chooses."

All this was said for effect, for Ayyub knew that some of the jealous emirs would be sure to write and report the whole proceedings to Damascus. When he was alone with his son, he took him to task for letting the officers see his secret ambition, and reiterated his conviction that not a man of the army would dare to take up arms against the King of Syria, and that the only prudent course was conciliation. He repeated the message he proposed before, and then added: "When he reads this he will give up his project. Meanwhile time is on our side, and every moment God is doing something." Then the old warrior broke out: "By Allah! if Nur-ed-din attempted to take but a sugar-cane of ours, myself should fight him to the death!" Saladin followed his father's counsel, and, as Ayyub had foreseen, the King thought it wise to accept the message of submission,—without risking the experiment of the dromedary.

The reality of Saladin's obedience was soon put to the test. In May or June, 1173, he set out, by Nur-ed-din's instructions, to lay siege to Karak. This celebrated fortress, north of Mont Real, and close to the southern extremity of the Dead Sea, was also on the caravan route, the very key of Syria, and a perpetual thorn in the side of the Saracens. It stood, and still stands, on the site of Kir Moab, which, in the days of Mesha, repelled the attack of Jehoshaphat, King of Judah; and it nobly sustained its tradition. "The Crow's Castle," as the Arabs called it, was rebuilt on Roman foundations by Payen, King Fulk's cupbearer, on a lofty hill of the range of Mount Seir, nearly three thousand feet above the sea, and overlooking a fertile valley, warmed by hot springs, where fruits grew in abundance. The position and the strength of the fortifications, the towers of which, carved with lions, may still be seen, made the fortress almost unassailable; a deep moat divided it from the town below, which was also fortified, and whence access was obtained to the castle only by two steep and narrow tunnels cut in the living rock. A sheer precipice defended the east side. In its general construction it was a typical Crusading fortress; and, well supplied with water and provisions, it resisted siege after siege.

Saladin was not destined to take it yet. Scarcely had he begun to skirmish with the enemy's outposts, when the news came that Nur-ed-din, as arranged beforehand, was approaching with his Syrian army. Up to this, Saladin had seemingly braced himself up to meet his suzerain, but at the last moment his heart failed him. He feared a snare, and hastily beat a retreat to Egypt.* His excuse was valid enough—the illness of his father, whom he had left in command at Cairo, and whose death might entail a revolution. Nur-ed-din took the desertion in good part, saying, "The holding of Egypt is our paramount object." As it was, Saladin returned too late to see his father alive. Ayyub had been thrown from his horse outside the Gate of Victory, whilst taking his daily ride to exercise his troops, and died on the 9th of August, before his son's arrival. The loss of his politic sagacity could not easily be replaced.

Saladin was well aware that, in spite of smooth words, Nur-ed-din still cherished feelings the reverse of friendly towards him, and he cast about for a safe refuge in the event of the threatened invasion. He continued to strengthen the fortifications of Cairo, to increase his army, and to accumulate stores and arms; but he was far from confident in his ability to resist an attack from Syria, and he turned his mind to preparing a place of retreat in case he were forced to abandon Egypt. He had already conquered the provinces on the African coast, Barka and Tripoli, as far as Kabis (Gabes), in an expedition commanded by a second Karakush (not the builder of the citadel of Cairo) in 1172–3; but this strip of territory was too open to invasion by sea and land to offer a secure asylum, and the expedition was undertaken chiefly in order to keep his numerous troops occupied, and to supply them with fresh booty and prize-money. The same objects, and the removal of intriguing officers to a safer distance, as well as the castigation of the still rebellious Blacks, no doubt prompted in some measure the expedition which he sent into the Sudan about the beginning of 1173; but in this he had a deeper design. If Egypt proved untenable, then the Sudan, or perhaps southern Arabia, might serve as a place of retreat, whither Nur-ed-din would not be likely to follow. The Sudan, however, proved anything but a desirable sanctuary. Saladin's elder brother, Turan Shah, a brave and dashing soldier, but rash, and unstable as water, successfully accomplished his immediate object, reduced the Blacks to submission, and occupied Ibrim, as has been related. But to live permanently in a country which produced nothing but maize, and where the only occupation was fighting and enslaving an irreconcilable population under a blazing sun, was not at all to his mind, so he returned to Cairo with a caravan of slaves, and reported that the Sudan would not answer Saladin's purpose.

---

* There is evident confusion in the accounts of the Arabic historians of the two similar expeditions to Mont Real and Karak in 1171 and 1173, and some of the incidents may have been transposed. It is probable that Saladin never really intended to meet Nur-ed-din on either occasion.

There remained the resource of Arabia. Omara, a poet and historian of the Yemen, then living at Cairo, exhausted the refinements of language in extolling the beauty and fertility of his native land, renowned in antiquity as Arabia Felix. It was afterwards believed that his enthusiasm was partly dictated by a wish to remove so fierce and warlike a leader as Turan Shah to a distance before a conspiracy that was hatching came to the birth. The poet's representations, however, which were true enough, were taken in good faith, and Turan Shah organised a well-found expedition, which left Egypt on the 5th of February, 1174, for Mekka, on its march to the Yemen. There he was joined by a powerful Arab chief, and the two made short work of the resistance of the Yemenites. Zebid, Jened, Aden, Sana, and the other strongholds fell one after the other, in May to August, and Turan Shah established his seat of government at Taizz and ruled Arabia Felix until his return to his brother early in 1176. The province remained under the authority of the Ayyubid dynasty for fifty-five years, but was never put to its intended use as a refuge from the vengeance of Nur-ed-din.

Meanwhile insurrection and intrigue had troubled the serenity of Egypt. The plot was ripening of which Omara was believed to be the instigator. A number of Egyptians and Sudanis, and even some of the Turkman officers and troops, joined in the conspiracy; the Kings of Sicily and Jerusalem were engaged to assist by promises of gold and territory; and preparations were a-foot for a combined attack by sea and land, in which Saladin was to be enmeshed. Fortunately the whole plan was betrayed to the intended victim by a divine to whom the conspirators had unwisely confided their secret. Saladin waited until his information was fully confirmed, and then swooped down upon the plotters, seized the leaders, including the too political poet, and had them all crucified on the 6th of April, 1174. The revolting Egyptians and black slaves were exiled to Upper Egypt.

The sea attack, which was to have supported the Cairo conspiracy, did not take place till the late summer. The Franks of Palestine did not move when they heard that the plot had failed; but the King of Sicily, less well-informed, despatched a large fleet, estimated at 282 vessels,* which arrived off Alexandria on the 28th of July. The inhabitants of the scanty garrison were completely taken by surprise, but they tried to resist the landing, which was nevertheless effected near the pharos. The catapults and mangonels which the Sicilians had brought were soon playing upon the curtain of the city walls, and the defenders were obliged to fight desperately all the first day till night fell, to resist the storming

---

* Ibn-el-Athir's account of the siege of Alexandria is here followed. Baha-ed-din puts the ships at 600, and the troops at 30,000, and dates the beginning of the siege at 7th September.

parties. The next day the Christians advanced their machines close up to the walls, but reinforcements had joined the garrison from the neighbouring villages, and again the attack was beaten off. On the third day, there was a vigorous sortie: the machines were burnt, the enemy lost severely, and the garrison returned flushed with triumph. Scarcely were they within the gates, when an express arrived from Saladin, to whom they had sent for support. The courier had ridden from Cairo that same day with relays of horses, and, reaching Alexandria between three and four in the afternoon, loudly proclaimed the approach of Saladin's army. The tidings put fresh heart into the defenders, and they rushed out again in the gathering darkness, fell upon the camp of the Sicilians, and drove them, some to the ships, some into the sea. The news that Saladin was on the march finished the fiasco: the Sicilians slipped their moorings and fled, as suddenly as they had come.

The danger from the Franks was over, but it had been very grave. Nevertheless the Sicilian invasion, the conspiracy at Cairo, and the insurrection up the Nile, weighed nothing in the balance against the important news which had been brought from Syria. The greatest of dangers was past, the greatest of rivals was no longer formidable; for on the 15th of May the Sultan of Syria lay dead.

SIEGE OF A SARACEN FORT.

FROM A 13TH CENTURY MS.

PART III

EMPIRE
1174–1186

CHAPTER IX

THE CONQUEST OF SYRIA
1174–1176

T HE NEWS OF THE DEATH of Nur-ed-din fell like a thunderbolt among the Saracens. It was wholly unforeseen. On the 6th of May, 1174, he was out riding with one of his courtiers, discoursing in his philosophic way upon the uncertainty of human life: on the 15th he was carried off, in his fifty-sixth year, by a contemptible quinsy. No sovereign since Melik Shah had been so revered. To his subjects he was a model of all virtue, the embodiment of Moslem piety, "a second Omar ibn Abd-el-Aziz," as religious, just, and clement a king as ever ruled. Even the Crusaders bore witness to his chivalrous character, and William of Tyre admits that, in spite of his race and creed, "Noradinus was a just prince, wise, and religious," though a great oppressor of Christians. Justice was the quality he valued next to—indeed as a part of—godliness. He would himself appear in the kady's court to answer the process of a subject, and he insisted on no favour being shown to his rank. He remitted all customs' dues and tithes throughout his dominions, and lived simply and frugally on his private means, without touching the public revenue. When his wife complained of her poverty, and disdained his offer of three shops at Emesa, belonging to his estate, and worth about twenty gold pieces a year, he rebuked her: "I have nothing more, for all the rest I hold only in trust for the people." In pursuance of that trust he built citadels for their defence, and founded many colleges, convents, hospitals, and caravanserais, for their spiritual and bodily welfare. No man delighted more in the conversation of the learned and devout. None was more diligent in the observance of the minutest rules of his religion. There was a holy calm in the grave but gentle eyes, which relieved the massive brow and ennobled the swarthy, almost beardless, face. He possessed the dignity and serenity of the true Eastern gentleman; in his presence there was silence and stillness—

> "Tum, pietate gravern ac meritis si forte virum quem
> Conspexere, silent, arrectisque auribus adstant;
> Ille regit dictis animos, et pectora mulcet."

Nur-ed-din's greatness consists rather in his just and able administration than in his victorious campaigns. Yet he was a bold and fearless warrior, a splendid horseman, ready to expose himself in the front of every battle; and he organised his feudal levies very carefully, made the soldiers' fiefs hereditary, and kept a strict register of the men and arms that each of his vassals was bound to furnish at his demand.* But his power of conquest was restricted at the very outset by the division of his father Zengy's dominions, and the jealousy of his elder brother of Mosil. He had to build up a kingdom, and secure it from attack both on east and west, before he could attempt larger schemes; and to this Jerusalem owed its temporary safety. His early wars with the Crusaders had been little more than forays; and after he had taken Damascus (1154) and reduced the rest of inland Syria, his attention was chiefly occupied with Egypt; as a rule he only skirmished with the Franks, and kept them at arm's length. He had indeed taken Harenc and Banias, and in the north he had made his power felt as far as Marash. At the time of his death, however, he was preparing for greater efforts. He had overrun Mesopotamia on his brother's death in 1170, and though he left the brother's son in nominal authority at Mosil, all Jezira and Diyar-Bekr were really under the sway of Damascus. Relieved from any menace from this quarter, and strengthened by the widened area for recruiting his army, he was gathering forces to reduce Saladin to more becoming humility when the hand of death arrested his plans. Whether he would have succeeded, and whether after deposing Saladin he would have led a united Egyptian and Syrian army against the Franks and expelled them from the Holy Land, are merely speculative questions; but the Christians, we may believe, had less to fear from the cautious policy of Nur-ed-din than from the zeal of his great successor.

Upon Nur-ed-din's death, Saladin became the most powerful ruler between Baghdad and Carthage. Es-Salih Ismaïl, the heir of the late King, was a child of eleven years, a luckless shuttlecock between rival guardians. The dominions of the descendants of Zengy in Mesopotamia were cut up among jealous factions. The knell of the Latin Kingdom tolled in July, when the Franks lost Amalric, and Raymond of Tripolis became regent over Baldwin, the afflicted heir, a boy of thirteen, and a leper. Two children with cliques of envious counsellors formed no very formidable obstacles to the progress of a determined ruler, backed by a powerful and seasoned army. Mere personal ambition would have led most men in Saladin's position to take advantage of the weakness of his neighbours, but to ascribe any such conscious motive to him would be to misread his character.

---

* Ibn-el-Athir, *Atabees*, 308.

Unless he could persuade himself that the general interests of the Saracens, and especially of the Moslem faith, required his intervention, he would hesitate to aggrandise his power at the expense of one with whom he was nearly connected and whose father had once been his lord and benefactor. The state of Syria left him no alternative, unless he were content to look on whilst the kingdom laboriously built up by Zengy and his son fell piecemeal to rival emirs, or even to the "infidels." Disunion and anarchy prevailed; the young King's cousin of Mosil threw off his allegiance and even annexed Edessa and other dependencies of Syria: the emir who had charge of Aleppo was at enmity with those who surrounded the boy sovereign at Damascus; many of the great vassals made themselves independent; Islam in Syria had no leader, and if the Franks had not been in a similar case they might have done what they pleased with the fragments of Zengy's realm.

In these straits, Saladin, as the chief among the officers of the late King, naturally came forward with advice and proffers of assistance, which might almost be interpreted as commands, despite the respectful terms in which they were couched. He sent an ambassador to the young King with assurance of his loyalty, and ordered the name of "es-Salih, son of Nur-ed-din," to be recited in the prayer and engraved upon the money of Egypt.* He wrote to the lords of Damascus to upbraid them with their jealousies:

> "If Nur-ed-din," he said, "had thought any one of you capable of taking my place or of being trusted as he trusted me, he would have appointed him to the government of Egypt, the most important of all his possessions. If death had not prevented him, he would have bequeathed to none but me the guardianship and bringing up of his son. I perceive that to my hurt you have arrogated to yourselves the care of my Master, the son of my Master. Assuredly I will come to do him homage and repay the benefits of his father by service which shall be remembered for ever; and I shall deal with each of you according to his work, [especially] the abandoning of the defence of the King's dominions." †

Not only had the council of Damascus sat tamely still whilst the Mesopotamia prince was filching cities; they even purchased with gold the goodwill of the Franks, to Saladin's fierce contempt. They were indeed equally afraid of their neighbours on either hand, Seyf-ed-din of Mosil and Saladin of Cairo, and to protect themselves from both they had made terms with the "infidels," as their predecessor Anar had done in the days of Zengy.

---

*There are copper coins in the British Museum bearing the joint names of es-Salih and Saladin (see my *Catalogue*, vol. ix., *Additions*, p. 308), but these were probably issued, after the occupation of Damascus, from the mint of that city.

† *Kamil*, 607, 608

But when in August the child-King was removed to Aleppo, a more imminent danger threatened them. The vigorous captain of Nur-ed-din's veterans, who ruled Aleppo and now assumed the guardianship of the King, was prepared to trample on all rivals, and would certainly begin at Damascus. In this emergency they appealed to the King of Mosil to come to their aid; and when he refused, they invited Saladin. He waited for no second bidding, but, taking only seven hundred picked horsemen, rode straight across the desert for Damascus, trusting to his luck to bring him safe through the Frank borders. He came out of the waste untouched, and, entering the Ancient city amid general acclamations, rested at his father's old house, until the citadel also opened its gates to him, on the 27th of November.* Then he installed himself in the castle and received the homage and salutations of the citizens, winning general applause by a liberal distribution from es-Salih's royal treasury. All this he did as the agent of the youthful King, whose "mamluk" he still professed himself to be, and whose sovereignty was formally attested by prayers and coinage.

Leaving his brother Tughtigin, surnamed the "Sword of Islam," as governor of Damascus, Saladin instantly pressed forward to reduce other cities which belonged to Nur-ed-din's kingdom, but were now practically independent. It was the depth of winter, and the cold and snow were severe on the highlands; but his business brooked no delay. Traversing the beautiful Bikaa, the wooded valley of the Litany river, on the 9th of December he victoriously entered the opulent city of Emesa, where Aurelian once made sacrifice to the gods for his victory over Zenobia; and then, masking its castle, which was too strong to be taken by assault, descended the fertile valley of the Orontes to the land of lush fields and water-wheels, to Hamah,—the same Epiphania where the heroic queen of Palmyra lost her throne and liberty. The city opened its gates, and the citadel presently surrendered, on Saladin's oath that he came as the viceroy and servant of es-Salih. Then he passed on to Aleppo, to the famous "Grey Castle" towering on its round hill above the plain, "a very bride for beauty," which held within its strong walls his nominal sovereign. The Governor and Vezir Gumushtigin had no mind to abdicate his authority to so dangerous a visitor, and prudently shut the gates in his face. Saladin opened a siege on the 30th of December, on the plea that he had come to rescue his liege-lord from evil counsellors; but es-Salih, as much afraid of his deliverer as he was distrustful of his governor, came out of the palace, and riding amongst the people threw himself on their mercy. The child

---

* Different dates are assigned by Ibn-el-Athir and Baha-ed-din for the entry into Damascus. Ibn-el-Athir's "end of Rabi I," *i. e.*, end of October, may be a miscopying of Baha-ed-din's more precise 30th of Rabi II," *i. e.*, 27th of November.

made so moving an appeal to the crowd, entreating them with the tears running down his cheeks, not to deliver him up to this fierce invader who had stolen his heritage, that their hearts were touched; they redoubled their efforts, and their vigorous and repeated sorties made the invader pause.

The energy of the defence, joined to a new and disquieting danger, decided Saladin to abandon the siege. Gumushtigin, the vezir, resolved to leave no stone unturned to escape falling into the hands of the Egyptians, sought help from the Sheykh Sinan, the so-called "Old Man of the Mountain," Grandmaster of the Assassins of Syria. This redoubtable secret society, partly religious, still more political, had spread abroad from its cradle at the castle of Alamut in the mountains on the south of the Caspian Sea. Its corps of *fidawis*, or emissaries, trained to murder as a fine art, had used their daggers to some purpose in the wars which had tormented Syria, and the Society had been rewarded by the gradual acquisition of nine forts among the Ansariya Mountains, forming an almost impregnable chain of fortresses from Valenie (taken in 1125), on the coast, to Masyaf inland. These "Assassins"—*Hashshashin* or smokers of hashish (their name among the vulgar), more properly Ismaïlis, or Batinis, "Esoterics"—had taken firm root in Syria at the time of Saladin's invasion, and were the terror of the country. Nur-ed-din had vainly attempted to subdue them, and had gained nothing by his endeavour except the unpleasant discovery of a warning pinned to his pillow by a poisoned dagger. In Egypt they had supported the lost cause of the Fatimids, from whose sect they were derived, and they probably had a share in instigating Omara's conspiracy. The Master was therefore willing enough to assist the vezir of Aleppo by sending his fanatics to murder Saladin in his camp. They gained admission without difficulty, but were detected just in time. One of the wretches was cut down by Tughril, the lord chamberlain, at the very tent of Saladin, and the rest made a desperate defence before they were overpowered and slain.

This narrow escape may well have deterred him from incurring further risks. He was threatened from other quarters, moreover: the King of Mosil was raising troops to defend his cousin of Aleppo; and the Franks had already cut the road to Saladin's base at Damascus. Raymond, Count of Tripolis, had been for many years a captive of Nur-ed-din at Aleppo, and after his release on ransom (which was not paid) had become regent of the Latin Kingdom during the minority of Baldwin IV. The vezir of Aleppo, hard pressed by Saladin, appealed to the Count for assistance, and Raymond saw advantages, political and pecuniary, in helping the beleaguered city against the new aggressor. He therefore made a diversion, marching upon Emesa, which was still masked and blockaded by part of Saladin's army.

The governor seems to have had some negotiations with Raymond, involving, as usual, solid cash. Cheered by this golden hope, the Christians opened the attack on the 1st of February, 1175, and had the satisfaction of succeeding in their main object—of raising the siege of Aleppo; for Saladin was heard of next day. He had already reached Hamah, and was taking up a strong position near the great stone bridge over the Orontes, where lies the village of Arethusa (er-Rastan). The Franks immediately deserted the famous city, which once gave birth to Julia Domna and taught the child Elagabalus those Syrian rites which he afterwards brought as Emperor to Rome. Saladin entered Emesa, and reduced the citadel, after a stubborn resistance, in the middle of March. At the end of the month he occupied Baalbekk. He was now master of all Nur-ed-din's Syrian kingdom, except the districts immediately depending on Aleppo.

These successes finally roused Seyf-ed-din Ghazy II., the Atabeg of Mosil, who, as head of the descendants of his grandfather Zengy, regarded Syria and Mesopotamia in the light of a family estate. As a member of the family he had felt no scruple in taking advantage of his cousin's youth and annexing his Mesopotamian possessions; but it was another matter when an upstart, who had no drop of Zengy's blood, ventured to usurp the family prerogatives. Seyf-ed-din accordingly mustered a large army and despatched it to Aleppo, where its arrival was anxiously expected. The combined forces marched against the common enemy, and found him near Hamah. Though he had recently been reinforced by the arrival of a contingent from Egypt, Saladin was evidently outnumbered; for he made overtures for an accommodation, even offering to abandon all his conquests north of the province of Damascus. The enemy, however, would listen to no terms, and roughly told him to retire to Egypt. Driven to an issue at arms, he took up a position by the gorge of the Orontes, on the hills called the Horns of Hamah, where a superior position made up for disparity in numbers. On the 13th of April, 1175, the troops of Mosil and Aleppo marched to the attack, confident in their strength; but taken at a disadvantage and caught in a ravine between the tried veterans of Damascus and Cairo, they were cut to pieces, and the battle ended in a shameful rout. Saladin pursued the fugitives to the gates of Aleppo, and es-Salih's advisers were compelled to agree to a truce, whereby each side retained the territory it then possessed. By this agreement Saladin remained the undisputed master, not only of the provinces of Damascus, Emesa, and Hamah, but even of the towns of Kafar Tab, Barin, and Maarra, not far from Aleppo itself.

Now, for the first time, Saladin asserted his independence, proclaimed himself King, and suppressed the name of es-Salih in the prayer and coinage.* This year he was prayed for in all the mosques of Syria and Egypt as sovereign lord, and he issued at the Cairo mint gold coins in his own name: "el-Melik en-Nasir Yusuf ibn Ayyub, ala ghaya," "*The King Strong to Aid,*† *Joseph son of Job; exalted be the Standard!*" So far as his words prove, he had done his best to convince the young King at Aleppo that he was ready to serve him loyally, though he had made it clear enough that he would allow no rivals near the throne. Es-Salih naturally perceived that such nominal service meant real mastery, and would have nothing to do with him. Positively repulsed in every overture of conciliation, Saladin felt himself absolved from further fealty, and in the circumstances there was no reason why he should not take to himself the dignity of King.‡ His assumption of royal prerogatives received the gracious sanction of the Caliph of Baghdad, who sent him the customary diploma and robes of investiture as King of Egypt and Syria; they reached him at Hamah, where he was organising his new possessions, in May, 1175.

Administrative duties and the mustering of troops occupied the rest of the year, and nothing of any moment happened until the following spring. But the contest between the houses of Zengy and Ayyub was not ended by Saladin's victory at the Horns of Hamah. Both sides were actively gathering strength for a fresh struggle. Seyf-ed-din was levying troops among the minor states of Diyar-Bekr and Jezira, with which, in the spring of 1176, he was able to cross the Euphrates at Bira. His army numbered 6000 men, and was further reinforced when he picked up es-Salih's contingent at Aleppo. Saladin, who left Cairo with only 700 horsemen, had by this time brought up his forces from Egypt to join the troops of Damascus.

As he crossed the Orontes on the 11th of April, 1176, to meet the approaching storm, the sun was eclipsed, the earth was in darkness, and the stars shone clear in the midday sky.§ Despite this omen, he continued his march, but he

---

* There are gold coins of this date (A.H. 570), struck at Cairo and Alexandria, in the Khedivial Collection and that of Artin Pasha at Cairo.

† It is difficult to render the exact meaning of Arabic titles. *En-Nasir* is *one who aids* another to victory, especially who aids in the triumph of Islam, a champion of the faith. It connotes the idea of success, and hence is often rendered "Victorious." A coin with this inscription, struck at Cairo in 570 of the Hijra, *i. e.*, 1175 A.D., is preserved in the Khedivial Library at Cairo. I think Sir Charles Wilson suggested the appropriate rendering " Strong to aid."

‡ Saladin has often been charged with disloyalty, but with little reason. The nominal King was in the hands of Saladin's rivals, and never gave him the opportunity to be loyal. Had Saladin left Syria alone, it would have fallen, not to the boy King, but to other ambitious emirs.

§ Imad-ed-din makes this eclipse occur on Saladin's return from Hamah to Damascus in May, 1175; but no total eclipse of the sun occurred in 1175, whilst there was a total eclipse visible in northern Syria on April 11, 1176. *Cp.* Oppolzer's *Canon der Finsternisse.*

had not advanced far beyond Hamah when the sinister import of the eclipse was revealed, for he narrowly escaped a serious disaster. Seyf-ed-din came up unexpectedly whilst Saladin's men were dispersed at the Turkman's Wells (Jibab et-Turkman) watering their horses. Had he attacked at once, the result must have been a victory; but he hesitated, and when he took the field next morning, Thursday 22nd April, he found Saladin ready for him near the Little Caravanserai on the "Mound of the Sultan," fifteen miles from Aleppo. A bloody hand to hand fight ensued. The lord of Irbil overthrew Saladin's left wing, and was driving it before him, when the King himself charged at the head of his guard and turned the fortune of the day. A sudden panic seized upon the enemy, and every man ran for his life. Most of the Atabeg's officers were killed or taken prisoners, and Seyf-ed-din with difficulty made his escape from the field. The camp and horses, baggage, tents, and stores, all fell into the conqueror's hands.

Saladin showed himself worthy of victory. He treated his prisoners generously, set them free, and sent many of them away with gifts. The wounded, especially, owed their lives to his care, and many were eager to enter his service. As for the rich booty of the enemy's camp, he gave it all to the army, and kept not a thing for himself. In this he displayed alike the instincts of a generous nature and the foresight of a statesman. He bound both his own troops and the enemy's to him with ties of gratitude and personal devotion. The prisoners he had freed, some of whom were men of rank and influence, went back to their homes by the Great River full of his praises, extolling his clemency and greatheartedness, and prepared to be his willing subjects. His own men, flushed with triumph and enriched with spoil, were ready to follow him anywhere.

After a few days' halt before Aleppo, which still closed its gates, he led them on whilst their blood was hot. A day's march brought them to Buzaa, which they took; next day they stormed Manbij; then they turned west to the strong fortress of Azaz, which cost them thirty-eight days' siege and heavy losses, and nearly sacrificed Saladin's life. The leaguer began on the 15th of May,* and on the 22nd Saladin was resting in the tent of one of his captains, when a fanatic rushed in upon him and struck at his head with a knife. The cap of mail which the King wore under his *tarbush* saved him for the moment, and he gripped the assassin's hands; but, seated as he was, he could not prevent his going on stabbing at his throat. The dagger slashed the collar of his gambeson† but the rings of the

---

* Baha-ed-din says the siege lasted from May 15 to June 24 ; Ibn-el-Athir, May 14 to June 21. Neither period exactly agrees with the 38 days stated by the latter to be the length of the siege; but a compromise between the two meets the difficulty.

† Persian *kazaghand*, a thick quilted tunic, always worn by Saladin on horseback.

armour kept it out of his neck. All this was the work of an instant, and in another, Bazkush had grasped the knife and held it, though it sawed his fingers, until at last the desperado was killed, with the knife still clenched in his hand. Another cut-throat followed, and fell dead; and yet a third; but the guard was now on the alert. Saladin mounted and rode to head-quarters in panic fear, scarcely realising that he was alive. The sudden assault of the secret assassin had terrors which he never felt on the battle-field, and this second attempt by the agents of the "Sheykh of the Mountain" unnerved him. It was found that the three desperados had contrived to be enrolled in the bodyguard itself: Saladin hastened to change it, and searched the ranks for suspicious faces; but the emissaries of Sinan had the art to assume every disguise and elude all precautions, and there could be no real sense of security until their master was either crushed or propitiated.

Convinced that Gumushtigin was at the bottom of this dastardly attempt, Saladin redoubled his assaults against Azaz, and at last on the 21st of June the fortress capitulated. Then he hurried to Aleppo, to punish the plotter, and on the 25th began his third siege of the Grey Castle. His attacks were resisted as before, but sooner than risk being starved out, the garrison consented to treat. A general agreement was arranged (29 July) between the young King of Aleppo, the neighbouring Ortukid princes of Keyfa and Maridin (who had throughout supported him), and Saladin, by which he was finally recognised as sovereign over all the dominions he had conquered, and the four signatories bound themselves solemnly by an oath of mutual alliance.

When the treaty was concluded, there came to Saladin a young girl, the little sister of es-Salih. He received her with honour, and asked her "What is thy wish?" "The Castle of Azaz," she said. So he restored the castle to its old owners, loaded the princess with presents, and escorted her back to the gate of Aleppo at the head of his staff. The great Constable Humphrey of Toron had cause to be proud of his Knight,

CHAPTER X

TRUCES AND TREATIES
1176–1181

F OR SIX YEARS there was peace between Saladin and the house of Zengy. Es-Salih remained at Aleppo in undisturbed enjoyment of what was left to him of his father's kingdom. The Atabeg of Mosil did not invite a repetition of the disasters at the Horns of Hamah and the Sultan's Mound. There was also a nominal truce with the King of Jerusalem, which Saladin had concluded in the summer of 1175, with the assistance of handsome presents and the mediation of Humphrey of Toron, with whom he probably maintained the friendly relation which dated from the time of his own knighthood. His object was to secure himself in the rear whilst he was occupied in the north. Treaties with the soldiers of the Cross, however, were worse than useless, so long as the doctrine prevailed in Christendom that no faith need be kept with the "infidel"; and scarcely had they concluded the pact of amity, when they began to ravage the beautiful valley of the Litany, burned the standing corn, set fire to the villages, and returned in triumph, laden with booty, and driving great flocks of stolen sheep and cattle.

The raids of the Franks, however, cannot have been very serious, or involved any loss of territory, for Saladin seems to have paid no attention to them. There was another power, independent both of the Franks and the Zengids, with which he was forced to deal. It was impossible to carry his life at the disposal of the Sheykh of the Assassins. Saladin accordingly determined to enter their country and destroy them root and branch. As soon as he had concluded his treaty of peace at Aleppo, and dismissed his Egyptian troops to recruit their strength at home, he marched with the rest of his army into the rocky passes of the Summak range, or Ansariya mountains, where the fanatics had their forts. He went into this gloomy region in August, and in August he came out; but the Old Man still ruled on his Mountain, and the Assassins were unconquered. What happened is variously related. It is agreed that Saladin laid waste much of the country and that he set siege to Masyaf, the chief among the nine castles of the society—a veritable eagle's nest, perched on a scarcely accessible peak, and commanding a desolate ravine. It is equally certain that his siege artillery and storming parties made no impres-

118

sion on the rocky fortress. The divergence arises when the cause of his abrupt retreat is explained. The Moslem historians naturally put the best colour on it, and assert that Sinan obtained peace through the mediation of Saladin's uncle; but even by these apologists the humility of the Master's overture is considerably weakened by his accompanying threat of a wholesale murder of the Ayyubid family in the event of refusal. The story told by Sinan's panegyrist* is more probable, when divested of its supernatural absurdities. This story is as follows.

When Saladin laid siege to Masyaf, Sinan was absent, and the King's summons to surrender reached him at a village near Kadamus. He told the messenger that he must have a personal interview with Saladin; and then, since access to Masyaf was blocked by the leaguer, he retired with only two companions to the top of a neighbouring mountain, whence he looked down upon the siege and awaited the event. Saladin, believing that he had the arch-enemy in his power, sent a body of troops to surround him; but hostile soldiers and peaceful messengers were alike held back by a mysterious force which numbed their limbs. Such was the miraculous power of the holy Master, in whom his followers were taught to recognise a veritable incarnation of the Divine Reason. The awed reports of his baffled and perplexed envoys worked upon Saladin's fears. He remembered the two former attempts upon his life, and began to doubt whether anything human could save him from the supernatural agencies of this devil or saint. He had chalk and cinders strewed around his tent, to detect secret footsteps; his guards were supplied with linklights, and the night watches were frequently relieved. But unearthly terrors surrounded him, and his sleep was troubled. One night the watchers on the battlements of Masyaf perceived a spark like a glow-worm slowly gliding down the hill where the Master sat. It vanished among the tents of the Saracens. Presently Saladin awoke from his uneasy dreams to see a figure gliding out at the tent door. Looking round he noticed that the lamps had been displaced, and beside his bed lay some hot scones of the shape peculiar to the Assassins, with a leaf of paper on the top, pinned by a poisoned dagger. There were verses on the paper:

> " By the Majesty of the Kingdom! what you possess will escape you, in spite of all, but victory remains to us;
> We acquaint you that *we hold you*, and that we reserve you till your reckoning be paid."

Saladin gave a great and terrible cry, and the guard and the officers rushed in. He showed them the scones, the dagger, the verses. The dread Master had

* Abu-Firas, published by S. Guyard: " Un Grand-Maître des Assassins" in the *Journal Asiatique*, 1887.

been actually at his pillow: it was nothing short of a miracle. No one had heard a step or seen a living soul: there were footprints on the cinders but they all pointed *outwards*. Then Saladin said: "I have *seen* him—and that is very different from hearing of him. Go to this man and ask him for a safe-conduct, and pray him not to punish me for my past errors." A messenger went to seek Sinan on the mountain, but the Master made answer that there could be no warranty for the King's life so long as he continued the siege. Saladin therefore departed, in such haste that he even left his artillery behind him; and at the Bridge of Ibn-Munkidh he received a safe-conduct from the Master of the Assassins.

This is the narrative of a partisan and a visionary, but it may well be based upon fact. Sinan may actually have groped or bribed his way to Saladin's tent, and thus convinced him in person that no precautions could avail him against the knives of the secret society. The dread of assassination, joined to the impracticable character of the district and the strength of its fastnesses, may reasonably have induced the King to abandon his design of uprooting the abhorred sect; and if he could not wholly destroy them, the only prudent alternative was to make them his friends. As a political measure, moreover, the binding of the Master by ties of mutual toleration was a master-stroke. It cut away from the still disaffected Shiïtes in Egypt their hope of Sinan's sinister support, and deprived the Crusaders of a secret weapon.

After leaving the mountains Saladin returned to Damascus (25 August), dismissed his Syrians to their homes, left his brother, Turan Shah, the conqueror of the Yemen, in command in Syria, and taking with him only his personal followers, went to Cairo (22 September). He had been absent two years, and there was much to organise and superintend. He now was able to devote his energies to the fortification and reconstruction of the city which he had already designed. The walls were repaired, and their extensions were laid out, and the building of the Citadel was begun. The Moor traveller, Ibn-Jubeyr, in 1183 saw Christian captives sawing stones and quarrying out the moat or fosse beneath the massive walls of the castle.* It was reserved, however, for a nephew thirty years later to complete the fortifications which his famous uncle had planned, and at the present day, so often has the Citadel been remodelled by Mamluk Sultans, and finally by Mohammed Ali, that it is difficult to identify with precision any large part of the original defences.†

The founder's inscription, however, may still be read over the old "Gate of

* Ibn-Jubeyr, *Travels*, ed. W. Wright, 49.
† The subject has been elaborately treated by M. P. Casanova in the *Mém. de la mission archéol. au Caire*, vi. See also Lane's *Cairo Fifty Years Ago*, ch. iv.

the Steps," Bab el-Mudarraj, a dark mysterious portal in the west face of the original enceinte. It records how "the building of this splendid Citadel,—hard by Cairo the Guarded, on the terrace which adds use to beauty, and space to strength, for those who seek the shelter of his power,—was commanded by our Master the King Strong to Aid, Honour of the World and the Faith (el-Melik en-Nasir Salah ed-dunya wa-d-din), Father of the Conquering, Yusuf son of Ayyub, Restorer of the Empire of the Caliph; with the direction of his brother and heir the Just King (el-Adil) Seyf-ed-din Abu-Bekr Mohammed, friend of the Commander of the Faithful; and under the management of the Emir of his Kingdom and Support of his Empire Karakush son of Abdallah, the slave of el-Melik en-Nasir, in the year 579 (or 1183–4 A.D.)."* The famous "Well of the Winding Stairs," 280 feet deep, still called the Bir Yusuf, "Joseph's Well," was certainly excavated in the solid rock by Karakush under Saladin's orders†; but the other buildings lately existing in the Citadel and called after his name really belonged to later times. The people of Egypt were accustomed to name public works after the famous Sultan. His memory, but not his act, is preserved in the long aqueduct of Cairo, and even in the great canal of Upper Egypt, still known as the "River of Joseph," Bahr Yusuf, though it dates from the time of the Pharaohs. The chief public work, however, that he carried out, beyond Cairo itself, was the great bridge or dyke of Giza, which was built, like the Citadel, with stones from the pyramids, in 1183–4, and carried on forty arches along the border of the desert, seven miles from Cairo, and was intended to form an outwork of defence against an invasion of the Moors, which never happened.‡

Saladin remained at Cairo, occupied with these improvements, building colleges like the Medresa of the Swordmakers, and ordering the internal administration of his principal province, for a whole year, till November, 1177, when he set out upon a raid into Palestine. The Franks had lately forayed the Damascus country, and the pretence of a truce was no longer worth preserving. The Christians had now sent a large portion of their forces north to besiege Harim, a fortress belonging to the King of Aleppo, and the south of Palestine was comparatively bare of defenders. The occasion was propitious, and Saladin marched gaily to Ascalon, "the Bride of Syria." William. of Tyre says that he heard, on careful inquiry, that the Saracens numbered 26,000 fighting men, of whom 8000 were *Toassin*§ or élite, including the bodyguard of a thousand Mamluks in yel-

---

* See Berchem in the *Mémoires de la miss. archéol. au Caire*, xix. 80*ff.*

† El-Makrizy, *Khitat*, ii., 204

‡ Ibn-Jubeyr, 49; el-Makrizy ii, 151.

§ Perhaps *Tausiin*, "Peacocky," for *taus* is used of " goodly men." *Toassin* can hardly be from *Tawashi*, "eunuch," though many of this class commanded in Saladin's armies.

low tunics—Saladin's colour—and 18,000 were *Caragholam* (black slaves) of inferior rank—doubtless the old Egyptian heavy-armed infantry from the Sudan. Meeting with no opposition, they began to raid the country in perfect confidence, sacked and burned Ramla and Lydda, and dispersed over the land, even up to the gates of Jerusalem, in a joyous orgy of plunder and devastation.

So secure were they in their strength that they treated the enemy with contempt, and allowed King Baldwin to get into Ascalon, and the Templars of Gaza to join him, without taking any precautions against a sudden attack. It is true the King of Jerusalem had only 375 knights to his back; but Saladin must have known by this time that 375 knights were not to be despised, especially when led by such warriors as Balian, Reginald of Sidon, Odo the Master of the Temple, and Joscelin the Seneschal, and encouraged by the presence of "the True Cross," borne by the Bishop of Bethlehem. How it happened is not clear, but this much is certain, that on the 25th of November, 1177, in the absence of the greater part of his army, Saladin's men were surprised at Tell Jezer, near Ramla,* and before they could form up, the knights were hacking them down. At first the Sultan retired fighting, and tried to get his men into order of battle; but his bodyguard was cut to pieces around him, and he was himself all but taken prisoner. Seeing that the day was lost, he turned at last, and mounting a swift camel rode for his life. A remnant of his troops escaped with him, and throwing away armour and weapons, and leaving the wounded to their fate, fled under cover of night pell-mell to Egypt, where they arrived after great privations. Of the rest of the army that had marched so gleefully to the despoiling of the Holy Land, few survived. Famine, cold, and heavy rains completed what the sword began. Never had Saladin's arms known such disaster.

Far from giving way to discouragement, however, the great captain, who had for once thrown away an army, hastened to collect another. Writing to his brother Turan Shah at Damascus, Saladin admits the desperate character of the battle, but is equal to quoting poetry on the subject—"I thought of thee," he wrote (and Ibn-el-Athir saw the very letter)—

> "I thought of thee, amid the thrusting of their spears,
>   While the straight browned blades quenched their thirst in our blood"—

and adds "again and again we were on the verge of destruction; nor would God have delivered us save for some [future] duty." In three months he was ready to meet the Franks again, and the spring of 1178 found him encamped under the

---

* *Mons Gisardus*, according to the report of Roger de Molines (Röhricht, *Regesta Regn. Hieros.*, 564).

walls of Emesa. Some skirmishes took place between his generals (who were also his kinsmen) and the Franks. The troops of Hamah won a victory over the enemy, and brought the spoils, together with many heads and prisoners, to Saladin, who ordered the captives to be beheaded. They were "infidels," and they had been plundering and laying waste the lands of the Faithful. The rest of the year was spent in Syria, without any considerable action on either side. Saladin wintered at Damascus, and in the spring prepared to undo the latest manœuvre of Baldwin.

The King of Jerusalem had followed up his triumph at Ramla by pushing forward towards the Saracens' country and setting an outpost on the road to Damascus. There was a passage over the Jordan called "Jacob's Ford," because here Jacob wrestled with the angel*; it was also known as the "Ford of Sorrows"; and here the King restored a fort which not only defended the passage of the river, but commanded the approach to the plain of Banias, the granary of Damascus, where rice and cotton fields and groves of lemon trees lay thick at the foot of the "Mount of Snow." Hitherto this fertile plain had been divided in the friendliest manner between the Franks and Moslems, and a mighty oak tree marked the boundary between the two nations, whose flocks grazed side by side. Saladin had vainly offered first 60,000 and finally 100,000 gold pieces to induce the King to abandon a project which was peculiarly offensive to the Saracens. . He now resolved to raze the fortress to the ground. His nephew Ferrukh Shah had already won a success over the Franks by an ambuscade in April, 1179: he had caught King Baldwin with a scanty following in a rocky gorge near Belfort, and it was only the courage of the valiant Constable Humphrey of Toron that rescued his young sovereign from capture, at the cost of his own life. The loss of this gallant knight was a heavy blow to the Franks. "No words can describe Hunfary," says the Arab historian; "his name was a proverb for bravery and skill in war. He was indeed a plague let loose by God for the chastening of the Moslems."†

Following up this advantage, Saladin, who had now removed his headquarters to Banias, pushed forward, and in June again encountered the King of Jerusalem. For Baldwin, hearing that the Saracens were pillaging in the direction of Sidon, went forthwith to the rescue, burning to wipe out his late disgrace. Marching north by way of Safed and Toron, he ascended a height of the mountains to

---

* "Cil lius qui est apielés li Gués Jacob, c'est là u Jacob luita à l'angle, et là u il ot brisie le cuisse, quant il repairait d'Aran, là u il estoit fuis pour Esaü, son frere." Ernoul, ed. Mas Latrie, 52. Ernoul adds that the King rebuilt the castle despite the treaty with the Saracens, and against his own judgment, but was overpersuaded by the Templars. Chesney says the ford is 80 ft. wide and 4 deep.

† Ibn-el-Athir, *Kamil*, 635.

the village of Mesafa ("the station"), whence he commanded a wide view, and beheld the camp of Saladin, as it were at his feet, spread out on the "Meadow of Springs" (Marj Oyun, Mergion). Hurrying down to the attack, his troops fell into disorder, the infantry dropped behind, and the army went into battle piecemeal. At first they had it all their own way and put part of the enemy to flight; but Odo at the head of his Templars rashly pursued the fugitives too far, and severed still further the already scattered forces of the Christians. Saladin, taking advantage of this, rallied his flying troops, and calling upon them for a great effort, made one of his furious charges. The enemy, who had thought the day won, were taken by surprise; and burdened by the spoils of the slain, had no time to form up. Many were killed or made prisoners, and the rest, escaping over the Litany river, sought refuge in the neighbouring stronghold of Belfort; some did not stop till they reached Sidon. The victory was specially notable for the high rank of the prisoners. The Masters of the Hospital and the Temple, Raymond of Tripolis, Balian of Ibelin, Baldwin of Ramla, and Hugh of Tiberias, were among the seventy knights whom the Secretary Imad-ed-din counted as they stood in Saladin's tent.* Baldwin obtained his liberty on paying a ransom of 150,000 Tyrian gold pieces and setting free a thousand Saracen prisoners; but when Saladin offered to exchange Odo for an emir who had been taken by the Franks, the Master—"a haughty, arrogant man, with the breath of fury in his nostrils, who feared not God nor respected man"† whose frantic fighting had been the wonder and the ruin of the day, replied proudly: "A Templar can give for his ransom nought but his belt and dagger."‡ Odo died in captivity: "he went from his prison to Hell," says Abu-Shama.

The road was now clear to King Baldwin's Folly, the Castle of Sorrows at Jacob's Ford. On the 25th of August Saladin marched thither, and as soon as his pioneers had collected enough vine-poles to make screens for the sappers, he began the attack. At the first assault a man in the crowd, in a tattered shirt, sprang on to the outwork and began to engage the enemy on the curtain; others followed, and the outwork was won. The Franks, however, still defended the walls resolutely, in confident expectation of being relieved. The next morning the Saracens mined the wall, and made the mine deep and filled it with burning wood, and waited for the wall to fall. But they waited two days, the fire burning all the time, and still the wall stood firm, for it was nine cubits thick, not ordinary cubits neither, but carpenters' cubits half as long again; and the mine was

---

* Quoted by Abu-Sharna (Goergens, *Arabische Quellenbeitrage*, 10).

† William of Tyre, xxi., 29.

‡ "Non esse consuetudinem militurn suae religionis, ut aliqua pro eis daretur redemptio præter cingulum et cultellum." (Robert de Monte, in *Mon. German.*, ad 1180.)

but a third through it. Saladin saw that it was useless, and called for water: "Every man who brings me a skin of water, shall have a gold dinar." Water was brought with such enthusiasm that the works were fairly flooded. Then the sappers returned and deepened the mine and pierced the wall, and put fire in again, and at last it fell on Thursday, the 30th of August, 1179. The Saracens poured in through the breach and took the castle by storm, and made prisoners of the defenders to the number of seven hundred, and set free the Moslem captives; but of the Franks, Saladin killed many and threw them down the castle well, and sent the rest to be imprisoned at Damascus. He remained on the spot till the Castle of Sorrows was razed level with the ground, and not a vestige of it remained. As Aly of Damascus, the clockmaker, sang:

"How can we leave in the Patriarch's house those who break faith after they have
    sworn it?
I admonish you sincerely—sincerity is part of religion—quit Jacob's House, for
    Joseph is come."*

When the King of Jerusalem at last arrived to raise the siege of his favourite castle, he found only heaps of stone blackened with fire. The Crusaders tried no more conclusions with Saladin that year. Their King's disease was increasing, and there was anxiety about the succession; a truce would be welcome. There was rest during the winter, indeed, which Saladin devoted to equipping a powerful navy to assist in the next expedition. His fleet of seventy vessels had done considerable execution in the autumn of 1179; harried the coast, and brought back a thousand Christian prisoners.† This encouraged him to try combined action by sea and land. In the spring of 1180 he was once more in the parts about Safed, waiting for his fleet to arrive off the coast, before opening a vigorous campaign. Baldwin wisely chose the prudent course, and sent messengers to propose peace. Saladin was not sorry to agree, for droughts and bad harvests were seriously hampering his commissariat. In the summer he consented to a truce for two years by sea and land, for natives and new-comers alike, and it was confirmed by solemn oaths. For the Franks it was an humiliating concession: never before had they set seal to a treaty drawn up on equal terms which reserved no advantage for themselves. It was no wonder that their pride rebelled. The Count of Tripolis, no friend to the King, loudly denounced the compact; but a rapid raid of the Saracens upon his territory in May, and the appearance of Saladin's fleet off Tortosa, brought Raymond to reason. The Holy War ceased for a while.

---

* Ibn-el-Athir, *Kamil*, 636–9; Imad-ed-din in Abu-Shama, 16, 17.
† Ibn-Aby-Tay in Goergens, 16.

There were other parties to the peace which now reigned over the Hither East, and the immediate cause of this widespread pacification was—a singing girl. Nur-ed-din, Prince of Keyfa, had been given to wife a great lady, the daughter of Kilij Arslan, the Seljuk Sultan of Konia. Unhappily he did not treat her well, but bestowed his affections upon a singing girl of no family at all. The neglected wife appealed to her father, and Kilij Arslan declared war. By the treaty of Aleppo, Saladin had agreed to stand by his allies, among whom was the Prince of Keyfa. Moreover he had himself a quarrel with the Sultan of Konia concerning the fortress of Raaban on the northern marches, and blood had been spilt. He was therefore in no humour to hear of a punitive expedition against his ally. "Tell your master, in God's name," he said to the Seljuk's envoy, "by my faith in two days I will march with my men into his capital and seize all his dominions." So in his wrath he had come as far north as Raaban, where he was again met by the ambassador, this time with peaceful arguments. Saladin, seeing the situation, put pressure upon his amorous ally, and the quarrel was compounded by the summary dismissal of the singing girl. This happy result was followed by an expedition into Cilician or Lesser Armenia, as far as Mopsuestia (el-Massisa), to compel its king Rhupen to keep faith with the Turkmans who pastured in his territory and under his protection. After the destruction of the castle of el-Menakir, Rhupen submitted.

Saladin's power had now made itself felt as far as Asia Minor; he was admittedly the chief of Saracen rulers from the Euphrates to the Nile, and was invited by other princes to act as arbiter in their disputes. This high position he used for a noble purpose, whatever motive urged him. He brought about a general peace, a *Truga Dei*, among all the peoples whom he could influence,

"nexuque pio longinqua revinxit."

On the 2nd of October, 1180, he presided over a memorable Congress, on the banks of the Senja, near Sumeysat, at which the princes of Mesopotamia— Mosil, Jezira, Irbil, Keyfa, and Maridin,—the Sultan of Konia, and the King of Armenia set their seals to a solemn pact, whereby they bound themselves on oath to keep peace one with another for the space of two years. For this time war was to be unknown within their borders, and a holy truce, a *Magna Pax Saracenica*, was to reign throughout the land.

"Hæ tibi erunt artes, pacisque imponere morem. . . ."

It was a great conception: but how it was observed will be seen.

CHAPTER XI

THE CONQUEST OF MESOPOTAMIA
1181–1183

HE GREAT TRUCE was made, and Saladin was free to return to Egypt. He left his nephew Ferrukh Shah in charge of Syria, and reached Cairo at the beginning of 1181. The year that was past had brought changes to many thrones. Louis le Jeune of France had died and Philip Augustus had succeeded; Pope Lucius had followed Alexander, and Alexius II. sat in the seat of the Emperor Manuel Comnenus. In Asia there had been a succession in the Caliphate; el-Mustady was dead, and en-Nasir, the most energetic of the later Abbasids, was pontiff at Baghdad. Seyf-ed-din, the Atabeg of Mosil, was gathered to his fathers, and Izz-ed-din his brother reigned in his stead. The close of 1181 witnessed an event of still greater importance to Saladin. On the 4th of December Nur-ed-din's heir, es-Salih Ismail, ended his gentle inoffensive life at Aleppo in a mortal attack of the colic—not without the usual suspicion of poison. When he knew his death was at hand, he sent for his chief officers and made them swear the oath of fealty to his cousin of Mosil—the only prince of the house of Zengy powerful enough to cross swords with its great supplanter. The dying youth could not forgive Saladin his trespass against the sovereign rights of the dynasty.

The Atabeg of Mosil hastened to take possession of Aleppo, where he was joyfully welcomed by his cousin's retainers. Other cities of Syria were disposed to revert to their old allegiance, and Hamah openly avowed its sympathy. The Atabeg nevertheless remained true to the treaty which he had sworn, and refused all inducements to invade Saladin's dominions. His later conduct suggests that fear had its share in this moderation, for he never ventured to meet his rival in the open field. Even the possession of Aleppo was too great a strain upon his energy, and harassed by the apprehension that he could not defend at once both his Syrian and Mesopotamian capitals, he yielded to the urgency of his brother, Imad-ed-din, the ruler of Sinjar, and consented to exchange cities with him. Imad-ed-din entered Aleppo on the 19th of May, 1182.

To these transactions Saladin offered no opposition. He was bound by his treaty to respect his ally of Mosil and he never broke a treaty in his life. At the same time he was closely watching events on his northern frontier. He had of course determined, long before, that the death of es-Salih should be the signal for his own advance to Aleppo. Its possession by so ambitious and unscrupulous a ruler as Imad-ed-din was an unforeseen obstacle to his plans. But nothing could be done so long as the peace was in force; and it would not expire till the 9th of September, 1182. It is true the other parties to the treaty would have justified him in tearing it up. The Franks had again broken their faith. Reginald of Châtillon, released from his weary captivity at Aleppo, and thirsting for revenge, had now become master of the Dead Sea fortresses, by virtue of his marriage with Stephania, the widow of the third Humphrey of Toron and heiress of Karak. He used his position unscrupulously, and had lately captured a peaceful caravan of merchants in time of truce; in return, Saladin had detained a pilgrim ship that had run ashore at Damietta.* When he prepared to re-enter Syria to protect his subjects, he learnt, further, that the Zengid princes had so far forgotten their honour and their religion as to make a formal treaty with the Christians and even with the Master of the Assassins for joint opposition to the common enemy†—himself. Even this did not tempt him to depart from his word. He advanced into Syria, to be on his guard; but he took no measures against his deceitful allies until the treaty lapsed.

On the 11th of May, 1182, Saladin left Cairo. The chief officers and grandees of his court assembled at the Lake to bid him farewell. One after the other they advanced to his stirrup and took their leave of the sovereign whom they had learnt, during fourteen years of glory abroad and equity at home, to honour and admire. Odes were recited, rhapsodies declaimed. Suddenly a discordant voice jangled the harmony of gracious words. "Enjoy," it cried, in the lines of the old Arab poet,

> "Enjoy the perfume of the ox-eyes of Nejd:
> After to-night, there will be no more ox-eyes."

The discordant note jarred upon Saladin, sensitive like all Easterns to the presage of ill-omen, and he rode away from Egypt with a weight at his heart. The prophetic verse did not err. There were no more ox-eyes for him in Egypt: he never saw Cairo again.

---

* William of Tyre admits the report (*dicebatur*) of Reginald's outrage, but charges Saladin with breach of faith in seizing the ship, as a hostage against further infractions of the treaty. It is clear, however, from the Latin account itself, that Saladin held the ship and captives as a set-off against previous breaches of the treaty by the Franks. Ernoul, 96, 97, distinctly records the breach of faith.

† Baha-ed-din, 68 ; Imad-ed-din and Kady el-Fadil, in Abu-Shama (Goergens, 28, 35, 37).

Knowing that the Christians were massed upon the frontier to intercept him, Saladin took the desert route across the peninsula of Sinai to Eyla at the head of the gulf of Akaba, and thence marched north over the barren flinty plain beside Mount Seir (the Shera range), reconnoitring in search of the enemy. Meeting with no opposition, he ravaged the country about Mont Real, whilst Baldwin's army watched him from their entrenchments near Karak, without moving a finger, either to fight him or cut him off from the wells. Profiting by their lethargy, he marched unmolested through Moab to Damascus in the middle of June. He found that his active nephew Ferrukh Shah had seized the opportunity of Baldwin's absence in the south to cross the Jordan, lay Galilee waste, sack Deburiya among the oaks and myrtles of the wooded western slopes of Mount Tabor, and even to secure possession of a rocky fortress (Habis Jeldek), to which the Franks attached great importance. Thee raiders lifted twenty thousand head of cattle and a thousand captives.

Following up this advantage in July, Saladin despatched Ferrukh Shah again into Palestine. He went by way of Ras-el-Ayn, and crossed the Jordan towards Beysan (Bethsan), once Scythopolis, the third city of Palestine, but then a small town situated in the rich champaign beneath the naked peaks of Mount Gilboa. The Franks meanwhile broke up their camp at the Springs of Saffuriya, and hurried south to protect Belvoir, a new castle near Beysan, where they had large stores of ordnance. Following the Jordan down stream, they camped beneath the hill of "the Star," whereon stood the ramparts of Belvoir. Saladin was himself near Tiberias, but he sent his two most capable generals, Taki-ed-din and Ferrukh Shah, at the head of a large body of horse-archers, to attack the position. The Saracens, according to their enemies, had 20,000 men in battle array, to their own 700 knights with their followers; but William of Tyre would have us believe that, thanks to the valour of the brothers Balian and Baldwin of Ramla, and other gallant warriors, the Christians had much the best of the skirmish, in spite of the defection of "many whose names for very shame we will not write." The Moslems, on the other hand, whilst admitting heavy losses, claimed the victory. Both sides retired after the battle, the Franks to Forbelet (Afrabela) and Saladin to Damascus.

The Saracens do not seem to have been disheartened; for in August Saladin led his troops in person across the Bikaa. His object was to seize Beyrut, which he hoped to surprise and storm with the assistance of his Egyptian fleet, with which his brother el-Adil was harrying the coast of Palestine. The ships bombarded Beyrut; whilst Saladin coming down from the hills, whence his scouts had signalled the fleet, directed a general attack on the land-side. The arrows fell so thick that the inhabitants "dared not lift a finger," but the town was well fortified and garrisoned, and made a sturdy resistance. The Saracens, expecting to storm, had brought no mangonels for a regular siege. Moreover, King Baldwin was hastily equipping ships at Acre and Tyre for the relief of the port, and the Christian army was approaching. The surprise had failed, and Saladin, having more important affairs to attend to in the north, abandoned a leaguer which promised little success.

His change of plan is explained by the fact that he had received an invitation from Kukbury, the Emir of Harran to enter and occupy Jezira. Any reason was good enough for Saladin, who was counting the hours till he could pay off his reckoning with the house of Zengy. At last the truce had come to an end; there were allies actually impatient to welcome him at the Great River; and the moment he could advance with honour he collected a siege-train and set out. After a feint attack on Aleppo, before which he lay but three days (19–21 September) he crossed the Euphrates at Bira. His partisans hastened to meet him. First Kukbury, whose fear of Mosil had led him to invite invasion; then Nur-ed-din of Keyfa, brought their war-bands to his colours. One after the other the cities of "the Island" fell before them. Edessa, Saruj, Rakka, Karkisiya, Nisibin, one and all bowed down, as subjects in a royal progress. In the midst of this triumph, the news came that the Franks were again foraying about Damascus. "Let them," said Saladin: "whilst they knock down villages, we are taking cities; when we come back we shall have all the more strength to fight them."

So he pushed on to Mosil, the capital of his only Moslem rival. Once more strong walls proved a match for his sappers. Karak first, then Beyrut, and now Mosil, resisted all assaults. The double ramparts were closely packed with zealous defenders, and there was not a weak joint in the armour. The place was crammed with stores, provisions, ammunition, and engines of war, providently prepared for this very emergency. Nevertheless Izz-ed-din would gladly have spared his city the rigours of a siege if an honourable arrangement could be come to; but Saladin's one persistent demand was the cession of Aleppo, which Izz-ed-din had not the will, nor perhaps the power, to force his brother to abandon. The neighbouring rulers of Armenia and Persia vainly endeavoured to mediate; Saladin had but one answer: "Aleppo—or Mosil."

The investment was therefore begun on the 10th of November, 1182. Saladin himself took the position over against the Kinda gate; his brother Bury "Crown of Kings" (Taj-el-muluk) commanded the attack on the Imadiya gate; whilst Nur-ed-din, of Keyfa, took charge of the gate of the Bridge. All their efforts, however, made no impression on the solid masonry, and after a month of fruitless endeavour, Saladin drew off his army and marched three days to Sinjar, thinking to break the spirit of the Mosilis by reducing the surrounding country on which they depended for supplies. Sinjar made a spirited defence, and for fifteen days Saladin lay before the walls under which Constantine once fought his great battle with Sapor; but on the 30th of December the ancient city was stormed and sacked by the irritated soldiery, who broke all discipline in greed of plunder. Saladin only succeeded in protecting the governor and his officers, and sent them to Mosil with every mark of honour. After establishing a garrison at Sinjar, he prepared to meet a coalition which had been formed by the Atabeg of Mosil and the Shah of Armenia, aided by the retainers of the Prince of Maridin and troops from Aleppo. By the end of February, 1183, a large army had assembled on the plain of Harzem, below Maridin; but, on hearing of Saladin's approach, they hastily sent messengers to treat for peace. He said they should have their answer on the plain of Harzem. The menace was sufficient. Each of the allies fled incontinently to his own city, and when Saladin reached the rendezvous, there was no enemy. "They advanced like men," says the Chancellor; "like women they vanished."

The Atabeg had once more retreated behind the walls of Mosil; but Saladin did not pursue him. He abandoned all attempts upon that city for the present, and when he had completed the organisation of his Mesopotamian conquests in his usual system of military fiefs, he marched north, and after eight days' siege, on the 6th of May, 1183, took the city of Amid, in spite of the double enceinte of its massive walls of black basalt, its iron gates, and the natural moat formed by the crescent bend of the Tigris. The place was full of precious spoil, of weapons and engines of war, stores and treasure. The famous library of "a million volumes" was made over to the learned Chancellor, the Kady el-Fadil, who took away a mere selection of the books on seventy camels.* This stronghold Saladin gave to his loyal and gallant ally the Prince of Keyfa. At this moment, news reached him that Imad-ed-din of Aleppo had arranged an understanding with the Franks, and was laying fire and sword to the Sultan's lands in Syria; so he hurried across the Euphrates at Bira, and, taking Ayn Tab on his way, on the 21st encamped once more on the Green Meydan before Aleppo. Imad-ed-din did not offer a long resistance. He was unpopular with his new subjects, and wished to get back to his old quarters at Sinjar. On his side, Saladin was eager to consolidate his empire by the acquisition of the capital of northern Syria. An exchange was negotiated, by which in return for the surrender of Aleppo, the

---

* Ibn-Aby-Tay, in Abu-Shama, 48.

principality of Sinjar, with its dependent cities of Nisibin, Saruj, and Rakka, was restored to Imad-ed-din, who was to hold it as Saladin's vassal on terms of military service.

On the 12th of June, the city was formally placed in Saladin's possession. The garrison paraded on the Green Meydan and paid him homage; a great banquet was given to celebrate the event; and general rejoicings prevailed. The people had never taken kindly to their late prince; they lamented the glorious days of Nur-ed-din, and hoped for their revival under a powerful and generous king, such as Saladin promised to be. Imad-ed-din became a butt for the scorn of the crowd, who jeered about "the ass who bartered fresh milk (in Arabic, Halab, *i.e.* Aleppo) for sour (Sinjar)," and even paraded a wash-tub before him, saying: "You were never meant for a King! Try taking in washing!" He was glad to escape from the torrent of ridicule, and taking leave of Saladin on the 17th he departed for Sinjar, richly equipped with choice horses and robes of honour presented by his generous adversary. The next day Saladin entered Aleppo. The crowd acclaimed him; poets sang his praise. The governor entertained him with splendour in the castle, and the whole city went mad with delight: was not Saladin their King? and was there any other so mighty, so just, and so generous in all the earth?

The possession of Aleppo made Saladin the most powerful ruler of Islam. From the Tigris to the Nile, and along the African coast as far as Tripoli, many great cities and different peoples owned his sway. His name was prayed for in the mosques from Mekka to Mesopotamia. When he wrote to the Pope,* he even used the style "*Rex omnium regum orientalium*," and of all the eastern princes within his reach he was undoubtedly King. But to be incontestably supreme over this wide dominion he must still take another step. He had nothing to fear from the east or the north: Mosil was cowed, and the Seljuk of Konia was friendly; but there yet remained that narrow strip of land stretching beyond the mountains along the Syrian coast from Antioch to Ascalon,—the cities beyond the Orontes and the Jordan, and the barrier heights of Lebanon,—above all Jerusalem itself, holy to Moslems and Christians alike. That strip of hostile territory which severed his kingdom from the great sea; those forts and cities and holy places, which still were gripped in the mailed hands of his enemies; that happy valley of the Jordan where the wooden bells of Christians harshly clashed in-

---

* Some of Saladin's despatches have been published in Latin. One to the Pope in 1183 acknowledges the receipt of a letter through Oliver Vitalis in reference to captives in the war. An earlier despatch from el-Adil to Lucius III. relates to the same subject. There are also two letters to Frederic Barbarossa and one from the Emperor to Saladin. They may be read in Ralph de Diceto, ed. Stubbs, ii., 25–27, 156, 57, and *Itinerarium Regis Ricardi*, i., 37–42.

stead of the sweet and solemn chant of the Muezzin—all these were as a rock of offence to "the Sultan of Islam and of the Moslems." Until the Holy City were once more in the keeping of the Faithful, until the rule of the Frank were brought low, for him at least there could be no rest.

SIEGE OF A CASTLE.
FROM A 13TH CENTURY MANUSCRIPT.

CHAPTER XII

DAMASCUS
1183–1186

SALADIN STAYED two months at Aleppo, ordering the government, award-ing offices and fiefs, and regulating the various dependent cities and forts. On the 14th of August, 1183, he left for Damascus, which was to be his capital and headquarters for the rest of his life. Much had happened during his long absence in the north. His brave viceroy Ferrukh Shah was dead, and the Franks had grown bolder. They had ravaged Busra and Zora and all the coun-try, even to Darayya, a few miles from Damascus, destroying the crops and orchards, and laying everything waste. They had recovered the rocky fastness in the "Suhite" of which the Saracens had been so proud. Reginald of Châtillon had even conceived the daring project to invade Arabia, destroy the tomb of "the accursed camel-driver" at Medina, and raze to the ground the holy Kaaba at Mekka. He transported his ships in sections from Karak to the gulf of Akaba, and sending the fleet to sack the port of Aydhab on the African shore of the Red Sea, with two vessels he blockaded Eyla. The Egyptian fleet was soon in hot pursuit, and Admiral Lulu, after easily relieving the blockade of Eyla, came up with the main body of the expedition near el-Haura, a small port on the Red Sea, whence they intended to march on Medina. The sight of the Egyptian squadron drove them hurriedly on shore, and they made for the mountains. Lulu mounted his sailors on the horses of the Bedawis, and catching the enemy in the Rabugh gorge cut them to pieces. Reginald escaped, but most of his men were killed; no quarter was given, except to a few prisoners who were sent to Mekka, to be slaughtered like goats in the valley of Mina at the annual sacrifice of the Pilgrim-age.* Thus, should they expiate their intended sacrilege.

The Spanish Arab, Ibn-Jubeyr, was at Alexandria in May, 1183, when some of the prisoners taken from Reginald of Châtillon's expedition were brought in, lashed on camels, their faces to the tails, amid the beating of drums and the shouts of the populace. Never, he says, had there been such consternation as

---

* Ibn-el-Athir, *Kamil*, 658–9; Abu-Shama, 41–2.

when the news of the raid reached Egypt. People told each other, trembling, how the accursed lord of Karak had bribed the Bedawis to carry his ships across the desert to the Red Sea; how he had burnt sixteen Arab vessels, seized a pilgrim-ship off Jedda, landed at Aydhab and captured a caravan that had journeyed from Kos on the Nile, every soul of which was massacred; and how, after making prizes of two ships from the Yemen, laden with stores for the holy cities, he had crossed over to Arabia with the fell design of sacking Medina and dragging the blessed Prophet out of his grave! Never was such appalling news! Allah be praised, Lulu, the captain of the fleet, caught the miscreants with his swift vessels, manned by Moors from the Maghrib, and the catastrophe was averted.

Saladin's first object on his return to Syria was to punish the Franks for their temerity. He recalled the troops whom he had allowed to go home during his rest at Aleppo, and marching south by the desert route past el-Fawar, crossed the Jordan on the 29th of September, ravaged the fertile Ghaur, and finding Beysan deserted by its terrified inhabitants, sacked and burnt it. Advancing up the valley of Jezreel, he camped by the Well of Goliath (Ayn Jalud) at the foot of Gilboa. Hence his scouts, veterans from Nur-ed-din's armies, ravaged the country round, as far as Tabor and the hills above Nazareth, captured Forbelet, and encountering a body of Franks marching from Karak to join the main army at the Springs of Saffuriya, defeated them (30 September) with the loss of only one man. On this Guy of Lusignan, who commanded during the illness of King Baldwin, immediately broke up camp, crossed the hills of Nazareth into the plain of Esdraelon, and advanced to "the castle of the Bean," el-Fula, (which the Franks called Faba and La Fève,) where Saladin gave battle.

> "Never, so old men said, had Palestine seen so vast an array of Crusaders; there were one thousand three hundred knights, and over fifteen thousand well-armed foot; among them were great nobles from Europe: Henry, Duke of Louvain, and Ralf de Maleine from Aquitaine, together with the lords of the land, Guy de Lusignan, Reginald de Châtillon, Baldwin and Balian of Ibelin, Reginald of Sidon, Walter of Cæsarea, and Joscelin de Courtenay."*

Nevertheless the battle was indecisive. It was a hand-to-hand fight, where "eye looked into eye." Saladin's vanguard of five hundred horse did much execution, but could not penetrate the serried ranks of the enemy's spears; and eventually both armies encamped opposite each other, at Tubania and Goliath's Well, scarcely a mile apart. Here an extraordinary delay occurred. For five days the Christian army lay motionless, whilst their leaders were wrangling amongst them-

---

* Archer and Kingsford, *Crusades*, 262; Imad-ed-din gives nearly the same numbers.

selves, united only in one purpose, to defy the authority of Lusignan.* Meanwhile Saladin had occupied the heights, and the Crusaders found themselves hemmed in and cut off from supplies. Their ranks were swelled by crowds of Italian merchants, Pisans, Lombards, Venetians, and Genoese, who had left their ships and hurried to join the army of the Cross, without taking thought for food, and unaccustomed to bear arms or endure privation. These were the first to feel the pressure of fatigue and want, and as no supplies could penetrate the close ring of the watchful Saracens, a grievous famine fell upon the camp. It was mid October, too, and the rainy season would soon be at hand. Saladin seems to have tried every device to bring them to the fighting point, but in vain: they contrived at last to escape, pursued by his arrows, and retreated in shame to Saffuriya, whence they had set out in glorious array but a week before.

In the same month of October the Sultan left Damascus to settle his score with Reginald of Châtillon at Karak; but all attempts to capture that crafty freelance or to gain an entrance into his fortress failed, though an Egyptian army under el-Adil co-operated in the siege. Their seven mangonels played in vain upon the stout walls, and when it was known that the royal forces were marching to its relief, Saladin drew off his army (4 December) and fuming at the repulse led it back to Damascus. In the following summer (13 August, 1184) he made another effort to reduce the fortress, for there could be no peace so long as Reginald of Châtillon held it; but the siege—the fifth that Saladin had begun— ended like all the rest. At first, indeed, it seemed as if success were about to crown the perseverance of the Saracens. The town was in no mood for battle: it was full of dancers and musicians, making merry for the wedding of the King's half-sister Isabella with the fourth Humphrey of Toron. The wedding feasts were like to be turned into funeral rites. Saladin and his mamluks forced their way into the town, and Reginald retreated over the fosse into the castle. Even so he hardly escaped, and but for the valour of a solitary knight, who held the bridge like Horatius of old, whilst the garrison sawed it behind him, the fort must have fallen to the Saracens. In curious illustration of the chivalrous manners of the time, Reginald sent Saladin meat and wine,—as it were a piece of the bride-cake,— to share in the feast; and in return the Sultan gave strict orders, proclaimed to the army, that the nuptial tower of the bride and bridegroom should be scrupulously respected by his archers and artillery!†

Saladin found himself in possession of the town and suburb, and master of every sort of festal luxury and wedding cates; but he was as far as ever from

* William of Tyre, xxii., 27; Abu-Shama, 52; Ibn-el-Athir, 663.
† Ernoul, 103.

taking the castle. He began indeed to fill up the fosse and to set up his engines; and his faithful ally, Nur-ed-din of Keyfa, showed himself brilliantly in combats with the garrison. Nine mangonels bombarded the gate and burst it open, but the enemy held the breach. The fosse was so far filled that a prisoner was able to jump from the ramparts and escape. But it was labour thrown away: the rock defied assault. Meanwhile couriers had carried the news to Baldwin, and in September a relieving force stationed at el-Wala, without risking a pitched battle, supplied the castle with food and tired out the besiegers. Saladin abhorred a waiting game, and failing to draw the Christians from their entrenchments, soon decamped from his positions at Heshbon and Main, and went off to lay waste Samaria, pillage and burn Nablus (Shechem) with its famous olive groves and melons, and thence returned to Damascus on the 16th of September, 1184.

After this there was peace between Saracen and Christian for a time. King Baldwin's misery came to an end in the winter of 1184–5. The crown was now on the head of a child, and Guy of Lusignan and Raymond of Tripolis, the Regent of the infant Baldwin V., headed rival factions. It was no time for a Holy War, said the old Crusading houses; better to make a truce and at least wait till a favourable occasion. So thought the Prince of Antioch, the Counts of Tripolis and Sidon, and the brave brothers of Ibelin. So did not think the two great fighting Orders of the Temple and the Hospital; nor new-comers like Guy of Lusignan, though his only campaign had been a ridiculous farce; much less Reginald of Châtillon, who still felt, at his stronghold of Karak, the iron of his unforgotten chains eating into his soul, and thirsted unquenchably for revenge. For the present the prudent policy prevailed, and at the Regent's motion a treaty was concluded with Saladin for four years. With Raymond himself, it was more than a truce; it was an offensive and defensive alliance. Saladin was to support him in his designs on the crown, and Raymond in, return set free all the Saracens he held captive in Tripolis, and even supplied Damascus liberally with food during the dearth of 1185. Nevertheless, whatever the amity of Saladin and Raymond, the truce was like the troubled sleep of a soldier, which might be broken in an instant by the call to arms. It was no real peace whilst the Patriarch Heraclius scoured Europe to beat up recruits, whilst English knights from the Cheviots to the Pyrenees took the Cross, whilst the two great Military Orders were burning to strike a blow for the faith. The Holy War was sleeping, but it was sure to awake.

Saladin, meanwhile, made the most of his leisure to set the affairs of his realm in order. Once more Damascus had become the seat of sovereignty. Saladin used to say that Syria was the Root and Basis of Empire: Julian had called Damascus the Eye of the East. Before the beginning of history, Damascus was a city. From the time when Abram took his servant Eliezar from among its citizens the ancient Syrian capital has been renowned. In the days of Ezekiel its commerce was famous, and to the port of Tyre it was written: "Damascus was thy merchant in the multitude of the wares of thy making, for the multitude of all riches." In all the ancient empires of the East, Damascus has played its part, as the natural metropolis of its region, the meeting-place of the people. Through its busy markets passed the trade of Babylonia and Persia and furthest India, borne from immemorial days by endless caravans, journeying from the Euphrates by Palmyra or Aleppo, and carrying their precious bales onward to the Mediterranean ports, or turning south to Egypt and Arabia. To Damascus came the wandering nation of the Bedawis in their countless tribes, who grazed their flocks in spring and winter on the light fodder of the desert, roaming every year between Arabia and the Great River along the familiar chains of wells; a race of cattle-dealers and camel-drivers, carriers of other men's wealth and sellers of their own pastoral produce in exchange for the goods of the merchants.

Rich and populous, Damascus owed all to its central situation and its natural advantages. The Greeks called it "Most Beauteous," Καλλιδτη, and the Arabs named it "The Bride of the Earth," "The Garden of the World." And looking down upon the ancient city from the Dome of Victory which crowns the near range of Antilibanus on the west, one understands the pride of the Damascene in his earthly Paradise. The famed level plain, the Ghuta, richly fertile, though it forms part of the high Syrian plateau rising two thousand feet above the sea, gains in beauty by contrast with the brown desert and the girdling rocky hills, through which the Barada, well-named "Gold-streaming" by the Greeks, forces its path, and spreading in seven streams over the plain gives it abundant life. A great green field stretches for miles from the mountains to the desert, and in its midst, in an emerald girdle of gardens and orchards, of orange and citron and jessamine, in a babel of gurgling brooks, rise the old Roman walls of the city, the yellow sea of its clay houses, a forest of minarets, and the great dome of the Omayyad Mosque, once the Church of St. John the Baptist, and before that, perhaps, the House of Rimmon .* "Though old as history itself, thou art fresh as the breath of Spring, blooming as thine own rosebud, fragrant as thine own orange flower, O Damascus, Pearl of the East!"

Every age of its varied history has left its vestiges in Damascus:—Roman gates of polished red sandstone, and doors plated with heavy iron; ancient walls fifteen feet thick and twenty high, built upon still older foundations of cyclopean

---

* The city has been well described by Kremer and Dr. Wright, and there are charming verbal pictures in Lady Burton's books.

masonry; square bastion towers, whence medieval archers drove back many a storming party by their flanking fire. The *Via Recta*, "the street which is called Straight," still leads from the east gate, as it did in the time when St. Paul was yet Saul of Tarsus; and on a wall of the Arab Mosque the pilgrim to the tomb of Saladin may still read the inscription which overhung the lintel of the older Church, and which thirteen centuries of Moslem rule have not erased:

H· BACIΛEIA· COY· X͞E· BACIΛEIA· ΠANTΩN· TΩN· AIONΩN· KAI· H· ΛECΠOTIA· COY· EN· ΠACH ΓENAI· KAI· ΓENEAI

"Thy kingdom, O Christ, is an everlasting kingdom, and thy dominion endureth throughout all generations."*

The city in Saladin's time must have shown much the same mixture of colours and races as now. The dress and customs of the Moslems change very slowly, and the same peoples, clad in the same way for many centuries, must have thronged its bazars, and dwelt in the exquisitely carved and painted rooms round the shaded courts of the houses. Then, as now, the city was divided into numerous walled quarters, closed at night by heavy gates, and occupied originally by members of a separate clan. Then, as now, the clear water of the Golden Stream flowed through a network of carefully planned channels, and was brought to every street and even to the poorest houses. But invasion and fire, Tatar vandalism and Ottoman neglect, have dimmed the splendour of the mosques and palaces; and now even the noble Omayyad Mosque, where the great Caliphs of the seventh century preached as leaders of the faithful, where Moawiya held up before the trembling congregation the bloody shirt of the murdered Othman, and pinned Naila's severed fingers to the pulpit,—the mosque where Saladin worshipped the God of Battles, has been seared and ruined by a consuming fire. Its mosaics were the triumph of artists from Persia, India, and Byzantium, and exhausted the revenues of Syria for seven years, besides eighteen shiploads of gold and silver from Cyprus.

The Spanish Arab, Ibri-Jubeyr, who visited Damascus in 1184, when Saladin was living there, has left us a minute description of the wonders of this marvellous mosque, not least among which was the clock in which brazen falcons struck the hours, and a brass door shut for each hour past, whilst at night red lamps marked the time, measured by subsiding water. He mentions twenty colleges, two free hospitals, and many monasteries.

"Damascus," he adds, "possesses a castle, where the Sultan lives, and it stands isolated in the modern quarter of the city, and in it is the Sultan's mosque. Near

---

* Ps. cxlv., 13.

the castle, outside the town towards the west, are two Meydans that are like pieces of silk brocade rolled out, for their greenness and beauty. The river flows between the two Meydans, and there is a grove of poplar-trees extending beside them, most beautiful to behold. The Sultan is wont to go out there to play the game of Mall and to race his horses; and nothing can be pleasanter to see than this. Every evening the Sultan's sons go out there to shoot the bow, and to race, and to play Mall."8

The Spanish traveller gives us but a glimpse of the great Sultan, playing polo on the silky lawn of the Meydan, nor do Saladin's biographers and chroniclers tell us much more. We hear indeed of evenings spent in literary discussions, of Saladin's intimacy with the old warrior-poet Osama, of recitations of poetry, and of frequent games at chess, to which the Sultan was passionately devoted.† But the echoes of these voices are faint indeed. To gain a picture of a Moslem ruler's life and occupations in Crusading times we must turn to the historian of the Mamluk Sultans, and see how Beybars, Sultan of Syria and Egypt, kept his state in the thirteenth century. He was a mamluk of Saladin's family, and he modelled his court upon the example set by his great predecessor.

The Sultan of those days enjoyed no sinecure; he was as hard a worker as his meanest subject. He sat in the Hall of Justice two days in the week to hear the complaints and right the wrongs of his subjects. His correspondence was immense, and though Saladin had indefatigable chancellors and secretaries in the Kady el-Fadil, Imad-ed-din, and latterly Baha-ed-din, he must have taken a large personal share in the despatches. In Beybars' time there was

"a well-organised system of posts, connecting every part of his wide dominions with the capital. Relays of horses were in readiness at each post-house, and twice a week the Sultan received and answered reports from all parts of the realm. Besides the ordinary mail, there was also a pigeon post, which was no less carefully managed. The pigeons were kept in cots at the various stages, and the bird was trained to stop at the first post-cot, where its letter would be attached to another pigeon for the next stage."

Fortunately we know something of Saladin's chief secretaries who managed his vast correspondence. What el-Jawad was to the warlike Zengy, the learned

* Ibn-Jubeyr, in Le Strange, *Palestine under the Muslims*, 255. Mall or polo was an ancient Persian game, there called *chogan*, and by the Byzantine Greeks *tzukanion* (τζονκανιον). Saladin was famous for his skill at polo, but he is said to have ridden too recklessly after the ball, like his father (*Kitab er-Raudateyn*; see Quatremère's admirable dissertation, *Hist. des Sultans Mamlouks*, i, 121–132).

† Abu-Shama (Cairo text), i., 252, 264, 270; H. Derembourg, *Vie d'Ousama*, 369, 396, Cp. Lessing, *Nathan der Weise*, Act ii, Sc. I.

judge, Kady el-Fadil, was to the wider imperial administration of Saladin. El-Fadil was not a Turk or a Persian, like so many of the statesmen of that time, but a pure Lakhmy Arab, born at Ascalon, a member of a family of judges. His colleague in the Council, Aluh, extols his exquisite style—then considered a prime qualification in a Secretary of State—in his own inflated manner:

> "Sovereign of the pen and lucidity, of eloquence and of style, his genius was resplendent, his sagacity profound, and his diction as novel as it was fascinating. . . . He was like Mohammed's law, which annulled all others and became the root of all knowledge. His thought was original, his ideas were new; he showered forth brilliance, and put forth the fairest flowers. He it was who led the empire by his counsels, and threaded discourse with the pearls of style," and so forth.

In spite of fine writing, and much curious euphuism, the Kady was an admirable public servant, and Saladin frequently left him in supreme charge of the government in Egypt whilst himself absent on campaigns in Syria. Egypt, indeed, was his adopted country; there Saladin found him in the chancery office; and he was never happy away from his beloved Nile. "Bear me a message to the Nile," he cries in one of his poems, written during a campaign in Mesopotamia; "tell it that Euphrates can never quench my thirst."

Another learned man, whose advice, it is said, Saladin never rejected, was el-Hakkary, the Arab jurist, who treated his master with an unceremonious familiarity which none other dared to use. His quaint figure, with the lawyer's turban surmounting a soldier's uniform, was seldom absent from the Sultan's councils. But Saladin's right-hand man in Syria, the counterpart of the Kady el-Fadil in Egypt, was the Secretary of State Imad-ed-din of Ispahan, commonly called Aluh ("Eagle"),—a poet, a master of style, a doctor learned in the law and deep in the mysteries of astrology, and a formidable gladiator in theological polemics. From being merely a professor at the college at Damascus to which he gave his name, "The Imadiya," he became President of the Council of State and Chancellor of the Syrian kingdom. His admirable skill in conducting diplomatic correspondence in Persian and Arabic, in the turgid and inflated style admired by Orientals, added to his learning and sagacity, made him invaluable to the Sultan who finally gave him his entire confidence.

Besides necessary business, state ceremonies formed a heavy burden upon the Sultan. The medieval Muslim court was minutely organised, and the selection of officers to fill the numerous household posts, the allaying of their jealousies and quarrels, the rewarding of their services with robes of honour, titles, and fiefs, cost time and thought. Everybody, from the Commander-in-Chief to the Cupbearer, Taster, and Polo-master, wanted something, or envied someone else, and must be attended to, however summarily, in the interests of general good humour and loyalty.

Reviews of troops and state progresses were matters which involved much ceremony. The Sultan himself (at the time of Beybars at least) rode in the midst of the procession, dressed in a plain black silk tunic with large sleeves, a turban over his steel cap, a hauberk under his tunic, and a long Arab sword at his side. In front some great noble displayed the royal saddle-cloth, covered with precious stones and gold brocade; and the Sultan's head was shaded by the state parasol of yellow silk with gold embroidery, crowned with a golden eagle, and carried by a prince of the blood, whilst another noble bore the imperial standard. The royal horse was housed in yellow silk and red atlas satin, and the regimental colours of the escort were also of yellow Cairo silk, embroidered with their colonel's badge.

> "Just before the Sultan rode two pages on white horses, with rich trappings; their robes were of yellow silk with borders of gold brocade, and a *kuffiya* or kerchief of the same. It was their duty to see that the road was sound. A flute-player went before, and a singer followed after, chanting the heroic deeds of former kings, to the accompaniment of a drum: poets sang verses antiphonally, accompanying themselves with the *kemenga* and *mosil.* Tabardars carried halberds before and behind the Sultan, and the state-poniards were supported by the polo-master in a scabbard on the left, while another dagger with a buckler was carried on the monarch's right. Close beside him rode the macebearer, who carried the golden mace aloft, and never withdrew his eyes from the countenance of his master. The great officers of the court followed with hardly less pomp.
>
> "When a halt was called for the night, on long journeys, torches were borne before the Sultan, and as he approached the tent, which had gone on in front and been pitched before his arrival, his servants came to meet him with wax candles in stands inlaid with gold; pages and halberdiers surrounded him, the soldiers sang a chorus, and all dismounted except the Sultan, who rode into the vestibule of the tent, where he left his horse, and then entered the great round pavilion behind it. Out of this opened a little wooden bedroom, warmer than the tent, and a bath with heating materials was at hand. The whole was surrounded by a stockade, and the mamluks mounted guard in regular watches, inspected periodically by visiting rounds, with Grand Rounds twice in the night."[*]

We do not know how much of this state ceremonial was observed by Saladin, but, however simple his own tastes might be, no Oriental sovereign could afford to neglect those outward trappings which have always produced a vivid impression of power upon the popular imagination, especially in the East where sym-

---

[*] S. Lane-Poole, *Cairo*, 3rd. ed., 1898, 82–90, etc.

bolism is peculiarly studied. Saladin, though he dressed very simply in linen or wool, doubtless maintained all the usual state of a Mohammedan King, and would be careful to display the full court ceremonies when receiving embassies from foreign princes. It was on such an occasion that he first met Baha-ed-din, who afterwards became his secretary and biographer. Baha-ed-din was a resident at Mosil when Saladin invaded Mesopotamia, and had been employed by the Atabeg to carry an appeal for help to the Caliph at Baghdad. When Saladin was settled at Damascus, Baha-ed-din was again sent on a diplomatic mission. He was empowered by his sovereign, the Atabeg of Mosil, with the approval of the Caliph, to arrange terms of amity with Saladin. He arrived at Damascus on the 25th of February, 1184, accompanied by Bedr-ed-din, the "Sheykh of Sheykhs," and was received by the Sultan with every mark of gracious hospitality. Although unable to come to any arrangement, he impressed Saladin so favourably that he offered him a post in his own service. Baha-ed-din, as ambassador of a rival prince, could not accept the honour, and the mission departed on its return to Mosil on the 22nd of March.*

Other embassies followed, from the Atabeg's nephew, Sinjar-Shah of Jezira, and from the lord of Irbil (Arbela), who did homage as vassals of the Sultan. The Prince of Mosil naturally resented these defections and set about chastising the Irbil chief, whose appeal eventually brought Saladin again into the field. Crossing the Euphrates as usual at Bira, on the 15th of April, 1185, he was joined by Kukbury, and at Ras-el-Ayn he learnt that there was a general coalition of the eastern princes to defend the Atabeg of Mosil. Disregarding their threats, he marched onwards to Duneysir at the foot of the hill of Maridin, the troops of which joined him, and arrived before Mosil in June, 1185. In vain the Atabeg sent his mother and other great ladies to humble themselves before him and pray for peace. They were received with all deference, but no promise was given: Saladin was inflexible.

Prepared for the worst, the Mosilis exerted themselves with the strength of desperation, and the siege proved as fruitless as before. A dispute in Armenia furnished an excuse for withdrawing the exhausted army away to the cooler climate of Diyar-Bekr. Saladin occupied Mayyafarikin at the end of August, and then returned to the siege of Mosil. But now the rainy season had followed the burning heats of summer, and neither the general nor the troops were able to support the unhealthy climate. Saladin became seriously ill, and was forced to remove to Harran for change of air; scarcely able to sit his horse, he arrived

---

* The ambassador did not join Saladin as his secretary till 1188.

nearly dead at his friend Kukbury's castle. His brother el-Adil hastened from Aleppo with the court physicians, but for a long time Saladin lingered between life and death. At one time the rumour spread that the end had come, and many a kinsman weighed his own chance of succession. Saladin himself gave up hope, and assembling his captains made them take the oath of fidelity to his sons.

At last he began very slowly to recover, and by the end of February, 1186, he was able to receive an embassy from Mosil, headed by Baha-ed-din, who came to treat for peace. Too weak as yet to dream of a campaign, and softened perhaps by suffering and danger, Saladin consented to a treaty (3 March), by which he took all the country about Shahrzur, beyond the Zab, but left the Atabeg Izz-ed-din in possession of the territory he then governed, between the great rivers, subject to his fully acknowledging the Sultan's sovereignty in the prayers and on the coinage. By this treaty the whole of northern Mesopotamia and part of Kurdistan were joined to Saladin's empire, and the Atabeg of Mosil swelled the muster of his vassals.*

Slowly returning from Harran to Damascus, Saladin paused at Emesa. He had lately given the city in fief to his cousin Nasir-ed-din, son of Shirkuh, whose kinship had been strengthened by marriage with one of Saladin's daughters. Nevertheless, during his cousin's illness, Nasir-ed-din had intrigued for the throne of Syria. Retribution followed swiftly; for retiring, full of wine and good cheer, on the Feast of the Victims (4 March, 1186), the pretender was found dead in his bed next morning.† On his way to the city Saladin was met by the son, a boy of twelve, whom he had appointed to his father's fief; appropriating, however, for the purposes of State a large part of the father's treasure. It is related that Saladin was kind to the boy, and interested himself in his studies. But when he questioned him about his reading, and asked how far he had gone in the Koran, the child replied, "As far as the place where it is written, *As to those who swallow up the goods of orphans unjustly; verily they shall swallow down fire into their bellies and burn at the Blaze.*"‡ The Sultan marvelled at the boy's quickness, and did not rebuke his presumption. Leaving him in possession of Emesa, he went on to Aleppo and thence in April to Damascus, where he was welcomed with tumultuous rejoicings, like another Lazarus come back from the grave.

---

* Coins in the British Museum show that Saladin's name appeared as suzerain on the currency of the following vassal lords in the years stated: the prince of Maridin (Yuluk-Arslan) in A.H. 581, 583, 584, 585, 586, or A.D. 1185–90 ; the prince of Keyfa (Sukman) in A.H. 581, 584, or A.D. 1185–8 : the prince of Jezira (Sinjar Shah) in A.H. 584, 585, or A.D. 1188–9; the lord of Irbil (Kukbury) in A.H. 587, A.D. 1191; and the Atabeg of Mosil in A.H. 585, 586, 587, or A.D. 1189–91.
† The improbable suggestion of Ibn-el-Athir that he was poisoned by Saladin's orders hardly deserves notice.
‡ *Koran*, iv., 9.

PART IV

THE HOLY WAR
1187–1191

CHAPTER XIII

THE BATTLE OF HITTIN
1187

THE GREAT CRISIS was at hand. Saladin was at last in a position to attack the Franks. The object of his campaigns on the Tigris and Euphrates had been attained. He had now allies instead of enemies on his northern flank. Before this no invasion of the Christian territory could safely be undertaken without posting an army of observation to guard against an attack from the north; but now he could advance with confidence. He had also more troops at his back, and could not only command the full strength of his Syrian and Egyptian levies, but also count upon large contingents from the Mesopotamian provinces. We shall see how at the siege of Acre the great barons of these parts came to reinforce the Moslem army, and how the princes of Zengy's line, the lords of Mosil, Sinjar, Jezira, Irbil, and Harran, and the Kurds from beyond the Tigris, swelled the general muster with their vassals and retainers. This was indeed the most important result of his northern campaigns. He had opened up new recruiting grounds; and without this added strength he could never have met and resisted the fresh forces from Europe brought against him in the Third Crusade.

The Holy War had long been a fixed resolve with Saladin, but the immediate provocation came, as usual, from Reginald of Châtillon. The lord of Karak had won for himself an unenviable reputation as a breaker of treaties. It was his delight to seize peaceful caravans of merchants and pilgrims on their way into Syria from Egypt or Mekka. He had done this in 1179, in a time of truce. A caravan encamped trustfully beneath his castle, and he took every man, woman, and beast, with goods to the value of two hundred thousand gold pieces; and when King Baldwin remonstrated, and sent an embassy to make him restore the stolen spoil and captives, he flouted the royal messengers. In 1182 he repeated this performance, also in a time of truce—"aussi com il avoit autrefois fait en trives"*; he had even dared to push his troops into Arabia to within a day's

---

* This is the admission of the Christian chroniclers (e. g., Ernoul, 54–5, 96–7, and the *Itinerarium*, i., 5), who are confirmed by the Moslem historians; see above, pp. 128, 134–5.

LESSER ARMENIA

Tarsus
Adana (Sarus)
El-Massisa (Pyramus)
R. Saihūn (Sarus)
R. Daihūr

Saladin's Frontier

Rabān
Duluk (Tulupa)
Ayn Tab
Edessa
El-Bira
Tell-Bāshir (Turbessel)
Sarūj
Harrān
Rāwenda (Ravendal)
Axāx (Hazart)
Tell-Khālid
Manbij

Baghras
Daribessak (Trapessac)
Antioch L.
Kara Su

Antioch
el-Amk
Jisr d-Hadid
Hārim (Harenc)
Halab (Aleppo)

(R. Orontes)
Shughr
El-Athārib (Cerep)
Sarmin
Er-Rakka
K. Jabar
Euphrates

Bakas
R. el-Makūb or Asi

Sahyūn (Saône)
Maarra en-Nomān
Tell-es-Sultān
Er-Rusāfa

Lādikiya (Laodicea)
Barzuya
Fāmiya (Apamea)
SYRIAN

Jebela
Bulunyās (Valenie)
Markab (Margat)
Sheyzar
Kurūn Hamāh
Kadmūs
Masyār
Hamāh

Antartūs (Tortosa)
Bārin (Mont Ferrand)

Hisn el-Akrād (Crac des Chevaliers)
Hims (Emesa)
Tadmūr (Palmyra)

Tripolis (Tarābulus)
Arka
B. Kadas

Mont Pèlerin
Kariyateyn

Jubeyl (Gibelet)
Baalbekk
DESERT

Beyrūt
EL-BIKA
Antilibanus
GHŪTA

Saida (Sidon)
R. Barada
B. el-Marj

Sarafenda
Darayya
Dimashk (Damascus)

Sūr (Tyrus)
Shakif Arnūn (Belvort, 1190)
Bānūna (Belinds)

Iskandarūna (Scandalion)
Tibnin
Hunin (Château Neuf)
JAULAN

El-Kureyn (Montfort)
Jisr Yakūb
Safad (Dec. 1188)

Akka (Acre)
Hittin
Haifa
Safūriya
Nazareth
Tabariya (Tiberias)
Yarmūk
HAURAN

Kaisariya (Caesarea)
El-Fulah
Beysān
Kaukab (Belvoir, Jan. 1189)
Busrā

N. el-Fālik (Rochetaille)
Sebastiya

Arsūf
Nāblus (Neapolis)
N. el-Auja
Mijdelyaba (Mirabel)

Yāfa (Jaffe)
Er-Ramla
Lydda (S. Geo)
Beyt Nūba (Betenoble)

Yubna (Ibelin)
En-Natrūn (Toron Militum)
El-Kuds (Jerusalem)

Askalān (Ascalon)
Beyt Jibrin (Beth Hospitum)
Ghazza
Dead Sea

Dārūm

El-Arish
Karak (Crak. Nov. 1188)

SYRIA &
PALESTINE
TO ILLUSTRATE
SALADIN'S CAMPAIGNS
1187 - 1193

Scale of Miles
0   25   50   75   100

Shaubak
(Mont Real May 1189)

march of the holy city where rest the bones of the Blessed Prophet. In 1186 there was again a time of peace. Caravans passed freely between Egypt and Syria, with no thought of danger from the Dead Sea castle. Suddenly Reginald pounced upon a party of merchants and captured a rich prize. One of the Sultan's sisters was rumoured to be travelling in the closed litter under the convoy of the traders. To their remonstrances the lord of Karak jeeringly echoed the taunts of the chief priests at Calvary: "Since they trusted in Mohammad, let Mohammad come and save them!" A year later he had bitter cause to repent his jest. On hearing of the outrage, Saladin swore a great oath that he would kill the truce-breaker with his own hand; and the vow was kept.

"The taking of that caravan was the ruin of Jerusalem." Saladin had repeat-edly sought to reduce Karak and lay hands upon its master, and he had always failed. He was now resolved to try no more half-measures but to wage a war of extermination on the whole Christian kingdom. The winter must first pass, when field operations were almost impossible; but in March, 1187, he sounded the tocsin for the *Jihad*. His messengers sped to the princes of Mesopotamia, to his vassals and viceroys and governors in the cities of Jezira, Diyar-Bekr, Syria, and Egypt, to bid them assemble their forces for the Holy War. Troop after troop hurried to Damascus, and each as it arrived was posted on the frontier against the Franks. The Sultan himself marched out towards Karak, in April, to protect the caravan of pilgrims returning from Mekka. After they had safely passed, and he had laid waste the territory of his bitterest enemy, he set up his standard at Ashtara on the 28th of May, and marshalled his squadrons for the great cam-paign.

The Franks were in no state for combined resistance. There was strife and jealousy among their leaders. The child king, Baldwin V., had died in the pre-ceding September, and a faction headed by Gerard de Rideford, the Master of the Templars, Joscelin of Courtenay, and Reginald of Châtillon, set on the throne Sibylla, the elder daughter of Amalric; and she in turn crowned her husband Guy de Lusignan as King. Count Raymond of Tripolis, the regent of the late King, repudiating this irregular coronation, set up a rival sovereign in the fourth Humphrey of Toron, the husband of Amalric's younger daughter Isabella. It is true, Humphrey mistrusted the unwelcome honour, and hastened to do homage to Sibylla and Guy; but Raymond and Baldwin of Ramla nevertheless refused to recognise the new King. It was Raymond who had made the treaty with Saladin in 1184, and the relations between the two became exceedingly friendly now that the Count was almost isolated from his fellow nobles. Raymond visited Saladin, and was received with cordiality. It was even rumoured that the Count would have embraced Islam but for dread of European contempt. When Guy prepared to invade the Count's territory and conquer his submission by arms, it was on Saladin's promised help that Raymond relied.* The invasion was deferred, however, by prudent mediation, and the Count nursed his resentment at Tiberias during the winter of 1186–7.

In the spring a fresh effort was made to restore harmony, and Balian of Ibelin was sent to Tiberias, with the Masters of the two Orders, to conciliate the sulking Achilles. Ernoul, who accompanied Balian as his squire, has left a graphic narrative of the expedition in his chronicle.† He tells how Balian was detained at Nablus, whilst the others pressed on to Faba; how he stopped again at Sabat to visit the bishop and hear mass; and how when he reached Faba he found the castle gates wide open, and his companions' tents deserted. He sent Ernoul into the empty fortress, and the squire went up and down the passages shouting and hallooing, but no man answered. At last he found two sick men in a chamber, but they could tell him nothing of what had happened. So he rode on towards Nazareth, and on the way a brother of the Temple hailed him. When he came up, Balian asked him "What news?" and the Templar said "Bad." Then he told them that the Master of the Hospital had had his head cut off, that all the Templars with him had been killed, save only the Master and two others, and that forty of the King's knights were prisoners in the Saracens' hands.

It appeared that Saladin had sent forward his eldest son, el-Afdal, to the Lake of Tiberias, where his friend Count Raymond was still in open enmity with the King of Jerusalem. El-Afdal, as an ally, asked permission to cross the Jordan and make an excursion in Raymond's territory. What his object was is not stated‡ he may have been in want of forage or food, possibly he merely wished for a day's hunting—for every prince of the land at that time was a sportsman; but it has more the look of a reconnaissance in force. Raymond could not refuse him leave, without risking the loss of Saladin's friendship, his best protection

---

* Imad-ed-din, Abu-Shama, in Goergens, 58; Ibn-el-Athir, *Kamil* 675 ; Ernoul, 141, who even states that Saladin sent a body of Saracens to Tiberias to strengthen Raymond's garrison.

† Ernoul, 148–152.

‡ It is not stated by Ernoul, who is the best authority on this point. The anonymous author of the contemporary *Libellus de Expugnatione Terræ Sanctæ per Saladinum* makes it an expedition in force, 7000 strong (ed. Stevenson, in the Ralph of Coggeshall volume, Rolls Series, 210). Ibn-el-Athir, who was not with the army, says (678) that Saladin ordered el-Afdal to lay waste the country towards Acre, and that el-Afdal did not go himself, but sent Kukbury of Harran and two other emirs of note, with 7000 horsemen. El-Afdal's absence is confirmed by the statement that the battle of Hittin was his first set battle; but this statement also comes from Ibn-el-Athir. El-Afdal perhaps would not have dignified the skirmish at Cresson by the name of *masaff* or set battle. His presence or absence, however, does not affect the story.

against King Guy. Yet to diminish the danger of the excursion, he stipulated that the Saracens should cross and return in a single day, by sunlight, and that they should molest neither town nor house on the way. To this they agreed. The Count sent messengers to announce the excursion and its conditions, and to warn every Christian to keep within walls.

All would have been well but for the inopportune arrival of the two Masters at Faba. Unluckily, as it befell, one of Raymond's messengers brought the news to the castle at the very moment when they were resting there, and full of right-eous wrath they collected as many knights as they could, to the number of 130, and 300 or 400 foot, and sallied forth to attack the roving Saracens. They, at least, would have no pact with the "infidels." They came up with them at the Spring of Cresson,* whilst they were already on their way back from Cana of Galilee to their own country. It was not the first nor yet the last time that the hot-headed zeal of the soldier-monks brought about their own destruction. The knights rashly attacked, in their haste, without waiting for the infantry,— and were utterly cut to pieces. The Saracens quietly continued their march to the Jordan, and as they passed near Tiberias, Raymond could distinguish Chris-tian heads carried on their spears. They had strictly kept their word. They had done no injury to town or house or castle, and they went back before sunset as was agreed.† This was Friday the 1st of May, the Feast of St. Philip and St. James.

In the face of this disaster, for which he was held responsible, Raymond consented to waive his resentment and made outward peace with Guy. They embraced in the presence of a rejoicing multitude by Joseph's Pit, and concerted measures of defence. It was ordered that a general muster of the Christian forces should be held at the Springs of Saffuriya, about three miles north of Nazareth, to resist the invasion of the Saracens. The Master of the Temple made over to Guy the money which King Henry of England had sent him, in expiation of the martyrdom of Becket; and the men who were paid with this treasure wore the arms of England on their shields. The total muster may have amounted to 1200 knights, more than 18,000 foot, and a large number of light cavalry, or Turcopoles, armed in the Saracen manner.‡

---

* Cresson, Kerson, Kelson, Quelson, as different MSS. spell it, is not named by the Arabic histori-ans, who place the skirmish at Saffuriya, nor is it found on the maps. It was probably on the road to Tiberias.

† Ernoul, 146, 148, who was on the spot. The *Libellus de Expugn.*, 211 contradicts this.

‡ So the *De Expugn.*, 218, where we read of "Turcopulos innumerabiles." These may have raised the total to the 50,000 reckoned by Imad-ed-din (Abu-Shama, 70), but this estimate is probably excessive. Twenty-five or thirty thousand is more likely. The Turcopoles were evidently ineffective.

Meanwhile Saladin, as has been seen, returning from the Dead Sea district, had mustered his troops at Ashtara, in the Hauran, and, with the army of Aleppo and the contingents from Mosil and Maridin added to his main force, he found himself at the head of 12,000 horsemen, "all holders of fiefs and stipends," besides numerous volunteers for "the Path of God." He reviewed the troops at Tesil, and marshalled his army in the usual order of battle, with centre, right and left wings, vanguard and rearguard; Taki-ed-din and Kukbury commanded the two wings, whilst the Sultan himself led the centre. In this formation he began his march on the 26th of June, 1187. It was a Friday, at the hour of public prayer; and this was the day and the hour that he preferred above all others for warfare, that the supplications of the people and the prayers of holy men might intercede for him at the throne of God. The Saracen army camped the first night at el-Ukhuwana at the southern end of the Lake of Galilee. Here Saladin waited, whilst his scouts were collecting information as to the enemy's positions. They brought word of the great muster of the Franks at Saffuriya, and their martial spirit. A council of war was held in the Moslem camp, and it was resolved to advance and offer battle. The next step was to cross the Jordan to es-Sinnebra, whence Saladin moved his men to the hills at Kafar Sebt,* some six miles to the southwest of Tiberias, and commanding the road, on Wednesday, the 1st of July. Whilst waiting for the Franks to advance, he employed his troops in sacking and burning the city of Tiberias,† no longer the home of an ally. The castle itself held out under Count Raymond's wife, Eschiva, the daughter of Hugh of St. Omer Her appeal for help reached Guy, at Saffuriya, on Thursday evening, at vespers, and caused the immediate advance of the Franks. Saladin's outposts brought news of their approach the next morning, and leaving a small force to mask the castle, he hurried up to the main army on the hills and prepared for battle.

The country where the memorable battle of Hittin was fought has been picturesquely described by an officer who knows every inch of the ground.‡

"Saffuriya," he writes, "was an unwalled town on the low hills north-west of Nazareth. The Church of St. Anne stood in the midst, and a strong tower on the hill above overlooked the brown cornfields which stretched towards the rugged mountain chain of Upper Galilee, and eastwards to the plain over Tiberias—an open and waterless plateau. The Fountain of Saffuriya lay a mile towards the south, in an open valley full of gardens, with a stream which now drives eight

* According to an eyewitness quoted by Abu-Shama 69, 70.
† Ibn-el-Athir, 681. Henceforward all references to this historian are to his *Kamil* (not his *Atabegs*).
‡ Lieutenant-Colonel C. R. Conder, R.E., in his *Latin Kingdom of Jerusalem* (1897), 148–150. The spelling of Arabic names has been assimilated to that used in this book.

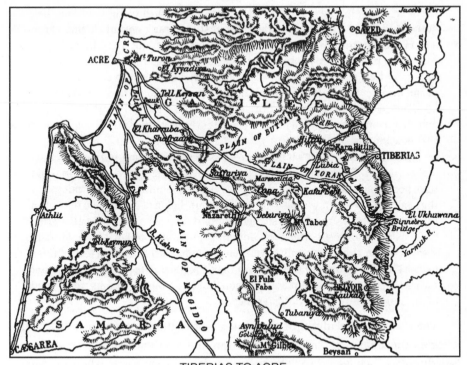

TIBERIAS TO ACRE.

Scale of English Miles.

0   5   10   15

mills, and which, therefore, was sufficient for so large an army as that which
gathered round King Guy. The surrounding lands also were full of villages, and
gave ample provisions.

"Saladin's camp was ten miles to the east, upon the plateau near [or rather
stretching considerably south of] the little village of Hittin. The place was surrounded with olives and fruit-trees, and a good spring—copious and fresh—flowed
on the north-west into the gorge of Wady Hammam. There was plenty of water in
the valleys beneath, and near Tiberias, where the wife of Raymond of Tripolis
was shut up in her castle upon the margin of the sacred lake. Just south of
Hittin rises the dark and rocky hillock famous in history as the 'Horn of Hittin,'
six hundred feet above the low-lying village, and overlooking the western plain a
hundred feet below. The highway from Acre led over the plain, and not a single
spring or stream of any size existed between the camps. It was the hottest season
of the year, and a long march for infantry divided the hosts of Christendom and
Islam.

"From the peak of Hittin the watchman looked towards the west over a sun-
burnt plain, with long grey ridges dotted with bush to north and south. Behind
him lay the Lake of Galilee seventeen hundred feet below, shut in with precipices

mirrored in its shining waters, with Hermon on the north rising snow-streaked over the valley of the Upper Jordan. Far east the craters of the Jaulan range stood up against the plains which stretch towards Damascus. The towers of Safed rose above the northern shores of the lake, and to the south the black walls and ditches of Belvoir frowned upon the rolling plateau. Defeat in such a position meant disaster to the Moslem forces, hurled down the slopes and driven into the lake; but in order to attack, the Christian army must cross the waterless plain, and after a long march would find the enemy covering all the springs and streams that flow into the lake.

"When we remember that the Franks possessed two strong outposts, at Fula [Faba] and at Belvoir; that an advance down the Valley of Jezreel to Beysan could have been made without any difficulty as regards plentiful supply of water; and that Saladin's position was also most dangerous, being at an angle to his line of retreat, it appears strange to a soldier that part, at least, of the Christian army was not despatched to attack the Jordan bridges, and to cut off the Moslem retreat, which could then only have been accomplished by the northern bridge guarded by the fortress of the Chateau Neuf.* A general like Godfrey would not have failed to take so evident a precaution, but probably the Franks were afraid of the summer heat in the Jordan valley."

The Franks were afraid of something worse than the summer heat: they dreaded the immense host which rumour said was following the standard of Saladin, and they feared to detach any portion of their force, when every man might be needed in the great battle that was before them. Nor is there any evidence that Saladin had not left a sufficient guard to defend the Jordan bridges: it was his custom to place corps of observation at dangerous points. The detaching of any considerable Christian force to cut off his retreat might have exposed the main army to defeat, and laid the whole of Palestine open to the invaders. The vital error of the Franks was their forgetting that their duty was to defend and not to attack. Had they chosen a strong defensive position and awaited Saladin's onslaught the issue might have been different; for the Saracens, man to man, were no match for the well-armed and high-mettled knights of the Cross, supported by steady and well-protected infantry. They threw away their advantage when, in spite of Count Raymond's urgent warning, the King yielded to the insistence of the Master of the Temple, and gave the signal for the fatal march over the waterless plain. "Better," said Raymond, "that my city of Tiberias fall, and my wife and all I possess be taken by the Saracens, than that the whole land be lost: for certes, if you go that way, lost it is." It was the counsel of a soldier, but the Master gave it the colour of treachery.

---

* Château Neuf was Hunin; perhaps Col. Conder refers to the new castle by Jacob's ford; but that was already destroyed (see above, pp. 124–5).

On Friday, the 3d of July, the Christian army broke up camp at Saffuriya, and began its disastrous advance upon Tiberias. Hardly had it set out, when the Saracen skirmishers were upon it. Ernoul's master, Balian of Ibelin, was with the vaward, under the command of Count Raymond, and lost many of his knights.* All that day the light horse of the Saracens harassed the troops, as they plodded along the shadeless, glaring limestone road, whilst the sun beat fiercely on the armour and headpieces, and not a drop of water was to be had. So hard pressed were the Templars and Turcopoles in the rear that they could not keep up with the King's battle in the centre, and were in sore danger of being cut off. Seeing their peril, Guy called a halt, though only half the distance to Tiberias was done; and it was decided to encamp under arms for the night. In vain Count Raymond, who was far ahead with the van, urged the vital necessity of pushing on to the water. The exhausted soldiers had no heart to face the Saracens who barred the way on the hills in front. The rearward was in difficulties. The whole army was demoralised. In desperation, Guy ordered the tents to be pitched at Marescalcia. Raymond rode in from the front in despair, crying out, "Alas! alas, Lord God! The war is over; we are dead men; the Kingdom is undone!"†

It was a night never to be forgotten. Through its long hours the one cry was for water. A raging thirst consumed man and horse. The voices of the Saracens could be heard close by as they patrolled the circle of the devoted host, triumphantly shouting, " *Allahu Akbar*, God is most great, there is no God but He." The enemy set fire to the scrub, and the smoke and fire increased the torment of the Christians. "Verily God fed them with the bread of tears and gave them to drink of the cup of repentance without measure."

The morrow came at last—the feast of the Translation of the Blessed Martin, Saturday the 4th of July.‡ The knights were early to horse, but the infantry was already worn out and gaping with thirst. The Saracens, who held the wells, were fresh and confident. Saladin had posted his men in the night, and carefully distributed their rounds of arrows. Every horseman's quiver was full; seventy camels stood at hand laden with arrows to replenish them; and there were four hundred loads of spare ammunition.§ All was ready, and the anxiety of the Moslems, who had been conscious of the peril of their position, where, they said,

---

* The march is vividly described by Ernoul, 166–8.
† *De Expugn.*, 223.
‡ Baha-ed-din is misled by his fondness for Fridays into placing the date of the battle a day too soon. Imad-ed-din, Ibn-el-Athir, Abu-Shama, Ernoul, and the *De Expugn.*, all say Saturday.
§ Imad-ed-din, Abu-Shama, 63.

"only God Most High could save them," was changed into jubilation when they realised the condition of the Franks. The two armies met near the village of Lubia, a couple of miles to the south-west of Hittin. Guy had been driven off the Tiberias road by the strong force of Saracens holding the hill of Kafar Sebt, and was now struggling towards the wells in the Wady Hammam to the north. The Moslems held off for a time, till the climbing sun should do its deadly work upon the weary Christians, and then they advanced, the centre a little "refused," and the wings thrown forward.* The battle began with a cloud of arrows from the Saracen archers, "thick as a flight of locusts," which unhorsed many of the enemy. Then with a shout the Moslems charged like one man, and a hand-to-hand fight ensued. Saladin was in every part of the field, exciting, encouraging, restraining his men, as the urgency required, and using the Arab's tantalising tactics—retreat before a charge, followed by instant pursuit of the retiring cavalry. Exhausted as they were, the Christian knights fought like heroes.

> "But† the grip of fear was on the throats of the crowd, who went Like driven beasts to shambles evident; They reckoned on sure disaster and dismay, And knew they would be among the visitors of the tombs next day: Yet the fury of the fight never slacked, And every knight his opposite attacked; Till the triumph (of the Faithful) was achieved, And ruin came on those who misbelieved."

The Frank infantry, maddened with thirst, scorched by the burning sun, and blinded by the flame and smoke of the bush which the Moslems had fired, lost their formation, neglected the combination with the knights which was the only hope of victory, and wildly struggled to push towards the lake in a desperate longing for water: but Saladin barred the way. They found themselves crowded in a heap on the top of a hill, and to the King's repeated entreaty that they would come down and do their devoir for Cross and Throne, they sent word that they were dying of thirst and could not fight. Thenceforth the infantry took no part in the battle: the Saracens eventually fell upon them, cast some down the precipice, and killed or captured the rest.‡ Many of them threw down their arms and surrendered, coming to the Saracens, their mouths hanging agape like thirsty dogs. Five of Raymond's knights even went to Saladin in their despair, and said: "Sire, why do you delay? Fall on them, they cannot help themselves; they are all dead men."§

---

* Abu-Shama, 70.

† Baha-ed-din rises into poetic language when he describes dramatic incidents, and he marks the occasion by the use of rhymed prose, each pair of clauses ending in the same rhyme.

‡ *De expugn.*, 225, 226.

§ Ernoul, 169; *cp.* Ralph of Coggeshall, *Chron. Anglic.*, 21.

In truth, not only the infantry, but the Templars and Hospitallers in the rear battle, and the King in the centre, were so hard pressed, and in such confusion and disarray, with swarms of Saracens surging in between them, that Guy, seeing it was hopeless to withstand their attacks without infantry, had tried to form a sort of lager of the tents huddled round the Cross.* There was yet one chance, a forlorn hope: the King called upon Raymond to charge; the field was in his lands, and by the laws of chivalry the post of honour was his also. The Count headed his knights in a last desperate effort, but Saladin's nephew was too quick for him: Taki-ed-din opened his ranks, and Raymond's division swept through; then, when the Christians were thus skilfully separated, the Saracens closed upon the King on all sides.† The last stand was made on the Horn of Hittin. The King and 150 of the bravest nobles and knights had gathered on this hillock round the royal red tent and the Holy Cross. "The Moslems revolved about them as a globe turns round its pole," and the unfortunate Franks vainly tried to break the cordon.

Saladin's son, a lad of sixteen, himself tells the piteous story‡:

"It was my first set battle," said el-Afdal, "and I was at my Father's side. When the King of the Franks had retired to the hill, his knights made a gallant charge, and drove the Moslems back upon my Father. I watched him, and I saw his dismay; he changed colour, tugged at his beard, and rushed forward, shouting, 'Give the devil the lie!' So the Moslems fell upon the enemy, who retreated up the hill. When I saw the Franks flying and the Moslems pursuing, I cried in my glee, 'We have routed them!' But the Franks charged again and drove our men back once more to where my Father was. Again he urged them forward, and they drove the enemy up the hill. Again I shouted, ' We have routed them!' But Father turned to me and said: ' Hold thy peace! We have not beaten them so long as that tent stands there.' At that instant the royal tent was overturned. Then the Sultan dismounted, and bowed himself to the earth, giving thanks to God, with tears of joy."

It was indeed the end. The Franks had spent their last strength in struggling to break through to the wells. The "Wood of the True Cross," which had been their gonfalon through the weary march and the hopeless battle, had fallen into the hands of the unbelievers; the Bishop of Acre, who bore it aloft, was slain, despite his armour; and God himself seemed to have deserted them. Tortured with thirst, parched with the heat and toil, they got off their horses and threw

---

* *De Expugn.*, 225.
† Ernoul, 169; Ibn-el-Athir, 684. The account in the *De Expugn.* describes the flight of the vaward as a desperate case of *sauve qui peut*, without orders from Guy (226).
‡ His narrative is reported by Ibn-el-Athir, 685–6.

themselves down on the scorched grass in sheer despair. The Saracens were upon them in an instant, and no defence was attempted. The knights were too weak to sell their lives dearly: they gave up their swords. The flower of chivalry was taken. The King and his brother, Reginald of Châtillon, Joscelin of Courtenay, Humphrey of Toron, the Masters of the Temple and Hospital, and many other nobles were among the prisoners. Count Raymond, after breaking through the Saracens, had seen the capture of the King, and never drew rein till he found himself safe at Tyre,—only to die of grief and shame. Legend did not deal gently with his memory. He became the Judas who betrayed Christendom, and for centuries minstrels told how Raymond basely plotted against King Guy, and sold the True Cross into the hands of the infidels. Balian of Ibelin, who had been in the advance guard, also escaped, with the Prince of Sidon. The rest of the chivalry of Palestine was under Moslem warders. Of the rank and file, all who were alive were made prisoners. A single Saracen was seen dragging some thirty Christians he had himself taken, tied together with a tent-rope. The dead lay in heaps, like stones upon stones, among broken crosses, severed hands and feet, whilst mutilated heads strewed the ground like a plentiful crop of melons.*

Saladin camped on the field of battle. When his tent was pitched, he ordered the prisoners to be brought before him. The King of Jerusalem and Reginald of Châtillon he received in his tent; he seated the King near himself, and seeing his thirst, he gave him a cup of water iced in snow. Guy drank, and passed the cup to the lord of Karak: but Saladin was visibly annoyed. "Tell the King," he said to the interpreter, "that it was he, not I, that gave that man drink." The protection of "bread and salt" was not to baulk his vengeance. Then he rose and confronted Reginald, who was still standing: "Twice have I sworn to kill him; once when he sought to invade the holy cities, and again when he took the caravan by treachery.—Lo! I will avenge Mohammed upon thee!" And he drew his sword and cut him down with his own hand, as he had sworn. The guard finished it and dragged the body out of the tent; "and God sped his soul to Hell."

The King, trembling at the sight, believed his own turn was now coming, but Saladin reassured him: "It is not the custom of kings to slay kings; but that man had transgressed all bounds, so what happened, happened."† The two military Orders were terribly punished for their daring and zeal for the faith. All the knights of the Hospital and the Temple that were prisoners were executed, to

---

* Imad-ed-din, Abu-Shama, 65.

† The accounts of Reginald of Châtillon's execution vary in details. Some represent Saladin as offering him the choice of Islam—a usual formality—and on his refusal cutting off his head. Others say he was killed outside the tent by the guard.

the number of two hundred, but the King and the chief nobles were well used and sent to Damascus. The field long bore the marks of the bloody fight where "30,000" Christians were said to have fallen. A year afterwards the heaps of bleaching bones could be seen from afar, and the hills and valleys were strewn with the relics of the horrid orgies of wild beasts.

The scene of the battle which overthrew the Christian Kingdom of Jerusalem had been sanctified by tradition for many centuries. The Horn of Hittin was believed to be the very Mount of Beatitudes where the Saviour taught the people the blessedness of peace. The Mount now bore witness to "not peace, but a sword."

SEAL OF REGINALD OF CHÂTILLON.
FROM ARCHER'S "STORY OF THE CRUSADES".

CHAPTER XIV

JERUSALEM REGAINED
1187

T HE SARACENS spent the night of the battle in rejoicing and giving thanks. The war-cry and the credo were shouted by thousands of triumphant voices; "God is Most Great," "There is no god but God," was echoed from mouth to mouth until the dawn. The Moslems might well rejoice. The victory of Tiberias had laid all Palestine at their mercy. The Kingdom of Jerusalem was at an end. Its King and almost all its nobles were prisoners, and hardly a leader was left to rally the broken remnant of the Crusaders. Since they entered the Holy Land ninety years before, they had never known such disaster. It was the death-blow to their dominion, and never to this day has Christendom recovered what it lost on the memorable Feast of St. Martin. In two months, from Beyrut in the north to Gaza in the south, the whole of Palestine, save a few isolated castles of the military Orders, was in the hands of Saladin, and only Tyre and Jerusalem itself remained to bear witness that there had been a Christian kingdom. The Holy City soon suffered the fate of its dependencies.

Saladin's first step was to take the castle of Tiberias. He went down on Sunday, the 5th of July, and the noble Eschiva, deserted by her husband and cut off from all hope of relief, could only surrender; the Sultan allowed her to depart in safety, with her children and attendants. Then, after one day's rest, the Saracens began to spread over Palestine in a great wave of conquest. It was not so much a conquest, indeed, as a triumphal progress. The resistance was of the feeblest. The Moslems had but to appear before a town, and, like Jericho, the walls fell down—the garrison surrendered. Only a few strong castles stood a siege, and even of these hardly one held out a week. The leaders of the Franks were dead or prisoners; their army was killed, captive, or dispersed; there were no reserves, no hope of reinforcement, no one to organise resistance. The people, too, the Moslem peasants and traders, were on the side of the conquerors. They believed after their fashion in Saladin's religion, they admired his courage and success, they recognised his clemency and even-handed justice. There were thousands of Moslem slaves in the cities who awaited with joy their liberation at his

160

hands. Even the scattered Christian sects had less to fear from the generous Sultan than from the rapacity and tyranny of their Christian masters, to whom heresy was almost as hateful as Islam itself. With the people to support him, and no one to oppose, save a desperate garrison here and there, it is not wonderful that Saladin's progress through Palestine was an almost uninterrupted march of triumph.

He gave the Franks no time to rally. On Wednesday, the 8th of July, 1187, four days after the battle of Hittin, he was before the strong walls of Acre; and on the Friday he celebrated the public prayers in the mosque that had been used as a church for three generations—the first Moslem prayers that had been offered on the coast of Palestine since the coming of the first Crusaders.* In Acre alone he freed four thousand Moslem captives. The treasure and stores of the great emporium and mart of the Mediterranean trade supplied him with the sinews of war and the means of rewarding and stimulating his army. He sent the troops in detachments in all directions to reduce the country, and summoned his brother el-Adil to bring the army of Egypt to aid in the subjection of Palestine. Some of his brigades occupied Nazareth, Saffuriya, el-Fula, inland; others entered Haifa and Cæsarea on the coast; another detachment seized Sebaste and Nablus; and el-Adil, marching from Cairo, took Castle Mirabel and Jaffa by assault. Saladin himself laid siege to Toron and after six days took it on the 26th of July. Returning to the coast, he next received the surrender of Sarafenda, Sidon, Beyrut, and Jubeyl, by the first week in August: Beyrut alone held out for eight days. In every case he granted honourable terms to the garrisons and people, and they learnt that the word of this Mohammedan could be trusted.†

The whole of the Kingdom of Jerusalem was now subdued, with the exception of a few castles, such as Belfort and Safed still held by Templars, and Hunin and Belvoir garrisoned by knights of the Hospital; the two cities of Tyre and Ascalon on the coast; and the Holy City itself. Tyre escaped by a hair's breadth. Saladin at first had avoided testing the endurance of his army by a long siege such as this strongly fortified city might be expected to stand. He preferred to keep up the courage of his men by easier conquests. Had he attacked Tyre directly after Acre, it would have capitulated, for Count Raymond had withdrawn to Tripolis, where he had quickly died of grief and shame; and the Prince of Antioch, who succeeded to the County of Tripolis, had not reinforced the small garrison of

---

* Ibn-el-Athir, 689.

† The authorities differ as to whether Toron capitulated or was stormed, and therefore whether the garrison was set free or made prisoners. Jaffa was severely treated, but this was by el-Adil.

Tyre.* Even when Saladin did venture to sit down before its walls, after the taking of Beyrut, its defenders despaired of resistance. "Reginald of Sidon and the commandant saw that all the knights were away, and that there were but few men, and little food, and they sent to tell Saladin that if he would withdraw they would surrender Tyre."† Matters had even gone so far that Saladin had sent two of his banners to be displayed on the castle the next day; when an unexpected event saved the city and changed the future of the Syrian coast.

Conrad, the young Marquess of Montferrat, who had won a great name in the Italian and Byzantine wars, finding himself involved in a blood-feud at Constantinople, escaped in a ship which was carrying some of his followers, ostensibly on a pilgrimage to the Holy Sepulchre. The news of Saladin's conquests had not yet reached the Golden Horn, and when Conrad arrived off Acre he was amazed to hear no harbour bells‡ and see no boats putting off to meet him. Suspecting that something was wrong, he did not venture to cast anchor, but lay off, awaiting events. Presently a Saracen officer of the port came out in a boat to ask who the visitors were. The Marquess himself answered that they were "merchants." "Then why do you not land and disembark?" Conrad replied that he did not know who was in possession of Acre. The Saracen assured him he could land, in all confidence, since the city belonged to Saladin, who had taken the King of Jerusalem and all his barons and put them in prison at Damascus, and had conquered all the land except Jerusalem and Tyre, which he was besieging. Therefore they could land in perfect safety. The grief which the Franks could not suppress at hearing this lamentable story betrayed them, and the Saracen hurried to the port to arm the fleet for pursuit; but Conrad had the start, and arrived safely at Tyre. His joy was unbounded at finding the place still in Christian hands, and he was welcomed with acclamation by the inhabitants, established with his knights in the castle, and given the supreme command. The castellan and Reginald of Sidon, who were preparing to surrender the city to Saladin on the morrow, in great alarm took ship by night and fled to Tripolis. Their cowardice was quickly exposed by the discovery of Saladin's banners, which the Marquess immediately flung into the moat. For "*the will of God is a fixed destiny*,"§ and Tyre was fated to be saved for the Christians by means of this "man of the Franks who border the Mediterranean, called el-Markis,—God's

---

* Ibn-el-Athir, 694. The historian was at Aleppo at this time, and evidently had good means of information.
† Ernoul, 179. *Cp.* Röhricht, *Regesta Regn. Hierosol.*, 660.
‡ Bells were rung at Acre when a ship came into port. Abu-Shama, 79.
§ *Koran*, xxxiii., 38.

curse upon him !" exclaims the pious Moslem historian, "for he was a devil of a man in caution and watchfulness, and of immense bravery withal."*

The effects of Conrad's energy were immediately felt. All thoughts of capitulation were abandoned, and the garrison, inspired with new courage, set about strengthening their defences and preparing for a stubborn resistance. Saladin perceived that the opportunity was lost: he tried one argument, and not a worthy one, by fetching Conrad's father, the old Marquess of Montferrat, from his prison at Damascus, and bartering his life against the city. But Conrad professed complete heartlessness, said his father had already lived quite long enough, and Saladin might kill him if he liked: not the smallest stone of Tyre should be given to save him.

The old man, however, was not sacrificed; Saladin was forced to raise the siege, and departed for Ascalon—the only other port of Palestine which still displayed the Cross. His biographer alleges another reason, which probably had its weight, when he states that the Sultan abandoned the leaguer "because his men were dispersed throughout the coast, each looting on his own behalf, and the army was tired of fighting and war without end."† It was also of the utmost importance to reduce both Ascalon and Jerusalem, since they barred the communications between his two great provinces of Egypt and Syria.‡ So he hastened to the southern frontier, occupied Ramla, Ibelin, and Darum, and sat down before Ascalon on the 23rd of August. El-Adil joined him with the army of Egypt, and the two brothers pressed the siege and directed the mangonels, whilst their foraging parties took Gaza, Beyt Jibrin and Natrun. Repeating the experiment of Tyre, Saladin had King Guy and the Master of the Temple brought from Damascus, and promised them their liberty if they could persuade the garrison to surrender; but Ascalon, like Tyre, at first rejected the temptation. The garrison held out nearly a fortnight, but finally empowered the King to treat for them. They were allowed to depart in peace, and the Saracens occupied Ascalon on Friday, the 4th of September. It is doubtful how far Guy had contributed to this result, but Saladin kept his promise, and after some further detention at Nablus, where he was allowed a "sad interview" with his queen, the King was released, together with his brother and the other nobles, in the following summer.

On the day the Saracens took possession of Ascalon, the sun hid his face, and the day became almost as night.§ An eclipse is always a sinister portent to

* Ibn-el-Athir, 694–5; Ernoul, 181–3.
† Baha-ed-din, 99
‡ Ibn-el-Athir, 696.
§ Ernoul, 185. A total eclipse of the sun took place on the 4th of September, but its totality passed

the credulous folk of the East, and it must have held a specially ominous significance to the burghers of Jerusalem who had come at Saladin's bidding to treat for peace. The Sultan was anxious to spare the Holy City the misery of a siege. "I believe," he told them, "that Jerusalem is the House of God, as you also believe, and I will not willingly lay siege to the House of God or put it to the assault." To obtain it "in peace and amity" he offered to leave the inhabitants free to fortify the city and cultivate the land for five leagues round, and even to supply them plentifully with money and food, until the following Pentecost, on condition that when Pentecost came, if they saw a prospect of being rescued, they should keep the Holy City; but if they saw no chance of succour, then they must surrender Jerusalem, and he would conduct them and their possessions safely to Christian soil.*

The offer was chivalrous, even quixotic, when the notorious bad faith of the Crusaders is remembered, and the lack of any security for their keeping a promise. But the delegates from Jerusalem refused it without hesitation. If God pleased, they said, they would never surrender the city where the Saviour died for them. So Saladin, pleased at their devotion, promised them on his oath that he would never take it except in the honourable way, by the sword. The Sultan's chivalry is the more remarkable, since Jerusalem itself had lately presented a signal example of bad faith. After Balian of Ibelin had escaped from the field of Hittin, he sent to Saladin, begging him to give him a safe-conduct to go to Jerusalem and bring his wife and children back to Tyre. The petition was at once granted, on the conditions that Balian should only stay one night in the city, and should never more bear arms against the Sultan. When he arrived at Jerusalem he was welcomed with delight as a deliverer, for there were no knights of rank there, and he was made commander and guardian of the city by universal acclamation. In vain he protested that he had given his oath to Saladin and could not honourably stay or help in the defence. "I absolve you," said the Patriarch, "from your sin and your oath, which it were a greater sin in you to keep than to break; for it were a perpetual disgrace upon you to leave Jerusalem in this strait and go away, nor should you ever have honour again whithersoever you went." So Balian stayed, and since there were but two knights in the place, who had also fled from Hittin, he knighted thirty burghers. The Patriarch opened the treasury for

---

a little north of Ascalon. The expression in Muratori's edition (1725) of part of Pipino's chronicle, "*tantam passus est eclipsim, ut fere nox esset,*" suggests an eclipse which was not quite total. Ernoul says, "*qu'il sambla bien qu'il fust nuis*"; the *Libellus de Expugn.* records, "*Feria sexta, hora nona, obscuratus est sol*" (238).

* Ernoul, 185–6.

him, and the garrison went out and bought provisions for the siege.* Fugitives had come in from all sides, and there were reckoned to be 60,000 men in the city, besides women and children.

The patience of Saladin was not exhausted even after this dishonour. Perhaps he believed that Balian could not help himself; and far from showing rancour, he gave him a fresh proof of his confidence. Balian again sent to him at Ascalon to beg him to give another safe-conduct, to remove his wife and children to Tripolis; he explained that he was forcibly withheld from keeping his former promise. Instead of reproaches, Saladin sent an escort of fifty horse, who carried out his wishes.

On Sunday, the 20th of September, 1187, the Saracens at length appeared before the walls of the Holy City. In seventy-five days they had overrun and subdued the Kingdom of Jerusalem; now they must have the capital itself, the cause and motive of the Crusades, the object of the veneration of Christian and Moslem alike. Saladin first took up his position on the west side, facing the line of walls from the gate of David to the gate of Saint Stephen. He was amazed to see the battlements packed with countless defenders, who indeed could not find room in the crowded houses and churches. He soon discovered that the ground was ill-chosen, for the great towers of Tancred and David (or the Castle of the Pisans, as it was then called) commanded his batteries, and the frequent sallies of the Christians drove back his engineers and opposed the erection of his mangonels. Moreover, the sun was in the eyes of the Moslems, and they could not see to fight till the afternoon by reason of the glare. He therefore reconnoitred the other sides of the city, and after five days transferred his army to the east, overlooking the valley of the Kidron, where the walls were less strong. He moved in the evening of the 25th of September, and the inhabitants, seeing him depart, thought he had abandoned the siege, and ran to the churches to pour out their thanksgivings and indulge in transports of joy. But on the morrow weeping followed hard upon laughter: the Saracen standards were flying on Mount Olivet; already two score mangonels were in position, and the engineers, who had worked all night, were beginning to mine the barbican.† Ten thousand Moslem cavalry masked the gates of St. Stephen and Josaphat, and prevented sallies, and the sappers pushed forward under a shield-wall, covered by the arrows of the archers and the stones and Greek fire discharged from the engines. It was impossible to keep a footing on the ramparts under the hail of stones and shafts, for "the arrows served as toothpicks to the teeth of the battle-

---

* Ernoul, 175–6.
† *Libellus de Expugnatione*, 243, where the writer says he was himself wounded in the siege.

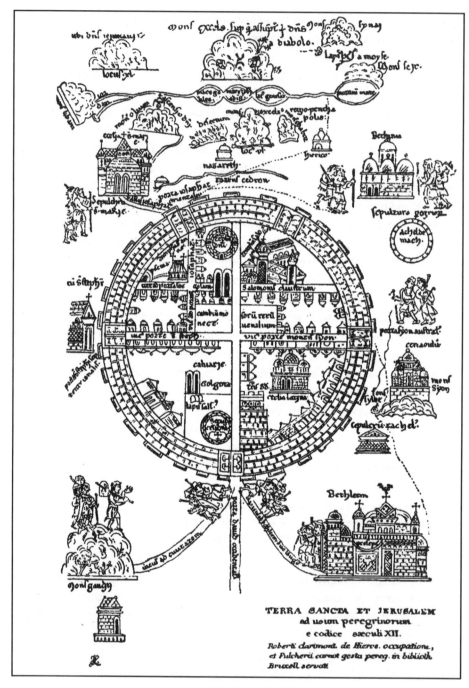

PLAN OF JERUSALEM.

(FROM A 12TH CENTURY MANUSCRIPT.)

ments"*; and the mining went on merrily, till in two days thirty or forty paces of the barbican wall were sapped; the mines were stuffed with wood and fired, and a great breach was made. The knights in vain attempted a sortie to cut off the engineers; Saladin's horsemen drove them in. Lamentation and despair fell upon the city. The people crowded to the churches to pray and confess their sins; beat themselves with stones and scourges, supplicating the mercy of God. The women cut off their daughters' hair, and plunged them naked in cold water, in the hope of averting their shame. The priests and monks paraded the city in solemn procession, bearing the *Corpus Domini* and the Cross, and chanting the *Miserere*. "But the wickedness and lewdness of the city stank in the nostrils of the Lord, and the prayers of the sinful people could not mount to the mercy seat."

At last the breach could not be manned; not for a hundred gold pieces would a citizen stand there for a single night. The common people were all for surrender. The leaders took counsel together, and resolved to sally forth and meet their deaths. But Heraclius the Patriarch showed them that they would thus expose their women and children to slavery—he had his private reasons—and they were persuaded to treat for terms. Balian went to Saladin's tent, but even whilst he was entreating him, the breach was carried and the Saracen flag appeared upon the barbican. "Doth one grant terms to a captive city?" scoffed the Sultan. Besides, he had sworn to take Jerusalem by the sword, and he must keep his vow. The city, however, was not yet taken: the garrison once more plucked up courage and drove back the assailants. Saladin wished to spare the devoted inhabitants, and sought counsel with his divines, if there might be another way to keep his vow. Balian's last visit had filled him with horror, for the baron had plainly spoken of the desperate resolution of the garrison:

> "O Sultan," he said, "know that we soldiers in this city are in the midst of God knows how many people, who are slackening the fight in the hope of thy grace, believing that thou wilt grant it them as thou hast granted it to the other cities— for they abhor death and desire life. But for ourselves, when we see that death must needs be, by God we will slaughter our sons and our women, we will burn our wealth and our possessions, and leave you neither sequin nor stiver to loot, nor a man or a woman to enslave; and when we have finished that, we will demolish the Rock and the Mosque el-Aksa, and the other holy places, we will slay the Moslem slaves who are in our hands—there are 5000 such,—and slaughter every beast and mount we have; and then we will sally out in a body to you, and will fight you for our lives not a man of us will fall before he has slain his likes; thus shall we die gloriously or conquer like gentlemen."†

---

* See a bombastic account of the siege written by Saladin's minister, the Kady el-Fadil, to the Caliph of Baghdad, quoted in Ibn-Khallikan, iv., 520–528.
† Ibn-el-Athir, 701; Abu-Shama, 84.

Balian's desperate threats, and the arguments of his own council, induced Saladin at length to modify his vow. It would be sufficiently kept, he announced, if Jerusalem surrendered at discretion, as though it had actually been taken by assault. In this case he would exercise his clemency and hold the population to ransom as prisoners of war. Each man should pay ten pieces of gold for his liberty, and two women or ten children should be reckoned as one man; whilst of the poor, who possessed not even a gold coin, seven thousand should be set free for the sum of thirty thousand besants, to be paid out of King Henry's treasure, the remnant of which was still hoarded in the house of the Hospitallers. Forty days were allowed for the ransoming; after that, all that remained became slaves. The articles of capitulation were signed on Friday the 2nd of October, the Feast of St. Leger. By a strange coincidence, it was the 27th of Rejeb, the anniversary of the blessed Leylat el-Miraj, when the prophet of Islam dreamed his wonderful dream, and visited in his sleep the Holy City which his followers had now recovered after ninety years of Christian occupation.

Balian returned to the city and announced the terms. They were accepted, with gratitude and lamentation. The people groaned and wept, and would not be comforted; they kissed the holy walls which they might never see again, and bowing their fates on the ground before the Sepulchre, watered the sacred spot with their tears. To leave Jerusalem was to tear the hearts out of them. But there was no help for it; the Moslem flag flew overhead, the keys were in the Saracens' hands, and in forty days the city must be delivered up. Never did Saladin show himself greater than during this memorable surrender. His guards, commanded by responsible emirs, kept order in every street, and prevented violence and insult, insomuch that no ill-usage of the Christians was ever heard of.* Every exit was in his hands, and a trusty lord was set over David's gate to receive the ransoms as each citizen came forth.

Then began a strangely pathetic scene. First Balian brought the thirty thousand gold besants, and the seven thousand poor who were ransomed by the King of England's treasure were allowed to shamble out. There followed burgher after burgher, money in hand, with their families and sometimes with poor dependents who could not ransom themselves. Saracen soldiers and merchants thronged the city and bought the goods of the departing citizens, so that each might raise the price of freedom. Kukbury ransomed a thousand Armenians of Edessa, and sent them to their homes; and others were not less benevolent. There was cheating and deceit, of course, and some of the Moslem emirs falsely

---

* Ernoul, 227.

claimed lost servants and took their ransoms privately, whilst others smuggled Franks out of the city in Saracen dress, and sucked them dry as soon as they were clear of the guard.* The Patriarch, who had neither morals nor conscience, carried off the treasures of the churches, gold chalices and monstrances, and even the gold plate of the Holy Sepulchre, besides a vast hoard of his own, which had been better spent on ransoming the poor who still remained. When the Saracen emirs urged Saladin not to let the old rascal make off with his plunder, he replied, "No, I will not break faith with him," and the Patriarch got off like the rest for his ten besants. It was left for the Mohammedan King to teach the Christian priest the meaning of charity.

For forty days the melancholy procession trooped forth from the gate of David, and the term of grace expired. Yet there still remained thousands of poor people whom the niggardly burghers and religious houses had left to slavery. Then el-Adil came to his brother and said: "Sire, I have helped you by God's grace to conquer the land and this city, I therefore pray you give me a thousand slaves from the poor people within." To Saladin's question, what he would do with them, he answered he would do as pleased himself. Then the Sultan gave him the thousand slaves, and el-Adil set them all free as an offering to God. Then came the Patriarch and Balian, and begged likewise, and Saladin gave them another thousand slaves, and they were set free. Then said Saladin to his officers: "My brother has made his alms, and the Patriarch and Balian have made theirs; now I would fain make mine." And he ordered his guards to proclaim throughout the streets of Jerusalem that all the old people who could not pay were free to go forth. And they came forth from the postern of St. Lazarus, and their going lasted from the rising of the sun until night fell. "Such was the charity which Saladin did, of poor people without number."†

> "Then I shall tell you," says the Squire of Balian, of the great courtesy which Saladin showed to the wives and daughters of knights, who had fled to Jerusalem when their lords were killed or made prisoners in battle. When these ladies were ransomed and had come forth from Jerusalem, they assembled and went before Saladin crying mercy. When Saladin saw them he asked who they were

---

* Ibn-el-Athir, 703; Abu-Shama, 85.

† This is the report of the Christian chronicler Ernoul, who was probably present (227–8). It is worth noting that, on the same authority, when the poor refugees whom Saladin released came to Tripolis, its Christian count shut the gates in their faces, and even sent out his troops to rob the burghers of the possessions which the Moslems had religiously respected. (*Ib.*, 234.) It is not to be understood, however, that Saladin freed *all* the poor; there was undoubtedly a large residue of young slaves, perhaps 15,000: so says Imad-ed-din, who himself received his share of women and children. Abu-Shama, 89.

and what they sought. And it was told him that they were the dames and damsels of knights who had been taken or killed in battle. Then he asked what they wished, and they answered for God's sake have pity on them; for the husbands of some were in prison, and of others were dead, and they had lost their lands, and in the name of God let him counsel and help them. When Saladin saw them weeping, he had great compassion for them, and wept himself for pity. And he bade the ladies whose husbands were alive to tell him where they were captives, and as soon as he could go to the prisons he would set them free. (And all were released wherever they were found.) After that he commanded that to the dames and damsels whose lords were dead there should be handsomely distributed from his own treasure, to some more and others less, according to their estate. And he gave them so much that they gave praise to God and published abroad the kindness and honour which Saladin had done to them."*

Thus did the Saracens show mercy to the fallen city. One recalls the savage conquest by the first Crusaders in 1099, when Godfrey and Tancred rode through streets choked with the dead and dying, when defenceless Moslems were tortured, burnt, and shot down in cold blood on the towers and roof of the Temple, when the blood of wanton massacre defiled the honour of Christendom and stained the scene where once the gospel of love and mercy had been preached. "Blessed are the merciful, for they shall obtain mercy" was a forgotten beatitude when the Christians made shambles of the Holy City. Fortunate were the merciless, for they obtained mercy at the hands of the Moslem Sultan.

> "The greatest attribute of heaven is Mercy;
> And 'tis the crown of justice, and the glory,
> Where it may kill with right, to save with pity."

If the taking of Jerusalem were the only fact known about Saladin, it were enough to prove him the most chivalrous and great-hearted conqueror of his own, and perhaps of any, age.

---

* Ernoul, 229–30.

CHAPTER XV

THE RALLY AT TYRE
1187–1188

W HEN ALL the Franks had departed, and only the slaves and rescued Moslem captives remained, with the native Christians, who begged to stay and pay tribute, Saladin ordered the holy places to be purified and restored for the worship of Islam. The golden cross had been torn down from the Dome of the Rock, and all traces of the Templars' additions were removed from the Haram where stood the ancient Mosque of Omar. Doctors and divines and pilgrims hastened from all parts to share in the great consecration. Deputations thronged the Sultan's tent outside the city, chanting the Koran, reciting poems, declaiming panegyrics in his honour. The secretaries laboured to spread the good news to the ends of the kingdoms of Islam: Imad-ed-din himself wrote seventy dispatches on the day of the recapture of Jerusalem. On Friday the 9th of October an immense congregation assembled to pray with Saladin in the sanctuary of el-Aksa. The chief Kady of Aleppo preached the sermon.* He praised God for the triumph of the faith and the cleansing of his Holy House; he declared the pure creed of the Koran, and pronounced the blessings upon the Prophet and the Caliphs, in the prescribed form of the Mohammedan bidding-prayer.

Then, "O Men," he cried, "rejoice at good tidings! God is well-pleased with what ye have done, and this is the summit of man's desire; he hath holpen you to bring back this strayed camel from misguided hands and to restore it to the fold of Islam, after the infidels had mishandled it for nearly a hundred years. Rejoice at the purifying of this House, *which God allowed to be raised and permitted his name to be said therein*, over which he spread his tent and wherein he established his holy rites; the house whose foundations were laid on the creed of the One God, the best of foundations, and the walls whereof were built to his glory, and stand firm upon piety from ancient times until now. It was the dwelling-place of your father Abraham, the spot whence your prophet Mohammed, God bless him, ascended into Heaven, the *kibla* to which ye turned to pray in the

---

* The sermon is preserved by Ibn-Khallikan, ii., 634–641, from whom the following extracts are abridged. The passages in italics are quoted from the Koran.

early time of Islam, the abode of the prophets, the resort of the saints, the grave of the apostles, the place where God's revelation came down, and where all mankind must gather on the Day of Resurrection and of judgment. . . . It is the city to which God sent his servant and apostle, the Word which entered into Mary, Jesus, the spirit of God, whom he honoured with his mission and ennobled with the gift of prophecy, yet without raising him above the ranks of his creatures: for the Most High hath said, Christ *will not disdain to be God's servant, nor will the angels who surround his presence.* . . .

"Had ye not been of God's chosen servants, he had not honoured you by this grace, wherein ye can never be rivalled nor shall any ever share in its perfectness. Blessed are ye, who have fought like those at Bedr, who have been steadfast as Abu-Bekr, victorious as Omar, who have recalled the hosts of Othman and the onslaughts of Ali! Ye have renewed for Islam the glorious memories of Kadisiya, of the Yarmuk, of Khaibar, and of Khalid, the Sword of God. The Almighty recompense you, and accept the offering of the blood ye have shed in his service, and grant you Paradise, happy for ever. . . .

"And prolong, O Almighty God, the reign of thy servant, humbly reverent, for thy favour thankful, grateful for thy gifts, thy sharp sword and shining torch, the champion of thy faith and defender of thy holy land, the firmly resisting, the great, the victorious King, the strengthener of the true religion, the vanquisher of the worshippers of the Cross, the Honour of the World and the Faith [SALADIN], Sultan of Islam and of the Moslems, purifier of the holy temple, ABU-L-MUZAFFAR YUSUF SON OF AYYUB, reviver of the empire of the Commander of the Faithful. Grant, O God, that his empire may spread over all the earth, and that the angels may ever surround his standards; preserve him for the good of Islam; protect his realm for the profit of the Faith; and extend his dominion over the regions of the East and of the West. . . . Save him, O God, and his children after him; may they rule the land till the end of time; preserve his days, and his sons and his brethren, strengthen his power by their long lives; and, inasmuch as by his means thou hast brought this lasting good to Islam, to endure whilst months and years shall roll, grant him, O God, the kingdom that never ends in the mansions of the blest, and hear his prayer that he prayeth unto thee:—*O Lord, help me to be thankful for thy favour wherewith thou hast favoured me and my fathers, that I may do that which is right and well-pleasing unto thee, and bring me at last of thy mercy to dwell amongst thy righteous servants.*"*

This noble *khutba*, with its beautiful peroration, was pronounced with such overwhelming effect, writes the Kady el-Fadil, that "the heavens almost cracked, not in wrath, but to drop tears of joy, and the stars left their places, not to shoot upon the wicked, but to rejoice together." The delight of the Moslems at the recovery of the Sanctuary was unbounded. Saladin restored it to its former beauty and simplicity, and brought from Damascus an exquisite carved pulpit which

---

* *Koran*, xxvii., 19: the prayer is there put into the mouth of Solomon.

Nur-ed-din had caused to be designed at Aleppo twenty years before. It is there to this day, and over the great niche of the Mosque may still be read the inscription:

"In the name of God, the Compassionate, the Merciful! Hath ordered the repair of this holy *Mihrab* and the restoration of the Mosque el-Aksa, founded on piety, the servant and agent of God *Yusuf son of Ayyub Abu-l-Muzaffar el-Melik en-Nasir Salahed-dunya wa-d-din*, when that God by his hand had triumphed, in the month of the year [of the Flight] 583: and he prayeth God to endue him with thankfulness for this favour and to make him a partaker in the remission of sins, through his mercy and forgiveness."8

Jerusalem and Ascalon were regained; Karak and Mont Real in "Oultre Jourdain" and Safed and Belvoir near Tiberias, alone of all the Crusaders' castles south of Tyre,† still held Christian garrisons; but every one of these castles was masked by a sufficient force, and it was only a question of time when they must be starved out. Tyre was the only important place in all Palestine that Saladin had not conquered; and to Tyre he despatched his jubilant army on the 1st of November, 1187. Twelve days later he arrived to take command. He found the city full of the garrisons which he had suffered to capitulate at other places. Conrad of Montferrat had worked night and day, strengthening the works, encouraging the defenders, and "directing them with superior ability." He had deepened and extended the moats till Tyre became "like a hand spread upon the sea, attached only by the wrist," an island approached by so narrow a spit that it could be easily defended by a small force, as well as covered by the cross-bows on the shielded Christian barges or *barbotes*. Saladin was supported by his brother, sons, and nephew, with their contingents from Egypt, Aleppo, and Hamah; but he was unable to bring his greatly superior strength to bear upon the enemy. He had indeed seventeen engines playing upon the walls day and night, but only a small number of men could advance at a time upon the spit of land, and these had not only to meet the frequent sallies of the Franks in front, led by the valiant Knight in Green,‡ but to protect themselves from the flank attacks of the barbotes drawn up on either side. Ten of the Saracen ships were brought from Acre, and soon drove the Tyrian galleys into port; but early on the morning of the feast of

* Vte. de Voguë, *Le Temple de Jerusalem*, 101; Le Strange, *Palestine*, 109.
† See Conrad's letter to the King of Hungary (Röhricht, *Regesta*, 670).
‡ This Spanish knight bore a shield vert, and a pair of stags' horns on his helmet, of the same. Saladin, says Ernoul, delighted to see the Green Knight's splendid sallies, for, be he Christian or Moslem, there was nothing he loved so much as a good knight (237–8).

the holy martyr, St. Thomas of Canterbury (Dec. 29th), half the Moslem fleet was surprised and captured by the enemy, and the rest were sent to Beyrut, as they were not strong enough to hold the galleys in check. Even as they went, they were pursued by the Tyrians, and in a panic all but two of their ships went ashore, where they had to be burnt. The failure at sea was followed by a reverse on shore: the Saracens, taking advantage of the diversion by sea, had scaled the barbican wall and were attempting the main wall, when Conrad sallied out at the head of his men and drove them out with heavy loss.*

Upon this Saladin called a council of war. Some of the emirs were for retreat; they alleged, with reason, the inclemency of the season—for it was now late in December, when rain and snow convert the plain into it sea of mud, and damp and cold breed sickness among the soldiers and horses;—they spoke of the number of dead and wounded, and the want of stores and money; and proposed to raise the siege, and return to the attack in the spring. Against these easy-going advocates, others urged that it was of the first importance to conquer Tyre, since it was the only hope of the Franks on that coast, and if it fell there would be no more reinforcements coming from beyond the sea. The timider counsels prevailed, however, and on New Year's Day, 1188, Saladin dismissed the various contingents to their homes in Egypt, Syria, and Mesopotamia, and withdrew with his own personal troops to Acre.†

The retreat from Tyre was the turning-point in Saladin's career of victory. It was a fatal, irremediable error. It was a fixed principle with him to avoid long sieges whenever possible, nor was the principle wrong. His troops consisted largely of an ill-disciplined feudal militia, of different races and dialects, who were bound together more by the hope of booty than by devotion to the Sultan or even zeal for the Holy War. Well led, they could fight with success on a pitched field, and when a town or castle could be taken by assault, the prospect of loot and sheer love of combat would lend the storming party a furious valour. But a long siege discouraged them, and opened occasions for the jealousies and discontents inevitable in so mixed an army. Instead of the incitement of rapid triumphs and frequent prizes, there were the weary sapping of strong walls, the daily exposure to sharpshooters on the battlements and desperate charges from the sally-port. In the case of a regular Crusaders' castle, well garrisoned and commanded by a capable leader, the odds were against the besiegers, whose clumsy mangonels were uncertain of aim and discharged stones, ponderous indeed, but doubtfully effective against a well-constructed wall of stone twenty

---

* Ernoul, 242–3.

† Ibn-el-Athir, 707–711, unsparingly condemns the policy of retreat.

feet thick. Mining, though wood had to be fired instead of gunpowder or dynamite, was more successful than bombardment, but it was conducted at great risk when a determined garrison harassed the sappers, nor was the modern science of trench approaches and zigzags and other protective devices familiar to the Saracen engineers. A close blockade, ending in starving out the garrison, was the surest method; but this involved keeping a large body of men in discontented inaction, perhaps in the trying winter season, and without a fleet it was of course useless against a coast town which could be provisioned by sea.

It is not wonderful, therefore, that Saladin avoided long sieges, for which, moreover, he did not show the same capacity that he displayed in set battles and rapid campaigns. His dislike to siege operations may account, as well as his natural clemency, for his usual practice of accepting the surrender of a fortress and letting the garrison go free, even when there was a near prospect of carrying a place by assault. He never seems to have considered that every garrison thus released went to swell the forces of the enemy, and that even if he exacted their parole they were certain to break it at the first opportunity for revenge. Obviously the prudent way was to hold them prisoners of war at Damascus, or some other distant city, until the campaign was over and peace was made. Tyre was full of these capitulated garrisons, and Saladin had chiefly himself to reproach for the strength of the defenders.

Nevertheless, whatever the difficulties of the siege, *Delenda est Tyrus* should have been his immutable resolve. He should have built a new fleet, destroyed the Tyrian galleys, filled the moats, breached the walls, if he lost half his army in so doing. The only answer is that Saladin knew his men, and felt that he could not count upon their endurance. But even this does not explain his neglect to blockade the city by sea and land, to keep off reinforcements, and to starve its crowded population. However we look at it, Saladin's measures against Tyre appear to be neither soldierly nor statesmanlike. Tyre became the rallying-point from which the Crusaders recovered part of their lost power and prestige along the coast of Palestine: and had this one city not held out, it is a question whether the Third Crusade would ever have been heard of at Acre.

The effects of this serious check were not, of course, immediately apparent. Europe took time to assemble its forces for the recovery of the Holy Land, and meanwhile Saladin, still ignoring the danger from Tyre, led a triumphant campaign in the north. Hitherto he had been content with the subjection of the Kingdom of Jerusalem; he now extended his conquests in the County of Tripolis and the Principality of Antioch. Bohemond III. was its Prince, and his son Raymond had succeeded to the County of Tripolis by the will of his namesake, the unhappy survivor of the battle of Hittin. Father and son had cheerfully left Tyre to its fate, and it was no thanks to them that Conrad had beaten off the invaders. Raymond indeed sent some galleys towards the beleaguered city, but an opportune storm had enabled them to return to Tripolis with a plausible excuse for doing nothing. So fearful was Bohemond of adding to his responsibilities that he had turned away the refugees from Jerusalem lest they should exhaust his store of food, and had at the same time relieved them of such money as they carried, in order to supply his own necessities. The northern princes had long pursued a policy of conciliation towards Saladin, and this meanness was perhaps intended as a proof of good feeling, which the generous Sultan can hardly have commended. It did not, at least, prevent him from attacking the northern provinces.

The winter was spent at Acre, where Saladin occupied the Palace of el-Afdal, which had been converted into a Templars' castle. The divines were installed in the Hospital of St. John, and the bishop's palace was made a hospital: both were richly endowed by Saladin out of the spoils. Meanwhile Karakush, the fortifier of Cairo, was sent for to strengthen the defences of Acre. Leaving the coast in the spring, and after inspecting in March the blockade at Belvoir (Kaukab), the castle of the Hospitallers south of Tiberias, which he found far too strong to be stormed, Saladin visited Damascus, and then on the 14th of May marched north.* The immediate cause was a movement of the Franks upon Jubeyl, but the direction of his march shows that his designs pointed towards Tripolis or Antioch. He camped near Emesa, whence he reconnoitred the country. Ernoul says that Saladin actually laid siege to Tripolis, but found it so largely reinforced that he withdrew. William of Sicily, first of all the princes of Europe to come to the rescue, had sent five hundred knights and a fleet of fifty galleys under his brave admiral Margaritus, whose exploits had won him the name of "the King of the Sea" and "a second Neptune," and the Sicilians brought invaluable aid to the survivors of the Crusades.† Conrad of Montferrat had also hastened to the assistance of his phlegmatic neighbour. With Conrad came the famous Green Knight, whose prowess again compelled the admiring notice of Saladin. The Sultan invited him to his tent; he came, and Saladin made him very welcome, gave him horses and jewels, and offered lands and possessions if he would take

---

* Before this campaign Saladin had been joined by his future biographer Baha-ed-din, who remained with him as his secretary (from June, 1188) in close intimacy until the Sultan's death. Ibn-el-Athir was also with Saladin (cp. 717) during at least part of his war against Antioch.
† *Itinerarium Regis Ricardi*, i., 13, 14; but Abu-Shama insists that the Sicilian fleet was useless for good or evil (Goergens, 100).

service with him. But the Green Knight refused everything; he said he had not come to the Holy Land to stay with Saracens, but to hurt and confound them; which he would do whenever he could.* So they parted in honest respect.

Abandoning any designs he had upon Tripolis, Saladin returned to his camp near the Hospitallers' virgin fortress, Crac des Chevaliers (Hisn el-Akrad, "the Kurds' Castle"), and, joined by his vassals from Mesopotamia under the leadership of Imad-ed-din of Sinjar, formed his army in order of battle. He set out on his campaign on Friday, his favourite day, the 1st of July. There was no Christian army to oppose him, and the campaign is a monotonous record of the storming or surrender of city after city, castle after castle. Tortosa (Antartus) was the first to feel the brunt of his wrath, for his unusually harsh treatment of the city shows that his ill-success at Tripolis had galled him. Arriving on the 3rd of July, he formed his army in a crescent round the place, from sea to sea, and ordered an immediate assault. It was carried before the followers had time to pitch the Moslems' tents; and they sacked, and burnt, and razed it to the ground. Of the two castles, however, only one was destroyed; the Templars' Tower resisted all assaults and had to be left, a standing support to the Christians. Valenia was deserted by its inhabitants; but the great fortress of Margat defied capture. Jebela opened its gates, and its citadel surrendered on Friday the 15th of July. On the following Friday the garrison of Ladikia capitulated, on the Friday after that, Saone (Sahyun), the great castle of the Crusaders on the hills, was carried by assault, but the Sultan held the garrison and people to ransom on the same terms as at Jerusalem.† On three Fridays in August fell the twin fortresses of the Orontes, Bukas and esh-Shughr, hitherto deemed impregnable, and the town of Sarmin. The capture of six strongholds on six successive Fridays assured the Moslems that the prayers of the faithful on the day of worship had been accepted, and they remembered the sacred promise that a good deed done on Friday would be doubly rewarded in Paradise.

Barzuya, on the east of the Orontes, a fort so strong that its impregnability became a proverb, was carried by assault after hard fighting on the 23rd of August; its defenders were made prisoners, and the Moslems were laden with the spoils. Only the governor and his relations, who were kin to the Prince of Antioch, were set free and escorted to their friends. Among them were a newly

---

* Ernoul, 251–2.

† Abu-Shama (103–4) says that Saone was protected by five walls, between which the space was filled with bears and lions! Imad-ed-din laments the wanton destruction wrought by the Saracens in the magnificent marble buildings of Ladikia—the most sumptuous and beautiful city he had ever seen.

married couple whom the Saracens had ruthlessly separated. Saladin pitied their misfortune, sought them out, and sent them, reunited, to safety.* Bohemond was not likely to forget this generosity, and after the Moslems had taken Darbesak and Baghras, important frontier fortresses commanding the Beylan pass north of Antioch, and were actually marching upon the capital itself, its Prince sued for peace. Saladin's army was glutted with booty, and weary of conquest. They had had three months of hard marching and not a little hard fighting. The officers were eager to go home with their spoils, and give their men time to rest and recruit their strength. Like all Moslem armies, it was a married army, and the troops wanted their wives. A truce for eight months was concluded on the 1st of October; the Prince of Antioch released all the Saracen captives in his power, and agreed to deliver up his city if it were not rescued before the end of the truce.†

At Aleppo, the Mesopotamian contingents under the Prince of Sinjar, who had been eager to depart, were dismissed to their homes; and after ovations in the Grey Castle, where Saladin's son ez-Zahir commanded, and at Hamah, which was under his bravest nephew Taki-ed-din, the Sultan returned to Damascus about the 20th of October. He had granted his vassals and kinsmen their well-earned repose, but he took no rest himself that winter. The month of Ramadan was at hand, but even the holy fast must give way to the urgent duty of fighting for the faith. North and south of the Lake of Galilee, Safed and Belvoir still held out against the long blockade of the Moslems. Setting aside the thoughts of rest and home which every Moslem cherishes during the sacred month, and despising the rigours of a Syrian winter, Saladin led his own guard against the Templars' fortress. The Saracens invested the rocky hill of Safed. Rain was falling in torrents, and the ground was a swamp, but the Sultan himself marked out the places for his five mangonels, and refused to sleep till they had been erected. Orderlies went backwards and forwards all night to report the progress of the work. The siege was pressed for a month, night and day without intermission, till the garrison at last surrendered (December 6th). They were suffered to depart to Tyre with the honours of war. Belvoir was next attacked, the fastness "set amid the stars, like a falcon's nest," "the city of barking, whose dogs ever yelped and bears growled."‡ The siege was carried on in storms of rain and wind, with a sea of mud under foot. After heavy losses a breach was at last effected, and the Hospitallers followed the example of the rival Order and capitu-

* Ibn-el-Athir, 729.
† *Itinerary*, i., 13; Baha-ed-din, 117; Imad-ed-din, Goergens, 109.
‡ Abu-Shama, 113.

lated (January 5, 1189). About the same time news arrived that the fortress which had so long troubled the peace of the Moslems, and which Saladin had so often besieged, had at length been starved out: Karak had surrendered to el-Adil. The garrison had been reduced to driving out their women and children, and eating their horses, before they would abandon their trust, though they had themselves been abandoned by the Christians and no lord was there to lead them. It is worthy to record that Saladin sought out these women and children, bought them himself, and gave them back to their stoical kinsmen. Then he sent them all safely into Christian territory.*

Thus the year 1188, after a series of conquests, closed with a triple crown of victory. Belvoir, Safed, and above all Châtillon's once dreaded eyry at Karak, would no longer menace the peaceful merchants and pilgrims on the roads from Egypt and Arabia, and along the Jordan valley. But events soon proved that even these gains did not outweigh the loss which the empire of Saladin was to suffer from the unchecked rallying of the Christians at Tyre.

---

* Baha-ed-din, 118–9; Ibn-el-Athir, 734–8; Ernoul, 187, 255; *Itinerary*, i.,15. Mont Real held out till the following May.

CASTLE OF SAHYUN (SAONE).

CHAPTER XVI

THE BATTLE OF ACRE
1189

W HEN THE FALL of Jerusalem became known in Europe, a universal cry of dismay was heard in every court and camp and village. The black sails of the ship which bore the Archbishop of Tyre, like Theseus of old, from the dismal scene announced from afar the "mortal news."

> "It is hard," says our most learned English authority on Crusading history, "at this distance of time to realise the measure of the disaster in the eyes of the western world. It was not merely that the Holy City had fallen; that all the scenes of that Bible history, which constituted emphatically the literature of medieval Christendom, had passed into the hand of the infidel. It was all this and something more: the little Kingdom of Jerusalem was the one outpost of the Latin Church and Latin culture in the East; it was the creation of those heroes of the First Crusade whose exploits had already been the theme of more than one romance; it lay on the verge of that mysterious East, with all its wealth of gold and precious stones and merchandise, towards which the sword of the twelfth-century knight turned as instinctively as the prow of the English or Spanish adventurer turned four centuries later towards the West. . . . Palestine inspired alike the imagination, the enterprise, and the faith of western Christendom."*

To recover what had been lost became the passionate desire of each pious knight, the ambition of every adventurer. The Pope issued a trumpet-call for a new Crusade, which should wash out every sin. Richard of England, then Count of Poitou, was the first to take the Cross. The Kings of England and France made up their quarrel and received the sacred badge from the Archbishop of Tyre. Baldwin of Canterbury preached the Crusade, in which he was later to die before Acre, and a "Saladin tax," a tithe of every man's wealth, was collected throughout the length and breadth of the land. The eloquence of Berter of Orléans roused the enthusiasm of France, which re-echoed with his chant—

---

* T. A. Archer, in *Crusades*, 305–6.

"Lignum crucis
signum ducis
sequitur exercitus,
quod non cessit
sed præcessit
in vi sancti spiritus."*

The zeal of Christendom was readily kindled, but its armies were slow to move. William of Sicily had been prompt to succour Tripolis; but England and France resumed their standing strife, and their sovereigns did not begin their leisurely Crusade till the summer of 1190. Alone among the great princes of Europe, the Emperor Frederick Barbarossa, whose seventy years had not quenched the fire of a chivalrous nature, led a vast army from Germany through the territory of the Greeks in May, 1189, but the brave old warrior met his death in the swift waters of the Salef, and only a remnant of his host slowly struggled onwards to the battle-fields of Palestine.

Meanwhile the Franks at the seat of war had not been idle. Queen Sibylla had claimed from Saladin the performance of the promise made at Ascalon; and her husband Guy with his ten fellow-prisoners at Damascus were brought before the Sultan at Tortosa in July, 1188, and after they had pledged their knightly honour never to bear arms against him, they were suffered to go free.† The Marquess of Montferrat was sent to his son at Tyre; Humphrey of Toron was restored to his mother, the widow of Reginald of Châtillon; and King Guy and his brother, with the Master of the Temple, joined Sibylla and concerted plans of vengeance at Tripolis and Antioch. They were all duly absolved from their oath‡ and lost no time in rewarding Saladin's good faith and generosity after their usual manner. A number of knights and volunteers gathered round Guy's standard and at their head the King and Queen proceeded to Tyre. Conrad of Montferrat, however, flatly refused to recognise their authority or to admit them into his city, which, he said, God had given into his charge. The King and Queen were forced to camp outside, and after some successful skirmishes with the outposts of the Saracens, who were lying before Belfort (Shekif Arnun) some fifteen miles off, Guy summoned the Sicilian fleet to follow him along the coast, and boldly marched upon Acre in August, 1189.

---

* See the vigorous sketch of this Crusade in Archer and Kingsford, 305 ff., and for the Archbishop's mission, Ernoul, 244 ff.

† Ernoul, 252–3; Baha-ed-din, 122–3.

‡ "The king was released by the sentence of the clergy from the enormity of his promise." *Itinerary*, i., 25.

The King's force was very inferior to the army which Saladin could bring against him. The estimates of the various chroniclers differ, and none, probably, can be taken as more than a very rough guess, but the statement in the "Itinerary" is perhaps as good as any other. Guy's army, including the Pisans of Tyre who had thrown in their lot with the King, is there reckoned at 9000 men of all nations, of whom 700 were knights; but in a few days "the Morning Star visited them from on high; for behold fifty ships, such as are commonly called coggs, having 12,000 men on board, are seen approaching." These were Danes and Frisians, "men of large limbs, invincible resolution, and fervent devotion."* The total was thus 21,000. Baha-ed-din estimated the Frank army at the same date at 2000 knights and 30,000 foot, and adds that he never heard anyone put them at a lower figure, and that "they were constantly reinforced by sea." It was true, for the famous knight James of Avesnes, "a Nestor in counsel, an Achilles in arms, and in honour a Regulus," soon joined the besiegers; and so did the Bishop of Beauvais, "who strove to be a Turpin, if he could but find a Charles," with many others. The Christians placed Saladin's army at a much larger number than their own, but neither side attempts to give accurate figures.

It is time to inquire what Saladin was doing to allow the assembling of the King's forces, and to let him advance upon Acre. After the surrender of Belvoir in January, 1189, the Sultan with his brother el-Adil visited Jerusalem and kept the Feast of Sacrifice there; he then inspected Ascalon, and stayed at Acre till March. He had placed his old officer Karakush, the founder of the citadel of Cairo, as commandant, with a garrison of tried veterans from Egypt and having ordered the repair of the walls of the great coast fortress, which was to be the capital of Palestine, returned to Damascus. In April, in an evil moment, he set out to reduce Belfort, a strong castle of the Templars, east of Tyre, which was the only inland fortress remaining to the Christians, except the famous Crac des Chevaliers perched on an inaccessible crag of the Lebanon, which defied the Moslems till 1285. If Saladin consulted an augury in the Koran on this occasion, as was his custom, the sacred book led him grievously astray. The place might have been masked by a moderate force whilst the Sultan devoted his energies to the far more important task of crushing the King's small army before it grew too strong. As it was, four precious months were wasted in front of Belfort, whilst the memory of Hittin, already two years old, was suffered to fade from Christian minds, and the enemy waxed bolder every day.

---

* *Itinerary*, i., 26, 27.

Reginald of Sidon, one of the few survivors of Hittin, commanded at Belfort, and he rendered an invaluable service to the cause. He saw that the great thing was to gain time, and being a wily diplomatic person, he set to work to "throw dust" in the good Sultan's eyes. He spoke Arabic, and had studied the history and literature of the Moslems. His intelligence was only equalled by his fascinating manners. Using these advantages, he came to Saladin's tent, professed himself his devoted servant, and promised to surrender the castle without a blow, if only he were allowed three months to bring his family and dependents from Tyre, for whom he dreaded the Marquess's revenge. After the surrender, there was nothing he would like better than to live at Damascus, at the Sultan's gracious Court,—with a suitable maintenance. Indeed, in his many conversations, the clever rogue discovered Saladin's blind side: he began to discuss serious questions of religion, and Saladin reasoned with him, and doubtless cherished the hope, dear to the lay missionary, of bringing a convert to the true faith.

The Sultan's "intelligence department" must have been singularly incompetent not to have warned him that the governor of Belfort was a particular friend and ally of the Marquess of Montferrat, and was not in the least likely to intrigue against him. Doubts, at last, of his fascinating guest began to disturb Saladin's mind, but he was pledged to the three months' truce, and could do nothing till it expired. It was then discovered that Reginald had been playing with him all the time, and that while the worthy governor had been opening his mind to theological debate the garrison had been strengthening the fortifications;—the castle was further from capitulating than ever. It was a melancholy disillusionment, and Saladin showed unusual generosity in sparing the diplomatist's life and only putting him into chains; but in the mean while April had passed into August, and King Guy was ready to advance upon Acre.

There had been ample notice of the attack. The King's movements about Tyre were no secret; Saladin had his outposts there, and early in July there had been more than one skirmish with his troops at the bridge over the Litany. Saladin was in the habit of riding out every day to reconnoitre, for his camp at Marj Oyun was within easy reach of the coast as well as of Belfort, and he had himself witnessed one of these encounters in which the Franks had the advantage.* He had even made a rapid ride to Acre in July, to order further fortifications, and enjoin the utmost watchfulness upon the garrison. He was clearly alive to the danger of a Christian attack. Yet he kept his army before Belfort until the guile of its governor was exposed, and it was not till the 27th of August,

---

* Baha-ed-din, 124–5.

after hearing that the Franks were actually on their way, that he finally gave orders for the march to Acre. He left a sufficient force to blockade Belfort, which surrendered seven months later, and no doubt he might have masked it in the same fashion three months before, and gone to meet the enemy.*

At last, however, the Saracens were on the road and marching night and day. They took the easy route by Tiberias, and then struck across by the great west road past Kafar Kenna (Cana) to el-Kharruba.† where they picked up a division which had come by the mountains of Toron to watch the enemy. Detachment after detachment was sent on, and men and stores were thrown into the threatened fortress; and the whole army was camped on the hills over against Acre three days after their departure from Belfort. King Guy had arrived there two days earlier, on the 28th, the feast of St. Augustine, and had established his camp on "Mount Turon," the Hill of Prayers (Tell el-Musalliyin), now Tell el-Fokhkhar, just opposite the city gate. Saladin's object was to outflank the enemy—to besiege the besiegers; he extended his lines from the river Belus to the hill of el-Ayyadiya, placing his headquarters on Tell Keysan; after a month he moved further north, so as to stretch his lines as far as the coast above Acre, and making his headquarters at el-Ayyadiya.

"If a ten years' war made Troy renowned; if the triumph of the Christians ennobled Antioch; surely to Acre belongs eternal fame—the city for which the whole world contended." It stands on a tongue of land jutting out to the southward, behind which the Mina or harbour is sheltered from the west and north. The northern or Musart quarter was not built in Saladin's time and the city measured three-quarters of a mile by a quarter;‡ strong walls and towers protected the city from the land, east and north; the sea washed the other sides. Among the defences, the *Turris Maledicta* or Accursed Tower at the north-east angle was so named because legend connected it with the bribe of Judas; and

---

* Baha-ed-din, wise after the event, remembers at a later page (152) of his history that he heard Saladin urge the council of war at Marj Oyun to adopt his counsel and attack the enemy on the march, before they could entrench themselves; but the council preferred to wait till the Franks were in position before Acre. Baha-ed-din, however, writes as a hero-worshipper, and the story has an *ex post facto* air. Its repetition with variations by Ibn-el-Athir (ii., 6) is perhaps a slight confirmation.

† El-Kharruba, an important position during Saladin's Acre campaign, is not found in the maps. The name means "the carob tree" and may have been given to many places where such trees grew. It was certainly a hill on the road between Saffuriya and Acre (Abu-Shama, 121) in the mountain range which borders the plain on its east side. The camp at Acre could be seen from this position, according to Baha-ed-din. Probably it should be placed some way north of Shafraamm, not far from the present Abelin.

‡ In the 11th century, Nasir-i Khusrau, ed. Schefer, 12.

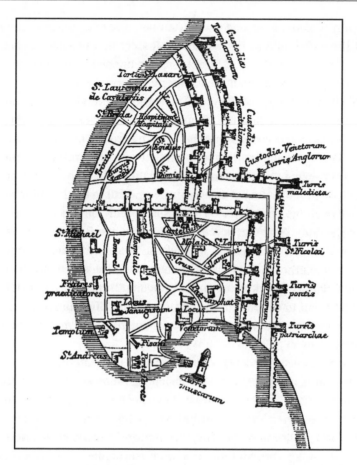

PLAN OF ACRE IN THE 13TH CENTURY.

the harbour was guarded by a chain and by a formidable rock fort, called the Tower of Flies, for the unsavoury reason that it had once been a famous place of sacrifice. The ramparts of the city overlooked the great plain of Acre, twenty miles from north to south, watered by the two great branches of the river Belus, with numerous tributary streams, and bounded on the south by the Kishon running parallel with the great barrier of Mount Carmel and falling into the sea at Haifa at the extremity of the bay. Isolated hills of no great height afford military positions at a distance of about five miles from the coast, and a couple of miles behind these the southern prolongation of the Lebanon range formed the eastern boundary of the plain, and served Saladin at once as a refuge from the malaria of the lowlands in winter, a retreat from superior forces, and a post of vantage and observation.

The Franks were not strong enough at this time to completely blockade the city, and the right wing of the Saracens, under the ever-valiant Taki-ed-din, easily forced their way in (15–16 Sept.). Saladin himself entered Acre and examined the enemy's position from the ramparts. Baha-ed-din also visited the fortress: "I climbed to the top of the wall," he says, "as every one did, and thence I hurled at the enemy the first thing that came to hand." The place was strongly garrisoned and well provisioned, and there was no present fear of its being stormed or starved. Perpetual skirmishing went on between the armies, and the soldiers on both sides became so accustomed to these little affairs that they would sometimes break off in the middle of an encounter and fall to talking. When they were tired of skirmishing, they diverted themselves with pitting boys of each side against each other, that they too might share in the fun, and the lads had a furious tussle whilst their elders formed the ring in a strictly sportsmanlike manner.* On the other hand we read of barbarous deeds on both sides—of wild Bedawis in Saladin's pay, who fell upon straggling Christians, cut off their heads, and brought them to the Sultan for reward; and of Christian women, dragging Turkish prisoners by the hair, shamefully misusing them, and hacking off their heads with knives.†

These varied encounters led up to a general engagement, which very nearly brought the war to an end. On the 4th of October, soon after sunrise, the Franks were in motion. Their army was extended in a semi-circle round Acre, over a line of fully two miles, from the sea to the river Belus, to match the length of the concentric Saracen line of battle. Their archers and cross-bowmen were as usual in front, and the knights and infantry were marshalled in close order behind them. They advanced in four divisions. The King commanded the right, with the Gospel borne before him under a canopy of satin. The two centre divisions were under Conrad of Montferrat and Louis, Landgrave of Thuringia, whilst the Templars mustered on the left. Saladin himself commanded the Moslem centre, with his sons el-Afdal and ez-Zafir on his right hand. On the right of the centre were the contingents from Mosil and Diyar-Bekr; and the right wing resting on the sea consisted of the fine troops of northern Syria under Saladin's best general, his nephew Taki-ed-din. The left of the centre was composed of Kurdish clans from the Tigris led by their chiefs, with the levies from Sinjar, and Kukbury's retainers from Harran; whilst the left wing was formed by picked veterans from Shirkuh's mamluks, the old conquerors of Egypt. Thus the most critical posts, the extreme right and left, were confided to the flower of the Saracen army; but

* Baha-ed-din, 139.
† Ibn-el-Athir, ii., 9; *Itinerary*, i., 34.

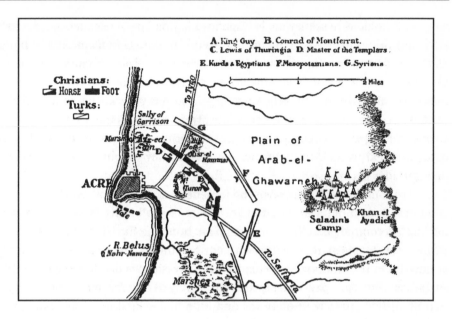

THE BATTLE OF ACRE, OCT. 4, 1189.
(FROM OMAN'S "ART OF WAR.")

the centre, apart from Saladin's bodyguard, contained doubtful elements in the less tried levies from Mesopotamia and Kurdistan.

The battle of Acre began at the fourth hour after sunrise with an attack of the Franks upon the Saracens' right wing. Instead of waiting for them, Taki-ed-din ordered his men back, in accordance with the usual Turkish tactics, intending to draw the enemy on, and then manœuvre to take them in flank. Saladin unfortunately mistook this movement for retreat, and sent part of his centre in support. Thus reinforced the left were able to drive the Franks in. But meanwhile the enemy had noted the weakening of Saladin's centre, and seizing the opportunity advanced upon it in strength, horse and foot keeping solidly together. When they came to close quarters, the infantry opened out, the knights rode through, and delivered the full shock of a mailed charge upon the Saracens. The brunt of this heavy attack fell upon the men from Diyar-Bekr, who broke in disorder and fled from the field: they were next heard from at the bridge by the Lake of Galilee, well on their way to Damascus! The knights, hot-headed and undisciplined as ever, pursued the flying enemy up the headquarters hill, rummaged the camp, and entered Saladin's tent, where the fiery Count de Bar disported himself in triumph. Looking round, they discovered that their charge had not been supported, and that they were separated from their friends. They had now to get back as best they could. Saladin's left had been untouched, and still stood firm. He rallied what remained of his centre, and held them tight in hand till the victorious Franks were passing on their return from his camp; then with his famous battle-cry of "*Yála-l-Islam,*" he hurled his whole force on their rear, calling up his right and his left wings to join in the general charge, whilst the garrison of Acre made a well-timed sortie. The result was the utter rout of the enemy. Seeing their comrades running, the other divisions were seized with panic and fled to their camp on the hill, where they just managed to beat off their pursuers.*

In the tumult the King himself rescued his rival, Conrad of Montferrat, from imminent danger. Andrew of Brienne, the pink of chivalry, was slain whilst rallying his comrades, in the very sight of his brother, who left him to his fate. A trooper saw James of Avesnes thrown from his charger and in utmost jeopardy; he gave him his own horse to escape on, and "by his own death nobly saved his lord's life." But the most notable loss that day was the Master of the Temple. Gerard of Rideford, whose ambition and hate had stirred up strife among the Christians and brought death to many a Saracen, ended his stormy life on the field of Acre. He refused to fly, and died like a soldier. Even women fought manfully on horseback beside their brothers in arms, nor were they discovered till they were made prisoners.† It was a day of Heroes and of Amazons. The Franks confessed to a loss of 1500 killed; but Baha-ed-din, who saw their bodies being carried to the river to be thrown in,‡ estimated their dead at over 4000. On the Moslems' side the loss was more by flight than slaughter. The Diyar-Bekr contingent had vanished; but of the rest, only the leader of the Kurds and one other emir were recorded as killed, with about 150 undistinguished warriors. Panic will account for a good deal, but the disproportion of these estimates is inartistic. The Christian estimate of the Moslem loss at 1500 horsemen is more consistent with the accounts of the battle.

---

* The battle is described with remarkable clearness by Baha-ed-din (140–6), who was present; but he does not mention any sortie of the garrison of Acre; this may be a mistake in the confused account in the *Itinerary* (i., 29, 30), which otherwise agrees in the main outlines with the Arabic description. What happened to the Christian right and left, after the advance of the centre divisions, is not clear; but in his admirable *History of the Art of War*, ii., 336, Mr. Oman has put forward a very ingenious explanation of the defeat of the Templars on the left by the garrison of Acre.

† Ibn-el-Athir, ii., 13.

‡ He says the man in charge of the dead-carts counted 4100 odd bodies from the left wing alone of the Franks. Imad-ed-din reckoned the total Christian loss at 10,000 (Goergens, 124), but round figures are to be distrusted

CHAPTER XVII

THE SIEGE OF ACRE
1189–1191

AFTER THE BATTLE Saladin failed to push his victory home. He even allowed the panic-stricken enemy to throw up earthworks and entrench themselves more securely, whilst he let his men rest, and restored order in the rifled camp. The army, it seems, was in no mood to follow up its success. It was exhausted, and the robbing of the camp by their own followers (who left little or nothing for the pursuing Templars) had exasperated the men. A week later a council of war was held, and the Sultan addressed the generals:

> "In the name of God, and praise be to God, and blessing on the Apostle of God.
> "Know that this enemy of God, and our enemy, hath entered our country and trampled on the soil of Islam: but already the star of victory (if God please) hath gleamed upon us. There remains but a handful of their force, and we must diligently destroy it. By God, it is our bounden duty! Ye know that this our army can now look for reinforcement only to el-Melik el-Adil, who is coming. As for the enemy, if it is left to hold its position till the sea is open, vast increase will come to it. My judgment is that we fight them. Each of you give his."

The council was divided, and there was much debate, but at last it was resolved to withdraw the army to the hills, to give the men rest, after fifty days under arms; when they were refreshed and the deserters had been brought in, the attack should be renewed. Once more Saladin allowed his sound judgment to be overruled by the council. He may have been more in their hands than is acknowledged; he certainly had a difficult task in keeping together so mixed a force and reconciling the jealousies and discontent of rival leaders and races. But the best explanation of his yielding to so unsoldierlike a decision, is that he was seriously ill. He was subject to violent attacks of what the Arab chroniclers call "colic,"—more probably the malignant Syrian fever,—and his doctors joined the emirs in counselling a change of air.* The constant fatigues and anxieties of the past two years had told heavily upon him. He was over fifty, and he had worked harder than any of his men. His long rides over the country and expo-

---

* Ibn-el-Athir, ii., 14.

sure to all weathers, the winter sieges he had undertaken, the forced march upon Acre in a sultry August, and at last the daily encounters with the Franks, where he was always in the thick of the fight, carrying heavy armour, and for days was too preoccupied to think of proper food*—all this was enough to wear out a younger man. But for this untoward weakness, Saladin might have insisted on carrying out his plan, and the result could hardly have been doubtful. Broken in spirits and crippled by the loss of thousands of their men, shut in between the Saracen army and the well-armed walls of Acre, the Crusaders must have suffered a second Hittin, from which there was no recovery: they must have been driven into the sea. The fatal error before Tyre was repeated before Acre. The Franks were given time to entrench themselves, and to hold the ground till reinforcements came. The siege might have been brought to a summary end on the 5th of October, 1189, instead of dragging on its weary length for nearly two more years, crowned at last by the victory of the Crusaders.

The retreat to the hills of el-Kharruba on October 16th meant more than a temporary rest. The rains began, and nothing further was done until the spring. The winter months were spent by the Franks in strengthening their position by digging a great trench, not without harassing interruption, and by Saladin in beating up recruits. El-Adil joined him with an Egyptian contingent, and Admiral Lulu, coming to Acre with fifty sail from Alexandria, captured a couple of valuable prizes, and landed a naval brigade of 10,000 sailors to harass the enemy.† Fighting soon became out of the. question, as the mud was so deep that the two armies could not get at one another. The Sultan visited Acre again in great state, and looked to its defences and stores, and then, dismissing his troops to their homes, remained at el-Kharruba with his guard till the spring reopened the sea and the roads. Meanwhile a fresh cause for anxiety had arisen. News had arrived of the march of Frederick Barbarossa through Asia Minor, and the letter of the Armenian Catholicos—who, like the Emperor of Constantinople, was on the side of Saladin—announcing the tragical death of the old Crusader, also informed the Sultan that Frederick's son was leading the army on into Syria. Had the extreme weakness of the remnant of the German host been known to the Sultan, he would hardly have crippled his fine army by sending a large division to cut off their approach. In response to his appeal and the efforts of his secretary Baha-ed-din, who visited the Caliph and the princes of Mesopotamia in the winter, and summoned all men to the Holy War, the troops from Aleppo, Harran, Sinjar, Jezira, Mosil, and Irbil, had been pouring into his camp (now at

* Baha-ed-din, 137, 147
† Imad-ed-din, Abu-Shama, 127.

Tell el-Ajjul near el-Ayyadiya) all May and June. The Caliph of Baghdad had sent lances and arrows and machines that discharged burning shafts. But the Syrian contingents were almost immediately sent north again to meet the imaginary danger of the German invasion, and the more urgent necessity of crushing the besiegers—who were really themselves closely besieged by the Moslems—before they could be reinforced, was neglected. The Crusading army must have been more formidable in reality than it reads in the chronicles to have thus intimidated the Saracens; indeed, the account of the eight days' fighting at Pentecost shows that the two sides must have been fairly matched.*

Saladin's mistake became painfully obvious when Henry of Champagne effected his landing at the end of July, with 10,000 men, and a number of knights, nobles, and fighting prelates. Up to this time the situation had remained unchanged; though partly surrounded, Acre was not cut off from communication with Saladin's forces, which in turn surrounded the enemy; and the skirmishes and sallies, the attacks on the trenches and destruction of siege-engines, had on the whole been in favour of the Saracens. The ingenuity of a young coppersmith of Damascus, who possessed the secret of making a kind of Greek fire, which burned up the enemy's siege-towers and machines, delighted Saladin, and still more did the young man's answer, when he offered him riches, that he would take no reward for what he had done in the cause of God. A fleet from Alexandria had successfully fought its way into the harbour in June, and replenished the stores of the besieged; and an attempt to surprise the right wing of the Moslem camp, weakened by the departure of the troops for the north, was repulsed by el-Adil with very heavy loss on the feast of St. James (25th July). At least four thousand of the Christians fell on that day, by their own admission†; but the Arabic eyewitnesses estimated the loss at more than double. Among the slain were some women, in armour, who had fought valiantly beside the knights. Imad-ed-din long afterwards recalled the piercing screams of a woman whom he saw dying on the field. But Saladin evidently did not feel himself strong enough to order a general assault of the King's entrenchments; the Franks could not be tempted again to risk a pitched battle; and two days after this engagement Count Henry arrived and took command of the army.

This large reinforcement, the first of several soon to follow, changed the situation. Saladin drew his army off once more to the hills (1 August), and Acre

---

* *Itinerary*, i., 38; Ibn-el-Athir, ii., 18.

† Letter of Archbp. Baldwin's chaplain, 21 Oct., 1191 (*Epp. Cantuar.*, 329). Imad-ed-din rode over the battle-field in the company of Baha-ed-din, and reckoned the number of the Christians slain to be 10,000 (Abu-Shama, 137),

was so far cut off that communications could only be maintained by the pigeon post, by strong swimmers, or by swift skiffs at night. It was small consolation to the Sultan to receive a friendly letter from his futile ally, the Greek Emperor Isaac, bidding him "not let the coming of the Germans weigh heavily on your hearts: their plans and purposes will work their own confusion"*: the French at least were already on the spot and had put Acre under strict blockade. Saracen ships indeed still forced their way in to the relief of the garrison; one was smuggled in under a French disguise, but generally they had to run the gauntlet. One such adventure happened in September. Three Egyptian *dromonds* or ships of burthen opportunely arrived, when there was not enough food in the city to last another day. The Christian galleys were upon the new-comers in a moment. The beach was lined with the Moslem army, calling aloud upon God to save the ships. The Sultan himself stood there in an agony of suspense, watching the struggle, "like a parent robbed of his child." The battle raged, but fortunately for the garrison there was a fair wind, and at last the three ships sailed into the harbour safe and sound, amid the furious shouts of the enemy and the loud thanksgivings of the Faithful.

Once in port they were protected by the celebrated Tower of Flies, which stood on a rock at the entrance to the harbour, and effectually shielded every vessel that got past it. The Crusaders retorted by a determined effort to destroy this obnoxious defence. The Pisans among them, ever adroit in seamanship, rigged tip turrets on their galleys, tall enough to overlook the Fly Tower, and to bombard or set it on fire, whilst a fire-ship was sent into the harbour to destroy the Saracen vessels which might put out to interfere. The device, however, failed signally. The Pisans managed to grapple the tower, and to get their scaling ladders up, under cover of a heavy bombardment from their turrets; but just as they were counting on success, the defenders rallied, crushed the storming party on the ladders with great rocks, and throwing their Greek fire, set ladders, turrets, and galleys in a blaze, amid the derisive shouts of the Moslems. The fire-ship went astray on a foul wind and was easily extinguished and captured.

At the beginning of October the dreaded Germans made their appearance: Frederick Duke of Suabia arrived at Acre with a bare thousand men. Inconsiderable as was this relief, the presence of Barbarossa's son raised the spirits of the besiegers, and his energy infused new zeal into the war. Nothing at first would content him but an engagement with the enemy in the open; but Saladin's advance guard, still posted at el-Ayyadiya, aided by the men of Mosil, who were

---

* Abu-Shama, 144.

ordered forward from Tell Keysan, beat back the Crusaders with little trouble. After this failure they turned their energies to pressing the siege with much ingenuity. For the first time they employed a battering ram—the garrison of Acre had evidently become very weak to allow them to get to close quarters: it was a huge beam with an iron head which weighed nearly three hundredweight, and had been constructed at great expense by the Archbishop of Besançon. Another ram, or bore, called the "cat," with a plough-shaped pointed head, and a penthouse or "sow" to cover a number of men, was also set to work; and a ship was fitted with a turret and drawbridge, to be dropped on to the Fly Tower. A grand assault was made early in October; the new machines were dragged up to the city, and the assailants dropped into the fosse to scale the walls; when the garrison suddenly opened a heavy fire of arrows, fireballs, stones, and bolts from bows, mangonels, slings, and arbalests, and sallying out in desperation drove the Franks back; then laying naphtha to the cat and ram they set them ablaze, and finally dragged the flaming ram in triumph within the gate.

The rejoicing of the garrison was almost immediately damped by the arrival of more reinforcements from Europe. At last an English fleet hove in sight. Baldwin, Archbishop of Canterbury, Hubert Walter, Bishop of Salisbury, and the Justiciar, Ranulf de Glanville, had reached Tyre with men and stores and money in September, and coming to the army before Acre on the 12th of October, announced that the Kings of England and France were verily on their way to the Holy Land. The Archbishop's chaplain gave a sorry picture of the Crusaders' camp:

> "We found our army (I say it with grief and groaning) given up to shameful practices, and yielding to ease and lust rather than encouraging virtue. The Lord is not in the camp; there is none that doeth good. The chiefs envy one another, and strive for privilege. The lesser folk are in want and find no one to help them. In the camp there is neither chastity, sobriety, faith, nor charity—a state of things which, I call God to witness, I would not have believed had I not seen it. The Turks are besieging us, and daily do they challenge us and persist in attacking us, while our knights lie skulking within their tents, and like conquered men let the enemy affront them with impunity. Saladin's strength is increasing daily, whereas our army daily grows smaller."*

The coming of the English put some spirit into the "skulking knights." The churchmen stirred up their zeal, if they could not mend their morals; the venerable Archbishop himself raised the standard of the holy martyr, St. Thomas of Canterbury, and sent the army forth with his blessing to do battle; whilst the

---

* *Epp. Cantuar.* ed. Stubbs, 328–9; Archer, *Crusade of Richard I.*, 18.

Bishop of Salisbury and many other priests and prelates manfully took part in the fight.* A general action near the Spring Head (or source of the southern branch of the river Belus), about six miles south of Acre, began on "the morrow of St. Martin's," the 12th of November. The enemy's object was to bring in provisions from Haifa, for they were running very short of food. Seeing them advancing in force, the Saracen outpost, after a sharp skirmish, withdrew from their usual station at el-Ayyadiya to Tell Keysan, and on the 13th, the army formed up in two positions almost facing each other and enclosing the enemy who nevertheless advanced to the Spring Head. Saladin's left wing stretched across from near the sea to the Belus, facing north-east, whilst the right, posted on the hills, faced west towards the river, which it touched on the east bank near the bridge of Da'uk. The centre was thrown forward beneath Saladin's reserve, which with his headquarters were on the summit of Mount Kharruba, whence he could view the whole plain below; and he also held the hill of Shafraamm, once a Templars' stronghold. This situation was maintained on the 14th, when the Franks, hearing that there was no food at Haifa, turned back by the east bank and made for the bridge of Da'uk. They were closely hemmed in by the Saracens all the way, whose light horse assailed them at close quarters with mace, sword, and lance, striving to break the solid and orderly formation†; and Saladin continually sent down supports from the hills behind; but they pluckily forced their way to the bridge, camped there for the night, and cutting it behind them on the morrow, retired much exhausted but in good order, and carrying many wounded, to their entrenchments. Here they were covered by their reserves, who came out under Godfrey de Lusignan, and drove back the Moslems' pursuit. Conrad and Henry of Champagne had themselves led the expedition, but the Franks had suffered heavily. Among the killed was a knight whose appearance astonished Baha-ed-din: he rode a charger with housings of chain mail to its hoofs. Saladin's picked guard had also lost severely.

Indecisive as the action was, it encouraged the Saracens, who wished immediately to follow it up. It was evidently a critical test, of doubtful issue, for Saladin had sent his baggage for safety to the rear, towards Nazareth; and the fact that he was himself again ill with colic or fever, and could not take part in the battle, added to his anxiety. Yet he kept his invincible spirit; and when some one spoke of the sufferings and deaths of the Moslems from the unhealthy state of the plain, he quoted the Arab proverb, "Kill me and Malik; kill Malik with me," allud-

---

* *Itinerary*, i., 62.

† The best account of the engagement at the Spring Head is by Imad-ed-din; *see* Abu-Sbama, 162–4, and Baha-ed-din.

ing to a famous historical combat in which the hero called upon his comrades to kill the adversary struggling with him on the ground, even if they also killed himself. Saladin was ready to die, with all his host, if only the Franks died too.*
Yet when some Crusaders of rank were taken in an ambush a little later, Saladin received them with stately courtesy, clothed them in robes of honour, gave them furs to keep out the bitter cold, allowed them to write to the camp for anything they wanted, and sent them in high good humour to Damascus. It was better to be the guest of Saladin than to shiver and starve in a Christian tent.

The winter of 1190–1, which stopped all active operations, was passed in great misery by the Crusaders. Many of their chiefs were dead. They had lost their Queen, Sibylla; Ranulf de Glanville, the earl of Ferrers, the earl of Clare's brother, among the English, were no more; and the aged Archbishop of Canterbury died in November, grieved unto death at the licence around him. Conrad of Montferrat had attained the first step in his ambition by his unscrupulous marriage with Isabella, now the heiress to the crown of Jerusalem, whose divorce from Humphrey of Toron he had successfully contrived; he then withdrew to Tyre to nourish schemes of kingship, leaving the army before Acre to its fate. The English "Itinerary" is full of curses upon the Marquess for his callous indifference to the perishing people, whom he might perhaps have relieved. For famine and disease were working havoc behind the entrenchments. Corn was selling for a hundred pieces of gold the sack, and a single egg cost six deniers. The greedy merchants kept up the prices, and the camp was starving. Blood horses were slaughtered for food, nor did the hungry people despise even the entrails of animals that died from age or disease. They ate grass like cattle, fought over the bakers' ovens, gnawed the bare bones abandoned by the dogs. Even nobles were reduced to stealing, and a pitiful story is told of how two friends, having come to their last coin, spent it on the purchase of thirteen beans and then, finding one bean bad, went a long way back to the seller to insist on his replacing it with a good one. A few even sought relief by going over to Islam. The prelates and some of the better nobles made contributions for the poor, but it was little they could do. This state of wretchedness, aggravated by the sickness and ague bred by perpetual rains, lasted until Lent, 1191, when at last the sea became navigable to the timid seamen of those days, and a cornship saved the camp from starvation.†

Meanwhile Saladin had dismissed most of his army to their homes, and remained only with his own guard. The Mesopotamian princes were the first to

---

* Baha-ed-din, 196–201.
† *Itinerary*, i., 67 ff.

leave in November: they had been with difficulty induced to stay so long. It was not to be expected that the vanquished descendants of Zengy should show much enthusiasm in their supplanter's service; but apart from such natural jealousy, Oriental troops cannot endure being long separated from their wives and homes The provisioning of Acre was Saladin's chief occupation during the winter. The Christian galleys had gone to escort Conrad to Tyre for his wedding, and the city was open to the sea. An Egyptian convoy failed to get in in December, but el-Adil, stationed at Haifa, contrived to send in stores, and Saladin in February introduced a fresh garrison under a new commander. The new garrison, however, was smaller than the old; many more came out than went in; nor were the newcomers adept in siege-work, and Saladin was accused of imprudence and carelessness in leaving too much to incompetent or interested subordinates.* Probably he was still suffering from the effects of illness. The relieving of Acre was not accomplished without assaults from the Franks, whose misery did not wholly paralyse their energy, for the famine was not then at its worst. On the other hand the garrison repulsed their attacks, and Saladin captured a few stray ships, aided by some deserters from the enemy's camp.†

So the weary winter months passed by. The spring found the contending forces in the same position: the city well garrisoned, and for the present sufficiently provisioned; Saladin on the hills, waiting for the return of his troops; the Christians, between the two, weakened, dispirited, and demoralised, but holding their entrenched camp unmolested, save for occasional sallies of the garrison or skirmishes with Saladin's outposts. The summer brought a complete revolution in the relations of the two forces, and the Saracens were soon to find themselves no longer the besiegers of the besieged, but the attacked. The Crusade of Richard Cœur de Lion was at hand.

---

* Ibn-el-Athir, ii., 33; Imad-ed-din, Abu-Shama, 165.
† Baha-ed-din, 207.

PART V

RICHARD AND SALADIN
1191–1192

CHAPTER XVIII

THE LOSS OF ACRE
1191

RICHARD OF ENGLAND and Philip of France were at last approaching the Holy Land. They had set out in the summer of 1190, but their advance was as leisurely as a yachting cruise. The long delays at Messina and at Cyprus, the subjection of the one and the conquest of the other, and the marriage with Berengaria, are commonplaces of history, but they nearly allowed the destruction of the army before Acre. A honeymoon at Cyprus was a strange manner of rescuing a starving camp. The King of France was the first to arrive. He was welcomed at Easter "with hymns and songs and floods of tears, as if he were an angel of God." He at once set up his siege-engines, and in May the city was assailed with renewed energy. Saladin's Chancellor records in a letter how the Franks attacked with wooden towers, stone-slings, rams, and other engines; how they strove by day to break the walls, and by night toiled in the trenches, filling up the moat, setting up scaling ladders, desisting neither by day nor night. They began to build an earthen dyke, which was like a wall, with round towers, and was heightened with wood and stones. It started from their camp, and as it progressed they dug the earth from behind it and cast it in front, and so pushed it forward to within half a bowshot of the ramparts. Neither stones nor fire had the least effect on it.* But whilst pressing the siege with vigour, Philip courteously awaited Richard's arrival before beginning the general assault.

How Cœur de Lion at last sailed from Cyprus to Acre, and how the siege was crowned with success, may best be read in the contemporary "Itinerary of Richard," which, however biased in favour of England's hero, presents the most detailed and picturesque narrative of the great siege that we possess.†

"And so, having concluded these matters, Richard straightway turned his thoughts towards his passage across [to the Holy Land]; and, when he had arranged his

---

* Letter from Kady el-Fadil, Abu-Shama, 173.

† The translations here extracted from the *Itinerary*, Bk. ii, c. 42, to Bk. iii., c. 18, are quoted by permission from Mr. T. A. Archer's admirable *Crusade of Richard I.*, in the series entitled "English History by Contemporary Writers" (1888).

baggage, set sail with a favourable wind. . . . And lo! there now went abroad a report that Acre was on the point of being taken; upon hearing which the king with a deep sigh prayed God that the city might not fall before his arrival, 'for,' he said, 'after so long a siege our triumph ought, God willing, to be one of exceptional glory.' Then with great haste he went on board one of the best and largest of his galleys at Famagusta, and being impatient of delay, as he always was, he kept right ahead, though other and better appointed galleys followed him from every side. And so, as they were furrowing the sea with all haste, they caught their earliest glimpse of that Holy Land of Jerusalem. The castle of Margat was the first to meet their eyes; then Tortosa, set on the sea-shore, Tripolis, Nephyn, Botron, and not long after the lofty tower of Gibeleth. At last on this side of Sidon near Beyrut they descried afar off a certain ship filled with Saladin's choicest warriors, the pick out of all his pagan realm, and destined to bring aid to the besieged in Acre. Seeing that they could not make direct for Acre on account of the nearness of the Christians, the Saracens drew back to sea a little and waited their time to make a sudden rush into the harbour. Richard, who had taken note of the ship, calling up one of his galley-men, Peter des Barres, bade him row hastily and enquire who commanded it. Word was brought back that it belonged to the king of France; but Richard, as he drew near eagerly, could neither hear any French word nor see any Christian standard or banner. As it approached he began to wonder at its size, its firm and solid build. For it was set off with three masts of great height and its smoothly wrought sides were decked here and there with green or yellow hides.* Added to which it was so well rigged out with every fitting appointment and so well furnished with provisions of every kind as to leave no room for improvement. . . .

"At the king's command a galley started after the strange ship at full speed. Seeing this, its sailors began to hurl arrows and darts against the crew of the galley, as it drew up alongside of them without offering any greeting. Noting this, Richard gave the word for an immediate onset. On either side the missiles fell like rain and the strange ship now went on at a slower rate, for the oarsmen had to slacken their efforts and there was not much wind. And yet, frequently as our galleymen made their circuits round the enemy, they could find no good opportunity of attacking; so strongly was the vessel built and so well was it manned with warriors, who kept on hurling their darts without a pause. . . . Our men began to falter and relaxed their efforts, wondering what the peerless courage of the unconquered king Richard himself would deem the best course under these circumstances. But he boldly called out to his own men as follows:

' What! are you going to let that vessel get off untouched and unharmed? Shame upon you! After so many triumphs will you let sloth get hold of you now and give way like cowards?

Never, so long as any foes
Remain, are you to seek repose.

* The hides were generally saturated with vinegar to protect the wood from Greek fire and naphtha.

Well do you know, all of you, that you will deserve to be hung on a gallows and put to death if you suffer these enemies to escape.'

"On hearing these words our galley-men, making a virtue of necessity, plunged eagerly into the sea and getting under the enemy's ship bound the helm with ropes so as to make the vessel lean to one side and hinder its progress. Others, pushing alongside with great skill and perseverance, grasped hold of the cordage and leapt on board. The Turks were ready for these and slew them promptly, cutting off one man's arms, another man's hands or head, and pitching the dead bodies out to sea. This sight roused the other Christians to greater valour . . . so that scrambling over the ship's bulwarks they hurled themselves upon the Turks and gave no quarter to those who offered any resistance.

"But the Turks emboldened by despair used every effort to repel the galley-men, and succeeded in cutting off a foot here, a hand or head there; whilst their opponents, straining every nerve, drove the Turks back to the very prow of the ship. Upon this other Turks came rushing up from the hold of the vessel and, massed into one body with their fellows, offered a stout resistance, being determined to die bravely or repulse their adversaries like men. For these were the very flower of the Turkish youth—a band skilled in warlike exploits and well armed. So the fight continued and warriors fell everywhere on either side till at last the Turks, pressing on with greater vigour, forced our men back and compelled them to quit the ship. Our galley-men accordingly betook themselves to their own galleys and again began to row round the ship, looking out for a place suitable for attack.

"Meanwhile the king, noting the danger of his men, and seeing that it would be no easy thing to take the Turkish vessel with all its arms and stores intact, gave orders for each of his galleys to prick the enemy with its beak. Accordingly the galleys, after drawing back a space, are once more swept forward under the impulse of many oars to pierce the enemy's sides. By these tactics the ship was stove in at once,* and, giving an inlet to the waves, began to sink; while the Turks, to avoid going down with their vessel, leapt overboard into the sea, where they were slain or drowned. The king, however, spared thirty-five of them, to wit the emirs and those skilled in the making of warlike engines. All the others perished; the warlike gear was lost, and the serpents were drowned or tossed about here and there on the sea waves.

"Had that ship got safe into Acre the Christians would never have taken the city. Thus did God bring disaster upon the infidels, while to the Christians who trusted in him he gave help at the hands of king Richard whose warlike endeavours prospered without intermission. . . .

"After destroying this ship, king Richard and all his company hastened with joy and eagerness towards Acre, where he longed to be. Thanks to a favourable wind on the very next night his fleet cast anchor off Tyre. Early next morning he

---

* Baha-ed-din confirms the loss of the great ship from Beyrut, with her 650 soldiers, stores, provisions, and machines of war; but he says her captain himself sank her, when he saw she must be taken, so that the enemy got nothing of her cargo (220–1).

hoisted sail once more, and had not gone very far before he caught sight of that place we have mentioned before—Scandalion; thence passing by Casal Imbert the lofty tower of Acre rose up in the distance, and then by degrees the other fortifications of the city.

"Acre was then girt round on every side by an infinite number of people from every Christian nation under heaven—the chosen warriors of all Christian lands, men well fitted to undergo the perils of war. . . . Beyond them lay an innumerable army of Turks swarming on the mountains and valleys, the hills, and the plains, and having their tents, bright with coloured devices of all kinds, pitched every-where. Our men could also see Saladin's own pair of lions and those of his brother Saphadin,* and Takadin the champion of heathendom. Saladin himself was keep-ing a watch on the sea-coasts and harbours without however ceasing to contrive frequent and fierce attacks upon the Christians. King Richard too, looking forth, reckoned up the number of his foes; and as he reached the harbour the king of France, together with the chiefs of the whole army, all the lords and mighty men, welcomed him with joy and exultation; for they had long been very eager for him to arrive. It was on [June 8] the Saturday before the feast of the blessed Barnabas the apostle, in Pentecost week, that king Richard with his followers reached Acre. On his arrival the whole land was stirred with the exulting glee of the Christians. For all the people were in transports, shouting out congratulations and blowing trumpets. He was brought ashore with jubilant cries; and there was great joy because the desired of all nations had come. . . ."

Since the opening of the season Saladin had again taken up his position on the hill of el-Ayyadiya (5 June), whence he made daily attacks upon, the enemy's trenches. The garrison was closely pressed; the daily labour of clearing the fosse of the bodies of horses and men with which the Franks filled it, added to the constant struggle to repulse the storming parties and destroy the machines, had tired them out; and Saladin's main object was to draw the enemies' attention to the rear by ceaselessly harassing the camp entrenchments, night and day, so as to relieve the garrison. He had not yet his full strength, though the North Syrian troops had rejoined him early; but at the end of June he received large reinforce-ments both from Egypt and from Mesopotamia. He was untiring in beating up recruits, and his despatches are full of reproaches for the luke-warm support of the Holy War by the Mohammedan princes. He even sent an embassy to the Almohade Caliph of Marocco to invite his assistance.

Hardly had Richard landed when he was taken ill with the fever of the coun-try, which the Franks called "Arnoldia": but "none the less did he during the whole course of his illness continue the construction of his stone-slings and mangonels and the erection of a castle before the city gate"—like the "Mate

* "Saphadin " is Seyf-ed-din el-Melik el-Adil.

Griffon" or "Kill Greek" tower which he had successfully set up against Messina and had now brought to Acre. Philip also fell sick in the same manner, but he was the first to recover.

"When the king of France got well from his sickness he devoted himself to preparing his engines and setting up his stone-slings in fitting places, from which he kept them working night and day. He had one very good engine of war called 'The Bad Neighbour'; and, within the city, the Turks had another which they called 'The Bad Kinsman,' by whose assistance they frequently managed to destroy the 'Bad Neighbour.' The king of France on his part kept rebuilding the latter machine till by constant blows he had partly overthrown the chief wall of the city and shattered the Accursed Tower. On one side the stone-sling of the duke of Burgundy used also to work, and not without effect; on the other that of the Templars wrought the Turks vast injury, whilst that of the Hospitallers— equally dreaded by the Turks—kept plying always. Besides all these there was a certain stone-sling, built out of common funds, which they used to call 'God's stone-sling.' Close by it a certain priest, a man of the greatest integrity, was always preaching and at the same time begging money for its reconstruction or for the payment of those who collected the stones it discharged. By its blows the wall near the Accursed Tower was shaken for a length of two perches. The count of Flanders, too, had a peculiarly choice stone-sling, to say nothing of a smaller one. King Richard took possession of the former on the count's death. These two stone-slings kept plying at a tower near one of the gates, much frequented by the Turks, till it was half smashed in. Moreover king Richard had made two other new stone-slings of remarkable material and workmanship, and these hit the mark at an incredible distance. He had also built an engine of the strongest construction of beams. It had steps fitted to it for getting up, and was commonly known as the belfry. This engine was covered with closely-fitting hides, with ropes, and strong planks of wood, so as not to be destroyed by the blows of the stone-slings or even by Greek fire. [Richard] had also got ready two mangonels—one of them of such power that it could hurl its charge into the very middle of the city market.

"King Richard's stone-slings were plying night and day, and it is a known fact that a single stone discharged from one of this king's engines slew twelve men. This stone was sent to Saladin for him to look at. The messengers who carried it said that that devil the king of England had brought from the captured city of Messina [a store of] such sea-flints and most lustrous stones for doing execution on the Saracens. Nothing, they went on, could resist the blows of these stones without being shattered or ground to powder. Meanwhile the king, whose fever was getting worse, lay on his bed, chafing sorely when he saw the Turks challenging our men, whilst his sickness prevented him from attacking them. For the constant onsets of the Turks caused him keener pangs than the most fiery throes of his fever.

"Acre seemed a city very hard to take, not only because of the natural strength of its position, but also because it was defended by the very choicest Turkish troops. It was all to no purpose that the French had spent so much pains on constructing engines of war and implements for pulling down the walls; because the Turks by a sudden volley of Greek fire would destroy everything their enemies had prepared, no matter at what expense, and consume it utterly with fire. Now among the other engines made by the king of the French was one which he had constructed with the utmost care. It was intended for scaling the walls, and for this reason was called "The Cat," because after creeping up in the manner of a cat it got a grip of the wall and stuck fast to it. He had also finished another contrivance of hurdles very strongly fastened together with twigs, and this the people used to call the *circleia*. Under this little hurdle, covered with raw hides, the king used to take his seat anxiously discharging bolts from his crossbow and watching his opportunity to strike any unwary Turk on the battlements of the city."

These engines worked havoc in the defences of Acre; the walls began to crumble, and the garrison, worn out with incessant vigils, sent despairing messages to Saladin in the extremity of their danger. In response he seems to have lost no opportunity of attacking the camp of the enemy and drawing their attention from the city. The garrison would beat their drums to give notice that they were being assailed; Saladin's drums would instantly reply, and his troops would forthwith charge the Franks' entrenchments. We read of such attacks on the 14th and 17th of June; the Saracens rushed the earthworks and plundered part of the camp; the enemy hurried back from the city walls; the engagements lasted till night, when each side retired to its position.* The most furious attempt upon the camp, however, took place on the 2nd and 3rd of July,† when the garrison were actually threatening to surrender unless Saladin could save them. It is described in the "Itinerary":—

"Now it chanced one day, while the French were drawing too close to the walls in their eagerness to bring up the *cat*, that the Turks cast a heap of dry wood over the walls on to the *cat*. Then, without any delay, they discharged a quantity of Greek fire down upon the *circleia* that had been prepared with such great care. After this they set up a stone-sling, taking aim at the same place, when lo! suddenly everything is in flames or destroyed by the blows of the stone-sling. Upon this the king of France, madly wrath, began to curse with horrid oaths at all who were under his rule and to chide them with shameful reproaches for not taking vengeance against the Saracens who had done him such a wrong. In the heat of his anger, as evening drew on, he proclaimed an attack for the morrow by herald's voice.

"Early next morning chosen guards were set at the outer ditches to keep off sudden attacks of the Saracens [outside].' For Saladin had bragged that on the same day he would cross the trenches in full force and shew his valour, to the

* Baha-ed-din, 222–4.
† Id., 229–32.

destruction of the Christians. But he did not keep his word; for he did not come himself,* but his fierce and persistent army, under his lieutenant Kahadin [Taki-ed-din], hurling itself in great masses against the trenches, was valiantly opposed by the French. There was no small slaughter on either side. The Turks, dismounting, advanced on foot. The fight went on at close quarters with drawn swords, daggers, and two-headed axes, not to mention clubs that bristled with sharpened teeth. The Turks press on; the valorous Christians drive them back; each side rages with a twofold fury; for it was the time of summer heat.

"That part of the army destined to take the city continued hurling darts, undermining the walls, pounding away with engines or creeping up to scale the walls. The Turks, dreading the courage of these assailants, signalled to their fellows outside by raising aloft the standard of Saladin in the hopes that [their friends] would come to their aid at once or draw off the enemy by an attack [in the rear]. Seeing this Kahadin and his Turks, pressing on with all their vigour, filled the ditch, but were resisted and driven back by our men, who, thanks to God, stood like an impenetrable wall. Meanwhile the king of France's diggers gradually burrowing by subterranean passages reached the very foundations of the walls and filled the chasm they had made with logs, to which they set fire. Then, when the fire had consumed the beams upholding the wall, a great part of, it gave way, sloping down by degrees, but not falling flat. Very many Christians ran up to this spot in the hope of entering, whilst the Turks came up to drive them back. Oh! how many banners might you then see and devices of many a shape, not to mention the desperate [valour] of the Turks as they hurled Greek fire against our men. Here the French brought up ladders, and attempted to scale the wall that was not quite prostrate; there the Turks on the other hand used ladders to defend the breach. . . ."

During this attack, el-Adil had led two gallant charges, in vain, and Saladin himself had gone from battalion to battalion, shouting his war-cry, and urging on his men. Looking towards the city he saw the terrible crisis and danger of the struggling garrison, and his eyes filled with tears, as he charged again and again. All that day he took no food, and nothing passed his lips but the doctor's stuff which he was forced to take.† Meanwhile the assault became fiercer and fiercer.

"King Richard . . . had a kind of hurdle-shed (commonly called a *circleia*) made and brought up to the ditch outside the city wall. Under its shelter were placed his most skilful cross-bowmen; whilst, to hearten his own men for the combat and to dispirit the Saracens by his presence, he had himself carried there on silken cushions. From this position he worked a crossbow, in the management of which he was very skilful, and slew many of the foes by the bolts and quarrels he discharged. His miners also, approaching the tower against which his stone-casters were being levelled, by an underground passage dug down towards the

---

* Baha-ed-din says Saladin commanded in person.
† Baha-ed-din, 230.

foundations, filling the gaps they made with logs of wood, to which they would set fire, thus causing the walls, which had already been shaken by the stone-casters, to fall down with sudden crash. . . .

"At last when the tower had fallen prostrate before the blows of our stone-casters and when king Richard's men began to stop digging, our men-at-arms, in their greed for fame and victory, began to don their arms. Amongst the banners of these were the earl of Leicester's; that of Andrew de Chavigny and of Hugh Brown. The bishop of Salisbury also came up, equipt in the noblest fashion, and many more. It was about the third hour, *i.e.*, about breakfast time, when these valorous men-at-arms began their work, going forth to storm the tower, which they boldly scaled at once. The Turkish watchmen, on seeing them, raised a shout, and lo! the whole city was soon in a stir. The Turkish warriors, hurriedly seizing their arms, came thronging up and flung themselves upon the assailants. The men-at-arms strove to get in; the Turks to hurl them back. Rolled together in a confused mass they fought at close quarters, hand against hand, and sword against sword. Here men struck, there they fell. Our men-at-arms were few, where-as the numbers of the Turks kept on increasing. The Turks also threw Greek fire against their enemies, and this at last forced the men-at-arms to retreat and leave the tower, where some of them were slain by weapons, others burnt by that most deadly fire. At last the Pisans, eager for fame and vengeance, scrambled up the tower itself with a mighty effort; but, bravely as they comported themselves, they too had to retreat before the onset of the Turks, who rushed on as if mad. Never has there been such a people as these Turks for prowess in war.

"Though its walls were partly fallen and partly shaken, though a great part of the inhabitants were slain or weakened by wounds, there still remained in the city 6,000 Turks. With these were the leaders, Mestoc [el-Meshtub], and Caracois [Karakush], who began now to despair of receiving aid. . . . So, by common con-sent and counsel, the besieged begged a truce while they sent notice of their plight to Saladin, hoping that, in accordance with their Pagan ways, he would ensure their safety—as he ought to do—by sending them speedy aid or procuring leave for them to quit the city without disgrace. To obtain this favour, these two noble Saracens, the most renowned [warriors] in all Paganism, Mestoc and Cara-cois, came to our kings, promising to surrender the city, if Saladin did not send them speedy aid. They stipulated, however, that all the besieged Turks should have free leave to go wherever they wished with their arms and all their goods. The king of France and almost all the French agreed to this; but king Richard utterly refused to hear of entering an empty city after so long and toilsome a siege. Where-fore, perceiving king Richard's mind, Caracois and Mestoc went back to Acre with-out concluding the business. Saladin, meanwhile, having received envoys from the beseiged, bade them hold out stoutly in the certainty that he would shortly send them efficient aid. He declared that he had certain news of the approach of a mighty host of warriors from Babylon [*i.e.* Cairo] in ships and galleys."

The succour had already come. Saladin received frequent reinforcements at the end of June and the beginning of July. On the 25th came the levies from

Sinjar; then a strong force from Egypt; the next day the lord of Mosil arrived with his division; on the 28th more troops from Egypt; on July the 9th came the Prince of Sheyzar with his Arabs, on the 10th Dolderim with a large squadron of Turkmans in Saladin's pay; on the 11th the young Prince of Hamah. Yet, with all this host of Saracens about it, Acre surrendered on the 12th. After a magnificent defence for nearly two years, the garrison laid down its arms in the sight of a great and unbeaten army of relief! Nay, the very spirits of dead heroes seemed in vain to lend mysterious aid to the beleaguered city. A mighty noise, like the tramp of many armed men, was heard at night within the walls. The Christian outposts sprang to arms, and wonderingly perceived as it were a regiment entering the gates, clothed in green robes; for such is the aspect of the martyrs of Islam who dwell in Paradise. Even the souls of the Faithful could not put faith into the panic-stricken people.

The story of this surrender, however, is not hard to understand. The large forces and improved siege-engines brought to bear upon the city by the Kings of England and France made the place untenable: it could only be rescued from without. Saladin's army seemed numerous enough for anything it might be called upon to do; yet it evidently could not fight against earthworks. A few bold leaders might force their way among the tents, but the enemy's entrenched camp was never really carried by the Saracens. Some of Saladin's men even mutinied, refused to attack, and accused him of "ruining Islam."*

Convinced that Saladin could not break through the iron ring that held them, the garrison foresaw nothing but a massacre. To hold out much longer was impossible. Three leading emirs succeeded in making a cowardly escape by night. A panic ensued. Some of the frightened people threw themselves from the battlements; others fled to the enemy's camp and begged to be baptised. Karakush, the governor of the city, and el-Meshtub ("Le Balafré") the commander of the garrison, resolved to make terms. They went to the Christian camp on July 4th, but were refused a capitulation. Saladin was no party to this: he urged resistance and promised relief. On the next morning, the 5th, he had his army ready for the effort, but the garrison failed to do its part. On the 7th a swimmer brought a despairing message: "We have sworn to die together; we will fight till we are slain; and we will not deliver up this city so long as we live. Look you to distract the enemy from us and prevent his attacking us. . . . Our turn is over." It was a last appeal. Still no relief came, and on the 12th, despite their desperate resolve, the same swimmer brought the message that the garrison had capitu-

---

* Baha-ed-din, 233–4.

lated. Saladin was in the very act of preparing a reply, denouncing* the terms of the treaty, when the banners and crosses of the Franks suddenly glittered upon the city walls and towers. The deed was done; Acre had surrendered without its sovereign's consent.

Thus, on Friday after the translation of the Blessed Benedict [July 12], the wealthier and noble emirs were proffered and accepted as hostages, one month being allowed for the restoration of the Holy Cross and the collection of the captive Christians. When the news of this surrender became known, the unthinking crowd was moved with wrath; but the wiser folk were much rejoiced at getting so quickly and without danger what previously they had not been able to obtain in so long a time. Then the heralds made proclamation forbidding any one to insult the Turks by word or deed. No missiles were to be hurled against the walls or against the Turks if they chanced to appear on the battlements. On that day, when these famous Turks, of such wonderful valour and warlike excellence, began strolling about on the city walls in all their splendid apparel, previous to their departure, [our men] gazed on them with the utmost curiosity. They were wonder-struck at the cheerful features of men who were leaving their city almost penniless and whom only the very sternest necessity had driven to beg for mercy; men whom loss did not deject, and whose visage betrayed no timidity, but even wore the look of victory. . . .

"At last, when all the Turks had quitted Acre,† the Christians entered the city in joy and gladness, glorifying God with a loud voice and yielding Him thanks for having magnified His mercy upon them and brought redemption to His people. Thus did the kings set their banners and varied ensigns on the walls and towers; while the city, together with all it contained in the way of victuals and arms, was equally divided among them. The captives too they reckoned up and halved the lot. To the king of France fell the noble Caracois and a great host of other folk; to king Richard, Mestoc and many more. Morever, the king of France had the noble palace of the Templars with all its appurtenances, while the royal palace fell to king Richard, who established the two queens there with their maidens and attendants. Thus each king had his own part of the city in peace, whilst the army was distributed over its whole area, enjoying pleasant rest after so long and continuous a siege."

---

* The *Itinerary* (iii., 17) says that Saladin had previously consented to the surrender; but every other evidence points to the contrary conclusion.

† This is a mistake. The inhabitants of Acre were detained prisoners (Ernoul, 274), as hostages for the execution of the treaty, as appears further on.

CHAPTER XIX

THE COAST MARCH
Aug.–Sept.,1191

THE SURRENDER of Acre took Saladin by surprise, but his anger was roused more by the terms that had been arranged behind his back, than by the act itself. He had evidently realised that the city could not hold out much longer, and that his army could neither break through the enemy's entrenchments, nor draw them into a pitched battle. So long as he had to deal with Guy de Lusignan and the Palestine Franks he had never thought of a truce; but the coming of the two Kings changed the situation, and he prepared to negotiate. The first overture, however, came from Richard. The King of England had sent very soon after he landed to request a personal interview. It was like his frank soldierly character to wish to be face to face with the man with whose courage and greatness of heart even the Christian camp was ringing. But Saladin declined the meeting: it was not well, he said, for kings at war with each other to meet in friendly converse until a treaty of peace was actually afoot.* Possibly he feared being won too far by the manly presence and chivalrous manner of the hero of whose exploits he too had heard so much: more probably his reply was thrown out as a feeler towards peace.

Other envoys came from the English camp during the King's illness. A meeting was arranged between Richard and el-Adil; it was to take place in the middle of the plain between the two camps, but the King's sickness postponed the interview. Some passages of wit were exchanged between the ambassador and the Sultan's brother, about a present of falcons which Richard wished to offer to Saladin, and the fowls which he required in return, and each tried to discover what the other was aiming at. On the 1st of July Saladin himself received the envoy and his Maghraby interpreter. "All these interviews," says Baha-ed-din, "were designed to find out our temper of mind, our strength and our weakness." It was doubtless to promote these *pourparlers* that the Franks stopped the bombardment for three days.†

---

* Baha-ed-din, 223-4; who extols Richard as a King "of mighty vast courage, and firm will; great battles had he fought, and daring was he in war."
† Baha-ed-din, 234; Ernoul, 274.

The ambassadors came again on the 4th, asking for fruit and snow, and the Master of the Knights of St. John was himself announced as coming on the morrow to treat for peace. Three envoys arrived instead, and had an hour's conference with el-Adil, but nothing was settled. There was a further discussion on the 6th, but the Christian terms were too hard. Saladin kept his army in battle array, and menaced the Franks as far as he dared, to induce them to lower their demands. But up to the 11th,

> "they stood resolute, not to make peace nor to grant a capitulation to the citizens, unless all the prisoners in the hands of the Moslems were released, and the cities of the coast-land were restored to them. It was proposed (on our part) to surrender the city and everything in it, save only its defenders, but they would not; and we offered besides the Cross of the Crucifixion, but they would not."

The next day came the news that the garrison had capitulated on these terms: (1) Acre to be surrendered with all its contents, ships, stores, and material of war; (2) 200,000 pieces of gold to be paid to the Franks; (3) 1500 prisoners, together with 100 prisoners of rank, to be delivered up; (4) the True Cross to be restored to them; (5) 4000 gold pieces to be paid to the Marquess of Montferrat. On these conditions, the inhabitants were to go free, and without molestation, taking with them their families and such private possessions as they could carry.*

Conditions such as these were naturally repugnant to the Sultan, still at the head of a strong army which had not lost a battle since the rout at Ramla fourteen years before. The terms had been made by Saladin's officers, and he did not repudiate them; but it was the greatest reverse he had ever experienced, and his grief was unconcealed. Having now no further need to guard the city, he at once moved his army to Shafraamm, and awaited the commissioners who should arrange the execution of the humiliating treaty. Agents passed between the two camps, and visited Damascus, drawing up full lists of the prisoners and paving the way for a permanent treaty of peace. This went on for a month, during which the outposts of the two armies faced each other in no friendly mood, and once even indulged in a regular set-to, when the Franks were driven to their trenches. Meanwhile the smothered quarrel between Philip and Richard had broken out again; the King of France was ill of a fever, such as had just carried off the Count of Flanders, and he made it an excuse to desert the Crusade and return home, there to stir up "confusion in Normandy." But if, in the words of Cœur de Lion,† Philip did "against the will of God and to the eternal dishonour of his kingdom,

---

* Baha-ed-din, 227, 228, 234–237; the 1500 prisoners are stated at 500 in one place by an obvious slip.
† Roger of Howden, iii., 128.

so shamelessly fail in his vow," he at least left behind him the greater part of his army under the Duke of Burgundy to carry on the Crusade. The French, unfortunately, were a source of weakness rather than strength, for they opposed the King of England at every step, and in this they were cordially abetted by Conrad of Montferrat, who withdrew to Tyre on the 1st of August, when he found that his schemes for the crown of Jerusalem received no countenance from Richard.

> "While the king of France was hastening home, king Richard was paying heed to the repair of the city walls, building them higher and stronger than before. He himself was always making the round of them, encouraging the workmen and masons, just as if his sole business were to regain God's heritage. He was still awaiting the end of the time fixed upon between himself and the Turks, occupying himself in the meanwhile with collecting his mangonels and baggage ready for carrying them away. After the period agreed upon for the return of the Holy Cross and the captives had been overpassed by three weeks [*sic*] to see if Saladin would keep his word; when the Saracens kept demanding a further delay, the Christians began to enquire when the Holy Cross was coming. One said ' Already has the Cross come!' Another said ' It has been seen in the Saracens' army.'* But each was deceived, for Saladin was not even setting about its restoration; nay, he neglected the hostages, in the hope that he would get better terms if he kept it in his possession. And all the while he kept sending frequent presents and envoys, while he made it his aim to waste time in long talks and ambiguous words."†

The Holy Cross (or a convincing imitation) was actually in Saladin's camp, for Baha-ed-din says it was shown to some English officers, who devoutly prostrated themselves in the dust. Whether Saladin was prolonging the negotiations merely to gain time can neither be proved nor disproved; but his secretary's account seems genuine and does not confirm the insinuation of bad faith By

---

* The fate of the "True Cross" is obscure. When it was taken at the battle of Hittin the sacred wood is described as mounted in red gold and adorned with pearls and precious stones. It was sent first to Damascus and then to Baghdad, where the Caliph buried it (4th of June, 1189) under the threshold of the Bab en-Nuby to be trodden under Moslem feet: a bit of the gold could be seen. Yet Baha-ed-din says the "True Cross" was exhibited in Saladin's camp at Acre and included in the first instalment of the proffered indemnity. When the negotiations were broken off, this Cross was sent to Damascus and exposed to contempt in the Omayyad Mosque. It should be noted that as the Moslems hold the story of the Crucifixion to be an unworthy fable, contempt for what they regard as a superstitious forgery involves no disrespect towards the honoured name of Jesus, whom they reverence. From Damascus the Cross is said to have been sent as a gift to Isaac the Emperor of Constantinople. Yet the Bishop of Salisbury is reported to have seen it at Jerusalem by permission of Saladin in September, 1192. Ernoul, moreover, has a curious story of a Frank soldier who undertook to find it on the field of Hittin at the spot where he had buried it with his own hands during the battle; but after three nights' digging he gave up the search. Another presumed fragment was shown to Richard by the Abbot of St. Elias at Beyt Nuba. There were doubtless several "True Crosses"—and imitations.
† *Itin.*, iv., 1.

this account* these English officers brought, on the 2nd of August, Richard's acceptance of Saladin's proposal to deliver up the prisoners and money specified in the treaty, in three separate instalments, at intervals of a month each. The first of these instalments was ready at the end of the first month. The officers sent by the Franks certified that the numbers were correct, except that certain prisoners specified by name were not yet included. On the 11th of August they came to exact their full due and Saladin, to meet the difficulty said "*Either* give us up our comrades (the captives at Acre) and take what has been agreed upon for this instalment, and we will give you hostages for the fulfilment of the remaining terms; *or* take what we offer you now, and give us hostages to hold until our comrades in your hands shall rejoin us." The commissioners replied, "We will not do that: but do you give us what is due for this term, and take our pledge that your people shall be given up to you." To this Saladin would not consent; he had already had too much experience of what a Christian oath was worth. Obviously neither side trusted the other, and Saladin's natural demand for some guarantee that his fulfilment of the treaty would be followed by a corresponding release of the captives at Acre was regarded by the Christians as an evasion. If we believe Baha-ed-din's statement, there was no reason for this suspicion; but, believe it or not as we may, there is no imaginable excuse or palliation for the cruel and cowardly massacre that followed. The horrible scene is described by the admiring chronicler:

"Orders were then given to cut off the heads of the hostages with the exception of a few of the nobler prisoners, who perhaps might yet be relieved or exchanged for captive Christians. King Richard, always eager to destroy the Turks, to confound the law of Mahomet utterly, and vindicate that of Christ, on the Friday after the Assumption† bade 2700 Turkish hostages to be led out of the city and beheaded. Nor was there any delay. The king's followers leapt forward eager to fulfil the commands, and thankful to the Divine Grace that permitted them to take such a vengeance for those Christians whom these very [captives] had slain with bolts and arrows."‡

When the Saracen outpost over against Acre saw their countrymen being butchered in cold blood beneath their very eyes, they rushed madly forward to

---

* Baha-ed-din, 241–2.
† 16th Aug.; Baha-ed-din and Howden date the massacre on Tuesday, the 20th.
‡ *Itin.*, iv., 2. In explanation of this atrocious crime it has been suggested that Richard could not safely leave so large a number of prisoners behind him when he marched south. One would rejoice to discover a less contemptible excuse for his barbarity. Another is alleged by Roger of Howden, who says that Saladin had massacred his Christian captives two days before. There is nothing to support this in any other authority.

prevent the slaughter; but though they fought till night they could not save them. "Only those had been spared who were of note or were strong to work" and the aged and weak, apparently even women and children, had been ruthlessly put to the sword. After Saladin's almost quixotic acts of clemency and generosity, the King of England's cruelty will appear amazing. But the students of the Crusades do not need to be told that in this struggle the virtues of civilisation, magnanimity, toleration, real chivalry, and gentle culture, were all on the side of the Saracens.

Immediately after the massacre, Richard prepared to march down the coast to Ascalon, on his way to the Holy City where Saladin had so conspicuously taught the lesson of mercy. There was great difficulty in getting the Crusaders to move. No less than 300,000 men were under the King's command, but they left the city "slowly and surlily." "The people given up to sloth and luxury, were loth to leave a city so rich in comforts, to wit, in the choicest of wines and the fairest of damsels. Many, by a too intimate acquaintance with these pleasures, became dissolute, till the city was polluted by their luxury, whose gluttony and wantonness put wiser men to the blush."* Richard's order that no women, save washerwomen, "who could not be an occasion of sin," were to follow the army, hardly encouraged the zeal of these worthy warriors. He managed to collect 100,000 however, and these he marshalled on the eve of St. Bartholomew.

On the surrender of Acre, Saladin had at once fallen back upon his line of retreat, and massed his main army on the hills which commanded the two great roads, the one leading east to Tiberias and Damascus, the other south-east through Nazareth to Jerusalem. The hill of Shafraamm overlooked both routes. Richard, however, did not gratify his adversary by attempting to force the passes; daring as he was, he would not risk an advance through hills completely held by the Saracens. He chose the longer but safer route by the old Roman road which skirts the coast, where if he had the enemy on the hills on his left, he had also the protection of the sea and the support of his fleet on his right. His plan was to descend the coast as far as Jaffa and Ascalon, and after making a fortified base, to strike across to Jerusalem. The distance to Jaffa, in a straight line, was a little over sixty miles; but there were eight rivers to be forded, the road was often difficult through brushwood and long grass, the season was the hottest in the year; and the whole route was commanded by a range of low wooded hills, which offered vantage ground for the Saracens, and, if Saladin had possessed field artillery, would have made the march utterly impossible. As it was, only the firm

---

* *Itin.*, iv., 7.

resolution of Richard in keeping his men in close order and pushing doggedly on, without attempting to follow the Moslems into the hills, saved him from disaster.

On Friday, the 22nd of August, the Franks crossed the Belus and encamped on the southern side. At daybreak on Sunday Saladin saw the fires of the enemy, which announced that they were breaking camp. He instantly loaded up his baggage and set out for the hill of Keymun, a spur of the Carmel range, which commanded the main southern road from Acre and Haifa into the interior of Palestine. The detachments he had sent out to harass the Franks brought word that the enemy had crossed the Kishon and camped at Haifa. Apparently they were not going to march inland. A line of troops was posted for the night to watch their movements, and next morning, leaving a strong detachment close to the enemy, under Jurdik, a trusty emir of Shirkuh's old Egyptian staff, Saladin himself rode across the hills towards Cæsarea, where the shoreland woods began, and where the Franks, if they kept the coast, must make their next camp. Here he examined the lie of the land to find a good position for a pitched battle. "He came back to the camp very tired after the time of evening prayer," and announced that the Franks were still at Haifa, and that nothing could be done till their movements were decided. The next day he reviewed his troops, and put them in heart by presents and compensations to those who had lost their goods and horses. On the 27th he rode out thrice towards the coast, searching for a suitable place to engage the enemy, who were slowly rounding the shoulder of land formed by the jutting spurs of Mount Carmel; and on the following day he moved the army on, so as to cover Cæsarea. Prisoners were brought in, who told him that the Franks were waiting for the fleet which carried their supplies. All prisoners, except women, were sternly executed: the King of England's cruelty was not to pass unavenged, even by Saladin. Eighteen Franks were thus put to death in one day.

At last, on the 30th the news came that the enemy were at hand. The Saracens were still near Cæsarea, and Saladin at once formed them up along the line of advance. Baha-ed-din was with his master close to the enemy, and describes the first engagement. He says that the Moslem archers could do little against the armour of the Franks:

> "their infantry drawn up in front of the horsemen stood firm as a wall, and every foot-soldier wore a thick gambeson and a hawberk, so dense and strong, that our arrows took no effect, whilst their cross-bows wounded both our horses and their riders. I saw soldiers with from one to ten arrows sticking in them, still marching on."

The divisions nearest the shore, being unexposed to the Saracen attack, relieved in turn the fighting battalions on the left, and the knights were kept in the centre protected by the infantry, and were not permitted to charge. In this formation the Christians marched steadily on, fighting on the left all the way. "The Moslem archers harassed them and tried to induce them to break the ranks, but the men controlled themselves admirably, and went on, without hurry, their ships following along the coast."*

This engagement is typical of the whole march. The Franks pressed doggedly on, whilst the Moslems, "like mountain torrents, raining down from the heights," worried them at every step. They came on in small parties, trying to tempt the Crusaders to break their impenetrable formation, but Richard's orders were strict. Yet we read in the "Itinerary" how

> "the Duke of Burgundy and his French who were in the rear followed at less speed, and thanks to their delay, came near to suffering a most terrible loss. The army was marching having the sea on its right, whilst from the mountain heights on the left the Turks kept a watch on all our movements. . . . The army had now reached a narrow passage along which the provision wagons had to go. Here on account of the narrowness of the way there was some confusion and disorder, which the Saracens noting swept down upon the packhorses and wagons, cutting off unwary men and steeds, plundering much of the baggage, breaking through and dispersing those who offered any resistance, and driving them in flight and slaughter to the brink of the sea. There both sides fought with manful courage for dear life. On this occasion when a Turk had cut off the right hand of a certain Everard, one of the Bishop of Salisbury's men, he without changing countenance seized his sword with the left hand and closing with the Turks stoutly defended himself against them all, brandishing his weapon."

Then King Richard came to the rescue, and

> "thundered on against the Turks, slaying them right and left with his sword. Nor was there any loitering, but right and left as of old the Philistines fled from the face of the Machabee, so now did the Turks scatter and flee from the face of king Richard till they gained the mountain heights, leaving, however, some of their number headless in our hands."

Richard, of course, was always to the fore in these emergencies, "thundering on like a wild boar," and taking heads as a Red Indian took scalps. Nor was Saladin behind-hand: he was often seen riding between the front ranks, with the arrows flying about his head and only a couple of grooms with spare horses as his escort. But it was not his habit to fight in person, and he certainly never

---

* Bah-ed-din, 250–2.

encountered Richard on the field of battle. The days were now intolerably hot, and both sides suffered severely; the unseasoned Franks fell fainting by the way, and many died of sunstroke. But they kept up their courage, and every night as they were turning in to sleep, a herald went through the camp crying in the midst "Help us, Holy Sepulchre!"

> "On hearing these words the whole multitude would take up the cry, stretching out their hands to heaven and, with copious tears, praying God for aid and mercy. Then a second time would the herald repeat the same words, calling out as before, 'SANCTUM SEPULCHRUM ADJUVA,' after which the words were repeated by the whole host; likewise, when he cried aloud for the third time, all imitated him with the utmost sorrow of heart and bursts of tears."

Meanwhile Saladin had at last chosen a site for a set battle. It was near Arsuf, where the downs shelve gently to the seashore; the dense woods of oaks offered shelter to within a couple of miles of the beach, yet there was space for the exercise of cavalry. Here, if anywhere, the Christian array might be broken and their advance stayed. The news that a Saracen army, magnified by rumour to the size of 300,000 men, was waiting for battle seems to have shaken the fortitude of the invaders, who reckoned their own numbers more modestly at 100,000. For on the 5th of September, Richard asked for a parley. He was weary of the daily fighting and grieved at the sufferings and losses of his troops. El-Adil went to meet him; but when the King proposed that peace should be made on the basis of the Saracens' restoring all Palestine and retiring into "their own country," Saladin's brother scornfully broke off the conference. Nothing remained but to leave the issue to the battle. The Franks were now at Rochetaillie, the "Stream of the Cleft" (Nahr el-Falik), halfway between Cæsarea and Jaffa. There they rested a day, protected by the great bog of Ramadan, and on the 7th they began the six miles' march along the road to Arsuf.* The Saracens were on the downs on the left, between Rochetaillie and Arsuf. The battle is finely narrated in the Itinerary":

> "On Saturday [Sept. 7] the eve of the Nativity of the Blessed Mary, at earliest dawn all prepared themselves most carefully as though the Turks were going to attack immediately; for they knew the enemy to have forestalled our path, and that the insolence of the Turks would not abate before a very severe contest had taken place. Indeed the Turks were already setting their men in order, and always drawing a little nearer. For this reason all our men looked to their own

---

* See the careful description in Oman, *Art of War*, ii., 308–316, whence I have been permitted to borrow the plan of the battle-field.

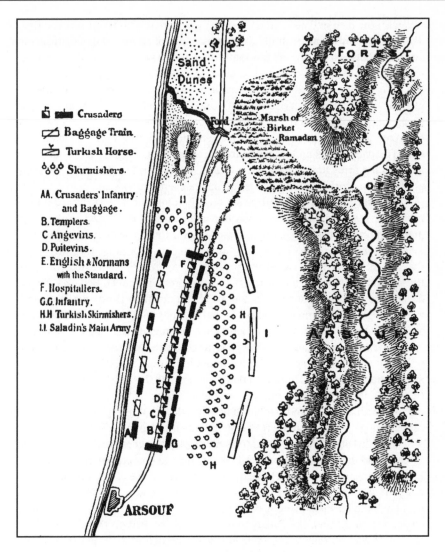

Crusaders

Baggage Train.

Turkish Horse.

Skirmishers.

AA. Crusaders' Infantry
and Baggage.
B. Templers.
C Angevins.
D. Poitevins.
E. English & Normans
with the Standard.
F. Hospitallers.
G.G. Infantry.
H.H Turkish Skirmishers.
I.I. Saladin's Main Army.

Sand Dunes

Ford

Marsh of Birket Ramadan

FOREST

ARSOUF

THE BATTLE OF ARSUF, SEPT. 7, 1191.
(FROM OMAN'S "ART OF WAR.")

affairs very carefully, and the ranks were ranged with the utmost precaution. King Richard, who was very skilful in military matters, drew up the squadrons according to a special scheme, arranging who had better lead the vanguard, and who bring up the rear. With this intent he appointed twelve squadrons; and arranged [his whole army] into five battalions, assigning to each men of great skill in warfare—warriors whose betters were not to be found on earth had their hearts only been firmly staid in God. On this day the Templars led the first rank; after them went the Bretons and the men of Anjolu in due order; next went king

Guy with the men of Poitou; in the fourth rank were the Normans and the English, with the royal banner under their charge. Last of all went the Hospitallers in due rank. This last array of all was made up of choice knights divided into squadrons, and its members marched so close together that an apple could not be thrown to the ground without touching the men or their horses. Our army occupied the whole space between Saladin's and the sea-shore. . . . Count Henry of Champagne kept guard on the side of the mountains: as did also the followers on foot. Last of all were drawn up the bowmen and the cross-bowmen closing the rear. The packhorses and wagons carrying provisions, baggage, &c., journeyed between the army and the sea so as to be safe from attack. Thus did the army advance at a gentle pace so as to guard against separation. . . .

"The third hour was now drawing on, when lo! a host of Turks, 10,000 in numbers, swept rapidly down upon our men, hurling darts and arrows, and making a terrible din with their confused cries. After these came running up a race of dæmons very black in colour; for which cause, because they are black, they are not unfittingly called the negro pack *(nigreduli)*. [Then too came on] those Saracens who live in the desert and are commonly called Bedawis, rough, darker than smoke, most pestilent foot-men with their bows and round targets— a people light of foot and most eager for battle. These were ever threatening our army. And beyond those we have mentioned, you might see along the smoother ground well-equipt phalanxes of Turks advancing with their several ensigns, banners, and emblems. They seemed to number more than 20,000 men. On steeds swifter than eagles they thundered down upon us, till the whirling dust raised by their rapid flight blackened the very air. Before the emirs there went men clanging away with trumpets and clarions; others had drums, others pipes and timbrels, rattles, gongs, cymbals, and other instruments fitted to make a din.

"That day our own losses and the sufferings of our horses, who were pierced through and through with arrows and darts, shewed how persistently the enemy kept up the attack: and then indeed we found out the use of our stalwart cross-bowmen, our bowmen, and those closely-wedged followers who at the very rear beat back the Turkish onset by constant hurling of their weapons so far as they could. Yet for all this, the enemy in a little while rushed on them again like a torrent of waters, redoubling their blows and so drunk with fury that at last many of our cross-bowmen could hold out no longer, but, throwing away their bows and cross-bow, in sheer dread of death, gave way before the intolerable onset of the Turks and forced a path within the close ranks of our main army, lest they should be cut off from their comrades. But the better men and bolder, whom shame forbade to yield, faced about and strove against the Turks with unflagging valour. So they marched backwards in their anxiety to keep themselves from the danger they would run by advancing too confidently in the ordinary method; and all that day they went on, picking their way rather than marching, with their faces turned toward the Turks, who threatened at their rear. Ay! in the stress and bitter peril of that day there was no one who did not wish himself safe at home, with his pilgrimage finished. . . .

"The Turks pressed on so stoutly that they nearly crushed the lines of the Hospitallers, who sent word to king Richard that they could bear up no longer unless their knights were allowed to charge the enemy:

> But he, forbidding, bids them wait
> In closer line and patient state.

Wherefore, for all the peril they were in, they endured on; though with many a heavy gasp, since they were not suffered to breathe freely. So they pursued their way, the excessive heat adding to their toil. Men might well augur that ill things were in store for so small an army hemmed in with so great a host. And now our assailants smote on the backs of our men as they advanced, as if with mallets; so that it was no longer a case for using arrows and darts from a distance, but for piercing with lances or crushing with heavy maces at close quarters: for hand to hand attacks with drawn swords, whilst the blows of the Turks resounded as if from an anvil. The battle raged most severely in the rear rank of the Hospitallers because they might not repay the enemy, but had to go along patient under their sufferings, silent though battered by clubs, and, though struck, not striking in return. At last, unable to bear up against so vast a host, they began to give way and press upon the squadron ahead of them. They fled before the Turks, who were madly raging in their rear. . . .

"At last more than 20,000 Turks made a sudden confused rush, battering at close quarters with clubs and swords, redoubling their blows against the Hospitallers and pressing on in every way, when lo! one of this brotherhood, Garnier de Napes, cried out with a loud voice, ' O illustrious knight St. George, why dost thou suffer us to be thus confounded? Christendom itself is now perishing if it does not beat back this hateful foe!' Thereupon, the Master of the Hospital going off to the king said, 'Lord king, we are grievously beset and are likely to be branded with eternal shame as men who dare not strike in their own defence. Each one of us is losing his own horse for nothing, and why should we put up with it any longer?' To whom the king made reply, ' My good master, it must needs be endured, [seeing that] none can be everywhere.' So the Master returned to find the Turks pressing on and dealing death in the rear, while there was no chief or count who did not blush for very shame."

At last two of the Knights of the Hospital could bear it no longer; calling on St. George, they spurred out against the Saracens; the rest would not be denied, and squadron after squadron wheeled round, until there was a general cavalry charge from end to end. Baha-ed-din witnessed this wonderful charge, which burst out when the Franks reached the woods and gardens of Arsuf.

"I myself saw their knights gather together in the middle of the infantry; they grasped their lances, shouted their shout of battle like one man, the infantry opened out, and through they rushed in one great charge in all directions—some on our right wing, some on our left, and some on our centre, till all was broken."*

---

* Baha-ed-din, 258–9.

The charge had anticipated Richard's signal, but the movement was not ill-timed, and he hastened to direct it.

"King Richard, seeing the army in confusion, put spurs to his horse and flew up to the spot, not slacking his course till he had made his way through the Hospitallers, to whose aid he brought his followers. Then he bore on the Turks, thundering against them and mightily astonishing them by the deadly blows he dealt. To right and left they fell away before him. . . . Fierce and alone, he pressed on the Turks, laying them low; none whom his sword touched might escape; for wherever he went he made a wide path for himself, brandishing his sword on every side. When he had crushed this hateful race by the constant blows of his sword, which mowed them down as if they were a harvest for the sickle, the remainder, frighted at the sight of their dying friends, began to give him a wider berth; for by now the corpses of the Turks covered the face of the ground for half a mile. . . .

"But still the Christians pounded away with their swords till the Turks grew faint with terror, though the issue is doubtful yet. Oh! how many banners and standards of many shapes, what countless pennons and flags might you see falling to earth; aye, and just as many good swords lying everywhere, lances of reed tipt with iron heads, Turkish bows and clubs bristling with sharpened teeth. Twenty or more wagon loads of quarrels, darts, and other arrows and missiles might have been collected on the field. There you might see many a bearded Turk lie maimed and mutilated, but still striving to resist with the courage of despair until, as our men began to prevail, some of the enemy, shaking themselves free from their steeds, hid among the bushes or climbed up the trees, from which they fell dying with horrid yells before the arrows of our men. Others leaving their horses strove to slip off by circuitous ways toward the sea, into which they plunged headlong from the promontories, some five perches high."

The rout of the Saracens is confirmed by their own historian. Baha-ed-din saw centre, left, and right wing all flying pell-mell, till only seventeen men stood by the standard, where the Sultan's drum still beat to action. Three separate charges he records, and each drove the Moslems further up the hillocks: but as each retired the Moslems rallied. Saladin remained immovable by his standard, trying to check the panic and bring the men back to the battle. At last he managed to collect a large number round the flag, and it is clear from the following passages from the "Itinerary" that the Saracens returned more than once to the attack.

"The Normans and English chosen to guard the Standard drew up gradually and with cautious steps towards that part of our army that was fighting, keeping no great distance from the battle, so that all might have a sure place of refuge. At last, having finished their slaughter our men paused, but the Turks continued their flight till, seeing our slackness, they regained their courage, and immediately more than 20,000 strong fell upon our men in the rear, threatening them with clubs in the hope of releasing our captives. With deadliest effect they kept launching forth their darts and arrows; smashing, lopping, bruising the heads, arms, and other limbs of our knights, till these bent stupidly over their saddle bows. At last our men recovering their courage, fierce as a lioness robbed of her whelps, rushed upon them again, forcing a way through them as if they were merely tearing through meshes. . . .

"Over this host of Turks there was a certain Emir, a kinsman of Saladin. This warrior had a banner marked with a wonderful device, to wit, a pair of breeches.* These he bore—a device well known to his men. This Tekedin pursued the Christians with a peculiarly fierce hatred; and he had with him on this occasion more than 700 choice and sturdy Turks attached to his person. They were selected from Saladin's special followers. Each squadron of this body carried a yellow banner in front with a pennon of a different colour. And now coming on at full speed, with noise and pride they fell upon our men who began to turn off from them towards the Standard. Then the king, sitting on his peerless Cyprian steed, with his chosen band made towards the hills, routing all the Turks he met; helmets clinked as the enemy fell before him, and sparks leapt out from the battery of his sword. So fierce was his onset this day that the Turks very soon all turned off from his irresistible attack, and left a free passage to our army. Thus at last, despite their wounds, our men reached the Standard, the ranks were formed again, and the host proceeded to Arsuf, outside which town it pitched its tents.

"Whilst busied in this work a huge mass of Turks fell upon our rear. Hearing the din of conflict king Richard, calling his own folk to battle, gave reins to his horse, and with only fifteen comrades rushed against the Turks, crying out with a loud voice 'GOD AND THE HOLY SEPULCHRE AID US.' This cry he uttered a second and a third time and, when the rest of his men heard his voice, they hurriedly followed him, fell upon the foe, and drove them in headlong rout right up to the wood of Arsuf, whence they had formerly come. . . .

"Then the king returned to his camp, and our men, wearied with so fierce a combat, rested for the night. Those who were eager for spoil went back to the battle-field and got as much plunder as they desired. Men who in this way returned used to say that they counted thirty-two emirs whom they found lying dead—all cut off on this day. These they reckoned to be men of the greatest authority and power, from their splendid arms and costly gear; and the Turks afterwards begged leave to carry them off because of their rank. In addition they brought back news of 7,000 Turkish corpses, to say nothing of the wounded, who, straggling here and there out of the fight, died later on, and lay scattered over the fields. But thanks to God's protection, hardly a tenth or even a hundredth of this number fell on our side."

---

* The chronicler has misinterpreted a well-known *renk* or heraldic badge, copied from an ancient Egyptian hieroglyphic cartouche. The use of armorial bearings was common among the Saracens, especially the Turkman mamluks.

No emir of the first rank fell, except Musik the Kurd; but the Christians lost that peerless knight James of Avesnes, whose body was found in a circle of fifteen dead Saracens. One Christian was taken prisoner, and beheaded. Saladin was so overwhelmed at the reverse that he would not listen to the well-meant consolations of his secretary. He sat under the shade of a cloth—for his tent had gone on—attending to the wounded, and giving his own horses to the men who had lost their mounts. Then the army passed on, and encamped on the green fields beside the river of Jaffa, some few miles from the enemy's camp under the walls of Arsuf.

The victory of the 7th of September was Richard's greatest achievement in Palestine, though it was brought on against his orders by a breach of discipline. But the Crusader did not follow it up. Far from being crushed by the disaster, Saladin, recovering from his momentary depression, marched his whole force the very next day back to Arsuf, drew them up in order of battle before the enemy, and challenged a renewal of the fight. He waited all day, but the Franks would not stir. On Monday he repeated his challenge, and harassed the enemy with his archers, but they preserved their former stubborn reserve, and succeeded in getting into Jaffa without a general engagement. Once there, they had walls to their back, and Saladin drew his army off to Ramla, a dozen miles to the south-east, to hold the road to Jerusalem, and await events. The coast-march had been accomplished, slowly and painfully, but with consummate generalship and final success.

SEAL OF RICHARD I. (1195.)
FROM ARCHER'S "STORY OF THE CRUSADES".

CHAPTER XX

IN SIGHT OF JERUSALEM
Sept., 1191–July, 1192

THE FRANKS were in no haste to follow up their victory. They declined Saladin's offers of battle, and shut themselves up at Jaffa for two months. They had succeeded, with much difficulty and at the rate of three miles a day, in pushing their way from Acre sixty miles south, and they set about fortifying their base before venturing to leave the coast and the fleet which had hitherto served them with intermittent supplies and reinforcements. The pleasant orchards of Jaffa were a refreshing change, after a diet of dead horses, and the weary troops showed little eagerness for the advance upon Jerusalem. "The army rested a long time in ease and pleasure; while day after day its manifold sins increased, to wit, drunkenness and luxury. For the women from Acre began to return to the army, and were a source of iniquity to corrupt the whole people, whose love for pilgrimage diminished as its religious zeal abated"*; indeed, a number of them began flocking back to Acre, "where they spent their time in taverns." Richard at least lent no countenance to this sloth and immorality. He sent King Guy to Acre to recall the deserters, and when this appeal proved unavailing, he went himself and preached "a most moving discourse," exhorting the backsliders to gird up their loins for the holy work.

By these exertions the army was restored to even more than its former strength. But up to the middle of November, beyond strengthening Jaffa, and restoring two or three fortified posts in the plain, a few miles out on the road to Lydda, this large and well-appointed army accomplished nothing.† There were some brisk skirmishes with the Saracen outposts, who did not allow them to rebuild the "Casal of the Plains" unmolested, and Richard indulged his love of adventure and deeds of "derring-do," whilst roving about the country. Once, when out hawking, he was surprised by the Saracens whilst asleep, and might have been taken prisoner but for the devotion of William de Préaux, who calling

---

* *Itin.*, iv., 26.

† According to Baha-ed-din (280) the outposts of the Franks had only advanced to Yazur, 3½ miles from Jaffa, by the 30th of October.

out in Arabic that he was the "Melik," passed himself upon the unsuspecting enemy as the King of England, and was carried off in triumph. But as for the object of the Crusade, the Franks never went further than one good day's march on the road to Jerusalem all the time they were in Palestine.

One reason for the inaction of the Crusaders is found in the negotiations for peace which were going on throughout October and part of November. Saladin's strength, despite his losses at Arsuf, was unbroken, and his army held the road to Jerusalem. He had shown that he would spare no sacrifice to worst his enemy, for immediately after his retreat to Ramla he had begun to raze the fortified city of Ascalon, to prevent its forming a support to the Franks. 'Fore God," he said to Baha-ed-din, "I had sooner lose all my children than throw down a single stone of it; but it is the will of God, and the safety of the Moslems hangs upon it." The work of demolition and burning took a whole month, amid general lamentations, and the people were transported to Egypt and other lands. The position of Ascalon, as a great port close to the Egyptian frontier, and a powerful base of operations by sea and land for southern Palestine, justified Saladin's precaution; but the Christians felt that the man who could destroy so noble a city would shrink from nothing.

But even before the razing of Ascalon was known at Jaffa, Richard had made overtures for peace. The example of Acre suggested a possible repetition of a similar bloodless success. Within a week of the battle of Arsuf, he sent Humphrey of Toron, to feel the way towards an arrangement. Saladin was then busy dismantling Ascalon, but his brother, el-Adil, who commanded the advance guard at Lydda, had full powers to treat, and from that time forth generally conducted the negotiations. According to Baha-ed-din, on whom we have mainly to rely for this diplomatic history, the Sultan was anxious for peace, in view of the worn-out state of his army, and indeed the haste with which he levelled Ascalon, and afterwards dismantled Lydda, Ramla, and Natrun, lest they should be taken and garrisoned by the enemy, seems almost a sign of panic. Thus Saladin, almost as impetuous as Richard, was for accepting terms, even though they included the surrender of all the coast to the invaders; but el-Adil was a more cool-headed diplomatist, and resolved to prolong the *pourparlers* in the orthodox manner, so as at least to give time for the thorough demolition of Ascalon.

Whilst thus engaged, a new factor complicated the negotiations, entirely to the advantage of the Saracens. On the 3rd of October Conrad of Montferrat opened from Tyre a separate correspondence with Saladin. He offered to break with the rest of the Crusaders, become the Sultan's ally, and retake Acre for the Saracens, on condition that Sidon and Beyrut were added to his dominion. Another ambassador from Richard arrived on the same day. Here was indeed a diplomatic godsend: el-Adil, evidently perfectly at home at such manœuvres, began to play the Marquess off against the King. All through October messages were passing between the camps. Richard scented the treachery of Montferrat, and became pressing in his attentions to el-Adil, called him "my true friend and brother," and urged a lasting settlement of the quarrel. "Both Moslems and Franks," wrote the King, according to the Arabic paraphrase,

> "are worn out; all their cities are being destroyed; lives and wealth are perishing on both sides. This matter has gone far enough. The only question is about the Holy City, the Cross, and the land. As for Jerusalem, we are firm; we will not recede, no, not if there were but a single man of us left. As for the land, give us back to the further side of Jordan. As for the Cross, to you it is only worthless wood, but to us it is priceless; let the Sultan then be gracious to us concerning it, and there shall be peace, and we shall rest from this weary toil."

To this appeal Saladin made answer:

> "Jerusalem is holy to us as well as to you, and more so, seeing it is the scene of our Prophet's journey, and the place where our people must assemble at the Last Day. Think not that we shall go back therefrom, or that we can be compliant in this matter. And as for the land, it was ours to begin with, and ye invaded it; nor had ye taken it but for the feebleness of the Moslems who then had it; and so long as this war lasts God will not permit you to set up a stone in it. And as for the Cross, our holding it is a point of vantage, nor can we surrender it except for the benefit of Islam"*

The secretary has doubtless infused into these despatches the tone which he considered appropriate to each side, and they are not to be implicitly accepted as literal copies; but they probably preserve the general sense of the correspondence. His next revelation, however, is more astonishing. He says that on the 20th of October el-Adil acquainted him with the latest proposals of the King of England. Richard offered peace on these terms: el-Adil was to marry his sister Joan, the widowed Queen of Sicily, who should be dowered with the coast cities, Acre, Ascalon, and Jaffa, and live at Jerusalem; Saladin, on his part, was to endow el-Adil with the rest of Palestine, besides what he already held in fief, and the wedded pair should reign together over the land; the Cross was to be surrendered; prisoners to be freed; the Templars and Hospitallers to be given establishments; these conditions settled, Richard would return to England.† El-Adil thought the scheme excellent, and sent Baha-ed-din to Saladin to obtain

---

* Baha-ed-din, 275; compare the *Itinerary*, iv. , 31, for a different version.

† Baha-ed-din, 277.

his consent; the Sultan said "*Na'm*" ("yes") energetically three times over, in the presence of witnesses. The secretary adds that Saladin took it as a bad joke on Richard's part, and the whole affair evidently caused much merriment in diplomatic circles. The fantastic humour of the notion struck Sir Walter Scott, who in the *Talisman* modified it into a projected alliance between Saladin and the imaginary Edith Plantagenet; whilst Lessing in *Nathan der Weise* adopts the true version.

The suggestion is not inconsistent, perhaps, with the character of a knight-errant; but it was plainly impossible for so strict a Moslem as Saladin to entertain it seriously. There is no doubt, however, that Richard struck up a warm friendship with el-Adil. Joan, it is true, is reported to have indignantly refused to marry a Mohammedan, and her brother's next idea, that el-Adil should turn Christian, was scarcely more practical. But he invited him to his camp, on the 8th of November, entertained him sumptuously at dinner in his own tent, and after a day of great festivity they parted in renewed love. This meeting is the only part of the negotiations which is alluded to by the English author of the "Itinerary," who deplores the successful manner in which el-Adil (or as he calls him "Saphadin," *i.e.*, Seyf-ed-din)

> "so imposed upon the unsuspecting king with his cunningly-fashioned speeches, that they seemed to have contracted an intimate friendship with one another. For the king consented to receive Saphadin's presents, and messengers were always running between them bearing little gifts from Saphadin to king Richard. The king's conduct seemed very blameworthy to his men, and it was a common saying that friendship with the Gentiles was a heinous crime. But Saphadin declared himself to be anxious to establish a fixed and lasting peace. So the king deemed himself acting wisely in making an open and fair peace for the enlargement of the bounds of Christendom."*

Richard's desire for peace was certainly not diminished by the knowledge that at the very moment when he was entertaining el-Adil, Conrad's ambassador was actually in Saladin's camp a few miles away. The Marquess was eager to secure the Sultan's support in his claim upon the crown of Jerusalem, against Richard's friend and vassal, the nominal King Guy, who had been playing a very minor part in recent events. His ambassador for this purpose was the same ingenious Reginald of Sidon who had passed so scurvy a trick upon Saladin at Belfort two years before. The Sultan, however, bore him no malice, received him hospitably, and provisionally approved the Marquess's renewed proposal of an alliance against the Crusaders, but postponed a definite reply. That same evening

---

* *Itin.*, iv., 31.

Humphrey of Toron arrived with fresh suggestions from Richard, in which he reiterated his wish to see el-Adil made King of Palestine, but insisted on the Christians having a share in Jerusalem. To him also Saladin was all complaisance and good will. He then called a council and set the two treaty proposals before the emirs. He found them of opinion that, if peace must be made, it were better to make it with Richard than with the Marquess, because experience had taught them that it was impossible to trust the good-faith of the Syrian Franks. The conditions thus accepted were those by which el-Adil was to marry Joan and be ruler of all Palestine, as previously proposed. The ex-queen's refusal does not seem to have been regarded as final. Richard, in his last communication to el-Adil, confessed that the Christians were all blaming him for wishing to give his sister to a Moslem; but he would try to get the Pope's dispensation; and if that failed, he would give el-Adil his niece instead of his sister. The niece was declined, but otherwise on this basis negotiations went on, and the sight of Reginald of Sidon riding beside el-Adil on the hills between the camps gave temporary wings to the slow-footed messengers of diplomacy. But nothing seems to have been definitely concluded when winter interrupted the negotiations.*

The seasons play an important part in Syrian campaigns. The beginning of the rains drove Saladin into winter quarters. Hitherto he had kept his advance guard at Lydda, but the main army had been camped on the hills, latterly at Tell Jezer, west of the Ramla road, for the sake of forage. These troops were now withdrawn to Jerusalem, whence after a time the more distant contingents were gradually dismissed to their homes as soon as they could safely be spared. Saladin had great faith in the protection of mud, but Richard had yet to learn the virtue of a Syrian winter. In December the Crusaders made their famous march upon the Holy City, the goal of all their pilgrimage. They ventured as far as Ramla, no less than eleven miles from their base at Jaffa, and after waiting six weeks there, in a ruined city, exposed to constant attacks from Saladin's outposts, they plucked up courage to penetrate seven or eight miles further, as far as Beyt Nuba; and then, almost in sight of Jerusalem, they turned about and went back again.

The "Itinerary"† tells the tragical story. After describing the delay in the ruined city of Ramla, and the hazardous adventures of the Earl of Leicester and other knights, it continues:

---

* All these separate stages in the negotiations are very precisely described, with dates, by Baha-ed-din (265, 270–9, 283–93), but the date of the council, " 11th Shawwal," is, as the context shows, a slip for 21st.

† Bk. iv., 34; v., 3.

"Our army in due order set forth for the Casal of Betenoble [Beyt Nuba], where we were discomforted by heavy rain and unwholesome weather, owing to which very many of our beasts of burden died. Indeed, so great was the tempest and such the downpour of rain and showers, coupled with the blasts of violent winds, that the stakes of [our] tents were torn up and whirled away, whilst our horses perished of cold and wet. A great part of our food and biscuit was also spoiled; and the swine flesh, commonly called bacon, grew rotten. Our armour and breast-plates became fouled with rust and could not be restored to their original bright-ness by any amount of rubbing; clothes began to wear out and very many people, from long sojourn in, a foreign land, lost health and were afflicted with great ills. This comfort alone sustained them: the hope that they were at last on the point of visiting the Lord's Sepulchre; for beyond measure did they desire to see the city of Jerusalem and finish their pilgrimage. . . .

"But the wiser set of men did not fall in with the too hasty zeal of the com-mon folk. For the Templars, the Hospitallers, and the *Pullani*,* having a sharper view of the future, dissuaded king Richard from going towards Jerusalem at that moment; because, they said, if he were to lay siege and set himself with all his might to take Saladin and all the Turks cooped up in the city with him, the Turkish army that lay on the mountain heights outside would be making sudden attacks. Thus there would be a double danger in every fight from the enemy in Jerusalem and the enemy outside. Nor, they continued, if they were successful in capturing the city would their success avail much unless they had very stout warriors to whose care they might entrust the city. And this they did not think was likely to be the case, for, in their opinion, the people were showing all eager-ness to get their pilgrimage finished, in order that they might get home without delay, being already unspeakably wearied at what they had undergone."

These prudent counsels prevailed, to the "great grief of the common people; all groaned and sighed at finding the dear hope of their heart to visit the Lord's Sepulchre so suddenly cast away. . . . They cursed the delay and those who brought about such untoward things." But the decree had gone forth, and the multitude was sorrowfully led back in snow and hail to the wretched ruins of what once was Ramla. This was before the feast of St. Hilary, which falls on the 13th of January.

"Now, whilst the army was staying at Ramla in the utmost grief, very many began to desert, either through a distaste for the tiresome march or indignation. Owing to this the army was diminished in no small degree; for the greatest part of the French went off in anger to Jaffa, and there abode at their ease. Some also went off to Acre where there was no lack of food. Some also accepted the urgent invi-tation of the Marquess of Tyre; whilst some, in their wrath and indignation, ac-companied the Duke of Burgundy when he turned off to the Casal of the Plains, at which place he dwelt eight days."

---

* Half-breeds, Franco-Syrians; or perhaps, in a wider sense, creoles—Franks born in Syria.

In order to retrieve this deplorable failure, and put heart into the army, Richard hit upon the plan of rebuilding Ascalon, and restoring it to its former power as a great Christian stronghold. At another season the policy had been admirable, but a winter march was not the most encouraging expedient that could have been devised. Richard and Henry of Champagne led the downhearted and diminished army to Ibelin.

> "So marshy and clayey did they find the ways that, at the time of pitching their tents they could think of nothing but how best to rest their wearied heads. At Ibelin he stayed for one night, outworn with grief and toil such as no tongue nor pen can describe. At earliest dawn the army went forward in due order, preceded by those whose business it was to pitch the tents. But the misery of the previous day was as nothing to this day's march. For, as our men plodded on wearily, bitter snow drifted in their faces, thick hailstones rattled down, and pouring rain enveloped them. The marshy land too gave way beneath their feet; baggage, horses and men sank in the swamps, and the more men struggled the deeper they became involved. . . . So battered, so weary, and so worn, cursing the day on which they were born, and smiting themselves, they at last reached Ascalon—only to find it so levelled by the Saracens that they could barely struggle through the gates over the heaps of stones."

The re-building of Ascalon, and difficulties with the French and with Conrad of Montferrat, occupied the next four months, and no attempt was made to molest the Saracens. There was civil war at Acre; the Duke of Burgundy and the French again deserted; and to crown all, the Prior of Hereford arrived from England with the news that the kingdom was being ruined by the oppression of John, who was plainly usurping the sovereignty. At this Richard declared he must go home and see to his own realm; but since no one would stay to carry on the Crusade unless there were a leader, and there were two claimants to the crown, he made the people choose their King. Without hesitation, one and all chose the Marquess of Montferrat, and Richard gave his reluctant assent. The unpopular widower of Sibylla, who had hitherto held if not enjoyed the title, was compensated with the kingdom of Cyprus. His supplanter was less fortunate. Hardly had Conrad attained his ambition when he was suddenly murdered by two emissaries of the Sheykh of the Assassins (27 April).* Henry of Champagne succeeded as King by general acclamation.

Whilst these things were happening on the coast, Saladin had spent the winter quietly at Jerusalem, after sending his army away to their homes. The

---

* The French accused Richard of prompting the murder, and Ibn-el-Athir charges Saladin with bribing the Assassins to kill Richard and Conrad. Neither charge deserves any more consideration than the forged exculpation ascribed to the Sheykh of the Assassins.

Franks were still in correspondence with him, for Conrad had not broken off his negotiations during the winter months. An offensive and defensive alliance was actually concluded in April, the details of which are of little interest, since the Marquess-King was murdered immediately afterwards. But the treaty, as epitomised by Baha-ed-din,* contains a reference to an understanding already existing between Saladin and Richard which probably explains a certain mysterious visit of Stephen of Turnham to Jerusalem. Stephen was astonished to see the envoys of the Marquess, Balian of Ibelin and Reginald of Sidon, "two miserable go-betweens," coming out of the city. It was apparently a case of Greek meeting Greek. The worthy Stephen was probably himself a "go-between," for the Arabic secretary mentions a message that was received about March from the King of England asking for an interview with "my brother" el-Adil, with a view to a treaty.

El-Adil set out on this mission on the 20th of March, with definite instructions. He was empowered to conclude a treaty of peace including a division of the country, the surrender of the Cross, with the right of pilgrimage to Jerusalem and of establishing priests in the Church of the Resurrection; if the King insisted on the cession of Beyrut, he must have it, but only on condition that it was destroyed. Thus far might el-Adil make concessions.† When he reached the plain of Acre, Richard was on the point of returning to Ascalon, but the conditions of the treaty were settled through an intermediary, Abu-Bekr the chamberlain, and el-Adil returned at the beginning of April, having apparently succeeded in his mission. Jerusalem was to be divided between the Christians and the Moslems, but the latter were to retain the sacred Dome of the Rock. That the treaty was not ratified is obvious from subsequent events; but a proof of the extraordinary amity then existing is found in the amazing words of the "Itinerary": "On Palm Sunday [March 29] King Richard amid much splendour girded with the belt of knighthood the son of Saphadin, who had been sent to him for that purpose."

It is hard to believe that, after so unprecedented—almost incredible—a mark of friendship, the King took advantage of a rumour of Saladin's temporary difficulties with a rebellious nephew in Mesopotamia, to postpone the conclusion of peace, in the hope of witnessing a civil war among the Saracens.‡ There is, however, no disputing the fact that in May, in spite of an all but ratified treaty, Richard again assumed the offensive, and sailing down the coast laid siege to

---

* P. 295 ; compare the *Itinerary*, v., 24.
† Baha-ed-din, 293.
‡ Baha-ed-din, 296.

the castle of Darum, where the Crusaders unhappily proved that they had lost nothing of their usual savagery in dealing with vanquished Moslems:—

> "Those Turks whom our men found holding out on the battlements they hurled down into the ditch there to be dashed to pieces. The number of Turks slain in the different parts of the castle was sixty. Those who had taken refuge in the tower, seeing that they were lost . . . surrendered themselves to perpetual slavery on the Friday before Whit-Sunday. . . . On the Friday night the king made his men keep watch over the Turks who were still in the Tower till early on the Saturday morning. Then on Whitsun Eve the Turks, coming down from the Tower at the king's command, had their hands bound so tightly behind their backs with leathern thongs that they roared for pain. They were three hundred in number, not reckoning little children and women. Thus, before the French came up, with the aid of his own men only did king Richard nobly get possession of Darum after a siege of four days."*

The capture of Darum so inspirited the Crusaders, unaccustomed of late to success, that they ventured to make a raid across the plain as far as Ibelin of the Hospitallers (Beyt Jibrin), and in June resolved to advance once more upon Jerusalem. Leaving Ascalon on the 7th, Richard marched by way of Blanche Garde and "Toron of the Knights" (Natrun), and camped once more near Betenoble, where he was joined by the French. Here the whole army waited a month for the new King, Henry, and during the delay Richard scoured the country in search of adventures. Once, "on the morrow of St. Barnabas," whilst hotly pursuing some Saracens on the hills, he raised his eyes and on a sudden beheld the Holy City afar off; or, as others say,† he would not see it, but holding his coat-of-arms before his face, wept and prayed, "O fair Lord God, I pray thee let me not see thy Holy City, if I may not deliver it out of the hands of thine enemies." But Jerusalem was not to be delivered by his sword. Whilst the Crusaders were lingering at Beyt Nuba, their enemy was daily gathering strength. Saladin's provincial contingents began to return from their homes after the breaking of winter, and were joining his colours in thousands. Dolderim, the lord of the old Courtenay fortress of Turbessel, was the first to arrive with his Turkmans at the end of May; others followed close on his heels. Careful preparations were made for the defence of Jerusalem, and the light troops were taken out by Saladin himself to skirmish with the enemy. Both sides scored successes in these affairs, but on the 23rd of June the loss of an important caravan from Egypt, laden with treasure and stores and arms, was the worst blow the Moslems received. After this, with thousands of fresh baggage animals at their command, Saladin made

---

* *Itin.*, v., 39.
† Joinville, 108.

no doubt that the Crusaders would march without delay on the Holy City, and he set about destroying the wells and cisterns in the neighbourhood, till there was not a drop of water left fit to drink. But the enemy still hesitated.

An anxious council was held at Jerusalem on Wednesday night, the 1st of July. Even Abu-l-Heyja "the Fat" attended, though he walked with difficulty and had to be given a chair in the Sultan's tent.* Baha-ed-din was ordered to address the assembled emirs, and he "spoke as God prompted him," urging to the Holy War. Saladin remained a long time deep in thought; then he made a short earnest appeal to the soldiers: "The lives and children and possessions of the Moslems rest upon you," he said; "if you fail, which God forfend, they will roll up the land like a scroll. . . . The Moslems over all the country hang upon your valour. *Wa-s-Selam.*" Then the Balafré, lately ransomed from his prison at Acre, spoke up:

> "O Maulana, we are thy mamluks and thy slaves. Thou hast been gracious to us, and made us great and powerful; thou hast given to us and made us rich; we have only our necks to offer, and they are between thy hands. By God, not a man of us will turn back from helping thee till we die!"

All the emirs said the like, and Saladin was comforted.

Thursday was spent in strenuous exertions, that no means of defence might be neglected, and after they had said the evening prayer together, Saladin and his secretary spent the night in anxious consultation. The Sultan was very uneasy; there were divided opinions among his officers as to the best way of meeting the attack; and the Kurds and Turks were not working well together. Dawn found him still deliberating. It was Friday, and in the mosque he prayed more earnestly than ever, in a low voice, his tears falling on the carpet. At any moment, he felt, the enemy might be at the gate, and Jerusalem might fall—"the Holy City for which he had an ineffable care."

That evening came a despatch from old Jurdik, who commanded the advance guard: "The enemy has ridden out and taken up a position on the hill, and then returned to camp." The next morning (Saturday the 4th) another message came: Jurdik's scouts had learnt that there was dissension in the Christian camp; some were for pushing on, others for going back; the French declared that they had left their country for the sake of Jerusalem, and they would not return without recovering it; the "Inkitar" (Englishman) had pointed out that all

---

*This emir's corpulence was so phenomenal that his stomach touched his horse's neck. When he was a governor in Mesopotamia, the potters of Mosil paid him the compliment of modelling a capacious jolly sort of bowl after his person, and these were known in commerce as "Abu-l-Heyjas." Abu-Shama (Georgens), 39 *n.*

the wells were fouled, and there was no water to be had; finally a jury was appointed to decide the issue.

The scouts spoke truth: another spell of fatal vacillation had come over the purpose of the Crusaders, and in the mist of divided counsels the decision had been committed to a jury chosen equally from the knights of the Temple and Hospital, the French, and the Syrian Franks. They decided* to abandon the advance upon Jerusalem, which was now almost in sight, and recommended a march upon Cairo—250 miles away, across the desert! The French knights protested in vain.

The next day they were in full retreat.† The Sultan rode out at the head of his men to see the wonderful sight. The rejoicing passed description. The danger was over, and Saladin felt that his prayers had indeed been heard. The Holy City was saved.

---

* *Itin.*, vi., 2.

† I have followed the chronology of Baha-ed-din, who was present and is generally accurate. It agrees with the statement in the *Itinerary* (vi., 9) that the Crusaders reached a castle near Lydda on the 6th of July. The previous statement (vi., 7) that "the feast of St. John was close at hand" (*i. e.*, 24th June) must be taken to refer, as the context shows, to a time before the decision of the jury to abandon the advance.

CASKET OF EL-'ADIL

CHAPTER XXI

THE LAST FIGHT AT JAFFA
1192

HARDLY HAD the Crusaders retired, when an ambassador to Saladin was announced from Henry "King of Jerusalem." He sent to inform the Sultan that the King of England had given him all the lands he had conquered on the coasts; "Give me back, therefore, my [other] lands," was his modest request, "that I may make peace with thee, and become as one of thy children." Saladin was so furiously indignant at this demand, coming hard after an ignominious retreat, that he could hardly keep his hands off the ambassador. He controlled himself with an effort, and sent the envoy away on the 6th of July with the reply that, as the successor of the Marquess, Henry must conform to Conrad's agreement, and that nothing beyond Tyre and Acre could be the subject of discussion. Three days later another but very different message came from Richard himself, recommending "his sister's son Count Henry" to Saladin's good graces, and urging an arrangement in a friendly and conciliatory spirit. The Sultan's council were all for peace, and an amicable answer was returned: Saladin would treat Henry "as a son," give up the Church of the Resurrection to the Christians, and divide the country; the coast would belong to the Franks, the hills to the Saracens, as then, and the lands between would be shared equally between them; but Ascalon would be demolished, and belong to neither side. Yet a third and a fourth embassy arrived within a few days, with a present of falcons from Richard; their object was to discuss details and above all to retain Ascalon. Saladin, however, remained firm; he offered Lydda in exchange, but Ascalon must inevitably be dismantled. On this rock the negotiations foundered. Richard refused to let a single stone of Ascalon be pulled down.

The King of England and most of his army had retired to Acre, where they were eagerly preparing to return to Europe, heartily sick of campaigning. Richard intended to embark at Beyrut, which he proposed to seize by a *coup de main.* Saladin, hearing more of the meditated raid upon his city than of the sailing that was to follow, took the opportunity to make a dash upon Jaffa. Leaving Jerusalem on the 27th of July, he was before the walls of Jaffa the same day. He met more resistance than he expected, but after three days' hard sapping and bombarding, in which Saladin himself took a vigorous part, the curtain was breached and the Saracens rushed forward to the assault. They were met by a wall of steel; when one man fell, another took his place. The constancy and courage of the garrison filled the Moslem chronicler with admiration. What soldiers they were, he cries, how undaunted and valiant! At last, however, there was no hope of keeping out the besiegers, and a capitulation was arranged on the same terms as at Jerusalem five years before. But the Moslems were hot with battle; they were in no mood for quarter; and Saladin confessed that he could not hold them. "Retire to the Citadel," he told the besieged, "and give up the town, for nothing will stop the Moslems going in."

It was indeed no time for peaceful citizens to be about. The town was full of wild Kurds and Turkmans, ranging the streets sword in hand, and plundering every house they entered: "stores of fine stuffs, corn in plenty, even the remnant of the plunder of the Egyptian caravan—all fell into their hands." It is no wonder that a few stray citizens were killed "by mistake."* In an orgy of victory such mistakes are apt to occur. The Sultan meanwhile had received news which made it urgently necessary to get his troops in hand. The officers commanding the corps of observation near Acre† sent word that on the very eve of his departure King Richard had heard of the perils of Jaffa and was on his way to the rescue. It was now essential to gain possession of the citadel, without which the town could not be held; but the difficulty was to get the garrison and refugees away. Though they had surrendered,‡ they were not likely to leave the safety of its walls without strong pressure, and the Moslems were gorged with spoil and weary with looting, and paid no attention to Saladin's repeated orders. He tried to get a force up to the citadel till late in the evening, but he spoke to deaf ears.

All night that worthy man, the secretary Baha-ed-din, lay sleepless with anxious forebodings. At daybreak Richard's trumpets were heard at sea. The King was at Acre, actually on the point of embarking for England, when breathless messengers arrived from Jaffa, rending their garments, and bewailing the extremity of their city. Richard did not wait to hear them out, but burst forth, "As God lives and by His help, I will set out and do what I may"; the herald sounded the assembly; knights ran to the summons; and with such force as he

---

* Baha-ed-din, 328.

† Throughout the war Saladin constantly kept bodies of troops watching the chief places of the enemy, Acre, Tyre, Antioch, and others when necessary. (Ibn-el-Athir, ii.,10.)

‡ According to the *Itinerary*, Saladin had accorded the garrison a day's delay; but this is contradicted by Baha-ed-din. The Latin statement is, however, very circumstantial, and though it is almost inconceivable that Saladin broke his word, there may have been a misunderstanding.

could hastily gather the King instantly set sail. It was the trumpets on his galleys that roused the Saracens on that Saturday morning.

There was no time to be lost. Saladin at once sent for Baha-ed-din. The man of peace, who had surveyed so many bloody fights from his mule's back, not always at a safe distance, was now entrusted with an aide-de-camp's task. While Saladin despatched troops to the shore to oppose Richard's landing, Baha-ed-din was to help to secure the citadel and bring out the garrison. He was to take three emirs and pick up the prince ez-Zahir, on the way. The prince was found asleep in his armour, wrapped in his wadded gambeson; and, still but half awake, he mounted his horse and joined the others. They rode through the glutted streets and reached the citadel. On their summons to surrender, the garrison, who were ignorant of Richard's arrival, obeyed, and prepared to leave. Had they been allowed to go forth at once, the issue might have been different. But one of the emirs, old Jurdik, who had served with Saladin in the invasion of Egypt nearly thirty years before, was a man of bowels, and he declared that he could not let the people go out from the citadel into the gathering crowd of Moslems, where they would be robbed and roughly handled. He began beating back the crowd to carve a safe retreat for the garrison, but the troops were in very ill-humour and out of control. At last forty-nine of the garrison were gotten out, with their horses and wives; but so much time had been lost in the hustle that it was now nearly noon, and as they marched out, the fleet of Richard, consisting of as many as thirty-five ships and fifteen swift galleys, could be descried close in shore. This cheering sight gave the rest of the defenders new courage, and one of them came up to Baha-ed-din and courteously informed him that they had changed their minds. In a few minutes the walls of the citadel were manned again; and the next thing was a charge of the garrison, which drove the Moslems out of the town. They were soon chased back to the fortress and the place was furiously attacked; indeed so desperate was the situation, so slow the succour, that they had just sent again to Saladin to beg for the same terms as before, when the face of fortune changed.

At this very moment the English galleys suddenly fell to their oars. Richard had waited and wondered to see Moslem banners floating from the towers, and feared that the citadel was already taken. The noise of the sea, the yells of the combatants, the shouts of the Moslem battle-cries, drowned the appeals of the men at bay. To land in face of the Saracen army, if nothing was left to be rescued, was an adventure too foolhardy even for Cœur de Lion. In this uncertainty and dismay, his quick eye caught sight of a man who plunged boldly from the castle into the sea and swam lustily towards the fleet. He was soon pulled on board, and proved to be a priest. "O noble King," he panted, "the remnant hunger for thy coming. They are borne down by the brandished swords of yonder butchers; their necks are stretched out as sheep for the slaughter; they will perish on the spot unless God helps them, through thee." And he showed the King where the garrison still stood at bay "in front of yonder tower." That was enough for Richard: "Perish the hindmost!" he shouted, and the King's red galley pulled hard for the shore. Ere it was beached, Richard was up to his middle in the sea; his knights leaped after him, and they set upon the Saracens with might and main. Right and left the King laid men low with swinging blows from his famous Danish axe.* The Moslems scattered in all directions, the beach was cleared:—"under my very eyes," says the astonished secretary, "they drove us out of the harbour." Up a stairway of the Templars' house the King rushed alone, and in an instant the English flag was waving on the walls, a signal of salvation to the garrison. Down they came at the charge, and meeting their deliverer hacking with his sword, as only Richard knew how to do, they all joined together and soon there was not a live Moslem in the streets.

What Saladin was about to allow all this can only be guessed. He may have been deceived by the long inaction of the fleet, and believed they dared not land in face of his troops. At the critical moment he was called away, and it was the man of peace who warned the general of his danger. "I galloped to the Sultan," writes the secretary, "and found him with the two envoys," who had even then come from the garrison to treat for terms. A whisper told Saladin what had happened, but he went on talking lest the envoys should guess the truth. Crowds of fugitives running headlong past the tent left no further doubt, and the Sultan formally ordered the retreat that was already a rout. The great bales of booty were abandoned; the army vanished to Yazur; only Saladin himself remained on the spot with a division of light cavalry.

Thus was Jaffa taken and re-taken in two days. The gallant rescue crowned Richard's Crusade with a glow of setting glory. He had routed a Moslem army with a handful of heroes, and had put them to flight, with three horses!†

The flight was over, but not the fight. Richard knew this as well as anyone. Abu-Bekr the chamberlain went to visit him—evidently with proposals for a truce—the very night of the rout, and brought back a quaint tale. He found the

---

* Ernoul, 281; Ralph of Coggeshall, 43. The *Itinerary* says Richard brandished a cross-bow.

† Ralph of Coggeshall, who took his account from an eyewitness, Hugh Neville, puts Richard's strength at 80 knights and 400 crossbowmen, and Saladin's army at 62,000 (*Chron. Angl.*, 44) He evidently does not reckon the Genoese and Pisans who swelled Richard's forces to between two and three thousand. (*Itin.*, vi.,20.)

King, he said, conversing in his jovial way with some of the Moslem emirs—prisoners, probably—and reported his talk, half serious, half rallying: "Why did this mighty Sultan of yours run off at the mere sight of me? By God, I was not even in armour or ready for fight—I had only my boating-shoes on! Why did you bolt?" Then he went on, "Great God, I thought he could not have taken Jaffa in two months—and he did it in two days!" Addressing Abu-Bekr he said, "My compliments to the Sultan and say that I beg him in God's name to make peace. There must be an end to all this. My country over the sea is in a bad way. There is no use to us or to you in going on with this."*

Saladin did not reject the overture, but he narrowed the limits of negotiation to the coast between Tyre and Cæsarea. It was not the attitude of a beaten general. Richard then proposed that the Sultan should fief him Jaffa and Ascalon, whereby he would become his "man," after the custom of the Franks, and he and his troops would be at Saladin's service, As the King was soon going away, the proposed vassalage (even if truly reported) could hardly be of much value, but Saladin did not wholly reject it; he offered to give Jaffa and keep Ascalon. On Sunday an ambassador came to Ramla, reiterating the demand for Ascalon. Saladin's reply was given without hesitation: we cannot give up Ascalon, he said, and your King cannot go away as he proposes without leaving *all* the country he has won to fall into our hands. If *he* can spend a winter here, far away from his country and his people, when he is still in the midst of his youth and pleasures, how much more can I stay here, both winter and summer? "I am in the heart of my own country," he added, "my children and folk are about me, I can obtain all I wish. And I am an old man; the pleasures of this world are nothing to me—I have enjoyed them to the full and have renounced them utterly. . . . I believe in my soul that I am doing the best of good works, and I will not desist until God grants the victory to whomsoever he willeth."

This negotiation split upon the rock of Ascalon, like its predecessor. Possibly it was merely intended to gain time, for on the Monday there was a report that reinforcements were marching from Acre to the King's support. Saladin sent his baggage into the hills, and taking only his cavalry went out to meet the new danger. The Franks, he found, had already reached safety at Cæsarea; and leaving them there, he turned back and resolved to make another attempt upon Jaffa. The Saracens were now well aware of the weakness of the force from which they had fled on Saturday, yet even so, they preferred to seek the advantage of a surprise. A certain Genoese prowling about at daybreak on Wednesday

---

* Baha-ed-din, 334.

(5 Aug.) heard the neighing of horses and the tramp of men, and saw the glitter of steel in the slanting rays of the sun. Running back to the camp he gave the alarm, and the knights sprang out of their beds. They had no time to gird all their armour on. Richard and many others went forth with no guards to their eyes; some had no breeches and the keen morning air struck cold upon their naked thighs; each picked up the weapon nearest to hand and sallied forth.

The King had only fifty-four knights in all, of whom only fifteen had horses, and some two thousand stout soldiers; but at their head stood Henry of Champagne, the Earl of Leicester, Bartholomew de Mortimer, Ralph de Mauléon, Andrew de Chavigny, Gerard de Furnival, and many another trusty sword. The Saracens came on at the gallop in seven divisions, each of a thousand horsemen; but their spears rattled upon an iron fence. Behind a slight palisade, hastily set, of tent-pegs, to hamper the cavalry, the Franks were formed up on one knee to receive cavalry, the butts of their spears firmly planted in the earth, their shields locked before them. Between each pair Richard placed an archer, who plied his cross-bow over the shields; another man stood behind to stretch and load a spare bow. Squadron upon squadron came thundering on, only to be brought up sharply by the wall of spears.

For a time they sat like paralysed men, locked spear to spear, able only to shout and curse, and at such close quarters that no one loosed a bowstring; then they sullenly wheeled off. Five or six times the charge was repeated, with the same result; but at last, at three in the afternoon, Richard made his cross-bowmen pass through to the front and deliver a volley of bolts at the galloping line. The spearmen then let the archers pass between them, and following up the attack completed the discomfiture of the enemy. At the moment of retreat, Richard sallied out with his fifteen mounted knights, and fell upon the Saracens with his incomparable fury, cleaving heads and chopping off limbs in every direction. In the heat of battle, he must have had his horse killed; for suddenly a Turk rode up to him on a foaming charger, leading another; seeing the King unmounted, Saladin had sent him two swift Arabs, thinking it shame that so brave a warrior should fight on foot.* Richard accepted them in the same spirit, and the battle went on. Meanwhile the Moslems tried to seize the town behind, but Richard with a handful of knights drove them out; the craven galleymen made off in alarm, but the King brought them back to hold the town; the day is one long record of Richard's exploits. "Velut leo ferocissimus invadit, invadendo

---

* The story is told in a different form by Ernoul, 281–2, who makes el-Adil the generous, or, as some suggest, the treacherous, giver; but as el-Adil was lying sick near Jerusalem at the time this version is clearly wrong.

prosterait, prostratos interficit."* Nor is this the coloured imagination of the
Christian chronicler. Baha-ed-din admits the total failure of the Moslem attack,
which he ascribes to the clemency shown to the garrison of Jaffa; some of the
soldiers, he says, even taunted the Sultan—"Make your slaves charge who beat
off our people on the day we took Jaffa! "Whatever the cause, Saladin could not
get his men to return to the attack, and his secretary tells, in admiration and
disgust, how the King of England rode along the whole front of the Saracen
army, lance at rest, defying them, and not a man attempted to touch him!†
Saladin at last left the field in a fury, and on the Friday he was in Jerusalem
ordering fresh fortifications. He had now no faith in Richard's going away without taking the Holy City.

The next day the Sultan was back at the camp near Ramla, praying for
reinforcements: he could not trust the men who had twice failed him. Supports
came in the nick of time—troops from Mosil, from Egypt, the old mamluks of
Shirkuh, the levies from northern Syria: in a few days he had a new army to
shame the men who had skulked before Jaffa. But they were not needed. The
King of England was seriously ill; health, as well as troubles at home, urged a
speedy move; the other Crusaders were impatient to be off; the new King of
Jerusalem and even the two Military Orders refused to be responsible for the
conquered cities on the coast unless Richard were there to lead them: "they
rejected his proposals and walked with him no more."

With so small a following, and so many friends estranged; lying on a sick bed
with "swarming hordes of Turks" all round; the King could only make terms with
Saladin and go. The second failure at Jaffa had taught the Sultan a lesson, and
even with his fresh troops he was not eager to carry on the war *à outrance*. There
had been enough of fighting, in all conscience, and no one could say that for five
years the Moslems had not trodden "the path of God" with the zeal and endurance of martyrs. The illness of the King softened the hearts of Saladin and el-
Adil, always disposed to friendship with so frank and soldierly an adversary. In
his burning fever Richard craved for cooling fruit, and Saladin constantly sent
him pears and peaches and refreshing snow from the mountains. It is said that
el-Adil was afflicted at the King's danger, and Richard of Devizes‡ relates a pretty
tale of one of his visits to the sick man's tent:—

> "Meanwhile there came down to see the king, as was his wont, a certain gentle
> Saffadin, Saladin's brother, an old soldier, very courteous and wise, and one

---

* See the vivid account, from an eyewitness, in Ralph of Coggeshall, 45–50.
† Baha-ed-din, 338.
* *Chronicon*, 88–92.

whom the king's magnanimity and munificence had won over to his side. When the king's servants received him with less glee than usual, and would not admit him to speech with their master, he said: ' By the interpreter I perceive ye are in great sorrow, nor am I ignorant of the cause. My friend your king is sick, and it is for this reason ye close the door against me.' Then bursting into tears, 'O God of the Christians,' he said, ' if thou indeed be God, thou canst not suffer such a man, and one so needful, to die so early."

It is a pity, but it is quite certain that el-Adil was never at Jaffa during the King's illness.

It was to el-Adil, nevertheless, though he lay ill at Mar Samwil, that Richard turned in his distress; he begged him to make "the best terms he could"* with Saladin. "Ask my brother, el-Adil," he urged Abu-Bekr the chamberlain, "to see how he can bring the Sultan to make peace, and beg him to leave me Ascalon." But Ascalon was not to be his. Diplomacy was busy from Friday the 28th of August to the following Wednesday; a swift courier sped between el-Adil and the two camps; and finally the treaty of peace for three years was signed on the 2nd of September, 1192. The coast cities he had conquered from Acre to Jaffa were given to the King of England; Ascalon was to be demolished; Moslems and Christians were to pass freely in each others' territories, and pilgrims might visit the Holy Sepulchre at Jerusalem. When the messenger placed the draft treaty in his hands, the King was very ill and said, "I have no strength to read it, but here is my hand on the peace." When the embassy came for the signing, Richard gave his hand to each, and they all pledged their word to him. He would not take an oath himself, saying that it was not the way of kings, but Henry of Champagne, King though he was, Balian of Ibelin, the knights of the Temple and Hospital, and all those present, took the oath. In the evening the Franks sent their ambassadors for the Sultan's ratification, and the next morning Saladin gave his hand on it, and the peace was proclaimed throughout the camp. "It was a joyful day: God alone knoweth the measureless delight of both peoples."

King Richard went on board his ship at Acre on the 9th of October: but before he sailed away he sent a message to his chivalrous adversary that when the three years' truce was over he would come again and rescue Jerusalem; and Saladin said in answer that, if he must lose his land, he had liefer lose it to Richard than to any man alive. And so they parted, and the land had rest.

---

* *Itin.* vi., 27.

CHAPTER XXII

AT REST
1192–1193

T HE HOLY WAR was over; the five years' contest ended. Before the great victory at Hittin in July, 1187, not an inch of Palestine west of the Jordan was in the Moslems' hands. After the Peace of Ramla in September 1192, the whole land was theirs, except a narrow strip of coast from Tyre to Jaffa. Saladin had no cause to be ashamed of the Treaty. The Franks indeed retained most of what the Crusaders had won, but the result was contemptible in relation to the cost. At the Pope's appeal, all Christendom had risen in arms. The Emperor, the Kings of England, France, and Sicily, Leopold of Austria, the Duke of Burgundy, the Count of Flanders, hundreds of famous barons and knights of all nations, had joined with the King and Princes of Palestine and the indomitable brothers of the Temple and Hospital, in the effort to deliver the Holy City and restore the vanished Kingdom of Jerusalem. The Emperor was dead; the Kings had gone back; many of their noblest followers lay buried in the Holy Land; but Jerusalem was still the city of Saladin, and its titular king reigned over a slender realm at Acre.

All the strength of Christendom concentrated in the Third Crusade had not shaken Saladin's power. His soldiers may have murmured at their long months of hard and perilous service, year after year, but they never refused to come to his summons and lay down their lives in his cause. His vassals in the distant valleys of the Tigris may have groaned at his constant requirements, but they brought their retainers loyally to his colours; and at the last pitched battle, at Arsuf, it was the division of Mosil that most distinguished itself for valour. Throughout these toilsome campaigns Saladin could always count on the support of the levies from Egypt and Mesopotamia, as well as from northern and central Syria; Kurds, Turkmans, Arabs, and Egyptians, they were all Moslems and his servants when he called. In spite of their differences of race, their national jealousies, and tribal pride, he had kept them together as one host—not without difficulty and twice or thrice a critical waver. But, the shirking at Jaffa notwithstanding, they were still a united army under his orders in the autumn of 1192,

242

as they had been when he first led them "on the Path of God" in 1187. Not a province had fallen away, not a chief or 3 had rebelled, though the calls upon their loyalty and endurance were enough to try the firmest faith and tax the strength of giants. The brief defection, quickly pardoned, of a young prince of his own blood in Mesopotamia only emphasises, by its isolation, Saladin's compelling influence over his subjects. When the trials and sufferings of the five years' war were over, he still reigned unchallenged from the mountains of Kurdistan to the Libyan desert, and far beyond these borders the King of Georgia, the Catholicos of Armenia, the Sultan of Konia, the Emperor of Constantinople, were eager to call him friend and ally.

To such allies he owed nothing: they came not to aid but to congratulate. The struggle was waged by Saladin alone. Except at the last, when his brother came prominently to the front, one cannot point to a single general or counsellor who can be said to have led, much less dominated, the Sultan. A council of war undoubtedly guided his military decisions, and sometimes overruled his better judgment, as before Tyre and Acre, but in that council it is impossible to single out a special voice that weighed more than another in influencing his mind. Brother, sons, nephews, old comrades, new vassals, shrewd Kady, cautious secretary, fanatical preacher—all had their share in the general verdict, all helped their Master loyally according to their ability, but not a man of them ever forgot who was the Master. In all that anxious, laborious, critical time, one mind, one will was supreme, the mind and the will of Saladin.

When the struggle at last was ended, when the Franks had been driven to the seashore, and the places holy to Moslems as well as to Christians were once more in his own keeping, Saladin may well have dreamt of wider empire, larger schemes. The memories of the first great tide of Saracen victory, even the late example of Seljuk triumphs, might awaken thoughts of other worlds to conquer. But such imaginings were not ripe to trouble his newly found peace. Saladin's first concern was for the repose of his weary troops. Hardly had the Treaty been signed when he dismissed them to their homes, and on the 10th and 11th of September the long procession of the men of Mesopotamia began the glad march to their villages by the great rivers and in the upper highlands. His next care was for the crowded caravans of Christian pilgrims who were at last to content their souls' craving to see the place where the Lord died. There were rough Saracen soldiers at Jerusalem, hungry for vengeance upon the slaughterers of their kindred upon the plain of Acre; but Saladin's escort on the road, and honest Jurdik's humane rule in the city, brought the pilgrims through all dangers.

The Sultan himself was in Jerusalem in September, when Hubert Walter the Bishop of Salisbury brought the third of the pilgrim caravans to the Holy Places

"To this bishop, on account of his uprightness, his reputation for wisdom and his wide renown, Saladin sent, offering him a house free of cost. But the bishop refused on the ground that he and his company were pilgrims. Then Saladin bade his servants shew all kinds of courtesy to the bishop and his men. Saladin also sent him many gifts of price and even invited him to a conference in order to see what kind of a man he was in appearance. He had the Holy Cross shewn him, and they sat together a long time in familiar conversation. On this occasion Saladin made enquiries as to the character and habits of the king of England. He also asked what the Christians said about his Saracens. To him the bishop made answer, 'As regards my lord the king, I may say that there is no knight in the world who can be considered his peer in military matters, or his equal in valour and generosity. He is distinguished by the full possession of every good quality. . . . If any one could give your noble qualities to king Richard and his to you, so that each of you might be endowed with the faculties of the other, then the whole world could not furnish two such princes. At last Saladin, having heard the bishop patiently, broke in: 'I know the great valour and the bravery of your king well enough; but, not to speak too severely, he often incurs unnecessary danger and is too prodigal of his life. Now I, for my part, however great a king I might be, would much rather be gifted with wealth, so long as it is alongside of wisdom and moderation, than with boldness and immoderation.'

"After a long interview by means of an interpreter Saladin bade the bishop to request any gift he liked and it should be granted him. For this offer the bishop gave many thanks, begging to have a space of time—till the morrow—granted him for deliberation. Then, on the next day, he begged that two Latin priests and two Latin deacons might be permitted to celebrate divine service with the Syrians at the Lord's Sepulchre. These priests were to be maintained out of the offerings of the pilgrims. For, in visiting the Lord's Sepulchre, the bishop had found only the services half celebrated after the barbarous fashion of the Syrians. He made a similar request for Bethlehem and Nazareth. This was a great petition to make, and, as is believed, one very pleasing to God. When the Soldan consented, the bishop, in accordance with his request, established priests and deacons in each place, thus inaugurating a fitting service to God."*

Four months before these Latin priests were installed, an ambassador from the Greek Emperor had preferred a similar request to Saladin on behalf of the priests of the Orthodox Church, and had been refused. It is curious to discover in the twelfth century the same contest over the Holy Places which was among the Russian pretexts for the war with Turkey in 1854. When he was assured that the King of England had really taken ship and left the country, Saladin began a progress

---

* *Itin.*, vi., 34.

through the land which had been won and held at so great cost. He visited all the strongholds and chief cities, examining their defences, giving orders for fortifications, and placing in each a strong garrison of horse and foot. At Beyrut, on the 1st of November, he received the Prince of Antioch, Bohemond the Stammerer, who participated in the treaty of peace; the meeting was cordial, and the Prince was presented with lands in the plain of Antioch to the value of 15,000 gold pieces a year. At Kaukab—no longer to be called Belvoir—he found his ancient servant of early days, Karakush the builder of the walls of Cairo, who had languished in prison at Acre ever since the surrender. There were no reproaches, but only the welcome due to old and tried devotion. On the 4th of November Damascus once more acclaimed its Sultan. He had not been within its gates for four years, and his public levee the next day was thronged with old friends and joyous subjects. The poets had no words rare and rich enough for the great occasion.

Once more Saladin was at home among his children. We see him sitting in his summer-house in the castle grounds, with his younger children about him. Envoys from the Franks were announced, but when they came into his presence, their shaven chins, cropped hair, and strange clothes frightened little Abu-Bekr, who began to cry. The father, thinking only of the child, dismissed the ambassadors with an excuse, before they had even delivered their message. Older sons were there, grown men who had fought in his battles, and with these and his brother, el-Adil, he went day after day hunting the gazelle in the spacious plains about Damascus. He had thoughts of going to Mekka on pilgrimage, the supreme duty of the pious Moslem; he wished to visit again that Egypt which had been his stepping stone to power; but the time passed and the pilgrims came back from Arabia, and Saladin was still at Damascus, revelling in the delights of a peaceful home.

On Friday the 20th of February, he rode out with Baha-ed-din to meet the caravan of the Hajj. He had not been well of late, and it was the wet season; the roads were streaming after heavy rains, and he had imprudently forgotten to wear his usual quilted gambeson. That night he had fever.* The next day he

---

* It was probably an acute remittent fever, of the bilious type,—the "yellow fever" of Arabic writers,—due to blood poisoning. His previous malarial attacks and exposure to constant and intense fatigue and hardships, and recently to wet and cold, may have produced organic complications. The symptoms, recorded very fully by Baha-ed-din,—suppression of the excretions with retention of the poison, which increased until it burst through the skin in exhausting perspiration, followed by death,—are common to various forms of virulent fever. So I am informed by Sir William Gowers, M.D., F.R.S., who kindly interested himself in the subject of Saladin's fatal illness, and consulted the local experience of Dr. F. J. Mackinnon, of the Victoria Hospital, Damascus, who confirmed his diagnosis.

could not join his friends at dinner, and the sight of the son sitting in the father's seat brought tears to many eyes—they took it as an omen. Each day the Sultan grew worse, his head was racked with pain, and he suffered internally. On the fourth day the doctors bled him; and from that time he grew steadily worse. The fever parched his skin, and he became weaker and weaker. On the ninth day his mind wandered; he fell into a stupor and could no longer take his draught. Every night Baha-ed-din and the chancellor el-Fadil would go to see him, or at least to hear the doctors' report; and sometimes they would come out streaming with tears, which they strove to command, for there was always a multitude outside the gates waiting to learn from their faces how the Master was. On Sunday, the tenth day of the illness, medicine gave some relief, the sick man drank a good draught of barley water, and broke into a profuse perspiration. "We gave thanks to God . . . and came out with lightened hearts." It was but the last effort. On Tuesday night the faithful secretary and chancellor were summoned to the castle, but they did not see the Sultan, who was sinking fast. There was a divine with him, repeating the confession of faith and reading the Holy Word; and when he came to the passage "He is God, than whom there is no other God,—who knoweth the unseen and the seen,—the Compassionate, the Merciful," the Sultan murmured, "True"; and when the words came, "In Him do I trust," the dying man smiled, his face lighted up, and he rendered his soul to his Lord.

Saladin died on Wednesday, the 4th of March, 1193, at the age of fifty-five.

They buried him the same day in the garden house in the Citadel of Damascus, at the hour of the *asr* prayer. The sword which he had carried through the Holy War was laid beside him: "he took it with him to Paradise." He had given away everything, and the money for the burial had to be borrowed, even to the straw for the bricks that made the grave. The ceremony was as simple as a pauper's funeral. A striped cloth covered the undistinguished bier. No poet was allowed to sing a dirge, no preacher to make oration. When the multitude, who, thronged about the gate, saw the bier, a great wailing went up, and so distraught were the people that they could not form the words of prayer, but only cried and groaned. All eyes were wet, and there were few that did not weep aloud. Then every man went home and shut his door, and the empty silent streets bore witness to a great sorrow. Only the weeping secretary and those of the household went to pray over the grave and indulge their grief. The next day the people thronged to the tomb, praying, lamenting, reciting the Koran, and invoking the blessing of God upon him who slept beneath.

It was not till the close of a second year that the body of the Sultan was interred by a son's loving care in the oratory on the northern side of the Kellasa, beside the great Omayyad mosque, where it lies now. Over it the faithful chancellor, who was soon to follow his master, wrote the epitaph: "O God, accept this soul, and open to him the gates of heaven, that last victory for which he hoped."

"I entered into this oratory," says a later biographer, "by the door which gives on the Kellasa, and after reciting a portion of the Koran over the grave, I invoked God's mercy on its dweller. The warden showed me a packet containing Saladin's clothes, and I saw among them a short yellow vest with black cuffs, and I prayed that the sight might be blessed to me."*

The wise physician Abd-el-Latif wrote, somewhat cynically, that to his knowledge this was the only instance of a King's death that was truly mourned by the people. The secret of Saladin's power lay in the love of his subjects. What others sought to attain by fear, by severity, by majesty, he accomplished by kindness. In the memorable words which he spoke, not long before his death, to his best-beloved son, ez-Zahir, on dismissing him to his provincial government, he revealed the source of his own strength.

"My son," he said, "I commend thee to the most high God, the fountain of all goodness. Do His will, for that way lieth peace. Abstain from the shedding of blood; trust not to that; for blood that is spilt never slumbers. *Seek to win the hearts of thy people,* and watch over their prosperity; for it is to secure their happiness that thou art appointed by God and by me. Try to gain the hearts of thy emirs and ministers and nobles, I have become great as I am because I have won men's hearts by gentleness and kindness."

Gentleness was the dominant note of his character. We search the contemporary descriptions in vain for the common attributes of Kings. Majesty? It is not mentioned, for the respect he inspired sprang from love, which "casteth out fear." State? Far from adopting an imposing mien and punctilious forms, no sovereign was ever more genial and easy of approach. He loved to surround himself with clever talkers, and was himself "delightful to talk to." He knew all the traditions of the Arabs, the "Days" of their ancient heroes, the pedigrees of their famous mares. His sympathy and unaffected interest set every one at his ease, and instead of repressing freedom of conversation, he let the talk flow at such a pace that sometimes a man could not hear his own voice. Old-fashioned courtiers regretted the strict propriety of Nur-ed-din's levees, when each man

---

* Ibn-Khallikan, iv., 547.

sat silent, "as if a bird were perched on his head," till he was bidden to speak. At Saladin's court all was eager conversation—a most unkingly buzz. Yet there were limits which no one dared to transgress in the Sultan's presence. He suffered no unseemly talk, nor was any flippant irreverence or disrespect of persons permitted. He never used or allowed scurrilous language. He kept his own tongue, even in great provocation, under rigid control, and his pen was no less disciplined: he was never known to write a bitter word to a Moslem.

The Baghdad physician has left a record, far too brief, of his first impressions of Saladin, in which we see the Sultan in his social aspect.

> "I found him," wrote Abd-el-Latif, "a great prince, whose appearance inspired at once respect and love, who was approachable, deeply intellectual, gracious, and noble in his thoughts. All who came near him took him as their model. . . . The first night I was with him I found him surrounded by a large concourse of learned men who were discussing various sciences. He listened with pleasure and took part in their conversation. He spoke of fortification, touched on some questions of law, and his talk was fertile in ingenious ideas. He was then [1191–2] absorbed in strengthening the defences of Jerusalem, and personally superintended the work, even carrying stones on his own shoulders; and everybody, rich and poor, followed his example, even Imad-ed-din the Katib, and the Kady el-Fadil. He was on horseback before dawn, superintending the work till noon, . . . and again from afternoon prayer till he returned by torchlight. Then he would spend a great part of the night in arranging the morrow's labours."

His whole life was simple, laborious, ascetic. When he was shown a beautiful pavilion that had been built for him at Damascus, he scarcely glanced at it: "We are not to stay here for ever," he said. "This house is not for one who looks for death. We are here to serve God." Luxury and self-indulgence he despised. When he found that one of his sons was neglecting his duties in his passion for a slave-girl, he sternly upbraided the voluptuary, and separated the girl.

"Our Sultan," says Baha-ed-din, "was very noble of heart, kindness shone in his face, he was very modest, and exquisitely courteous." The histories are full of his goodness. He could not bear to have his servants beaten, in an age when the beating of servants was a matter of course. If they stole his money, he dismissed them; but the whip he abhorred. His indulgence and patience knew no bounds, and he never set store by his own dignity, Baha-ed-din relates with horror how, when they were riding together into Jerusalem on a rainy day, his mule splashed the Sultan with mud; but Saladin only laughed, and would not let the abashed secretary ride behind. Another time a servant threw a shoe and almost hit the Sultan, but he turned smiling to the other side, as though he had not noticed it. An old mamluk importuned him with a petition when he was worn out with fatigue, but he fetched the ink-horn himself and granted the request without a sign of irritation. Petitioners would so crowd him when he sat in audience, that they even trampled his divan, but he always took their petitions with his own hand and attended to their grievances, and none went empty away. Every day he received these troublesome documents, and set apart a certain time to go through the papers with his secretary and endorse them with the proper answers.

On Mondays and Thursdays he sat on the judgment seat, with the Kadis and jurisconsults, in the court of law, and administered justice to all comers. He claimed and allowed no privileges before the court, and if a man had a suit against one of the royal princes, or even against the Sultan himself, they had to appear before the Kady like any ordinary defendant and submit to the law. But if Saladin won the case, he would clothe the defeated suitor in a robe of honour, pay his expenses, and send him away happy and astonished. From such a judge people could not fear sternness. Yet in the war for the Faith he could be stern, almost implacable, and the list of executions, especially of Templars, shows how religion may embitter even the gentlest of men. But it was not always so. It is related how a Frank prisoner was brought trembling before Saladin, and then cried out, "Before I saw his face I was sore afraid, but now that I have seen him I know he will do me no harm." He went off a free man.

These pages have recorded instances of his clemency and tenderheartedness, but many might be added. There is the touching story of the woman who came from the Crusaders' camp at Acre seeking her baby, who had been carried off by the Saracen soldiery. The pickets let her pass and led her to the Sultan, to whom she had appealed,—"for he is very merciful," they said. Saladin was touched by her anguish; the tears stood in his eyes; and he had the camp searched till the little girl was safely restored to her mother, and both were led back to the enemy's lines. His love for children was a beautiful part of his character. Every orphan child he felt was his special charge. He was devotedly attached to his own little ones: of his wives we read nothing*; Eastern gentlemen do not talk of their wives; but there are many references to his pleasure in his children. He would not allow them to see deeds of blood—a precaution natural enough in our

---

* The only one of Saladin's wives whom we know by name is the princess Asimat-ed-din, daughter of Anar, the celebrated vezir of Damascus. She married the Sultan Nur-ed-din in 1147, and after his death she became in 1176 the wife of Saladin, by whom (though she must have been at least 45) she was recorded to be with child in 1182. No child, however, survived her, when she died in 1185. Like Saladin's sister, the "Lady of Syria," she was a pious founder of mosques. At his death, Saladin left seventeen sons and one little daughter; and several children died earlier. (Abd-el-Basit, *Description de Damas*, trans. Sauvaire, 198, 248; Imad-ed-din in Abu-Shama, 40.)

eyes, but very rare in his age. "I do not wish them," said Saladin, "to become accustomed to bloodshed, young as they are, or to delight in the taking of life, when as yet they know not the difference between Moslems and infidels." He used to teach them himself and delighted, more perhaps than they did, in instilling into their infant minds a certain compendium of theology, which they had to learn by heart.

For above all things Saladin was a devout Moslem. His religion was all the world to him. In this alone he was fanatical; and the only act of severity, not done in war, that can be alleged against him was the execution of the mystic philosopher es-Suhrawardy, on the ground of heresy. Saladin hated all eclectic philosophers, materialists, and free-thinkers, with a holy horror. His own faith was as rigidly orthodox as it was simple, strong, and sincere. Islam, in its essence and as professed by such a man as Saladin, is a religion of noble simplicity and austere self-sacrifice. To say that he was regular in its ceremonious observances is little, except that his determination to make up for the two, months of fasting, which he had been forced to omit during the war, probably hastened his end. His frequent illnesses and arduous exertions alike made fasting dangerous to his health; his doctors warned him in vain, and his persistence in this religious duty whilst at Jerusalem in his last year weakened his constitution and made him less able to resist the fatal fever. No one was more assiduous in the five daily prayers and the weekly attendance at the mosque; and even when seriously ill, he would send for the Imam and force himself to stand and repeat the fatiguing service of Friday. He delighted in hearing the Koran read to him, but his reader had to be a practised expert. Saladin would listen till his heart melted and the tears rolled down his cheeks. He had this womanish weakness, yet one likes him none the less for his emotional, sensitive nature. "His heart was humble and full of compassion, and tears came readily to his eyes."

It was a grief to him that he was never able to perform the religious duty of pilgrimage; but at least he was a benefactor to the pilgrims. One of his early acts of sovereignty was to abolish the onerous tolls which had for centuries burdened the Faithful who visited Mecca, and his last public appearance was to welcome the returning Hajj. As the pilgrims greeted him, it was noticed how radiant he looked. He had but a week to live.

In nothing did he show his religious zeal more fervently than in the chief and supreme duty of Moslems, the *Jihad* or Holy War. Naturally averse to bloodshed, even unwarlike, as he was, he was a changed man when it came to fighting the infidels. "I never knew him," says Baha-ed-din, "show any anxiety about the numbers and strength of the enemy. He would listen to plans of all kinds and discuss their consequences without any excitement or loss of composure." He used to ride, as we have seen, between the lines of battle, attended only by a page; and once he sat there on horseback surrounded by his staff and listened calmly whilst the sacred Traditions were read aloud to him in face of the enemy. To wage God's war was a genuine passion with him; his whole heart was wrapped up in it, and to this cause he devoted himself, body and soul. During those last years he could hardly speak or think of anything else, and he sacrificed every pleasure, comfort, and domestic happiness, to its service. He even dreamed of wider battles for the faith: when the Franks should be driven out of Palestine, he told his secretary, he would pursue them over the sea and conquer them, till there should not remain one unbeliever on the face of the earth. "What is the most glorious death?" he asked his friend, who replied, "To die on the Path of God." "Then I strive for the door of the most glorious of deaths," said Saladin. When he was so prostrated with a painful illness at the siege of Acre that he could not come to table, he would yet sit his horse all day before the enemy; and when men marvelled at his fortitude, he said, "The pain leaves me when I am on horseback. It comes back only when I dismount." So long as he was doing God's work, he felt no pain; but inaction tortured him.

On that Holy War he spent everything, strength, health, one may even say life itself. He emptied his treasury in the cause. But it was natural to him to give, and he gave ungrudgingly, with open-handed, both-handed generosity, as freely when he was poor as when he was rich. Money he compared to mere dust, and he hated to refuse it to him who asked. He would always give more than was expected, and he never said "we have given to him before." He was preyed upon by greedy beggars, and Baha-ed-din was ashamed at the importunity of the petitions that passed through his hands. Had he been left to himself his campaigns would have been ruined for lack of funds—for it was his rule that his commissariat should pay for the provisions they took from the country people. His treasurers used always to keep a secret balance for emergencies, and even then the Sultan would sell his last farm sooner than turn away a poor man. So it happened that when he was dead there was found but one Tyrian dinar and 47 silver dirhems in the treasury. He left neither house, nor goods, nor acres, nor villages, nor any sort of personal property. The great Sultan died almost pennyless. It would be hard to imagine a nature more unselfish, devoted to higher aims, or more wholly lovable. Had he been made of sterner stuff, or skilled in the prudent economics and saving foresight of mere selfish statesmanship, he might perhaps have founded a more enduring and united empire, but he would not have been Saladin, the type of generous chivalry.

The faithful secretary, when he finished his Story of his Master's life, wrote, "I have ended my record on the day of his death, God's mercy be on him. My aim was to deserve the compassion of the Most High God, and to stir men to pray for Saladin and to remember his goodness."

THE TAKING OF JERUSALEM.

FROM A PAINTED WINDOW AT ST. DENYS, 12TH CENTURY.

CHAPTER XXIII

SALADIN IN ROMANCE

THE MOST CELEBRATED English romance of the Middle Ages relating to Saladin is the "Romance of Richard Cœur de Lion," which appears to have taken its present shape about the beginning of the fourteenth century. In this dreary poem we find Richard, lying sick before Acre, demanding pork with an invalid's persistence. His attendants are in despair, because pork is not easily procured in a Mohammedan country. A crafty old knight hits upon a perfect substitute. He kills a plump young Saracen, and Lionheart finds it excellent "pork." With a refinement of hospitality he tries the new dish on his Saracen prisoners, and bids them to a state banquet, where each man's plate is garnished with the head of a particular friend. Richard himself presides at this Pelopeian feast, and gracefully carves a Saracen's head by way of encouragement. "Friends!" he exclaims, seeing a not unnatural hesitation among the convives:

> Frendes, be nought squoymous!
> This is the maner of my hous,
> To be servyd ferst, God it wot,
> With Sarezynes hedes abouten al hot.

The "Romance of Richard Cœur de Lion" is more than satisfying in regard to its hero, but disappointing in its vague account of Saladin. Like the *Itinerarium Regis Ricardi*, on which its more historical—or less unhistorical—incidents are perhaps distantly founded, it is wholly occupied with the heroic deeds of

> Kyng Rychard, the werryor best
> That men fynde in ony jeste.

When he met Saladin in single combat (which, as we know, he never did) the Sultan was miserably discomfited. At the battle of Arsuf, for example, Richard did not miss the opportunity of personally worsting his "heathen" antagonist as well as routing his army:

> Off a footman a bowe he took,
> He drowgh an arwe up to the hook,
> And sente it to the Sawdon anon,
> And smot hym thorwgh the schuldyr bon.

Whereat Saladin, in great dolour, fled to Cairo:

> The cheff Sawdon off Hethenysse
> To Babyloyne was flowen, I wysse.

He presently plucked up courage, however, to come back and challenge Richard to single combat. Here the true story of the horse which Saladin sent to Richard, when he saw him fighting on foot at Jaffa, is introduced with variations. Saladin sends for his astrologer, "a maytyr Negromacien," who conjures "twoo stronge feendes off the eyr" into the forms of two chargers. One of these is sent to King Richard, and is warranted to come to the neigh of his mate, the mare whom Saladin was to ride, and thus would the King be snared at the critical moment of the encounter. An angel, it is needless to say, warns Richard of this trick, and instructs him how to manage the strong fiend with a huge pole.

> Ther myghte men see, in a throwe,
> How Kyng Richard, the noble man,
> Encounteryd with the Sawdan
> That cheef was told off Damas.
> Hys trust upon hys mere was.
> Therfoore, as the booke telles,
> Hys crouper heeng al full off belles
> And hys peytrel, and hys arsoun;
> Three myle myghte men here the soun.

The event of the duel was never doubtful: no man could withstand Richard's arm. He soon

> Gaff the Sawdon a dynt off dede.
> In his blasoun, verrayment,
> Was i-paynted a serpent.
> With the spere that Richard heeld,
> He bar hym thorwgh and undyr the scheelde.
> None off hys armes myghte laste:
> Brydyl and peytrel al to-brast,
> Hys gerth and hys stiropes also:

and, to make a long story short, the mighty Sultan, transfixed by his adversary's spears, tumbled over his mare's crupper, and lay in the most undignified attitude, his "feet toward the fyrmament." Yet Saladin challenged Richard again at Jaffa, to whose ambassador the Lionheart made answer.

> God geve the wel evyl pyne!
> And Saladyn yowr lorde,
> The devyl hym hange with a corde. . . .
> Now go and say to Saladyn,
> In despyte of his god Appolyn
> I wyl abide hym betime. . . .
> And if the dogge wyl come to me
> My pollax schal hys bane be.

The famous poleaxe, however, the two-handed Danish axe of Ernoul's story, was less baneful to Saladin than to his sons, two of whom Richard slew offhand, according to the Romance.

One finds a much richer store of Saladin legends in the French romances. To take but a thread or two of the mythical skein, the "Tales of a Minstrel of Rheims"* give a good idea of the recitations which used to delight gentle audiences in courts and castles, the Society of the thirteenth century. Indeed, the very same tales were evidently current two centuries later, as anyone may see by a reference to Pierre Cochon. They are much more artistic than the clumsy English romance of Richard, and as their object was by no means to belaud that hero, or the "caudate" Britons—who were supposed (by Frenchmen) to put their tails between their legs and run,—they had to resort to other characters and incidents to excite and retain the interest of their hearers. In matter of history the Minstrel sticks at nothing. He begins Saladin's adventures at a precocious age, and connects him in a discreditable manner with Eleanor of Aquitaine, afterwards the Queen of Henry II. and mother of Richard I, but at the time of the story wife of Louis le Jeune of France.

Eleanor, he explains, "qui mout fu male famme," when she went to Palestine on crusade with her husband, was much annoyed at Louis's slothfulness. He stayed at Tyre all winter (1148–9), doing nothing but spend money, while Eleanor became a prey to melancholy. Her wandering thoughts would stray to the gallant person of Saladin, who openly rallied the French king's unwarlike luxury, "sa molesce et sa nicetei," and vainly challenged him to come out and fight. Eleanor was so much impressed with the gossip she heard of Saladin's prowess and generosity, that she fell in love with him *durement*, and, in the good frank medieval way, sent a dragoman to tell him so; offering to have him for her lord,

---

* *Récits d'un Ménestral de Reims* edited by M. N. de Wailly for the Société de l'histoire de France, Paris, 1876.

and to change her religion for his sake. Saladin, of course, could only be delighted, *moult liés*, at such a proposal from so fair a dame, with such a dower—"la plus gentis dame de crestienté et la plus riche." He straightway sent a swift galley from Ascalon to fetch her. In not going himself he showed more prudence, perhaps, than gallantry; but Saracen lovers, no doubt, had their own canon of etiquette. The galley arrived at Tyre in the dead of night, and the dragoman hastened by a secret passage to the Queen's chamber. When she heard that the galley was waiting she was in ecstasies: "Parfoi," quoth she, "c'est bien fait." Taking two demoiselles, and two coffers well stuffed with gold and silver, she hurried to the strand, when, just as she stood there, "one foot on sea and one on shore," the King her husband laid hands on her and brought her back. A talebearing maid of honour had roused the good man, and told him that his Queen was off to Saladin, and Louis had scrambled into his breeches and armour just in time. Restored to a *tête-à-tête* in the castle, he naturally asked her what she did it for. "God's name! "cried the Queen, "because of your poltroonery: you are not worth a rotten apple. And I have heard such fine things of Saladin, that I love him better than you." The enormity of her vice, however, is only fully appreciated when history informs us that, at the date of this amour, Saladin was a good little boy of eleven, going regularly, no doubt, to the mosque school at Baalbekk.*

The Minstrel is not, it will be observed, very careful of chronology, and he thinks nothing of taking us at a leap from 1148 to 1187, in order to tell the story of Count Raymond's treason. When Sibylla had crowned her husband Guy King of Jerusalem, there was great discontent among the old nobility of Palestine; and Raymond of Tripolis, it seems, took counsel with the Patriarch and the barons, and plotted against the new King. They appointed a secret interview with Saladin, and proposed to surrender the land to him, "car li rois est nices et mauvais, et n'a point de pouoir se par nous non." Saladin had no objection to offer: on the contrary, he promised the conspirators immense rewards. "Tell us what pledge you require," said the Count of Tripolis. "By Mahom my god," cried Saladin, "you say well. You shall all of you swear by your religion, and more, for we will be blooded together, and will drink each other's blood in token of amity and union." This was done: all swore by their faith and drank each other's blood, and the plot was settled. When the great battle took place "before Acre," three

---

* It is possible, as Mr. Archer has suggested to me, that the romancers have confused our Saladin with an older namesake, Salah-ed-din el-Yaghisiyany, a prominent general in Zengy's campaigns against the Franks. But we do not hear of him at the date of Louis's Crusade, and if he was then alive he must have been a very old man.

leagues from the city, on the day of "Sant Jehan Decollace," the time came for the pledge to be kept. Saladin called out in the thick of the fight, "Count of Tripolis, Count of Tripolis, fulfil your oath!" Whereupon Count Raymond vailed his banner, and all the other traitors did the like; so the Christians were defeated, and the King and his knights were sent prisoners to "Babiloine." But Saladin despised traitors and treachery, and was moved by Guy's misfortune, finding him indeed to be a "prudhomme and good knight." So he shortly set him free, with twenty of his knights, all well furnished with arms and provisions, and sent them back to their friends on the Syrian coast.

We next hear of Saladin in connexion with the Hospital at Acre. Ralph de Diceto ascribes the foundation of this famous house of charity to his own chaplain, one William, who "on his way to Jerusalem vowed that should he come to Acre harbour safe and soon, he would there build, as well as he could afford, a chapel to St. Thomas the Martyr," and arriving there he did so, and became its prior, and served the sick. The Minstrel makes Saladin its pious benefactor. His authority is an imaginary uncle of Saladin, a venerable man of ruddy face (*vermauz en vis*) and a great white beard, which reached half-way to his feet, besides a fine long *tresse* hanging down to his waist. In spite of these eccentricities, he looked the thorough gentleman (*preudons*), and was most courteously communicative about his famous nephew, when questioned as a prisoner at Acre in the days of the merry Bishop of Beauvais.

Saladin, it appears, had heard of the boundless charity of the Hospital, and resolved to test its generosity. So he put on pilgrim's garb, and took a palmer's staff, "*bourdon, escharpe, et esclavine,*" and presented himself in an exhausted condition at the Hospital. They took him in and attended him with assiduous care, but for three days he refused all food. The Master feared he would die, and every means of persuasion was used to tempt him to eat. At last he confessed he had a longing, a sick man's longing, for one special dish. The good brothers gladly promised to gratify his desire. Then he said he must have a dish of the off forefoot of the Grandmaster's horse, and nothing else would he touch. Yet he protested he had rather die, for he knew how choice and rare a steed he was, and how dear to his master, who had given a thousand gold besants for him. But the Grandmaster said the life of a man was worth more than a horse, and at once sent his favourite to the sick man's room. They cast him and tied him down, and a man came with an axe and asked which foot was wanted. "The off forefoot," they said. Then he swung the axe in both his hands and was bringing it down for the stroke, when Saladin cried out: "Hold! My wish is satisfied, and now I crave other meat: I would eat sheep's flesh." So the horse was unbound and led back to the stable, and Saladin ate mutton. Four days later he departed with grateful leavetakings, and coming to his own kingdom he caused a charter to be drawn up, granting a thousand besants of gold, charged on the revenues of Babylon, to be paid to the Hospital at Acre each year on St. John Baptist's Day. Whereat the Grandmaster and the brethren rejoiced, "for they knew that Saladin did not lie," and the thousand pieces of gold were duly paid each year, and are so paid to this day.* At least, so said our Minstrel to his thirteenth-century listeners, and very likely they believed his pretty tale.

Another story of the white-haired prisoner has a family likeness to other legends. The Marquess of Cæsarea was a miserly man, who lightened his garrison while he weighted his coffers. Saladin warned him that if he went on in this way, he would lose the city. "Peace!" quoth the Marquess, "I can make a thousand knights leap out of my coffers when I please!" In due time Saladin took the city by storm, and the miser was brought a prisoner before him. "Marquess, Marquess," said the conqueror, "where are the thousand knights whom you were to bring out of your chests? By Mahom, your covetousness has misled you. You were never glutted with gold or silver but I will glut you yet more to-day." Then gold and silver were melted down in an iron pail and poured down the Marquess's throat, *et maintenant le convint mourir.*

There is an old legend recorded by Vincent de Beauvais and Pippin,† that when Saladin lay dying "he called his standard-bearer to him and charged him, saying: Do thou, who art wont to bear my banner in the wars, carry also the banner of my death. And let it be a vile rag, which thou must bear through all Damascus set upon a lance, crying: 'Lo, at his death the King of the East could take nothing with him save this cloth only.'"

The Minstrel also knows the story, and puts it into the mouth of his confidential prisoner. In this version Saladin is represented as sending a servant through all his cities, with a strip of linen on the point of a lance; the man stood at all the street corners and proclaimed these words: "Of his kingdom and all his treasure, Saladin will carry nothing away, save only these three ells of linen for his shroud." The idea is in perfect keeping with the devout and humble character of the Sultan, and it is a pity that it finds no confirmation in the Arabic records.

---

* The Minstrel may have got this idea from the fact that Saladin, during his occupation of Acre, did actually endow the hospitals there, but of course as Moslem institutions. See above, p.176.

† It is quoted in that delightful little volume of English History from Contemporary Writers, *The Crusade of Richard I.,* by Mr. T. A. Archer, a book full of interest and humour, and packed with solid learning. I am much indebted to its author.

The prisoner gave other details of Saladin's last moments. The dying Sultan, he said, called for water, and they brought it in a silver bowl. He took it in his left hand, and with his right he made the sign of the cross over the water, touching the rim of the bowl in four opposite places, saying the while, "As wide is it from here to there as from here to there," to mislead those who were looking on. "Then he poured the water on his head and body, and said three words in French, which we did not catch, but it seemed as if he baptised himself." "So died Saladin," the Minstrel concludes, "the best prince that ever was in pagandom, and was buried in the cemetery of my lord Saint Nicholas of Acre, beside his mother, who was there very sumptuously interred. And there is a beautiful tall dome over them, where burns a lamp of olive oil day and night, furnished and lighted by them of St. John of the Hospital of Acre, who hold large revenues which Saladin and his mother bequeathed them."

Saladin lies buried at Damascus, and assuredly neither gave nor bequeathed a single dirhem to any Christian charity. But the legend of his baptism probably comes from the widely believed story of his having solemnly received the Christian Order of Knighthood. At first sight it seems incredible that a devout Moslem, who carried his religion into his every act, and consecrated the last five years of his life to the Holy War for the faith, could possibly consent to perform the ceremonies involved in the Christian initiation to knighthood, as practised by the Crusaders. Yet the author of the "Itinerary of King Richard" (i., 3) states definitely, and without a syllable of surprise or explanation, that when Saladin came to mature years and was fit for bearing arms, "he came to Humphrey of Toron, the illustrious noble of Palestine, to be mantled, and after the manner of the Franks received from him the belt of knighthood." If this were a solitary instance, it might perhaps be dismissed as fiction; since the chronicler was not then present in Palestine. But later on, at a time when the author of the "Itinerary" was himself probably with the Crusading army, he records (v., 11), "On Palm Sunday, King Richard, amid much splendour, girded with the belt of knighthood the son of Saphadin, who had been sent to him for that purpose." Thus it appears that not only did Saladin voluntarily seek knighthood at the hands of Humphrey of Toron, but he (or his brother el-Adil, the "Saphadin" of the chronicles) also voluntarily sent his nephew to be knighted by Richard himself. There is naturally not a word of this in the Arabic contemporary histories: if they knew it, as good Moslems they would feel it their duty to conceal such painful backsliding in their hero and master. But if such doings were to be, Humphrey of Toron was the very man to do them. He had been bound in brotherly pact (*fraterno fœdere junctus erat*, according to William of Tyre, xvii., 17) with a powerful

Saracen Emir as early as 1152; he spoke Arabic, and his influence was exerted in 1175 to arrange a truce between the Moslem Sultan and the King of Jerusalem. The friendship may have begun in 1167, when Saladin was honourably entertained as guest or hostage in the camp of Amalric before Alexandria. Here he may have acquired an admiration for the ideals of chivalry, which he certainly carried into practice. There were also rites of initiation in the East, which may have prepared his mind for the ceremony of knighthood; and the feudal system of the Turks in which he was brought up, and on which he organised his own empire, may have suggested further assimilation to the military customs of Europe.

The most detailed account of this surprising ceremony is given in the early metrical romance "L'Ordene de Chevalerie." The knighting is here performed by Hugh the son of Raymond, Count of Tripolis and (through his wife) lord of Tiberias, the same Raymond whose supposed treachery on the field of Hittin has been described. The youthful Hugh of Tiberias, for several reasons, was a much less likely actor than Humphrey of Toron; but the ceremony, and not the officiator, is the point of interest. Hugh of Tiberias had been taken prisoner by Saladin (this actually happened in 1179), and before releasing him on promise of ransom, the Sultan took him aside, and begged him, by his faith towards God and his religion, to show him how knights were made. "Beau Sire," said Hugh stoutly, 'I will not;" and he explained that Saladin being void of baptism and Christianity, it was folly to talk of knighthood, "car mout en seroie blasmés," Saladin, however, urged that he could not be blamed for doing it under compulsion, as a prisoner, and Hugh at length gave way. Then the ceremony began. First he arranged the Sultan's hair and beard.

> Cheveus et barbe et le viaire
> Li fait appareiller mout bel
> Chest droit à Chevalier nouvel.

Then he laved him in a bath; for, said he, just as the little child comes forth after baptism pure from sin, so must the knight be purified symbolically, and come forth full of courtesy and goodness.

> Sire, tout ensement devés
> Issir sans nulle vilonnie
> Et estre plains de courtoisie,
> Baigner devés en honeste,
> En courtoisie et en bonté,
> Et faire amer à toutes gens.

Saladin, who showed much curiosity to learn the precise meaning of each act in the initiation, was much impressed: "By God most great," he exclaimed, "this beginning is beautiful." Then, after laying him on a bed, the type of the everlasting rest of Paradise, Hugh clothed him in white raiment, to signify purity, and then in scarlet, in token that he must ever serve and honour God and defend Holy Church. Next he shoed him with dark shoes, "to keep you in memory of death, and the earth in which you must lie, whence you came and whither you must go;" for no knight may cherish pride, but must ever strive after humility. "All this is good hearing," said the Sultan, who was next girt, standing, with a slender white girdle, a sign of chastity and contempt of luxury—

> Car Chevalier doit mout amer
> Son cors a netement tenir
> Qu'il ne se puist en chou honnir.

The gilt spurs were next put on, that he might be spurred to ardour in the service of God—"mout plaisoit bien Salehadin"—and then Hugh girded him with the sword, which stood for Uprightness, Trustiness, and Loyalty, and signified that a knight must hold his own against the powerful, and succour the weak, "ch'est œuvre de misericorde." A pure white coif completed the dress, the symbol of a white soul, pure of great sins and fleshly follies, fit to appear before God at the Last Day.

Saladin at each step cheerfully assented, and now he asked whether there was no more. "Yes, Sire," was Hugh's answer, "but I dare not do it." "What is it then?" " 'T is the accolade." The prisoner could not give a blow, even of knighthood, to a king. But the old French is worth quoting:

> Li Rois très tou chou escouta,
> Et en après li demanda
> S'il falait plus nule cose?
> "Sire, oil, mais faire ne l'ose."
> "Que chou est dont?" "Chest li colée."
> "Pourquoi ne le m'avés donnée,
> Et dite la senefianche? "
> "Sire, chou est li remembranche
> De celui qui l'a adoubé
> À Chevalier et ordonnéé;
> Mais mie ne le vous donron,
> Car je suis chi en vo prison,
> Si ne doi faire vilonnie
> Pour cose qu'on me fache et die,
> Si ne vous voel pour chou ferir."

Though too respectful to dub him, Hugh instructs Saladin in the four devoirs of a true knight. First, he shall never take part in injustice or treason: if he cannot turn away wrong, he must at least turn himself away from it. "The next thing is very beautiful: he shall on no account deceive matron or maid, but if they have need of him, shall aid them to the utmost of his power, if he would win glory and regard; for women one must honour, and adventure great deeds in their cause." Fasting and hearing Mass were the last duties enjoined upon the new knight. All this much delighted Saladin—"Si en a eu joie mou grant." If he entered upon the ceremony merely out of curiosity, he was now evidently impressed, and romance and history are at one in the main point, that Saladin became a Knight.

It would be interesting to trace the effect of these medieval tales upon the two great writers who have introduced Saladin among the *dramatis personæ* of European classics. Scott, of course, had read the chronicles and romances, as far as they were readily accessible, and incidents in "The Talisman" may be plausibly traced to the legends of the minstrels. Saladin's visit to Richard's camp in the disguise of a *hakim* may have been suggested by the Minstrel's tale of the equally imaginary visit to the Hospital of St. John at Acre. The quarrel over the banner of Austria is found in the "Romance of Richard Cœur de Lion," published at Edinburgh, in Weber's "Metrical Romances," fifteen years before "The Talisman." But his main source was clearly, not the romances, but the chronicles, which he used as far as they suited him, and very properly threw over whenever they did not fit his scheme. As he wrote himself in the Preface of 1832:

> "One of the inferior characters introduced was a supposed relation of Richard Cœur de Lion; a violation of the truth of history, which gave offence to Mr. Mills the author of the History of Chivalry and the Crusades, who was not, it may be presumed, aware that romantic fiction naturally includes the power of such invention, which is indeed one of the requisites of the art."

Scott boldly asserts that he "had access to all which antiquity believed, whether of reality or fable," about Richard I.; but he can hardly have gone very thoroughly into the Oriental sources, although some were even then easily accessible in Latin. It is obvious, however, that when he sins against "the truth of history," in regard to his European characters, it is of malice prepense. He admits that he knowingly killed Conrad of Montferrat in the wrong way, and the wrong time, and the wrong place, and his other deviations from history are probably no less intentional. He places the scene of the novel at Jaffa, in the autumn of 1192, as various indications prove; and he must have known that Philip of France and Leopold of Austria had both left the Holy Land after the surrender of Acre more than a year before. He sets "the Diamond of the Desert" close to the Dead Sea, on the road to Jerusalem, half way between the camps of the Crusaders and the Saracens; which would place Saladin's camp, "over against Jaffa," somewhere in Moab on the other side of the *Mare Mortuum*. Nor could Ilderim have been deceived for a moment by the notion that the Knight of the Leopard could possibly find himself beside that inhospitable water if he was riding from Jaffa to Jerusalem, since he must have left the Holy City directly behind him. At that time, moreover, no "pilgrimage to the Holy Sepulchre" was to be thought of. But a crusading tale without a desert, no sand, no oasis, no Dead Sea, no pilgrimage, would lack the essential local colour, and Scott very properly put it in. And so all the quarrelling between the rival nations, which was true enough of the French and English, is infinitely more interesting when the absent King of France himself leads his knights; no novel-reader would care a rush for the jealousy of a Duke of Burgundy—unless, of course, he were Charles the Bold.

Scott's treatment of the Oriental side of the picture is marked by fewer liberties, because there was less occasion. He has exercised a judicious caution in bringing practically only one Eastern figure, that of Saladin himself, upon his canvas, and avoiding the temptation to dwell upon anything but his personality. He says nothing definite of the Sultan's history, and by substituting him for his brother "Saphadin" in the story of the proposed marriage, he gets rid of the necessity for individualising a second important Moslem character; but Scott knew very well that it was to be an alliance between "Saphadin," not Saladin, and Joan of Sicily, not Edith. To avoid crowding the canvas with "inferior characters," to say nothing of lowering the dignity of the alliance, a stroke of the pen abolished both Joan and her proposed bridegroom. No one can deny that the story is all the better for it; and a footnote easily propitiates complaisant history.

But if Saladin was to marry Edith there must be a meeting; and so the ordeal by battle and the unhistorical slaughter of Conrad and the Master of the Temple (whose name was not "Sir Giles Amaury") serve also most conveniently to make the chief actors acquainted. It is possible that Scott was really unaware of the fact—somewhat singular, considering their close relations, both hostile and diplomatic—that Richard and Saladin never actually met face to face. The King twice proposed an interview, but in each case Saladin declined. It was "Saphadin" who really met Richard and exchanged much cordial hospitality, and who conducted all negotiations. Equally fictitious are Saladin's visit in the disguise of a *hakim*, and his solitary rides about the plains. The Sultan never travelled unattended; he generally had his guard of mamluks when he was anywhere near the enemy; and the chance encounter with Kenneth, the disguise and the talisman belong to the category of the "Thousand and One Nights." Nor can Scott honestly be justified in his description of Saladin's appearance. He says he was "in the very flower of his age," but Oriental flowers at fifty-four are apt to be faded; and he ventures to paint his portrait, which, to our loss, no contemporary Eastern attempted. All we know definitely about his face is that at fifty he wore a beard, and we only know this because he happened to tug at it during the battle of Hittin. Sir Walter has got the beard right, "a flowing and curled black beard," to boot, "which seemed trimmed with peculiar care"; but when he goes on to work in the nose, eyes, teeth, and forehead, he trusts to that admirable source, his own invention.

Setting aside these natural licences of the romancer, the portrait of Saladin is drawn with remarkable insight and accuracy. His gentleness, courtesy, and nobility of character, his justice, truthfulness, and generosity, which "The Talisman" has made familiar to so many readers who know nothing else in Mohammedan history, are set forth in every contemporary record. His rare bursts of passion, which Scott has finely rendered, were also historically part of his disposition. Unfortunately he seems to have never heard of Saladin's knighthood, and thereby we have probably lost a magnificent chapter. The general manner, dress, and so on are sufficiently Eastern, but show no minute study of the subject. The hatred of the Templars is another true touch. The two Military Orders were the only Christians to whom, as a class, Saladin showed no mercy: and he had his reasons. On the other hand, Scott is altogether wrong when he says that the Sultan "has been ever found" in "the front of battle," "nor is it his wont to turn his horse's head from any brave encounter." Saladin revelled in the sight of battle; "there was nothing he loved so much as a good knight" says Ernoul—witness his hearty admiration of the Green Knight of Spain—but he did not fight in person. He would fearlessly expose himself between the lines of battle, attended only by a groom with a spare horse, whilst the bolts and arrows whistled about his head; he would even make his chaplains read prayers under fire; and he would be seen in all parts of the field. But his duty as general, he conceived, was to lead, encourage, restrain, and order the disposition of the troops, not to engage in personal encounters; and so far as fighting went, a marshal's *bâton*, or Gordon's cane, would be his proper weapon. Conversing with the Bishop of Salisbury, after peace was made, he censured the rashness of the "Inkitâr" Richard in mixing personally in the fray. That Scott played tricks with history is really nothing to the point; but that he was able, through the confused and imperfect records he used, to see and depict the true character of Saladin with remarkable accuracy, is but another proof of his genius.

Lessing, in *Nathan der Weise*, had drawn a portrait of the chivalrous Sultan half a century before "The Talisman" was written, and the play shows signs of a German's serious study of *Quellen*. Lessing may have read Marin's *Histoire de Saladin* (1758), or even Schultens' Latin translation (1732) of the contemporary Arabic biography by Baha-ed-din. He falls into historical errors like Scott, but, unlike Scott, he does not do so on purpose, in deference to the requirements of romantic fiction. There is no artistic object served, for instance, in making Saladin's father act as his treasurer in 1192 in the Lebanon, an inconvenient centre for the paymaster of an army at Jerusalem; besides, the father had been dead nearly twenty years. But the very blunder shows that Lessing had read somewhere that Saladin's father was once governor of Baalbekk, and was after-wards his son's treasurer at Cairo, both of which are historical facts. Again, Lessing adheres to the historical version of the projected marriage, but adds a wholly unauthentic plan of a marriage between Saladin's sister Sittah (really Sitt esh-Sham, or "The Lady of Syria") and Richard's brother—presumably the bastard William Longsword. The whole story of the marriage is so bizarre, even in the Oriental authorities, that one can hardly wonder at any extravagance in the modern glosses.

> Wenn unserm Bruder Melek
> Dann Richards Schwester wär' zu Theile worden:
> Ha! welch ein Haus zusammen!

Saladin exclaims to Sittah. What a house indeed! The notion of Richard putting Joan of Sicily into "Saphadin's" harim, and the couple reigning jointly in Palestine, under the affectionate patronage of their Christian and Moslem brothers of England and Egypt, is delightful enough to tempt the poorest imagination to run riot.

There are many true touches, no doubt, in Lessing's portrait of Saladin: such as his love of kindred,

> Der sein Geschwister ingesammt so liebt,

and his generosity and contempt for money; though

> Ein Kleid, ein Schwert, ein Pferd,—und Einen Gott,
> Was branch ich mehr?

gives an impression of knight-errantry, which was not in the real character. The main defect, however, of Lessing's delineation (considered historically), is that it is too European. His Saladin is no real Saracen, as Scott's is. The set purpose of "Nathan the Wise," as a motive-drama, to preach toleration, and to silence the bigoted criticism of worthy pastor Goetze, compels Lessing to hold up Saladin as a type not only of a good Moslem, but a tolerant. The former he was, beyond question; but tolerance was not his virtue; his chivalry and clemency were in act, not in thought. He could be kind to Christians, but he never doubted that they must eventually go down into the Pit. He had a holy horror of philosophy, free-thought, "broad views," and all manner of heterodoxy. The only cruel act recorded against him, outside the retaliations of war, was the deliberate execution of a "philosopher"—a mystic Sufi. Like many fanatics, he could better tolerate the flat opposition of other religions than heresy within the pale of his own creed. His chivalry to crusaders was the good-breeding of a gentleman; it did not touch his intellectual appreciation of their errors. He had a gentle soul and a soft heart, but they did not dispel his conviction that Christians were "fuel for Hell." He is a type of a true Moslem of the purest breed; but Lessing gives him a theological latitude which he would have indignantly disowned. Of course, all this has nothing to do with the drama as a drama, any more than historical criticism of "The Talisman" touches in any way its merits as a novel. To the student of the widespread Saladin myth, both works have the great interest that they preserve, amidst some historical truth and some romantic legend, the general character which opinion in all times has ascribed to the great Sultan.*

It is singular that the East, the birthplace of Saladin, which has been the mother of so many admirable tales, has almost wholly neglected him in its fiction. The "Thousand and One Nights" do not disdain crusading stories, witness the "Tale of King Omar ibn en-Noaman and his sons Sharrkan and Zau el-Mekan"; but Saladin's name is not once introduced. The omission is the more singular when it is remembered that the "Nights" probably received their latest form at Cairo, where the founder of the Citadel has always been a favourite hero. Doubtless he has formed the subject of many popular tales, told in the coffee-houses and in the bazars of Egypt, but so far unpublished. One such romance, indeed, has come to light in an Arabic manuscript at Berlin,† but it is poor stuff. Richard's sister Rumina is brought captive before Saladin. Saphadin falls in love with her on the spot, strikes off her fetters, and leads her to his tent. There she promises to adopt his religion, but only to gain time. Whilst he sleeps, she escapes, dressed in men's clothes. Saphadin writes to Richard to demand her in marriage, but meanwhile is captured by guile. Rumina comes forth on horseback, clad in a knight's coat of mail, to do battle with Saladin. She is again

* The preceding pages originally appeared partly in *Literature*, May 28th, but principally in *Longman's Magazine*, August, 1898.

† Published in a German translation by Goergens, *Arabische Quellenheiträge*, 283 ff.

made prisoner, Saphad in is rescued, Rumina embraces Islam—and Saphadin, and the wedding takes place with great pomp. The interest in the story is the repetition of the original idea of a Christian-Moslem marriage between el-Adil and some relation of Richard I., which seems to be the most permanent and universal detail in the Saladin myth. It is strange, however, that no better example of Arabic romance should be connected with the subject. The character of the great Sultan, however, appeals more strongly to Europeans than to Moslems, who admire his chivalry less than his warlike triumphs. To us it is the generosity of the character, rather than the success of the career, that makes Saladin a true as well as a romantic hero.

TOMB OF SALADIN, DAMASCUS.
FROM A PHOTOGRAPH BY BONFILS.

APPENDICES

APPENDIX I.—DYNASTIES OF WESTERN ASIA

		SYRIA					MESO
EGYPT	PALESTINE	TRIPOLIS	ANTIOCH	DAMASCUS	ALEPPO	EDESSA	DIYAR BEK
FATIMID CALIPHS	KINGS OF JERUSALEM	COUNTS	PRINCES	SELJUK SULTAN	SELJUK SULTANS	COUNTS	ORTUKID PRINCES of KEYFA MARID
				1095 Dukak	1095 Ridwan		
		[1097 Raymond of St. Giles]	1098 Bohemond I.			1098 Baldwin of Boulogne	
	1099 Godfrey of Bouillon						
	1100 Baldwin I. of Boulogne			ATABEG BURIDS 1103 Tughtigin		1100 Baldwin du Bourg	
1101 el-Amir			1104 Tancred			1104 Tancred	1101 Sukman
		[1105 William Jordan]					1104 Ibrahim (
		1109 Bertram				1109 Baldwin du Bourg	1108 Dawud (K 1108 Il-Gha (M)
		1112 Pons	1112 Roger d.1119		1113 Alp-Arslan II. 1114 Sultan Shah		
	1118 Baldwin II. du Bourg				ORTUKIDS 1117 Suleyman I.	1118 Joscelin de Courtenay	
					1121 Suleyman II.		1122 Timur (M)
					1123 Balak		
			1126 Bohemond II. d.1130-1	1128 Bury	ATABEGS 1128 Zengy I. of Mosil	1131 Joscelin II.	
1130 el-Hafiz	1131 Fulk of Anjou			1132 Ismail			
				1134 Mahmud (*Muin-ed-din Anar, vezir*)			
		1137 Raymond I.	1136 Raymond of Poiters d.1149	1138 Mohammad 1139 Abak			
	1143 Baldwin III.					1144 Zengy I.	
1149 ez-Zafir					1146 N u r E d - D i n		1148 Kara-Arsl (K)
1154 el-Faïz		1152 Raymond II.	1152 Reginald of Châtillon	1154 Nur-ed-din			1152 Alpi (M
1160 el-Adid d. 1171	1163 Amalric I.		1163 Bohemond III. d. 1201				
AYYUBIDS 1169 SALADIN vezir 1171 viceroy 1175 king	1174 Baldwin IV.			1174 SALADIN	1174 es-Salih Ismail 1181 Imad-ed-din 1183 SALADIN	1174 Atabeg of Mosil 1182 SALADIN	1174 Nur-ed-din Mohamma 1176 Il-Ghaz (M)
							Vassals of SALAD 1184 Yuluk-Arslan 1185 Sukman II
	1186 Guy de Lusignan 1187 SALADIN	1187 Raymond III. of Antioch					
1193 d. 4 March	[At Tyre 1192 Conrad „ Henry of Champagne]						

...POTAMIA			ASIA MINOR			
MOSIL	BAGHDAD	PERSIA	ARMENIA	KONIA (RUM)	LESSER ARMENIA	GREEK EMPIRE
ZENGID ATABEGS	ABBASID CALIPHS	SELJUK SULTANS	SHAHS	SELJUK SULTANS	KINGS	EMPERORS
						1081 Alexius I. Comnenus
	1094 el-Mustazhir	1092 Bargiyaruk		1093 Kilij Arslan I.	1092 Gosdantin	
			1100 Sukman el-Kutby		1100 Thoros I.	
		1104 Mohammad		1106 Melik Shah I.		
				1109 Mesud I.		
			1112 Ibrahim			
		1117 Sinjar				
	1118 el-Mustarshid	1118 Mahmud				1118 John II.
1127 Imad-ed-din Zengy I.			1127 Ahmad			
			1128 Sukman II.		1129 Leon I.	
		1131 Dawud				
		1132 Tughril II.				
	1134 er-Rashid	1133 Mesud				
	1135 el-Muktafy	(1136 *Atabeg Ildigiz*)				
					1141 Thoros II.	
						1143 Manuel I.
1146 Seyf-ed-din Ghazy I.						
1149 Kutb-ed-din Modud I.		1152 Melik Shah II.				
		1153 Mohammad		1156 Kilij-Arslan II.		
	1160 el-Mustenjid	1159 Suleyman				
		1161 Arslan Shah				
					1167 Rhupen II.	
1169 Seyf-ed-din Ghazy II.	1170 el-Mustady				1169 Meleh	
		(1172 *Atabeg Pehlewan*)			1175 Rhupen III	
1180 Izz-ed-din Mesud	1179 en-Nasir	1177 Tughril III.				1180 Alexius II.
						1183 Andronicus I.
			1183 Seyf-ed-din Bektimur			
Vassal of SALADIN		1185 *Atabeg Kizl-Arslan*			1185 Leon II.	1185 Isaac II. Angelus
				1188 Melik Shah II.		
N		1191 *Atabeg Abu-Bekr*				

APPENDIX II.—THE FAMILY OF SALADIN

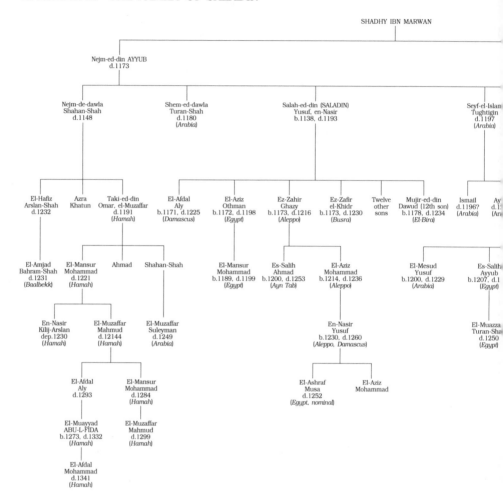

SHADHY IBN MARWAN

Nejm-ed-din AYYUB
d.1173

Nejm-de-dawla
Shahan-Shah
d.1148

Shem-ed-dawla
Turan-Shah
d.1180
(*Arabia*)

Salah-ed-din (SALADIN)
Yusuf, en-Nasir
b.1138, d.1193

Seyf-el-Islam
Tughtigin
d.1197
(*Arabia*)

El-Hafiz
Arslan-Shah
d.1232

Azra
Khatun

Taki-ed-din
Omar, el-Muzaffar
d.1191
(*Hamah*)

El-Afdal
Aly
b.1171, d.1225
(*Damascus*)

El-Aziz
Othman
b.1172, d.1198
(*Egypt*)

Ez-Zahir
Ghazy
b.1173, d.1216
(*Aleppo*)

Ez-Zafir
el-Khidr
b.1173, d.1230
(*Busra*)

Twelve
other
sons

Mujir-ed-din
Dawud (12th son)
b.1178, d.1234
(*El-Bira*)

Ismail
d.1196?
(*Arabia*)

Ay
d.1
(*Ara*)

El-Amjad
Bahram-Shah
d.1231
(*Baalbekk*)

El-Mansur
Mohammad
d.1221
(*Hamah*)

Ahmad

Shahan-Shah

El-Mansur
Mohammad
b.1189, d.1199
(*Egypt*)

Es-Salih
Ahmad
b.1200, d.1253
(*Ayn Tab*)

El-Aziz
Mohammad
b.1214, d.1236
(*Aleppo*)

El-Mesud
Yusuf
b.1200, d.1229
(*Arabia*)

Es-Salih
Ayyub
b.1207, d.1
(*Egypt*)

En-Nasir
Kilij-Arslan
dep.1230
(*Hamah*)

El-Muzaffar
Mahmud
d.12144
(*Hamah*)

El-Muzaffar
Suleyman
d.1249
(*Arabia*)

En-Nasir
Yusuf
b.1230, d.1260
(*Aleppo, Damascus*)

El-Muazza
Turan-Sha
d.1250
(*Egypt*)

El-Afdal
Aly
d.1293

El-Mansur
Mohammad
d.1284
(*Hamah*)

El-Ashraf
Musa
d.1252
(*Egypt, nominal*)

El-Aziz
Mohammad

El-Muayyad
ABU-L-FIDA
b.1273, d.1332
(*Hamah*)

El-Muzaffar
Mahmud
d.1299
(*Hamah*)

El-Afdal
Mohammad
d.1341
(*Hamah*)

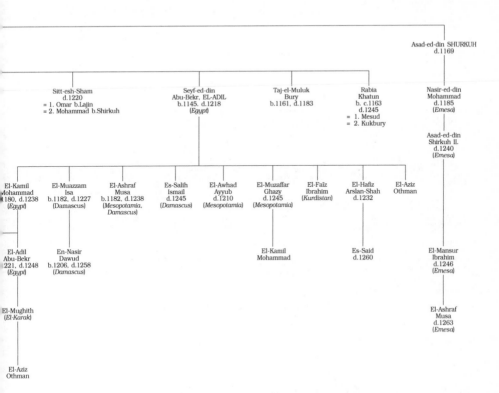

Asad-ed-din SHURKUH
d.1169

Sitt-esh-Sham
d.1220
= 1. Omar b.Lajin
= 2. Mohammad b.Shirkuh

Seyf-ed-din
Abu-Bekr, EL-ADIL
b.1145. d.1218
(*Egypt*)

Taj-el-Muluk
Bury
b.1161, d.1183

Rabia
Khatun
b. c.1163
d.1245
= 1. Mesud
= 2. Kukbury

Nasir-ed-din
Mohammad
d.1185
(*Emesa*)

Asad-ed-din
Shirkuh II.
d.1240
(*Emesa*)

El-Kamil
Mohammad
180, d.1238
(*Egypt*)

El-Muazzam
isa
b.1182, d.1227
(Damascus)

El-Ashraf
Musa
b.1182, d.1238
(*Mesopotamia,
Damascus*)

Es-Salih
Ismail
d.1245
(*Damascus*)

El-Awhad
Ayyub
d.1210
(*Mesopotamia*)

El-Muzaffar
Ghazy
d.1245
(*Mesopotamia*)

El-Faiz
Ibrahim
(*Kurdistan*)

El-Hafiz
Arslan-Shah
d.1232

El-Aziz
Othman

El-Adil
Abu-Bekr
221, d.1248
(*Egypt*)

En-Nasir
Dawud
b.1206, d.1258
(*Damascus*)

El-Kamil
Mohammad

Es-Said
d.1260

El-Mansur
Ibrahim
d.1246
(*Emesa*)

El-Mughith
(*El-Karak*)

El-Ashraf
Musa
d.1263
(*Emesa*)

El-Aziz
Othman

APPENDIX III.—KINGS OF JERUSALEM, PRINCES OF ANTIOCH, AND COUNTS OF TRIPOLIS*

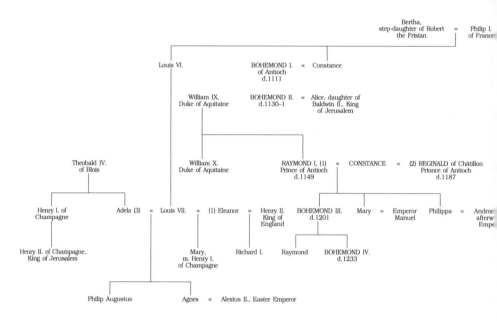

APPENDIX IV.—THE GREAT LORDS OF PALESTINE*

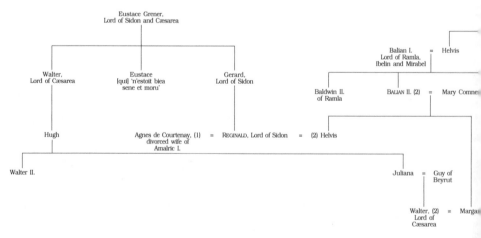

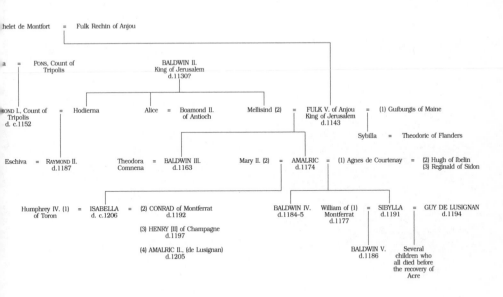

helet de Montfort = Fulk Rechin of Anjou

a = Pons, Count of Tripolis

BALDWIN II.
King of Jerusalem
d.1130?

MOND I., Count of Tripolis d. c.1152 = Hodierna

Alice = Boamond II. of Antioch

Mellisind (2) = FULK V. of Anjou King of Jerusalem d.1143 = (1) Guiburgis of Maine

Sybilla = Theodoric of Flanders

Eschiva = RAYMOND II. d.1187

Theodora Comnena = BALDWIN III. d.1163

Mary II. (2) = AMALRIC d.1174 = (1) Agnes de Courtenay = (2) Hugh of Ibelin
                                                                        (3) Reginald of Sidon

Humphrey IV. (1) of Toron = ISABELLA d. c.1206 = (2) CONRAD of Montferrat d.1192

(3) HENRY [II] of Champagne d.1197

(4) AMALRIC II., (de Lusignan) d.1205

BALDWIN IV. d.1184–5

William of (1) Montferrat d.1177 = SIBYLLA d.1191 = GUY DE LUSIGNAN d.1194

BALDWIN V. d.1186

Several children who all died before the recovery of Acre

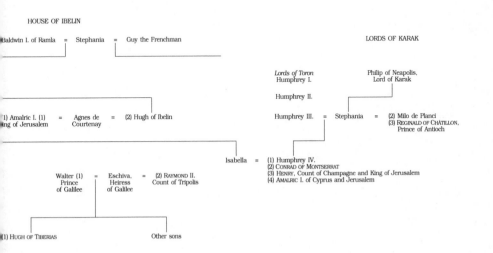

HOUSE OF IBELIN

Baldwin I. of Ramla = Stephania = Guy the Frenchman

LORDS OF KARAK

Lords of Toron
Humphrey I.

Philip of Neapolis, Lord of Karak

Humphrey II.

1) Amalric I. (1) King of Jerusalem = Agnes de Courtenay = (2) Hugh of Ibelin

Humphrey III. = Stephania = (2) Milo de Planci
                                 (3) REGINALD OF CHÂTILLON, Prince of Antioch

Isabella = (1) Humphrey IV.
             (2) CONRAD OF MONTSERRAT
             (3) HENRY, Count of Champagne and King of Jerusalem
             (4) AMALRIC I. of Cyprus and Jerusalem

Walter (1) Prince of Galilee = Eschiva, Heiress of Galilee = (2) RAYMOND II. Count of Tripolis

(1) HUGH OF TIBERIAS

Other sons

* From Archer's *Crusade of Richard I.*

INDEX

119–20

Sinjār, 58, 127, 131–2, 147, 186, 190, 207

Sinjār-Shah (Sinjār Shah), 143, 144 n.

Şinnebra, es-, 152

Sitt esh-Sham, "Lady of Syria," Saladin's sister, 249 n., 265

Slaves, 41–2, 50, 54, 63, 64, 90, 96, 102, 103, 168, 169, 171, 232, 240

black (Caraholam), 104, 122

Christian, 48

Moslem, 160, 167

White, 37; *see also* mamluks 37

Sorrows, castle of, 124–5

Sorrows, ford of, 123

Sow, or penthouse, 193

Spies, 37, 38, 54

Spring Head, 86, 194

Standard, 115, 142, 149, 154, 181, 193, 200, 205, 220, 221

see also Banner

Stephania, 128

Stephen, gate of St., 165

Stephen of Turnham, 230

stone-slings 60, 199, 202, 203, 204

Sūdān, 103, 122

Sūdānis, 81, 90, 96, 104

Suhite (Said?), 134

Suhrawardy, es-, 40, 250

Sūk-en-Naḥḥāsīn, 96

Sukmān, Ortukid, 57, 144

Summak mountains, 118

Sunnites, 76, 89, 93

Swordmakers' Medresa, 121

T

Ṭabary, el-, 98 n.

Tabor, mount, 129, 135

Ta'izz, 104

Takī-ed-dīn, 'Omar, 129, 152, 157, 178, 186–7, 205

"Tale of King Omar ibn en-Noaman and his sons Sharrkan and Zau el-Mekan," *see Thousand and One Nights*

Tales of a Minstrel of Rheims, *see Ménestral de Reims*

Talisman, The, 21, 226, 262–6

Tancred, 46, 165, 170

Ṭarsūs, 44

Saul of, 139

Taxation, 37, 55, 86

Tekrīt 31, 32, 46, 59, 69

Tell Bāshir (Turbessel), 62

Tell el-'Ajjūl, 191

Tell el-Fokhkhār, 184

Tell el-Muṣallīyīn, 184

Tell es-Sulṭān, *see* Mound of the Sultan

Tell Jezer, battle of, 122, 227

Tell Ḳeysān, 184, 193, 194

Templars, knights, 47, 92, 122, 123, 124, 149–50, 155, 157, 161, 171, 176, 177, 178, 182, 186, 188 n., 189, 194, 203, 208, 217, 225, 228, 237, 249, 264

Tesīl, 152

Thenaud, Jehan, 100

Thousand and One Nights, 266

Tiberias (Tabarīya), 45, 51, 59, 71, 124, 129, 150, 151–6, 160, 173, 176, 184, 213, 260

Timurtāsh, Ortukid of Maridīn, 54, 57

Toassin, 121

Toron (Tubnīn), 45, 123, 161, 184

Toron Militum, Toron of the Knights, *see* Nātrūn

Tortosa (Antartūs), 43, 44, 125, 177, 181, 200

Treaties, 22, 60, 61, 81, 82, 83, 92, 117, 118, 123, 125, 126, 127, 128, 137, 144, 147, 149, 208, 209–10, 212, 227, 230, 241, 242, 243, 245

Tribute, 48, 77, 78, 171

Tripoli, 103

Tripolis (Ṭarābulus), 43, 44, 137, 161, 162, 165, 169, 175–,7, 181, 200

Tubania 135

Ṭughtigīn, Atābeg of Damascus, "Sword of Islam," 58, 70, 112

Tūlūn, Ahmad Ibn- 98, 99

Tūrān Shāh, 90, 103, 104,

120, 122

Turcopoles, 82 n., 151, 155

Turkman's Wells (Jibāb et-Turkmān), 116

Turon, mount 184

Turris Maledicta, 184

see also Accursed Tower

Tutush, daughter of, Zengy's wife, 58

Tyre (Sūr), 15, 17, 43, 130, 138, 158, 160, 161–3, 164, 173–4, 175, 176, 178, 179, 181, 182, 183, 190, 193, 195, 196, 201, 211, 224, 234, 235, 238, 242, 243, 255, 256

archbishop of, *see* William

marquess of, 228

U

Ukhuwāna, el-, 152

V

Valenie, 113

Vassals, 23, 37–9, 41, 42, 43, 49, 50, 51, 57, 100, 110, 111, 132, 143, 144, 147, 149, 177, 178, 226, 242, 243

Venetians, 136

Vezīr, house of the ,98

Vezīrs, 22, 38, 39, 42, 71, 77–8, 79, 81, 84, 86, 88, 89, 90, 93, 94, 95, 112–13, 249

Victory, dome of 15, 138

Victory, gate of (Bāb en-Nasr), 103

Visions 64, 65, 81

Vitalis, Oliver, 132 n.

Voguë, Vte. de, 173

W

Wailly. M. N. de, 255

Wāla, el-, 137

Walls of Cairo, 78, 245

War-cry, 160, 205

Wāsiṭ, 51, 53

Wedding at Karak, 136

Wells

Joseph's, 121

of Goliath, 135

of the slain, 96

of the Winding Stairs, 121

William de Préaux, 223